MW00614385

ORIGINS

STUDIES IN THE HISTORY AND CULTURE OF THE ANCIENT NEAR EAST

EDITED BY

B. HALPERN AND M. H. E. WEIPPERT

VOLUME VI

ORIGINS

The Ancient Near Eastern Background of
Some Modern Western Institutions

BY

WILLIAM W. HALLO

E.J. BRILL
LEIDEN · NEW YORK · KÖLN
1996

The paper in this book meets the guidelines for permanence and durability of the Committee on Production Guidelines for Book Longevity of the Council on Library Resources.

Library of Congress Cataloging-in-Publication Data

Hallo, William W.
    Origins : the ancient Near Eastern background of some modern western institutions / by William W. Hallo.
        p. cm.—(Studies in the history and culture of the ancient Near East, ISSN 0169-9024; v. 6)
    Includes bibliographical references and indexes.
    ISBN 9004103287 (cloth)
    1. Civilization, Western—Middle Eastern influences. 2. Middle East—Civilization—To 622. I. Title. II. Series.
CB245.H25   1996
909'.09182—dc20   96-1921
                                              CIP

Die Deutsche Bibliothek – CIP-Einheitsaufnahme

Hallo, William W.:
Origins : the ancient Near Eastern background of some modern Western institutions / by William W. Hallo. - Leiden ; New York ; Köln : Brill, 1996
    (Studies in the history and culture of the ancient Near East ; Vol. 6)
    ISBN 90-04-10328-7
NE: GT

ISSN 0169-9024
ISBN 90 04 10328 7

PRINTED IN THE NETHERLANDS

Dedicated to the Memory of

Edith Sylvia Hallo
née Pinto

1928-1994

לכל יש תמורה חוץ מאשת נעורים

"For everything there is an equivalent,
save only the wife of one's youth."

Babylonian Talmud
Sanhedrin 22a

CONTENTS

ACKNOWLEDGEMENTS

The present work took shape over a number of triennial leaves generously granted by Yale University. The first two, in 1987-88, were spent as a Fellow of the National Humanities Center in Research Triangle Park, North Carolina, where I profited from the stimulating contact with other Fellows and the helpful ministrations of the devoted staff, beginning with then Director Charles Blitzer and the Associate Director Kent Mullikin. The third, in the Spring semester of 1990, was spent at the Netherlands Institute for the Near East in Leiden, whose outstanding facilities were put at my disposal by its Director, Professor J. de Roos and by the head of its Assyriological Section, Professor Klaas Veenhof. During the Summer Semester of 1990, I was invited to serve as the Franz Rosenzweig Guest Professor at the University of Kassel (Germany) by Professor Wolfdietrich Schmied-Kowarzik and the Fachbereich "Gesellschaftswissenschaften." Sabine Effenberger and Sabine Stange helped turn my manuscript into intelligible German so that I could test much of it on sizeable audiences of students and the general public. Other chapters were prepared for lecture trips during the Fall Semester of 1993. I am grateful to my various hosts on these and other occasions, and wish to mention here in particular Professor Yehoshua Gitay of the University of Cape Town (ch. V 3). Some of the individual chapters have recently appeared in print in other contexts, usually of Anniversary Volumes or Memorial Volumes not widely available; they are reproduced here with major or minor changes and with the kind permission of the respective publishers. The title of this book is chosen with apologies to Eric Partridge, whose *Origins: a Short Etymological Dictionary of Modern English* (New York, Macmillan, 1958) is always at my fingertips (cf. ch. X, n. 3). The translation of a passage from the Danish in ch. III 1 was provided by my associate, Ulla Kasten, and assistance in reading the proofs by my student, Madeleine Fitzgerald. At Brill, the project enjoyed the editorial ministrations and encouragement of Dr. F. Th. Dijkema, Senior Editor, and of Patricia Radder, Editorial Assistant. I cannot list all the students, colleagues, friends and relatives who have encouraged my efforts and stimulated my thinking on the diverse subjects of these essays, but I wish to single out the one to whose memory this book is dedicated and to thank Nahum Sarna for the motto which expresses my debt to her better than any words of my own could do.

"Lakeridge"
Torrington, Connecticut
July 1, 1995

PERMISSIONS

The following publishers kindly permitted the republication of material originally published by them and here reproduced with greater or lesser changes:

(1) University of Texas Press (Austin) (ch. I 3, in part): "First published as Foreword to *Before Writing*, vol. I, by Denise Schmanolt-Besserat (c) 1992. Reprinted by permission of the University of Texas Press."
(2) Université de Liège (ch. II 2, in part).
(3) Editions Recherches sur les Civilisations (Paris) (ch. II 3).
(4) Biblical Archaeology Society (Washington) (ch. III 2).
(5) Israel Exploration Society (Jerusalem) (ch. III 3).
(6) Eisenbrauns (Winona Lake, IN) (ch. V 2): "Previously published in *Texts, Temples, and Traditions: a tribute to Menahem Haran,* ed. by Michael V. Fox *et al.,* 1996."
(7) Augsburg Fortress Publishers (Philadelphia) (ch. VII 1): "Reprinted from *Ancient Israelite Religion,* ed. by Patrick D. Miller, Jr., Paul D. Hanson, and S. Dean McBride, copyright © 1987 Fortress Press. Used by permission of Augsburg Fortress."
(8) Scribners (New York) (chs. VII 2, 3): "Portions of these chapters have been revised from my article 'Lamentations and Prayers in Sumer and Akkad' in *Civilizations of the Ancient Near East,* Jack M. Sasson, Editor in Chief. Vol III, pp. 1871-1881. Copyright © 1995 Charles Scribner's Sons. Used by permission of Charles Scribner's Sons, an imprint of Simon & Schuster Macmillan."

INTRODUCTION

In 1975 and again in 1979, an ambitious book appeared under the title *The Timetables of History*. It was written by Bernard Grun and was, by its own acknowledgement, "based on Werner Stein's *Kultur-fahrplan*." It bravely attempted to highlight outstanding events in all parts of the world under the headings, respectively, of history and politics, literature and theater, religion philosophy and learning, visual arts, music, science technology and growth, and daily life. For the more recent past it ventured to do this decade by decade or even year by year, thus providing a useful synchronic and synoptic view of human accomplishments and setbacks across the face of the globe. But for earlier eras, it was necessarily and desperately abbreviated. It covered the last two thousand years of prehistory and the first two thousand years of history (5000-1000 B.C.) in four facing pages. It thus could hardly hope to live up to the promise of its preface: "The historian in his library ... has the opportunity to sort out origins and consequences." That preface and its optimistic programmatic statement came from the pen of Daniel J. Boorstin.

Daniel J. Boorstin took a B.A. summa cum laude at Harvard, received his Ph.D. from Yale University, and taught for twenty-five years at the University of Chicago before becoming Librarian of Congress in 1975. In 1983 he published *The Discoverers*, subtitled "A history of man's search to know his world and himself." I bought his book as soon as it appeared, took it with me to Cape Cod, and read it with fascination, not only because I have ties to Harvard, Yale and Chicago in my own right, but also because of the ground he covered. In four books within the one thick volume, he dealt successively with "Time," "The Earth and the Seas," "Nature," and "Society." Each time he traced the history of humanity's dawning awareness of the world around it, and its ceaseless efforts to organize its observations into an intelligible system. What impressed me most was his detailed chronicling of the painfully slow yet doggedly persistent way in which human beings have pursued these objectives. What I missed most was an adequate place for the ancient Near Eastern contribution to many of the insights and inventions that have given us the world as we know it today. (Much the same characterization applies to the companion volume, *The Creators*, published in 1992, though with no-

table exceptions like the architecture and sculpture of ancient Egypt.)
Then and there I determined that, given the opportunity, I would
make the attempt myself. What follows is the result of a scholarly
lifetime devoted to the study of the ancient Near East. Many of the
topics covered have been previously addressed in detailed studies of
mine that have appeared over the years in a variety of more or less
obscure professional journals and collective volumes. Here the same
findings are updated and recast with a wider audience in mind. At the
same time it is hoped that the extensive documentation will make the
essays helpful to further scholarly inquiry.

Like Boorstin, I am attempting to cover a vast panorama, and
have to subdivide it into a number of subtopics of more manageable
size. Where he began with "Time," I will explore various aspects of
the calendar. For his vast coverage of geography, I will substitute a
more modest synopsis of cartography. For the science of nature, I
have little to offer. By contrast, for the study of society, I will look
into the essentials of all civilization, its secondary aspects, and some
of its specific manifestations, like kingship and the special role of
women. Beyond these parallels, I will explore some areas left entirely
out of account in Boorstin's presentation. In the first place there is
the whole realm of religion, both the cult and the language of prayer,
agenda and *dicenda* as it were. Secondly, I will seek to accord a proper
place to the practice and study of creative literature. In a lighter vein,
I will delve into the earliest documented evidence for some of our
popular games, and even have something to say about the first cookbooks.

In all these areas, my object will be to show how ancient Near
Eastern innovations or their consequences have survived into our
own day and age. To put it another way, I will try to assess the extent
to which our modern western world is indebted to the ancient Near
East. This debt is often enough ignored. We are accustomed to ac-
knowledging our legacy from the classical world of Greece and
Rome, though even here there is the danger that the acknow-
ledgment will attenuate in the measure that classical learning diminishes. Who now recalls that "The Discoverers" was originally the
title of a chapter of the *Phoenician History* by Philo of Byblos in which
he traced the invention of basic artifacts to antediluvian sages? There
is also some disposition, at least in the English-speaking world, to
speak of a so-called "Judaeo-Christian heritage," by which is usually
meant the legacy of the Hebrew Bible and the New Testament as

filtered through subsequent liturgy and literature. But that heritage tends to be defined by and confined to the religious realm, and does not take account of the many secular institutions which can also be traced to these origins. As for the worlds of Mesopotamia and Egypt, they are most often relegated to the field of antiquarianism, or lumped together with non-Western, or at best pre-Western cultures. It is only in the last few decades that the startling discoveries in these parts of the ancient world have come to be appreciated for the pivotal and seminal role which they have to play in the writing and rewriting of the history of almost any human institution worth chronicling—and too often that recognition remains the privileged information of the specialists. Hence the attempt here made to give some of these insights wider currency.

I am well aware that many other insights remain neglected in this connection. Many of the areas lying on the periphery of ancient Mesopotamia and its sphere of influence have themselves become subjects of special disciplines, or sub-disciplines. The Assyriologist with a primary interest in Mesopotamia cannot hope to speak with equal authority on developments in ancient Turkey, Iran or the Arabian peninsula, to mention only the Asiatic Near East. In the African Near East, the field of Egyptology rivals Assyriology in the breadth and depth of its findings. Its findings can only be touched on in passing here. Readers who seek the origins of Western institutions in Egypt—whether from an Afrocentric perspective or for other reasons—will therefore need to look for them elsewhere. But they may wish to ponder the implications of the Sumerians' own self-designation: they called themselves the "black-headed" people—hardly a distinction from their neighbors if the allusion was, as generally thought, to the typical color of their hair, so just possibly—who knows!—to skin color. Those wishing to delve further into the many topics necessarily omitted here may wish to study such scholarly works as Samuel Noah Kramer's *History Begins at Sumer: Thirty-nine Firsts in Man's Recorded History* (1981) or such popular ones as Charles Panati's *Extraordinary Origins of Everyday Things* (1987). Those with a special interest in Biblical and post-Biblical data may wish to consult Judah Gribetz' *Timetables of Jewish History* (1993), organized like the *Timetables of History* (above).

As an Assyriologist with equal interests in the history and the literature of the ancient Near East, I will advance my arguments in the first instance by appeal to the historical (and archaeological) record, which includes both texts ("monuments" and "archives" in my taxonomy) and artifacts. But wherever possible, I will also listen to the ancient literary texts (the "canons"), taking the ancient documents seriously without necessarily taking them literally, on the proposition that literary sources may be used, with due caution, in historiographical reconstructions. I will rely in the first instance on the cuneiform evidence from Mesopotamia and its environs, but consider Biblical and other West Semitic evidence whenever possible. Indeed, having cultivated Biblical studies since the beginning of my own schooling, I am naturally inclined to pursue potential comparisons and contrasts of Biblical and other Near Eastern evidence by means of the comparative method or a modification of it that I prefer to call the contextual method, i.e., investigating the broadly contemporary context of a given institution or topos. The newer technique of intertextuality, by contrast, seeks the earlier antecedents of a given text—or institution—as a clue to its origins and its transformations over time. By a judicious combination of both approaches, one can hope to exploit both synchronic and diachronic relationships—both the horizontal and the vertical dimensions, as it were—of any given phenomenon.

But an Assyriologist is also, inevitably, a philologist, who approaches the sources in the first instance through an intensive study of the lexicographical evidence. I will therefore occasionally introduce the reader to the ancient terminology that corresponds to the modern concepts with which we necessarily operate. To the non-specialist, this may at first seem somewhat daunting, but it offers important compensations. In the first place it opens the door to the whole thesaurus of insights stored up in the great dictionaries of ancient languages now being compiled around the scholarly world. It thus provides a counterpart to the encyclopedias, organized as they are by entries (*lemmata*) in modern languages. In the field of Assyriology, the standard work of the latter type is the *Reallexikon der Assyriologie und vorderasiatischen Archäologie* (1928ff.) In Biblical studies, the latest and most comprehensive coverage is provided by the *Anchor Bible Dictionary* (6 vv., 1992). By a judicious use of both dictionaries and encyclopedias, it is possible to compare ancient and modern concepts, and to avoid as far as possible the imposition of our categories on the conceptual world of the ancients. Secondly, the history of the ancient terms often enough provides a fascinating thread for tracing the fate of the institutions and concepts that they identify; sometimes, indeed, that history reaches into our own day or into our own modern languages, so that we can appreciate the better the legacy that the ancient Near East has bequeathed to us.

Of course not every modern convenience or convention derives from this source. Where it does not, it may still be useful to compare and contrast it with a corresponding phenomenon of antiquity. In fact the contrast with such counterparts can sometimes be just as illuminating as comparison. In other words, a fully rounded picture requires both positive and negative comparison. This too is of the essence in the "contextual approach" which I have championed in Biblical studies and in my attempts to understand Biblical texts in the context of their ancient Near Eastern environment. The approach is here extended to the broader panorama of our origins: the ancient Near Eastern background of some modern western institutions.

CHAPTER ONE

THE ESSENTIALS OF CIVILIZATION

1. URBAN ORIGINS IN CUNEIFORM AND BIBLICAL SOURCES [1]

The essential ingredients of civilization are three: cities, capital and writing. Of these three, cities are in a sense the first and foremost requirement, since the very word civilization stems from Latin *civis*, "citizen," and *civitas*, "city-state." If the "agricultural revolution," as first described by the British anthropologist-archaeologist V. Gordon Childe, marked the transition from the Old Stone Age to the New Stone Age, or from the Palaeolithicum to the Neolithicum, [2] then his "urban revolution" marked the transition from the Stone Age to the Bronze Age, or from pre-history to history. And though there are disconcerting hints of earlier urban experiments at Jericho near the Dead Sea and at Çatal Höyük in Anatolia (Turkey), the development took place first in a systematic way in Southern Mesopotamia, in the lower valley of the Tigris and Euphrates rivers, the land known as Sumer.

The refinements that the urban revolution brought in its train are unthinkable without the stimulus and opportunities afforded and necessitated by the new concentration of populations around the monumental buildings and behind the sheltering walls that define the true city. By contrast the nomadic or semi-nomadic mode of life that continued to co-exist side by side with urban agglomerations seemed a rude throwback to more primitive ways, or at best an occasional test of manly virtues and martial strength to offset the debilitating ease of the urban setting. An Akkadian poem of the late second millennium B.C. sums up the latter aspect in the context of seven irresistible weapons presented to the divine Erra and urging him into battle in the following words: [3]

---

[1] This is a thoroughly revised and updated version of portions of Hallo 1970.
[2] See below, ch. II 2.
[3] Tablet I lines 46-60; translation mine. For other translations see Reiner 1967, Cagni 1977:86, Foster BM 2:774f, FDD 135f.

Arise, get up!
Are you perhaps going to stay in the city like a paralyzed old man?
Are you going to stay in the house like a feeble baby?
Are we to eat women's bread like one who will not take the field?
Are we to fear and tremble as if we did not know battle?
Taking the field of manhood is like a holiday!
The city-dweller, though he be a prince, can never eat enough.
He is despised and slandered in the talk of his own people.
How is he to match his strength with him who takes the field?
Let the prowess of him who stays in the city be ever so enormous—
How is he to overpower the one who takes the field?
The finest city food cannot compare with field rations.
The sweetest light beer cannot compare with water from the goatskin.
The palace (erected on) a high terrace cannot compare with the war-
   rior's pallet.
Warlike Erra, take the field, brandish your weapons!

With these resounding phrases, a relatively late Babylonian poet sil-
houetted the contrast between the debilitating security of the city and
the manly challenge of the open field. The passage represents one of
"the rare attestations for rejection of the city in cuneiform literature." [4] More often, Mesopotamian thought was marked by the absence of an anti-urban bias, [5] and the "Mesopotamian poet and his
relationship to nature" was at best ambiguous. [6] I am not, however,
concerned with his particular scheme of values, but with the contrast
which he draws between city and country as such and which is
stressed in the native sources from the very beginning—as it is, often
enough, in modern scholarship. [7] In what follows, the native Mesopotamian (and Biblical) views on the nature and origins of urbanism will
be studied, rather than the modern ones. [8]

   To begin, then, with the lexical evidence, it is worth noting that
the concept "city" is expressed by a single term throughout virtually
all the long history of cuneiform: *uru* in Sumerian, [9] *er-mu*, *ar-mu*(KI),
or *i-la-mu* in Eblaite, [10] *ālu* in Akkadian, [11] and *happiras* in Hittite, [12]

---

[4] Reiner 1967:118f.; cf. *eadem* 1985:44f.
[5] Oppenheim 1964:110f; 1970:7.
[6] Oppenheim 1978:636-641.
[7] Brentjes 1968; Komoróczy 1977, esp. n. 153.
[8] For the latter see e.g. Adams and Kraeling 1960, Jawad 1965, Adams 1966,
Erwin 1966, Lampl 1968, Lapidus 1970, Orlin 1975.
[9] For which *iri*, *eri* or *ere* are only allophones; cf. Lambert 1992.
[10] Pettinato 1974-77:27 (*ad* obv. viii 15) and 30f.; OLA 5 (1979) 205 n. 62; 1982:80
and 129 = 323:1151; Fronzaroli St.Eb. 1 (1979) 9.

where the word originally meant "market." [13] True, a dozen ostensible synonyms for the Akkadian term are provided by the canonical synonym list. [14] But with the possible exception of *māhāzu* (cf. Aramaic *mahôzā*), [15] these never occur in connected contexts in the sense of "city." Some are learned loan-words from technical Sumerian terms for "foundation" or "border"; others are terms for "herd" or "pasture" that in context occur mostly as antithetically paired with "city"; one is simply the word for "inhabited world" (*dadmē*), explained more accurately as "(all) the lands" or as "sum-total of all cities" elsewhere in the same source. The rest are rare and probably foreign equivalents with which the synonym lists are typically filled out. [16] As for Sumerian, the single lexically attested synonym for *uru* is *tir*. [17] It occurs in a Hittite vocabulary—a genre not always noted for its accuracy—[18] and in a damaged context where, in addition to its normal meaning of "forest," *tir* is equated with Akkadian (and Hittite) words for "dwelling-place," "city" and "country." If correctly restored, the passage may go back to the metaphoric use of "forest" in the sense of "prison, asylum, city of refuge" suggested by scattered literary allusions. [19]

This unanimity of designation in cuneiform contrasts with the situation in other ancient Near Eastern traditions, where there are many terms for "city" and few for "countryside." [20] The antonyms for *uru* and *ālu*, on the other had, are legion. [21] It would be impossible to document here all the descriptive data that these terms provide in the context of the literary and administrative sources. Suffice it to summarize the lexical evidence in its own right: on the one side a diffuse,

---

[11] For the derivatives *āliu, ālaju, ālajītu*, "city resident," see CAD s.v. **ālû* and add ARM 10:9:12, cited by A. Malamat, Fohrer AV 75f., n. 13a. Cf. also *ša libbi āli*, "city dweller," in CAD A/1:390.

[12] Cf. Hoffner 1967:30.

[13] Friedrich 1952:55; cf. now Steiner 1989:474-476.

[14] Kilmer JAOS 83 (1963) 428 lines 193-204.

[15] For the latest of the innumerable studies on *māhāzu* and its cognates see Klein 1980 (A) and Teixidor 1983. Note it also occurs as a toponym, e.g. in the Nahal Hever papyri.

[16] See Hallo 1970:58 for details, and add *qunduhu* to the last group.

[17] MSL 3:87:5'.

[18] Hoffner 1967a; Otten and von Soden 1968.

[19] Hallo 1979, 1985 and BP 96f. and 161.

[20] For some Hebrew terms see most recently Haran 1978:117f.; Mazar 1981; Levine 1993.

[21] Hallo 1970:58f. with nn. 12-33 for details.

subjective, functional diversity of descriptive terms for the country-side, reflecting the urban point of view and a succession of different linguistic strata; on the other, a single term for the city, reflecting a common distinctiveness that apparently outweighed whatever external differences divided the cities of one age or place from another.

Mesopotamian thought is sometimes accused (on the whole unjustly) of inability to generalize. But the lexical evidence is one indication, on one level of generalization, that the city had achieved identifiable, conceptual status. Other peculiarly Mesopotamian techniques of generalization or conceptualization could be cited to the same effect. Thus the generic term for city could be substituted for the generic term for deity in Sumerian personal names like Uru-KA-gina [22] as well as in Akkadian ones, [23] and specific city-names like Nippur could be substituted for the corresponding divine names like Enlil in a name such as Nibruta-lu, "from Nippur a man-(child)" in texts from Nippur of pre-Sargonic, [24] neo-Sumerian [25] and Old Babylonian date. [26] Outside of the onomasticon, the city was also occasionally deified in royal inscriptions [27] including, arguably, the "Bassetki inscription" of Naram-Sin; [28] in an *adab*-hymn which apostrophizes the city of Ur instead of, as customary, the king; [29] and in scattered passages elsewhere in Sumerian literature where *uru* is treated like a noun of the animate class or where it is in apposition to the word for "deity." [30] From the orthography, one can cite further the fact that the word for city served as a semantic indicator or "determinative."

But I wish to turn my attention to still another index of conceptualization, one which may be loosely described as aetiological. A peculiarity of the mythopoeic mode of thought [31] was to describe identifiably isolated phenomena in terms of their origins, as though a single imaginary event in past time were the necessary and sufficient

---

[22] Lambert 1992.
[23] Gelb MAD 3:3-5; J.J.M. Roberts, *The Earliest Semitic Pantheon* (1972) 15.
[24] TMH 5:113:5.
[25] NRVN 1:109:5.
[26] Civil, RA 63 (1969) 180.
[27] So according to Larsen 1976:103 and 128, n. 71.
[28] So according to B.R. Foster, RA 73 (1979) 179, n. 1. Differently Jacobsen 1978/79:12, n. 45; Farber 1983; Hirsch 1983/84.
[29] Hallo, JCS 17 (1963) 115, n. 59.
[30] Cf. e.g. l. 98 of the Sumerian Flood Story (below, at n. 36); l. 3 of the archaic temple hymns (for which see M. Krebernik, Hrouda AV (1994) 153-157 *contra* B. Alster JCS 28 (1976) 121; and in general van Dijk 1969:182-184.
[31] On this see Komoróczy, Or. 45 (1976) 86, n. 38.

explanation of any given phenomenon in the observed present. [32] The city, too, had its aetiology, though as it happens the mythical version of urban origins as preserved in the "Sumerian Flood Story" seems to refer to the first cities as "capitals" in Civil's translation. [33] But there are quite a number of different Sumerian terms for which this meaning has been claimed, [34] and the question may legitimately be raised whether the Flood Story's KAB-du$_{11}$-ga is one of them. [35] I therefore translate lines 88-98 with Jacobsen (lines 36'-46') [36] as follows:

> When the royal scepter was coming from heaven,
> the august crown and the royal throne being already down from heaven,
> he (i.e. the king) regularly performed to perfection the august divine services and offices,
> laid the bricks of those cities in pure spots.
> They were named by name and allotted half-bushel baskets.
>
> The firstling of those cities, Eridu, she (Nintur) gave to the leader Nudimmud,
> the second, Badtibira, she gave to the Prince and Sacred One,
> the third, Larak, she gave to Pabilsag,
> the fourth, Sippar, she gave to the gallant Utu.
> The fifth, Shuruppak, she gave to Sud.
>
> These cities, which had been named by names,
> and had been allotted half-bushel baskets,
> (Dredged the canals....)

In van Dijk's interpretation, the first city, Eridu, is regarded as a or the "capital city." [37] It may be asked, however, whether his sag$_x$ uru-bi-e-ne, any more than Civil's KAB-du$_{11}$-ga, refers in this context to a priority of rank. It may well be that it refers rather to a priority of time, for the cities in question were not in fact outstanding in importance, with the possible exception of Sippar, of which more pres-

---

[32] For this definition of aetiology, or more generally of myth, see most recently Hallo, Kramer AV 2 (1983/84) 170.

[33] M. Civil *apud* W.G. Lambert and A.R.Millard, *Atra-ḫasīs* (1969).

[34] See Hallo 1970:60f. for a detailed review of the evidence.

[35] Civil JCS 28 (1976):76f. Cf. CAD s.vv. *litiktu* and *kaptukku*. For the Sumerian reflex of the former, *(giš)li-id-ga*, cf. Jacobsen, Kramer AV 2 (1983/84) 196 (p). For the Hebrew cognate *letek* cf. Hosea 3:2.

[36] Jacobsen 1981:518; Harps 146f.; cf. also Kramer An St 33 (1983) 115-121.

[37] J. van Dijk, JCS 19 (1965) 19f.

ently. [38] They are distinguished, rather, for their antiquity. This antiquity is, for the most part, well attested in the archaeological evidence. My purpose here is to adduce, not this, but the literary
evidence to the same effect.

    There is, it is true, considerable vagueness and contradiction in
cuneiform literature about the antediluvian traditions. This is not
unexpected, even in light of the latest discoveries. These now make it
seem possible that a specific historic event provided the original inspiration for the Mesopotamian versions of the deluge, and that this particular event occurred about 2900 B.C. [39] Whether that event was a
natural disaster, or whether the deluge served as a metaphor for a
human " flood" remains to be seen. [40] But in any case the earliest
Sumerian literature, if not the story of the flood itself, can now be
traced back to approximately 2500 B.C. at Fara and Abu Salabikh, [41]
or only some four hundred years later.

    Four hundred years are, of course, still enough to account for the
legendary aura that surrounds even the earliest cuneiform allusions to
the flood and the flood-hero, and for the confusions and contradic-
tions concerning the antediluvian traditions. Such inconsistencies
characterize in the first place the number, the names, the order and
the lengths of reign of the antediluvian kings. [42] They apply in the
second place to the tradition of the seven antediluvian sages, which is
first attested in the Erra Epic (I 147 and 162) and then in a late
medical text, [43] and which even finds a Biblical echo in the "seven
pillars of wisdom" (Prov. 9:1), according to one interpretation. [44] They
apply in the third place to the secondary uses to which the antediluvian traditions were put.

    To begin with the antediluvian sages, whose names are fairly trans-
parent titles (incipits) of learned and in part late compendia, [45] and
who were considered "culture-heroes" bringing the arts of civilization
to Sumer, all seven were originally linked with Eridu as early as Old

---

[38] Even Sippar was relatively small and insignificant; cf. Adams *apud* Lapidus
1970:16f. Cf. also Harris 1975:10.
[39] Cf. ANEH 34-36 for a summary of the arguments and literature.
[40] Hallo 1990:194-197; cf.also Eichler 1993.
[41] For this date cf. Hallo Or. 42 (1973).
[42] See most recently Lambert 1973:271-275 and 280.
[43] AMT 105:22; cf. Reiner 1961:9f.
[44] Greenfield 1985.
[45] Hallo 1963:175f.; HUCA 48 (1977) 4, n. 9.

Babylonian times, as is clear from the Temple Hymn for Ku'ara. [46] Later texts make reference to the "seven sages of Eridu" [47] and to individual sages: the first one, Adapa, is called sage (NUN.ME = *apkallu*) of Eridu [48] and the sixth, An-Enlilda, is called purification priest (ME = *išippu*) of Eridu. [49] The first explicit linkage between sage and king in antediluvian times is provided by a neo-Assyrian text from Sultan Tepe. This is an "apocryphal letter" of "Adapa the sage," elsewhere identified with U'an = Oannes, [50] to Alulu, the first antediluvian king. [51] In Hellenistic times, the linkage was systematized by associating each of the seven antediluvian sages with one of the first seven antediluvian kings. This final stage in the process has long been known in a corrupt form from Berossos, who assigned one sage to the first king, one to the fourth, *four* to the sixth and one to the seventh. [52] More recently it was confirmed and corrected by a cuneiform text from Uruk dated to the 147th year of the Seleucid Era (= 165 B.C.). [53] Implicitly, this scheme also involves a link between the antediluvian sages and the first three or four antediluvian cities, excluding Larak (?) as well as Shuruppak, home of the eighth and last antediluvian, and ending instead with Sippar.[54] But it was only the *post*-diluvian *apkallu*'s who were each explicitly linked with cities of their own in the various cuneiform traditions. [55]

So much for the development of the *apkallu*-tradition. The history of the antediluvian royal names is also instructive. In Mesopotamia itself, they were simply added, by way of prologue, to the Sumerian King List [56] or, later, to the "Dynastic Chronicle." [57] King Enmenduranna of Sippar may have been regarded as ancestor of all diviners in one late tradition, but the older Babylonian traditions neither ex-

---

[46] See most recently Heimpel 1981.

[47] K 8444 (unpubl.), cited by van Dijk 1953:20, n. 56; LKA 146:5 as read by Lambert, BiOr 13 (1956)144.

[48] PBS 1/2:113 ii 58 = IV R 58:24; cf. BRM 4:3:5 and 11: *ap-kal-lum* (resp. *a-da-pa*) DUMU URU.DUG (Adapa legend).

[49] LKA 146:11 with van Dijk 1962:48 *contra* CAD I/J 243a; *bit mēsiri* III 19f. with Borger 1974:192 *contra* Reiner 1961:4.

[50] Written u₄-ᵈ60; see above, n. 45.

[51] STT 2:176:14'-21' + 185 rev. 1'-4' with Reiner and Civil, JNES 26 (1967)208.

[52] Burstein 1978:160f.

[53] Van Dijk 1962:44-52.

[54] Below, at nn. 92-96.

[55] Hallo 1963:175 with n. 75; W.G. Lambert, JCS 11 (1957) 8f.

[56] Hallo 1963a:54-56.

[57] See most recently Finkel 1980:68-70; Hallo, Sachs AV (1988)184f.

plicitly claim the total destruction of mankind at the flood nor, in consequence, that all of humanity therefore descended from a lone survivor. [58] In the Hebrew Bible, on the other hand, the antediluvians re-emerge as ancestors one of the other and, in the case of the "line of Seth," as ancestors of all of post-diluvian humanity in turn. The Biblical recasting of the traditions is quite in keeping with the genealogical orientation that makes its appearance in the ancient Near East with the coming of the Amorites. In the words of W.G. Lambert, "the idea that family descent somehow assured the legitimacy of the king arose only with the arrival of the Amorites in the Second Millennium." [59] It is reflected in the Mesopotamian king lists of the Old Babylonian and Old Assyrian periods as these have recently been recovered or reinterpreted. [60]

In light of all these vagaries of the other antediluvian traditions, the relative unanimity of the tradition of antediluvian *cities* emerges as all the more impressive. [61] This unanimity applies to the number, the names and the sequence of cities, in approximately that order. The number of cities is five in all the most reliable texts where the relevant section is completely preserved: the Weld-Blundell Prism version of the Sumerian King List (WB 444), the Sumerian Flood Story, and the Dynastic Chronicle. The same number can be restored where the the section is damaged (Ni. 3195). [62] It is increased by one in a Larsa version of the Sumerian King List (WB 62) where local pride apparently dictated the insertion of that city. It is decreased by one in a casual school-boy's version, apparently through simple omission (UCBC 9-1819). [63] It is decreased by two or more in the late Hellenistic versions tradited under the name of Berossos. [64]

The names of the antediluvian cities are Eridu, Bad-tibira (or Patibira), Larak, Sippar and Shuruppak, in the earliest traditions. They are regarded as substrate toponyms by Salonen. [65] The substitution of Ku'ara (HA.A.KI) for Eridu in one version may be no more than a

[58] Cf. in detail Hallo 1970:62, n. 74.
[59] Lambert 1974:434; cf. also Wilson 1975:175f.
[60] Hallo, Sachs AV (1988)180f.
[61] See the summary of the evidence by Finkelstein 1963:45f. and Table I, to which add above, nn. 53 and 57.
[62] Published in transliteration by F.R. Kraus, ZA 50 (1952) 31.
[63] Finkelstein 1963.
[64] Burstein 1978.
[65] Salonen 1972:11f., n. 1.

pars pro toto usage if Ku'ara was simply a subdivision of Eridu, [66] as it was later of Babylon. [67] This in turn may help to explain the late replacement of Eridu by Babylon. The addition of Larsa has already been noted.

As for the order, this is relatively fixed as to the first and last members of the series, no doubt because of firm notions, preserved outside the antediluvian scheme, as to the first of all cities and as to the home of the flood-hero. The maximum divergence occurs in the middle of the sequence, which seems to be arranged more or less at random. The analogy of similar discrepancies in post-diluvian historiography, notably in the "History of the Tummal," [68] suggests that here too we are to see the three cities as more or less contemporary, rather than successive. (In fact, van Dijk regards all five of them as an early amphictyony.) [69] This solution recommends itself if, as I tend to suppose, Mesopotamian urbanism was only some two centuries old at the time of "the flood," i.e. at the beginning of Early Dynastic times. [70] The Atar-hasis Epic seems to reflect a native understanding of antediluvian chronology in similar terms with its repeated assertion that "twice 600 years had not yet passed" since the creation of mankind (i.e., of cities and civilization?) before it provoked the Deluge.

This chronology admittedly flies in the face of the reigns attributed to the antediluvians in the King List traditions which, measured in millennia, are obviously fantastic and probably secondary. The shorter chronology can claim some support from archaeology, according to which it may or not be the equivalent of the brief but creative Jemdet Nasr Period, [71] and from other ancient Near Eastern traditions, such as the early Phoenician ones preserved by Philo of Byblos in the name of Sanchunjathon, in a chapter of his *Phoenician History* called "the discoverers." [72] These include the notion of the emergence of cities as one of the signal achievements of the semi-divine "culture-heroes" who resemble the antediluvian sages of Mesopotamia. [73]

---

[66] Hallo *apud* Finkelstein 1963:46, n. 22. Differently Burstein 1978:160, n. 29.
[67] Under the name Kumar; cf. Heimpel 1981.
[68] Sollberger 1962.
[69] Van Dijk 1982:110, n. 23.
[70] Cf. ANEH 34f.
[71] ANEH 27-34; Finkbeiner and Röllig 1986.
[72] Greenfield 1985:19.
[73] Clemen 1939:26:19; cf. Baumgarten 1981:140-179.

Sanchunjathon in turn may prove to be something of a bridge to Biblical traditions. The two parallel but separate versions concerning the generations before the flood preserved in Genesis 4 and 5 can no longer be regarded simply as variants of a single source. Rather they reflect, respectively, the two parallel but separate Mesopotamian traditions of antediluvian kings and antediluvian sages whose distinct histories we have traced. [74] That they are partly conflated in the Bible is merely another echo of a comparable process that can be detected on the Mesopotamian side as well.

What then of the even older Mesopotamian tradition of antediluvian cities? Has this, too, left its traces in the Biblical account? The peculiar phrasing of Genesis 4:17 is one clue to this effect. It does not simply say that Cain built a city, but that "he was (or became) the builder of a city" (*wayᵉhi bone ᶜir*). In the context of the Cainite/Kenite genealogy, which stresses the novelty of the arts and sciences attributed to this line of "culture-heroes" —and "euhemeristic" ones at that—[75] this can only imply that he became the first builder of a city. The building of cities, that is to say, began with him, whereas before that he and his brother Abel had known only agriculture and animal husbandry, for they had been the archetypical "tiller of the soil" and "shepherd of the flock" respectively (Gen. 4:2). In modern terms, we have here in capsule form the doctrine of the agricultural revolution followed by the urban revolution. Parenthetically, it is interesting to note that the Biblical account derives incipient urbanism from the domestication of plants, not of animals. [76]

But verse 17 has more to reveal, for it tells us that Cain called this first city "like (i.e., after) the name of his son Enoch (ḤNWK)." This Enoch, or rather his namesake in the Sethite genealogy of Genesis 5, bears comparison with king Enmenduranki (Enmenduranna) of Sippar. [77] In Hellenistic wisdom literature, he was also widely equated with the Oannes of Berossos, [78] the same Oannes who according to Berossos taught men to build cities. [79] Both Enoch and Oannes were

---

[74] Finkelstein 1963:50, n. 41; ANEH 32. For earlier views, see Hallo 1970:63f., n. 83.

[75] After Euhemerus, who regarded myths as traditional accounts of real incidents in human history; cf. Hallo, JAOS 101 (1981) 255.

[76] Cf. below, ch. II 2.

[77] Borger 1974:185f.

[78] Ben-Zion Wacholder, HUCA 34 (1963) 97, n. 86.

[79] Burstein 1978:156 (top).

regarded as the fountain-head of human wisdom, especially astrology. [80] Indeed, it would be possible to propose similar etymologies for both names, for Oannes is the Graecized form of Sumerian u_4-^dan which, in late texts, tended to be (playfully) equated with Akkadian *ummânu*, "sage, teacher," [81] while ḤNWK can be derived from a root meaning "to train, educate." It would be harder to derive ḤNWK from the name of an antediluvian city, as the Biblical text suggests.

Or as it seems to suggest. Cassuto noted, however, that Gen. 4:17 is a close parallel to Gen. 4:1-2. [82] These verses state: "And the man knew Eve his wife and she conceived and bore Cain ... and she continued to bear Abel his brother, and Abel became a shepherd of the flock while Cain became a tiller of the soil." Just so, the first part of our verse should then be understood thus: "And Cain knew his wife, and she conceived and bore Enoch, who became a city-builder." [83] If, then, it was *Enoch* who built the (first) city, it follows (though Cassuto does not draw this consequence) that it was Enoch who named it after his son, Irad. Ignoring the Masoretic punctuation, we should therefore understand the second part of the verse as follows: "and he called the name of his city according to the name of his son—did Enoch!" (Alternatively, Enoch may represent a gloss that has crept into the text.)

As for the name Irad, and its parallel Yered in the Sethite line, they have defied all explanations to date, [84] other than Midrashic ones. [85] I therefore propose to see in them, not in Enoch, a name equal to that of an antediluvian city, specifically Eridu, thus reviving a suggestion made over a century ago by A.H. Sayce. [86] And indeed, the notion that Enoch built the first city is preserved in Al-Asatir, a medieval Samaritan text, where "each of Adam's antediluvian descendants is associated with the building of a city, some of which are

---

[80] *Ibid.* and n. 10; above, nn. 45 and 50.

[81] Hallo 1963:176, n. 83; my reading of ABL 923 is not followed by ANET 3:606f. or CAD A/2:172d, but cf. A. Spalinger, BASOR 223 (1976) 64.

[82] Cassuto 1961:228-230.

[83] *Ibid.* Similarly already K. Budde, *Die biblische Urgeschichte* (1883)120-123. So now also Borger 1974:193, n.3.

[84] A. Poebel, JNES 1 (1942) 256, n. 17, wanted to link it with *wardu, mardu,* "slave, Amorite," B. Mazar, JNES 24 (1965) 299, n. 16, with the city-name Arad, M. Birot, RAI 26 (1980) 144, with Yaradi as an epithet of the Hanaeans.

[85] See Hallo 1970:64, n. 91 for one.

[86] Sayce 1884-85.

named for the builder's son... This tradition attributes the building of the first city to Enoch the son of Cain and not to Cain." [87]

As to the third and fourth names in this portion of the Cainite/Kenite genealogy, corresponding roughly to the first and fourth in the Sethite line, I make no claim to connect them phonetically with any antediluvian city-names. They are clearly intended as personal names, and in the case of Methuselah, the Sethite chronology even adds a biographical touch, for this longest-lived of all the antediluvians died precisely in the year of the flood, that is in 1656 according to the Era of Creation, [88] albeit seven days *before* the onset of the flood according to Rabbinic tradition. [89]

The last of the five names in both Biblical versions, by contrast, offers a multiple choice of contacts with Mesopotamian traditions. On the phonetic level, Hebrew Lamech (LMK) bears comparison with cuneiform Larak, especially if allowance is made for the uncertain spelling and pronunciation of the latter name. [90] As father of Noah or of the virtually synonymous Na'amah, [91] Lamech invites comparison with Shuruppak, father of the Sumerian flood-hero Ziusudra and at the same time last of the antediluvian cities in the cuneiform traditions. As father of Tubal-cain, the inventor of copper and iron implements, he recalls Bad-tibira or (Pa-tibira), the "fortress (or canal) of the metalworkers," or Sippar, the city whose name means bronze. Sippar deserves some further attention.

Alone among the antediluvian cities, Sippar boasted a sustained importance that matched its hoary antiquity. It was sacred to the sun-god. Though rarely if ever the seat of an independent kingdom in historic times, it was firmly and exclusively linked, in the cuneiform sources, [92] to the antediluvian king Enmeduranki (or Enme(n)duranna), hero of a considerable number of independent traditions, [93] and sometimes linked to the Biblical Enoch by the latter's solar symbolism

---

[87] Personal communication from my colleague Steven Fraade (June 5, 1980). Professor Fraade notes, however, that Cain is the builder of seven cities in a tradition preserved by Pseudo-Philo in his *Biblical Antiquities*.

[88] Cf. below, ch. IV 3.

[89] Hallo 1991:178-180.

[90] Hallo 1970:65, n. 94; for Larak in the later period (8th century) see A.J. Brinkman, *Prelude to Empire* (Philadelphia, 1984) 15, n. 59.

[91] The explanation for Noah's name in Gen. 5:29 actually suits Na'amah much better.

[92] Only Berossos diverges here; cf. Burstein 1978:161.

[93] Lambert 1967 and 1974; Borger 1974.

(cf. Gen. 5:23). It was in Sippar that, according to Berossos, the revealed wisdom of the antediluvian sages was buried for safekeeping during the Deluge, [94] for it was Sippar alone that was then spared, according to the Epic of Erra with which we started (IV 50). But the later Sippar was not so lucky, for the same Epic tells how Erra finally responded to the urgings of his weapons and put a number of cities to the sword in what may be the literary recasting of an event also recorded in a historical inscription of King Shimbar-shihu (ca. 1025-1008 B.C.). [95] The sack of Sippar was particularly inexcusable, for in both sources, as well as others, it is called "the eternal city," and there is even a part of the city called "Sippar of Eternity." [96] It is to the former concept that I now turn.

The concept of "eternal city" is expressed by *uru-ul* in Sumerian, [97] *āl ṣâti* in Akkadian, [98] and *ukturis happiras* in Hittite. [99] Other cities share the epithet with Sippar, though more rarely. [100] But its most intriguing occurrence is in the divine name *dEn-uru-ul-la*, "lord of the eternal city," or "lord of the primeval city," [101] a manifestation or atavar of the supreme sky-god An. According to a very suggestive hypothesis of van Dijk, the reference here is to a mythical "univers embryonnaire," a condition before the creation of sun and moon, before the separation of earth and sky, the emergence of gods and men, the introduction of agriculture or, what is more to the point here, of cities. [102] He essayed the first edition of an enigmatic fragment from pre-Sargonic Lagash [103] variously described as a hymn to the Sun or a lamentation over the destruction of Lagash, [104] but which was in fact one of the oldest pieces of Sumerian mythology then known. [105] Paraphrasing his translation, we read:

---

[94] Burstein 1978:162.

[95] Goetze 1965; Brinkman 1968:150-155.

[96] For this *Zimbir-u₄-ul-lí-a* see Hallo, JCS 18 (1964) 66 and nn. 13f.; Harris 1975:14 and n. 26. Cf. also MSL 11:12:11; 35:22; 63:9'; 101:170.

[97] Not to be confused with *uru-ul* in the sense of *ālu elû*, "lofty city," or the toponym "field of *Uru-ul-la*" for which see Hallo 1970:65 and n. 100.

[98] CADṢ 118c. Add the date formula for Hammurapi's last year!

[99] Archi 1983:24 and 26, line 14. The reference is to "Sippar, the eternal city of the Sun-god."

[100] See in detail Hallo 1970:65 and nn. 101-103.

[101] I.e., city of the dead according to Jacobsen TIT 115.

[102] Van Dijk 1964:20 and 42; 1976.

[103] Sollberger, CIRPL Ukg. (= Urukagina) 15.

[104] Sollberger, ICO 22 (1957) 33; cf. already idem, ZA 50 (1952) 26 and n. 2..

[105] Hallo 1963:167, n. 11.

The reptiles verily descend
The earth verily makes its (breast?) appear resplendent
It is the garden, it is the foundation-terrace
(Which) the earth-hole for its part fills with water
An (Heaven) is the lord, he is stationed like a young hero
Heaven and Earth cry out together
At that time Enki and Eridu(!) had not appeared
Enlil did not exist
Ninlil did not exist
Brightness was dust
Vegetation was dust
The daylight did not shine
The moonlight did not emerge.

The parallels with both versions of creation in Genesis which this tantalizing fragment evokes are too numerous to go into here. True, the crucial line mentioning Eridu (NUN.KI) is rendered differently in some translations, both older [106] and more recent. Thus Wilcke's German translation amounts to "At that time the lords of the locales, the princes of the locales did not reside (yet)," [107] Alster renders "At that time the (divine) earth lord and the (divine) earth lady (NIN!.KI) did not exist yet," [108] and even van Dijk has a new suggestion. [109] But if they have recovered the original understanding of the passage, that must have been lost long ago, for already the bilingual myth of "The Founding of Eridu," which Falkenstein ascribed to Kassite times, dates the foundation of Eridu and its sister cities in relation to the Creation, as we have previously seen it dated to the flood. [110]

In the Bible, the tradition of the antediluvian cities remained embedded, and for practical purposes concealed, within the context of the primeval history of humankind. The same fate would likely have befallen the tradition in Mesopotamia had it been confined to the myths cited above, each of them known to date from no more than a single fragmentary example. By being spliced into the framework of the Sumerian King List, however, it was saved from this fate. The

---

[106] Sollberger, ZA 50 (1952) 26, translated "en ce temps-là, Enki ne créait plus dans Eridu."

[107] Wilcke 1969:132, taking *sig₇* as plural for *ti*, "reside, live"; it can also function as plural for *gál*, "exist, be."

[108] Alster 1970.

[109] Van Dijk 1976:128, n. 22.

[110] CT 13:35-38; cf. van Dijk 1976:127f. and nn. 12, 20.

importance of the relationship beween kingship and the city is evident throughout the King List. Indeed, that List should more properly be called the "Sumerian City List" in terms of its own summary.[111] In its fullest form, the List begins with (the building of) Eridu and ends with (the destruction of) Isin, that is, it records the entire history of "The City."

For in the final analysis, the concepts of eternal city and first, head or capital city converge, not only in their common Akkadian equivalent *ālu elû*, "lofty city," but also in the notion of a "pristine heavenly city" *(uru-sag-an-na)* named, according to a lexical text, Dunnum. [112] In historical terms, this otherwise obscure city was regarded as the "ancient capital" *(uru-sag-mah)* or "bolt" *(gāmiru)* of the Isin empire, [113] and its capture by Larsa in 1795 B.C. was the prelude to the fall of thwe whole kingdom of Isin in the following year. [114] In mythological terms, however, it was the cosmic "eternal city" (URU *ṣa-a-tam*) according to a myth edited most recently by Jacobsen and called by him "the Harab Myth." [115] It was built by Heaven and Earth themselves as their third and climactic creation, Heaven appearing here under the otherwise unknown name of Harab. It does not begin, however, with Harab's name, as in Jacobsen's restoration, but with the words "in the beginning" *(ina rēš)*, to judge by the appearance of this incipit (twice) in a late literary catalogue. [116] It continues with a complicated theogony set in the primordial past. And that is, I daresay, as far back as even the cuneiform sources will allow us to trace our urban origins.

Bibliographical References

Adams, Robert M., 1966: *The Evolution of Urban Society: Early Mesopotamia and Prehispanic Mexico* (Chicago, Aldine).

———, and Carl Kraeling, eds., 1960: *City Invincible: a Symposium on Urbanization and Cultural Development in the Ancient Near East* (Chicago, University of Chicago Press).

Alster, Bendt, 1970: "e n - k i n u n - k i," RA 64:189f.

Archi, Alfonso, 1983: "Die Adad-Hymne ins Hethitische übersetzt," Or. 52:20-30.

---

[111] Buccellati 1964:54.

[112] See now MSL 17:226:188.

[113] Jacobsen 1984; for the concept cf. Hallo, RHA 1936 (1978) 2 (Simurrum); P. Steinkeller, ZA 72 (1982) 239f. and n. 11 (Arawa); Å. Sjöberg, Hallo AV 212, n. 7 (Huhnuri etc.).

[114] See the date-formulas of Rim-Sin 29 and 30.

[115] Jacobsen 1984.

[116] Van Dijk, BaMiBeiheft 2(1980) No.90; cf. Hallo, Sachs AV (1988)185, n. 78.

16 CHAPTER ONE

Baumgarten, A.I., 1981: *The Phoenician History of Philo of Byblos: a Commentary* (Leiden, Brill).

Borger, Rykle, 1974: " *Bīt Mesēri* und die Himmelsfahrt Henochs," JNES 33:183-196.

Brentjes, B., 1968: "Zum Verhältnis von Dorf und Stadt in Altvorderasien," WZUH 17/6:9-41.

Brinkman, J.A., 1968: *A Political History of Post-Kassite Babylonia 1156 - 722 BC* (= AnOr 43).

Buccellati, Giorgio, 1964: "The enthronement of the king and the capital city," Oppenheim AV 54-61.

Burstein, Stanley M., 1978: "The Babyloniaca of Berossus," SANE 1:141-181.

Cagni, Luigi, 1977: "The poem of Erra," SANE 1:61-118.

Cassuto, Umberto, 1961: *A Commentary on the Book of Genesis, Part I: From Adam to Noah* (Jerusalem, Magnes Press). Translated from the Hebrew edition of 1953.

Clemen, Carl, 1939: *Die phönikische Religion nach Philo von Byblos* (= MVAG 42/3).

Eichler, Barry L., 1993: "mar-URU5 : tempest in a deluge," Hallo AV 90-94.

Erwin, Robert, 1966: "Cities without vistas: a reconnoitering of Akkadian civilization," *Virginia Quarterly Review* 42:43-57.

Farber, W., 1983: "Die Vergöttlichung Naram-Sins," Or. 52:67-72.

Finkbeiner, Uwe and Wolfgang Röllig, eds., 1986: *Gamdat Nasr: Period or Regional Style* (Wiesbaden, Reichert).

Finkel, Irving L., 1980: "Bilingual chronicle fragments," JCS 32:65-80.

Finkelstein, J.J., 1963: "The antediluvian kings: a University of California tablet," JCS 17:39-51.

Friedrich, Johannes, 1952: *Hethitisches Wörterbuch* (Heidelberg, Carl Winter).

Goetze, Albrecht, 1965: "An inscription of Simbar-šīhu," JCS 19:121-135.

Greenfield, Jonas C., 1985: "The seven pillars of wisdom (Prov. 9:1)—a mistranslation," JQR 76:13-20.

Hallo, William W., 1963: "On the antiquity of Sumerian literature," JAOS 83:167-176.

———, 1963a: "Beginning and end of the Sumerian King List in the Nippur tradition," JCS 17:52-57.

———, 1970: "Antediluvian Cities," JCS 23:57-67.

———, 1979: "Notes from the Babylonian Collection I: Nungal in the egal," JCS 31:161-165.

———, 1985: "Back to the big house: colloquial Sumerian, continued," Or. 54:56-64.

———, 1990, "The limits of skepticism," JAOS 110:187-199.

———, 1991: "Information from before the flood," *Maarav* 7:173-181.

Haran, Menahem, 1978: *Temples and Temple-Service in Ancient Israel* (Oxford, Clarendon Press).

Harris, Rivkah, 1975: *Ancient Sippar: a Demographic Study of an Old Babylonian City (1894-1595 B.C.)* (= PIHANS 36).

Heimpel, Wolfgang, 1981: "Ku'ara," RLA 6/3-4:256f.

Hirsch, Hans, 1983-84: "Ideologie einer Stadt," AfO 29-30:58-61.

Hoffner, Harry, 1967: *An English-Hittite Glossary* (= RHA 25/80).

———, 1967a: "Ugaritic pwt: a term from the early Canaanite dyeing industry," JAOS 241-245.

Jacobsen, Thorkild, 1978-79: "Iphur-Kishi and his times," AfO 26:1-14.

———, 1981: 'The Eridu Genesis,' JBL 100: 513-529.

———, 1984: "The Harab myth," SANE 2:95-120.

Jawad, A.J., 1965: *The Advent of the Era of Townships in Northern Mesopotamia* (Leiden, Brill).

Klein, Jacob, 1980: "Some rare Sumerian words gleaned from the royal hymns of Šulgi," E.Y. Kutscher AV ix-xxviii.

Komoróczy, Geza, 1977: "Ummanmanda," *Acta Antiqua ... Hungaricae* 25:43-67.

Lambert, W.G, 1967: "Enmeduranki and related matters," JCS 17:52-57.

————, 1973: "Antediluvian kings and Marduk's chariot," Böhl AV 271-280.

————, 1974: "The seed of kingship," RAI 19:427-440.

————, 1992: "The reading of Uru-KA-gi-na again," *Aula Orientalis* 10:256-258.

Lampl, Paul, 1968: *Cities and Planning in the Near East* (New York, George Braziller).

Lapidus, Ira M., ed., 1970: *Middle Eastern Cities: a Symposium on Ancient, Islamic, and Contemporary Middle Eastern Urbanism* (Berkeley, University of California Press).

Larsen, Mogens Trolle, 1976: *The Old Assyrian City-State and its Colonies* (= Mesopotamia 4).

Levine, Baruch A., 1993: "On the semantics of land tenure in Biblical literature: the term *'aḥuzzāh*," Hallo AV 134-139.

Mazar, Benjamin, 1981: "The early Israelite settlement in the hill country," BASOR 241:75-85.

Oppenheim, A. Leo, 1964: *Ancient Mesopotamia: Portrait of a Dead Civilization*; 2nd ed., ed. by Erica Reiner, 1977 (Chicago, University of Chicago Press).

————, 1970: "Mesopotamia—land of many cities," apud Lapidus 1970:3-18.

————, 1978: "Man and nature in Mesopotamian civilization," *Dictionary of Scientific Biography* 15:634-666.

Orlin, Louis L., 1975: "Ancient Near Eastern cities: form, function and idea," in Orlin, ed., *Janus: Ancient and Modern Studies*, Part One: The City in History: Idea and Reality (An Arbor, Center for Coordination of Ancient and Modern Studies, The University of Michigan).

Otten, Heinrich and Wolfram von Soden, *Das Akkadisch-hethitische Vokabular KBo I 44 + KBo XIII 1* (= SBT 7).

Pettinato, Giovanni, 1974-77: "Il calendario di Ebla," AfO 25:1-36.

————, 1982: *Testi Lessicali Bilingui della Biblioteca L. 2769* (= MEE 4).

Reiner, Erica, 1961: "The aetiological myth of the seven sages," Or. 30:1-11.

————, 1967: "City bread and bread baked in ashes," Bobrinskoy AV 116-120.

————, 1985: *Your thwarts in pieces Your mooring rope cut: Poetry from Babylonia and Assyria* (Ann Arbor, University of Michigan Press).

Salonen, Armas, 1972: *Die Ziegeleien im Alten Mesopotamien* (= AASF 171).

Sayce, A.H., 1884-85: "Sprechsaal 10: Irad und Enoch im Genesis," *Zeitschrift für Keilschriftforschung* 1/1:404.

Sollberger, Edmond, 1962: "The Tummal inscription," JCS 16:40-47.

Steiner, Gerd, 1989: Kultepe-Kanis und der 'Anitta-Text'," Ozguc AV 471-480.

Teixidor, J., 1983: "Palmyrene *MHWẒ* and Ugaritic *MIḤD*. A suggestion," UF 15:309-311.

Van Dijk, J., 1953: *La Sagesse Sumero-Accadienne* (Leiden, Brill).

————, 1962: "Die Inschriftenfunde," UVB 18:39-62 and pls. 27f.

————, 1964: "Le motif cosmique dans la pensée sumériennne," *Acta Orientalia* 28:1-59.

————, 1969: "Les contacts ethniques dans la Mésoptamie et les syncrétismes de la religion sumérienne," in Sven S. Hartman, ed., *Syncretism* (Stockholm, Almqvist & Wiksell).

————, 1976: "Existe-t-il un 'poème de la creation' sumérien?" Kramer AV 125-133.

————, 1982: "Fremdsprachige Beschwörungstexte in der südmesopotamischen Überlieferung," RAI 25:97-110.

Wilcke, Claus, 1969: *Das Lugalbandaepos* (Wiesbaden, Harrassowitz).

Wilson, Robert R., 1975: "The Old Testament genealogies in recent research," JBL 94:169-189.

2. Capital Formation

Of course the amenities of civilization implied by the creation of cities were not solely due to these cities, but in equal measure to the concomitant accumulation of capital, which had helped to make the cities a possibility in the first place. Capital took many forms, beginning with "heads" of cattle which, as in the case of civilization, provide the Latin etymology for the concept in the first place. In similar fashion, the Akkadian word for "herd" (*sugullu*) reappears in Hebrew in the meaning "treasure" (*segulla*). [117] In English, too, the terms "chattel" and "cattle" have a common etymon.

But I am not concerned here with these basic forms of capital (we will return to agricultural wealth later), but with its earliest conversion into "money" in one form or another. And here we encounter an interesting phenomenon. While the origins of coinage are generally dated no earlier than the seventh century B.C., and attributed then to the Lydians of Western Anatolia, [118] there is certainly money before coinage—as there is today, we might almost say, money after coinage, i.e. the greater part of today's transactions are carried on with other instruments of payment.

In the view of historians of economics, the classical functions of money are three: as a medium of exchange, as a unit of account, and as a standard of value. There are many other ways to satisfy these three functions than only through minted coinage. [119] Fritz Heichelheim has argued that notably the so-called "exchangeable goods" or commodities served the purpose in pre-classical times. [120] They were characterized by being non-perishable and in fairly constant demand. While we lack assurance of the situation at the end of the fourth millennium when the process of capital accumulation was certainly in full swing in Sumer, we do have evidence from the end of the *third* millennium of commodities answering these descriptions. They are especially wool, dates, fish-oil, dried or smoked fish, skins, and above all: grains (barley and wheat). [121]

Of barley, the ancient Sumerian poet himself said: "Whoever pos-

---

[117] Greenberg 1951; reprinted 1995:273-278; cf. Hallo *apud* J. Lewy, JAOS 78 (1958) 93, n. 19.
[118] See most recently Kagan 1982.
[119] Meshorer 1976; cited but not used by Powell 1978:234, n.1.
[120] Heichelheim 1958:103-107.
[121] Curtis and Hallo 1959:111f.

sesses gold, or silver, or cattle, or sheep, / Shall wait at the gate of
him who possesses barley, and thus spend his day!" [122] The passage
concludes the disputation of Cattle and Grain, or Ewe and Wheat, as
Alster and Vanstiphout call it. Thus barley (*še*) conquers all, because
it is the standard of value for all, even for the stereotypical forms of
wealth, phrased in another Sumerian "wisdom text" as "silver, precious stones (literally: lapis lazuli), cattle and sheep" (Enlil and Namzitarra 13' -16'). [123]

Despite the poet, however, silver eventually won the day. It was
not only more durable and more constantly in demand than the other
"exchangeable commodities," but also had the virtue of being easily
carried about the person because of its high value per unit of weight.
This was theoretically also true of gold, but gold was generally from
seven to ten times as valuable as silver, in other words *so* valuable that
it was impractical to carry about. It was used as money only in the
Middle Babylonian period. [124]

Silver, on the other hand, not only could be carried on the person,
it *was*. We know this from the abundant testimony of both texts and
excavations. "The Neo-Sumerian Silver Ring Texts" [125] record mostly
gifts of such rings in amounts varying from five to ten shekels in
weight (i.e. ca. 37.5 to 75 grams) and usually on the occasion of a
journey. [126] As for the archaeological evidence, I long ago identified
these rings of silver (and gold, etc.) called *har* in Sumerian and *šewiru,
šemeru, semeru* in Akkadian, with "the spiral bands found frequently in
grave deposits throughout the Old World; they served the living as a
precursor of coined money not because they generally weighed five
gín [127]—in fact, an interesting group published by Sollberger enumer-
ates at least sixteen such objects and only two of them have this
weight—but because they were easy and relatively safe to carry and
because they could be broken off in the desired weight when payment
was called for," [128] citing Sollberger, [129] a neo-Sumerian letter-order [130] and "the *har* (ring) placed on the teacher's hand as an obvious

---

[122] Alster and Vanstiphout 1987:28-31, lines 189f.; they translate "grain."
[123] Klein 1990: 58f.
[124] Cf. especially Edzard 1960; Leemans 1957-71.
[125] Michalowski 1978.
[126] Cf. also below, n. 130.
[127] Limet 1960:212.
[128] Hallo 1963:138.
[129] JCS 10 (1956) 21-24.
[130] YOS 4:117, meantime edited by Sollberger as TCS 1:1.

bribe in "the first case of 'apple-polishing'." [131] Meantime such *har*-rings have also been identified in the texts from Ebla. [132]

Silver rings or rather spirals or coils of this sort were found at Ur and a number of other sites and identified as "money before coinage" by J. Dayton. [133] They were also in use at Mari, as noted by Stephanie Dalley. [134] But they were especially common at Tell Asmar (ancient Eshnunna) according to T. Jacobsen, [135] and these finds formed the basis of an extensive study called "A Contribution to the History of Money in Mesopotamia prior to the Invention of Coinage" by Marvin Powell. [136] Powell criticized Dayton's study; he showed that, at Ur, the 5-shekel *har* was indeed by far the most typical (541 out of 635 occurrences in the Ur III texts); [137] and he concluded that, as a forerunner of money, the coils went largely out of use after the Old Babylonian Period, when "scrap silver" *(šibirtu)* and eventually a mark of quality on such silver called *ginnu* (Persian period only) provided a gradual transition to coinage proper.

To return to the rings or coils, they sometimes come in pairs; they are then called *har é-ba-an* in Sumerian [138] or *tapal šemeri* in Akkadian. [139] It is even possible that the cuneiform script itself preserved a memory of the functional identity of these silver rings with money: while the basic pictographic meaning of the *har*-sign was "liver, millstone, ashes, etc." according to Deimel, [140] he assigns to the sign for "silver" *(kù(g))* the meaning of a bent silver wire, with calibration marks to indicate weight or value [141], and semicircular in form. [142]

Having shown that silver, in the form of rings or coils, served as a medium of exchange in ancient Mesopotamia, we should now demonstrate that it also served the other classical functions of money, as

---

[131] Kramer 1981: 11.

[132] Archi 1985.

[133] Dayton 1974.

[134] *Mari and Karana* (1984) 65-69: "currency and rates of exchange," with fig. 30.

[135] Assyriological Colloquium, New Haven, 12-15-75.

[136] Powell 1978; cf. also *idem*, Jones AV (1979) 95.

[137] Powell 1978:214f.

[138] Hallo 1963:138 and n. 30.

[139] Bezold s.v.; cf. B. Landsberger, JCS 21 (1967) 169, n. 128; P. Steinkeller, OA 19 (1980) 87f., n. 15.

[140] Deimel, ŠL 2/3:792f. (401:1) s.v.

[141] Deimel ŠG 2 s.v.: "e. gebogener Silberdraht mit Teilungstrichen als Gewichts/wertbezeichnungen."

[142] ŠL 2/3:916 (468:1): "e. halbkreisförmig gebogener Silberdraht, auf dem durch Teilstriche Gewichtsmasse, bzw. der Wert, angedeutet war."

a unit of account and a standard of value. That was done initially by Curtis and myself in 1959 and more recently and massively by Daniel Snell in his Yale dissertation published in 1982. [143] Snell subtitled his study "Early Mesopotamian Merchant Accounts," and it was indeed these more or less semi-annual [144] accountings where all manner of goods, both those "on hand" and those bought, were evaluated in terms of their silver equivalencies. It is my sense that the items bought by the neo-Sumerian merchants were primarily or even exclusively imports. [145] Snell does not necessarily share this view, but there is no dispute about the merchants' balanced accounts as a primary source for the reconstruction of a neo-Sumerian price index.

But we can go further. Silver as money is not only well attested for this period in the merchants' balanced accounts but also in other records associated with merchants. The conclusion seemed inescapable, already in 1959, that "silver as money was primarily used by the merchants in the neo-Sumerian period." [146] This conclusion was, at the time, once more buttressed by appeal to the native literary sources, in this case the millennial wisdom enshrined in the Sumerian proverbs. As we translated the appropriate adage (S.P. 1. 165), it complained: "How the merchant has reduced the (amount of) silver! How the ... (?) has reduced the(amount of) barley!" [147] Since then, the proverb has been republished with the help of newly discovered duplicates which corrected its unclear portions. It is now translated "How has the merchant robbed (me of my) silver and (at the same time) how has he robbed (me) of barley" and seen clearly to be the complaint of a woman, as it is in the so-called woman's dialect. [148] Indeed, it occurs at the conclusion of a group of proverbs about women. [149] It recurs in another proverb collection (S.P. 3. 65) in the midst of a trio of proverbs about merchants. [150] The proverb has meantime been quoted again often to describe the merchants' relation to silver: as evidence that "the merchant's business was to make

[143] Snell 1982.

[144] *Ibid.* 106.

[145] Curtis and Hallo 1959:112; more explicitly Hallo, JCS 17 (1963) 59; cf. previously A.L. Oppenheim, AOS 32 (1948) 137f.

[146] Curtis and Hallo 1959:108.

[147] *Ibid.* 103.

[148] Gordon 1959:512f.

[149] S.P. 1.142-165: *ibid.* 110-128, 466-469, 510-513, 549.

[150] S.P. 3. 64-66: Falkowitz 1980:190f.

money;" [151] that "cheating merchants .. were not unknown in Sumer"; [152] that it occasionally came to attempts at fraud in this connection. [153]

Nor was this the only proverb to stress the merchant's unpopularity and his intimate connection, not to say obsession, with silver as money. In Collection 3, it is preceded by one which reads in part: "The merchant has no one for his friend" (S.P. 3:64). [154] In S.P. 1.73, we read: "The merchant has departed from the city, (and so) prices (Gordon: trade-values) have become flexible!" [155] And S.P. 1.67 can best be rendered: "A city whose wills are not drawn up (Jacobsen : (whose) affairs are not attended to) [156]—its registrar of deeds is the merchant!" [157] This proverb is the third of a trio that begins: "In the city of the dogs, the fox is overseer" and continues with: "In the city of the lame, the halt is courier!" (S.P. 1.65-66; cf. S.P. 2.118-119), and the second of these is readily identified (via various intermediaries) as the ancestor of our own "In the country of the blind, the one-eyed man is king!" [158] The juxtaposition of the three proverbs shows clearly enough that, in the opinion of his contemporaries, having a merchant as registrar of deeds was as good as putting the fox in charge of the chicken-coop.

But if the existence of money is thus established for Mesopotamia in the neo-Sumerian period from both the excavations and the texts, it remains true that it plays a very modest role outside the world of the merchants. It is sometimes a factor in the court cases as assembled by Adam Falkenstein in his classic edition, [159] and regularly in the "private legal documents ... which record purchases of real property or chattels" more recently compiled by Piotr Steinkeller. [160] But for the rest the situation remains much as I described it already in 1958: "Not once in all the transactions which have been illustrated by the

---

[151] Powell 1977:25.

[152] Kramer 1977:64.

[153] "Dass es dabei zuweilen auch Versuche zu Betrügereien gegeben hat": Klengel 1979:59 and n. 55; cf. Hallo, Bi.Or. 38 (1981) 277.

[154] Falkowitz 1980:189f. For slightly divergent translations see M. Civil, JCS 28 (1976) 74 and B. Alster in Aleida Assmann, ed., *Weisheit: Archäologie der literarischen Kommunikation* 3 (Munich, Wilhelm Klink, 1989) 108.

[155] Gordon 1959:504f.

[156] *Ibid.* 548.

[157] *Ibid.* 74.

[158] Hallo 1969.

[159] Falkenstein 1956-57.

[160] Steinkeller 1989.

preceding texts do we meet a reference to silver, i.e., money. This is in contrast to the Old Babylonian period, which was pre-eminently a money economy, with a price on everything from the skin of a gored ox to the privilege of a temple office. Only a handful of Ur III texts before Ibbi-Sin's reign give us the money value of commodities involved in transactions (specifically the accounts of the traders ...), and the price and wage fixing so dear to the royal law-givers of the Old Babylonian period is unknown to the law-code of Ur-Nammu, as far as preserved. (The extant portions of the code include its prologue and opening paragraphs, which is where we might expect to find the section on prices.) But if money did not turn the wheels of economic activity under the Third Dynasty of Ur, something else must have, and the letters show the motivation for at least some of the innumerable transactions which are attested for the period. The letters, perhaps better described as letter-orders, are in effect drafts or orders to pay (in kind), drawn on the great storage centers of Drehem, Umma etc., in favor of the bearer. Whether they were drawn up in every case by royal officials only a systematic study of the category can determine." [161]

Such a study was published eight years later by Sollberger under the title of *The Business and Administrative Correspondence under the Kings of Ur.* [162] In a review-article on this book, I challenged its title, contending that "The neo-Sumerian letter-orders ... deal neither with business in the sense of the Old Assyrian correspondence between the merchants of Assur and their travelling salesmen in Anatolia, nor with administration in the manner of Hammurabi's correspondence with his lieutenants such as Shamash-hazir and Sin-iddinam." Rather, "the majority of the letters ... are characterized by one or more command or permission forms ... which justify their designation as 'letter-orders' first coined by Oppenheim ..., and their interpretation as 'bank-drafts and other missing links in the statist economy of Ur III." [163] I went on to note that Raymond Bogaert's history of ancient banking that had appeared meanwhile disagreed with my assessment, holding that Drehem and other entrepots served as a "caisse de l'État" rather than as a bank, [164] but wondered whether this was not

---

[161] Hallo 1958:98.
[162] Sollberger 1966.
[163] Hallo 1969a:171f.
[164] Bogaert 1966:67 and n. 142.

"a matter of definition, i.e. is banking a question of technique or of the private vs. the public sector of the economy?" [165]

In fact, the notion of the letter-order as the ancient equivalent of a modern bank-draft seemed nicely confirmed when David Owen published a letter-order enclosed in an envelope which described the same transaction as the letter-order, but this time in the form of a standard receipt, i.e., it indicated that the order had been carried out or, if one prefers, the draft had been paid! [166] Admittedly this is a unique situation, since envelopes, when they are preserved at all, rarely diverge so markedly from the message of the letter enclosed in them.[167] Owen suggests, in fact, that in this case the original envelope had been replaced by the receipt after the order had been filled. Be that as it may, it does go far toward justifying the close connection between the relatively rare letter-orders of the Ur III period and the vast numbers of receipts, accounts and other records of transactions carried out under official auspices at this time. If the merchants' balanced accounts thus represent a kind of forerunner to the practice of double-entry bookkeeping (otherwise traced no further back than Renaissance Venice), then the letter-orders may be said to attest to a prototypical banking system in the sense of a generally recognized means of authorizing drafts on the great storage centers under royal auspices situated all over the Ur III empire.

Bibliographical References

Alster, Bendt and H.L.J. Vanstiphout, 1987: "Lahar and Ashnan: presentation and analysis of a Sumerian disputation," *Acta Sumerologica* 9:1-43.

Archi, Alfonso, 1985: "Circulation d'objets en métal précieux de poids standardisé à Ebla," Birot AV 25-34.

Bogaert, Raymond, 1966: *Les origines antiques de la banque de dépôt* (Leiden, Sijthoff).

Curtis, John B. and William W. Hallo, 1959: "Money and merchants in Ur III," *HUCA* 30:103-139.

Dayton, J., 1974: "Money in the Near East before coinage", *Berytus* 23:41-52.

Edzard, Dietz Otto: 1960: "Die Beziehungen Babyloniens und Ägyptens in der mittelbabylonischen Zeit und das Gold," *JESHO* 3:38-55.

Falkenstein, Adam, 1956-57: *Die neusumerischen Gerichtsurkunden* (= VKEK 39, 40, 44).

Falkowitz, Robert, 1980: *The Sumerian Rhetoric Collections* (Ph.D. Thesis, University of Pennsylvania) (Ann Arbor, University Microfilms).

---

[165] Hallo 1969a:172, n. 2.
[166] Owen 1972; for the seal impression, see Mayr MS No. 611.
[167] See below, ch. I 3.

Gordon, Edmond I., 1959: *Sumerian Proverbs: Glimpses of Everyday Life in Ancient Mesopotamia* (Philadelphia, The University Museum).

Greenberg, Moshe, 1951: "Hebrew *s^e gulla*: Akkadian *sikiltu*," JAOS 71:172-174.

———, 1995: *Studies in the Bible and Jewish Thought* (Philadelphia/Jerusalem, Jewish Publication Society).

Hallo, William, 1958: "Contributions to neo-Sumerian," HUCA 29:69-107 + xxvii pls..

———, 1963: "Lexical notes on the neo-Sumerian metal industry," BiOr 20:136-142.

———, 1969: "The lame and the halt," *Eretz-Israel* 9:66-70.

———, 1969a: "The neo-Sumerian letter-orders," BiOr 26:171-175.

Heichelheim, Fritz, 1958: *An Ancient Economic History*, vol 1 (Leiden, Sijthoff).

Kagan, Donald, 1982: "The dates of the earliest coins," *American Journal of Archaeology* 86:343-360.

Klein, Jacob, 1990: "The 'bane' of humanity: a lifespan of one hundred twenty years," *Acta Sumerologica* 12:57-70.

Klengel, Horst, 1979: *Handel und Händler im alten Orient* (Vienna, Hermann Böhlaus Nachf.).

Kramer, Samuel Noah, 1956: *From the Tablets of Sumer* (Indian Hills, CO, Falcon's Wing Press).

———, 1977: "Commerce and Trade: gleanings from Sumerian literature," *Iraq*, 39:59-66.

———, 1981: *History Begins at Sumer* (3rd. ed.) (Philadelphia University of Pennsylvania Press).

Leemans, W.F., 1957-71: "Gold," RLA 3:504-515.

Limet, Henri, 1960: *Le Travail du métal au pays de Sumer au temps de la IIIe dynastie d' Ur* (Paris, Societe d'Edition "Les Belles Lettres").

Mayr, Rudolph, MS: *"Seal Impressions from Umma in the Ur III Period.*

Meshorer, Y., 1976: "Means of payment prior to coinage and the first coinage," *Qadmoniyot* 9/II-III:51-69 (in Hebrew).

Michalowski, Piotr, 1978: "The Neo-Sumerian silver ring texts," *Syro-Mesopotamian Studies* 2:43-58.

Owen, David I., 1972: "A unique Ur III letter-order in the University of North Carolina," JCS 24:133-135.

Powell, Marvin A., 1977: "Sumerian merchants and the problem of profit," *Iraq*, 39:23-29.

———, 1978: "A contribution to the history of money prior to the invention of coinage," Matouš AV 2:211-243.

Snell, Daniel C., 1982: *Ledgers and Prices* (= YNER 8).

Sollberger, Edmond, 1966: *The Business and Administrative Correspondence under the Kings of Ur* (= TCS 1).

Steinkeller, Piotr, 1989: *Sale Documents of the Ur-III-Period* (= FAOS 17).

3. WRITING

In thus relying on textual documentation for some of the characteristic traces of an emerging capitalism, we have already implied the third leg of the tripod of civilization: writing. And here we can take the evidence back, not only to the end of the fourth millennium, but well before it, relying on a new thesis to account for the emergence, at the end of the fourth millennium, of a full-fledged system of writing in lower Mesopotamia, specifically at the great urban center of Uruk. The new thesis is essentially the work of a single scholar, Denise Schmandt-Besserat, and while she had discussed and refined her thesis in a variety of articles scattered in the scholarly and popular press since 1974, it was only in 1992 that her results were updated and synthesized in monographic form in *Before Writing*. [168] I quote here from my preface to this volume. [169]

Every so often, a field of study is revolutionized by a single discovery or a unique hypothesis. *Before Writing* promises to play such a role in our understanding of the emergence of civilization. Writing itself is a crucial component of civilization, together with the formation of capital and the emergence of cities. All three of these innovations occurred together in lower Mesopotamia—the ancient land of Sumer—towards the end of the fourth millennium B.C. Most notably they can be traced at Uruk (the Biblical Erech) where German excavations have profited from a 100-year concession to unearth the transition to civilization in annual seasons of excavations since 1928—interrupted only by the exigencies of war.

The first epigrapher of the Uruk expedition was the noted German Sumerologist, Adam Falkenstein. As early as 1936, he published his pioneering study of the "archaic texts from Uruk" [170] which identified the basic character of the new invention. The tradition has been carried forward by subsequent expeditions and epigraphers, notably Hans Nissen and his team of specialists in Berlin. [171] But their researches have left open the question of how a fully-formed system of writing could have emerged at Uruk and elsewhere without any vis-

---

[168] Schmandt-Besserat 1992.
[169] *Ibid.* ix-xi.
[170] Falkenstein 1936.
[171] Cf. e.g. Green and Nissen 1987; Englund and Nissen 1993.

ible prehistory. This is the question to which   Denise Schmandt-Besserat devoted her research for nearly twenty years.

As long ago as 1974, she published the first of several articles on the earliest uses of clay in the Near East, which occurred at or just after the beginning of the neolithic or New Stone Age. From this preoccupation with the purely artifactual remains of preliterate cultures, she was led inexorably to a closer study of small clay objects recovered in large numbers from neolithic age sites all over the Near East, but often enough dealt with in the excavation reports cursorily—if at all—because of their inexplicable or even seemingly trivial character.

A first breakthrough occurred when these objects were linked with the stone pebbles of mid-second millennium date long known from a chance find at Nuzi as "an operational device in Mesopotamian bureaucracy." [172] Pierre Amiet, excavator of Susa and the author's teacher, had made the link in an oblique allusion as early as 1972, [173] but they became a cornerstone of the new theory as historic survivals of a prehistoric counting technique as well as the likeliest key to its explanation. Though the pebbles themselves had meantime been lost, they were described, on the round clay envelope in which they had been found, and on a related tablet, as "stones" (Akkadian *abnāti*). Her earliest papers in which this relationship was explored actually proposed to use the Akkadian term to designate the comparable prehistoric phenomenon.   Happily, she soon replaced it with the more serviceable (and less anachronistic) term "token." Recent collation of the texts by Tzvi Abusch has permitted further precision in the matter. [174]

In subsequent research, the author tirelessly reviewed the evidence of numerous museum collections, identifying, dating and comparing the clay tokens recovered in excavations all over the Near East. She attempted to develop a coherent hypothesis accounting for the evolution of the original tokens into a full writing system. In brief, it may be outlined thus. Writing was preceded by counting, and counting was done with clay tokens such as occur as early as the ninth millennium B.C. throughout the Near East, i.e., shortly after the neolithic revolution or "agricultural revolution" and probably as a consequence

---

[172] Oppenheim 1959.
[173] Amiet 1972:69, n. 3.
[174] Abusch 1981.

of it. After some millennia of simple token assemblages, it was found convenient, before the end of the fourth millennium, to string the tokens together and enclose the end of the string in a ball of clay ("bulla") [175] or to deposit them inside round and hollow clay envelopes. Before drying, these bullae and envelopes were impressed with stamp seals characteristic of the prehistoric period or, more often, with the cylinder seals which replaced them as the glyptic form most characteristic of Mesopotamia. Originally devised for impressing the wet clay which covered the neck of a clay vessel, that form proved equally serviceable for the rounded bullae and envelopes. On the evidence of later periods, the seals already performed their historic functions of signalling ownership, obligation or authority.

Some envelopes, in addition, were impressed with tokens like those enclosed in them to indicate what they contained. But their format itself was not ideal for record-keeping. To verify the contents and to reuse the tokens required breaking the envelope open. It was simpler to rely on the impression of the tokens on the outside of the envelope, and simpler still to dispense with the making and enclosing of ever new tokens and to rely exclusively on their impressions on the outside. That given, it was a short logical step to abandoning the envelope shape entirely in favor of a simple rectangular tablet whose shape was only slightly rounded on the writing surfaces. In short order the rounding of the obverse (front) writing surface was replaced by a flat obverse, probably to minimize contact between writing surface and palm of the hand when the tablet was turned over to impress the reverse while the clay of the tablet was still wet. The cylinder seal continued to be used for impressing the newly devised clay tablet, usually before the tokens were impressed on it. The final transformation occurred when a reed stylus was employed to impress the clay tablet with designs resembling in two-dimensional format the three-dimensional tokens that had preceded. With this step, full writing had been achieved. The subsequent history of the invention involves refinements that belong to the history of writing rather than to its prehistory.

The new thesis thus reviewed here in its barest outlines first appeared in 1978-9 in major refereed publications such as *Scientific American*, *Archaeology* and *The American Journal of Archaeology*. It was in

---

[175] Later called *šipassu* in Akkadian; cf. CAD s.v.; AbB 11:170:15f. 179:18f.

the last named journal that, a year later, it faced its severest challenge when Stephen J. Lieberman faulted it from the vantage-point of rigorous attention to the evidence of the subsequent history of cuneiform writing. The meanings attested for word-signs (logograms) in their fully developed cuneiform shapes could be reasonably argued to apply already to their linear and pictographic forerunners, but in no case was he prepared to see conclusive proof that the same meanings attached to their alleged three-dimensional prototypes. [176] He raised a second major objection as well. While number tokens had turned up inside bullae which were either opened or X-rayed in modern times to reveal their contents, such investigations had turned up not one example of tokens regarded in the hypothesis as prototypes of logograms *other* than numbers. He was therefore prepared to grant the possibility of a token system for counting, but dismissed as purely speculative the idea of a token system for representing and recording any other concepts. Additional reservations were expressed by I.J. Gelb, [177] Mark Brandes, [178] M. J. Shendge [179] and others. [180]

In her gradual refinement and development of the hypothesis, the author has confronted all of these challenges. She has identified envelopes, notably from Susa and Habuba Kabira, impressed with nonnumerical tokens, indeed with the very tokens enclosed inside. Not trained as an Assyriologist in her own right, she has wisely sought the collaboration of specialists in cuneiform writing and the Sumerian language, including Margaret Green, a former member of the Berlin team dealing with the archaic texts from Uruk. These texts may be said to stand midway between the tokens of the neolithic period and the fully evolved cuneiform script of the Early Dynastic and subsequent periods in Mesopotamia. The case for linking the tokens via the archaic Uruk texts to the clearly intelligible logograms of the third and second millennia is today substantially stronger than when the first tentative suggestions were advanced in this regard in the 1970's. In a special issue of *Visible Language* devoted to "aspects of cuneiform writing" in 1981, this point was already recognized by Green and by Marvin Powell. Powell's defense of the thesis (its *ad hominem* argu-

---

[176] Lieberman 1980.
[177] Gelb 1980.
[178] Brandes 1980.
[179] Shendge 1983.
[180] Among more recent critical reviews, cf. especially Englund 1993, Michalowski 1993, and Zimansky 1993.

ments apart) is particularly important for its numerical aspects, given his long involvement with the evolution of cuneiform numeration systems in the historic period. [181]

But what about the rest of the hypothesis? Here its latest refinement as first elaborated in the pages of Schmandt-Besserat's book is crucial. In effect, we are offered a credible hypothesis that provides a possible, even a plausible evolutionary model, not only for the emergence of literacy but of " numeracy." According to this working hypothesis, the earliest tokens represented given quantities of given commodities. It required another quantum leap to conceptualize or at any rate to represent the idea of quantity *apart* from any specific commodity. But once taken, this leap implied at the same time the ability to represent any specific commodity *apart from its quantity*. If so, then the prehistoric token system may be said to have bequeathed three-dimensional representations of *both* numbers *and* commodities to the writing system that emerged at the beginning of history.

The new refinement of the thesis will no doubt face its own challenges, not only from Assyriologists but from archaeologists, historians, linguists and even psychologists. The search for complex tokens contained in envelopes will continue; so far the efforts to this end have turned up some three dozen, or ten percent of the entire assemblage, at three different sites. Other early scripts may well have to be brought into the discussion, both as to their implications for the new thesis and vice versa. And if the conceptualization of pure number is indeed, as often averred, a very early attainment of human speech, it may need to be asked why its representation in token form should lag so far behind.

Whatever challenges have been or are yet to be encountered by the thesis, however, these would have to offer an equally systematic alternative to be convincing. The sudden appearance of the sophisticated script of the archaic texts from Uruk *ex nihilo* and *de novo* is an argument sustained neither by reason nor by the evidence. *Before Writing* furnishes to date the most coherent working hypothesis to account for the prehistory of the historic invention known as writing.

It may be interesting, once more, to compare this modern thesis

---

[181] Powell 1981, 1994; for other favorable reviews, see especially John R. Alden, *Natural History* March 1992:64-67; Carol F. Justus, *Diachronica* 10/1 (1993) 97-110; Winfred P. Lehmann, *General Linguistics* 34 (1992) 184-192; David I. Owen, *Religious Studies Review* 20/2 (April 1994) 127.

on the origins of writing in Mesopotamia, and hence of writing altogether, with native cuneiform traditions on the subject, as we did before in reference to urban origins. (We may ignore the late rabbinic legend or midrash according to which writing, or at least the alphabet, was invented by Abraham.) [182]

Here we may pause to contrast the modern scientific modes of explanation more generally with those of a pre-scientific antiquity. In drawing such a contrast, we are not making a value-judgment that assigns a higher order of truth to one or the other, but only describing their essential differences. The essence of scientific explanation is experimental verification, i.e., any explanation put forward by one theorist or theory should be able to be reproduced or "replicated" in the laboratory of any other investigator when the experiment is repeated. The essence of pre-scientific explanation is "historical"; so far from seeking to replicate an experiment, the ancient theorist postulated a prior stage of history in which the current phenomenon did not as yet exist, and a one-time event in the remote past which caused that prior stage to be forever replaced by the current state of affairs. Such an event can be a real or historical one, but more often it is an imaginary or hypothetical one, designed to satisfy a kind of child-like curiosity about the observed world of the questioner. A modern analogy, albeit not a serious one, would be the "Just So Stories" of Rudyard Kipling, "How the elephant got its trunk," for instance.

Imaginary and imaginative tales such as these were anciently enshrined in mythology, sometimes loosely defined as tales of the gods. But a more rigorous, and certainly a more serviceable definition holds that "myth presents a legendary occurrence as a paradigm for a continuing human experience, i.e., myth uses the punctual to explain the durative." [183]   Among myths in general, it is in particular the so-called aetiologies which answer to this definition. Aetiology is a concept borrowed from medicine, where it is described as "that part of medical science which investigates the causes of disease (1684)." [184] But it was used even earlier to identify "the science or philosophy of

---

[182] *Talmud Bavli*, Avodah Zarah 14b.
[183] T.H. Gaster paraphrased by Hallo, RAI 17 (1970) 117, n. 1; cf. *idem*, JAOS 103 (1983) 170.
[184] *The Oxford Universal Dictionary* (1955) s.v.

causation (1660)," [185] and so we are entitled to reclaim the term for Sumerian mythology. And there we have, albeit imbedded in epic, such aetiologies as those for the origins of fire-making, of foreign trade and of meat-eating. [186] And we have there as well an aetiology of writing. [187]

According to this version of matters, the lord of Kullab, a part of Uruk, wanted to send a message by envoy to distant Aratta. But: "That day the words of the lord ... were difficult, their meaning not to fathom, and, his words being difficult, the envoy was unable to render them. Since the envoy—his words being difficult—was unable to render them, the lord of Kullab smoothed clay with the hand and set down the words on it in the manner of a tablet. While up to then there had been no one setting down words on clay, now, on that day, under that sun, thus it verily came to be: the lord of Kullab set down words on clay, thus it verily came to be!" This is the translation of the Sumerian passage by Thorkild Jacobsen, albeit he regards it as referring to the invention of letter-writing rather than writing as such. [188]. Others would translate, instead of "his (i.e. the lord's) words being difficult" rather "his (i.e. the envoy or messenger's) mouth being heavy" or "the herald was heavy of mouth." [189] Such an understanding of the passage invites comparison with the Biblical tale of Moses' speech-difficulty. [190] But that is a detail. More importantly, the aetiology typically combines authentic and imaginary factors: we would agree that the invention of writing involved the city of Uruk and the use of clay; we would hardly associate it with Enmerkar, a ruler of the Second Early Dynastic Period (ca. 2700-2500 B.C.), nor would we associate the invention with the writing of letters.

But Sumerian literature not only provides us thus with the origin of letter-writing, it also suggests an aetiology for the enclosing of letters inside envelopes! In an epic text describing the rise of the first great Akkadian king Sargon, there is a passage clearly echoing—or even parodying—the passage we have just considered in what might almost be described as literature's first example of intertextuality. [191]

---

[185] *Ibid.*

[186] See below, ch. VII 1.

[187] Komoróczy 1975.

[188] Jacobsen, *Harps* 311f.; cf. Cooper and Heimpel 1983:82 for a slightly different rendering.

[189] Kramer 1952:37.

[190] Tigay 1974, 1978.

[191] For this concept in cuneiform literature see Hallo 1990.

Reading the preserved portion of the text with Cooper and Heimpel, [192] we have: "In those days, writing on tablets certainly existed, but enveloping tablets did not exist! King Ur-Zababa, for Sargon, creature of the gods, wrote a tablet, which would cause his own death, and he despatched it to Lugalzagesi in Uruk." As reconstructed, this aetiology corresponds to a familiar folklore motif: [193] a king despatches a potential rival to a third party carrying instructions to that third party to put the rival to death, so that the messenger becomes the means to his own demise. As such this tale too has parallels in the Bible, where King David rid himself of Uriah with a message that Uriah carried to David's general Joab; in the Iliad, where Bellerophon was sent to the king of Lycia with a similarly deadly message; and even in Shakespeare's Hamlet. [194]

In the case of Sargon, of course, the intended victim survived and the royal design was frustrated, presumably because the letter was *not* enclosed in an envelope. Alster, however, thinks that it *was*—indeed, that the tale furnishes an aetiology of envelope-making. Basing himself on the earlier aetiology of letter-writing, he reconstructs a lost passage reading: "But now, under the sun of that day, so it was! He put the tablet into an envelope, and so it was!" and inserts it into the middle of the pericope. [195]

How does this version of matters compare with the facts as reconstructed by archaeological discoveries? In this case we have no real quarrel with the chronology: apart from late literary conceits like a letter to the first king, Alulu, from Adapa, the first *apkallu* (sage/vizier), [196] and "parodies" like "a letter of Gilgamesh," [197] letters (if not envelopes) are not attested until shortly before the start of the Sargonic period, [198] and even then only a half dozen of them are preserved. [199] They become more numerous in Sargonic times. [200] While

---

[192] Cooper and Heimpel 1983:82; cf. Cooper in Liverani, *Akkad*, 17f.

[193] K 978 in Stith Thompson's *Index*.

[194] Hallo 1994; previously Alster 1987:170; 1990; Afanas'eva 1987; Vanstiphout 1986. There is also a Hittite parallel (M. Eilat, orally).

[195] Alster 1987:163.

[196] See above, ch. I 1, n. 51; Hallo 1981:19, n. 11.

[197] Gurney 1957.

[198] Hallo 1981:19, n. 14, based on Sollberger TCS 1:3 *sub* 6.1.2(a); for the alleged Fara letter alluded to by Ebeling 1938:65 see Hallo 1981:19, n. 13.

[199] For Sollberger TCS 1 N 12, see now the edition by Bauer 1971.

[200] Hallo 1981:19, nn. 15f.; add Owen, JCS 26 (1974) 65 and the editions by Edzard, SR Nos. 92-96. See now for both periods Kienast and Volk 1995.

none of the Sargonic letters known happen to come with envelopes, that is not necessarily to say that envelopes did not exist: in the nature of things, they are not often likely to be preserved together with the letters they once enclosed. [201] In the much more abundant corpus of neo-Sumerian letters, envelopes recur quite often, and they continue to do so in Old Babylonian times, [202] though even here only one in fifty letters is preserved with or in the form of an envelope. [203]

What is perhaps more interesting is to consider what these envelopes say. [204] The aetiology implies that they would *not* repeat more or less verbatim the message contained on the inside (as *is* the case later with contracts enclosed in envelopes), as otherwise the whole point of enclosing (or not enclosing) Sargon's death sentence in an envelope would be lost. And indeed such repetition is attested only twice in Sollberger's corpus of Ur III letters. [205] More often, the envelope bore no more than the seal impression of the sender, [206] a practice sporadically attested also in Old Babylonian times. [207] Only one Ur III letter is known with an envelope bearing both the seal impression of the sender *and* the name of the addressee. [208] This practice became standard in Old Babylonian times, when it is attested at Mari, [209] Karana (Qattara) [210] and elsewhere. [211] Kraus has identified some fifty examples of sealed envelopes. [212] The envelope of a letter-prayer to a deity may have carried the divine addressee's name but presumably no seal impression. [213] Old Assyrian usage was again slightly different: typically, preserved envelopes carry, in addition to the seal impression of the sender, an abbreviated text of the enclosed letter. [214] Neo-Babylonian usage knows of a letter enclosed in an en-

---

[201] Cf. already Klauber 1911, cited Kraus 1985:138.

[202] Kraus 1985; but contrast P. Steinkeller, BM 6 (1977) 41.

[203] 2.2% of the corpus according to Kraus 1985:144.

[204] Cf. in general Hallo *apud* Buchanan ENES 452 *ad* No. 649.

[205] Sollberger 1966 Nos. 53 and 83.

[206] E.g. *ibid.*, Nos. 61, 142, 281 = Buchanan ENES 649, 142, 281; cf. *ibid.* 761; Owen, NSAT 1.

[207] Greengus, OBTIV 1; TIM 2:158 (from Lagaba).

[208] Michalowski 1976:165.

[209] E.g. M. Birot, *Syria* 50 (1973) 8f. *contra* Kraus 1985:138f.

[210] D. Hawkins *apud* Dalley, *Tell Rimah* p. 247; cf. p. 250 No.5 and Dalley 1984:16.

[211] E.g. CT 52 (= AbB 7) 52, 187, 189, etc. For some good photographs see YOS 2 pl. lxi.

[212] Kraus 1985:144f. *sub* D and H.

[213] Hallo, Speiser AV 79.

[214] E.g. H. Lewy, HUCA 39 (1968) pp. 30-32; M.T. Larsen, *Mesopotamia* 4 (1976) 135; D.I. Owen, SCCNH 7 (1995) 65-67..

velope bearing the stamp seal and caption of the sender *and* the name of the addressee. [215]

Thus the evidence as excavated tends in this case to confirm the essentials of the aetiological tale.

The invention of cuneiform writing in Mesopotamia was followed in short order, and probably under Mesopotamian stimulus, by the invention of autonomous writing systems in Elam, the Indus Valley, and especially Egypt. Like cuneiform, all these varieties of writing used a combination of word-signs and syllabic signs, and thus required hundreds of signs in all, a technique inevitably mastered by only a small elite of trained scribes. It remained for the Levant, lying between the high civilizations of the great river valleys, to devise a purely syllabic script which could be mastered by the masses and which was ultimately to furnish the entire world with the advantages of a fully alphabetic script.

The first case in point is provided by the "proto-Sinaitic" inscriptions found in the Egyptian copper and turquoise mines of Serabit-el-Khadim and other sites in the Sinai Peninsula and dated to the 17th or 16th centuries B.C. [216] These inscriptions, although still not fully deciphered to everyone's satisfaction, are generally regarded as derived from Egyptian hieroglyphics, particularly in the form known as the "syllabic orthography," whether by the "acrophonic" principle as widely held [217] or otherwise. [218]

The second case in point is that of Ugaritic, which is sometimes traced to a Mesopotamian impulse, or a juncture of Egyptian and Mesopotamian influences, not only because of the outward resemblance of its signs to Mesopotamian cuneiform, but because it evolved in a setting where and a time when (in the 14th and 13th centuries B.C.) Mesopotamian cuneiform, its scholastic traditions and its literature were well known to the scribes of Ugarit and the rest of the Levant. These earliest forms of the syllabic script had a seminal role to play in the evolution of the West Semitic syllabary or "alphabet" and thereby indirectly influenced the outward form of the letters of the alphabet still in use today. But I prefer to deal with an aspect of

---

[215] CT 22:142, cited by M. Dandamayev, *Slavery in Babylonia* (1984) 20.

[216] For an early and still intriguing discussion of the texts and their implications, see Rudolf Hallo 1926; cf. *idem* 1924.

[217] E.g. Albright 1966, esp. p. 7; cf. also Rainey 1975.

[218] Gelb 1952:138-143; Hallo 1958:335f. and n. 29.

the Ugaritic script which *directly* bears on our modern heritage, namely the *order* of the letters, and the related question of the *names* of the letters. Much new material has been discovered since I surveyed these questions in 1958. [219]

'   Let us begin with the abecedaries, those exercise texts which arranged the letters in a fixed sequence, and which were originally designed, in my opinion, to help spread the knowledge of the new script, [220] although later, when the order of the letters was already widely known, they could serve other purposes as well, such as representing numerals or preserving the order in which blocks of stone were quarried so as to realign them the same way when used in masonry work, [221] or as decoration for a seal; 'BGD//HWZḤ on a limestone seal in the Israel Museum illustrates the latter function. [222] The order of the letters in the Ugaritic abecedaries is: 'a-b-g-KH-d-h-w-z-ch-ṭ-y-k-TH-l-m-D-n-Z-s-ᶜ-p-ṣ-q-r-sh-G-t-I-U-Ś.   Allowing for the elimination of those consonants which were not needed in later scripts (here indicated by capital letters), and for the addition of vowels (and certain other phonemes) not represented in the Ugaritic script, this order is clearly ancestral to that of the Hebrew and Greek alphabets and thus ultimately to our own.

New discoveries, and new insights into old discoveries, have significantly expanded the testimony of the abecedaries. In the first place we now have "a proto-Canaanite abecedary dating from the period of the Judges," to cite the title of the article by Aaron Demsky which first announced its discovery. [223] The inscription in question was excavated by M. Kochavi at Izbet Sarta, which he identifies with Biblical Eben-ezer, and dates to the beginning of the Iron Age (ca. 12th century B.C.) [224] Together with the abecedaries from Kuntillet Ajrud in the northeastern Sinai [225] dating to the time of the Divided Monarchy (ca. 9th-8th c.), [226] the new evidence attests to the diffusion of the new alphabetic order (albeit with minor and major modifica-

---

[219] Hallo 1958.
[220] *Ibid.*, 335; cited by Watt 1987:11; cf. *ibid.* 14, n. 43.
[221] E.g. Hallo 1958:332; cf. now in detail Millard 1995.
[222] Hestrin, *Catalogue*, 166, No. 129; cf. *ibid.* 161, No. 127.
[223] Demsky 1977; reprinted in Kochavi 1978; cf. Demsky and Kochavi 1978.
[224] Kochavi 1977; reprinted Kochavi 1978; cf. also Cross 1980, esp. pp. 9-15 and figs. 9f.
[225] *Ibid.* 13.
[226] Demsky and Kochavi 1978:30.

tions) at an early date far to the south of its first attested home in Ugarit.

But the Ugaritic evidence itself has also expanded southward (and eastward) in startling ways. It is now known that Ugaritic cuneiform writing was attested and attempted in places as distant from Ugarit as Tell Nebi Mend in Syria, Kamid el-Loz (Kumidi) and Sarafand (Sarepta) in Lebanon, and Hala Sultan Tekke on Cyprus. [227] And Canaan has also furnished examples, such as a tablet from the beginning of the 12th century at Taanach, [228] and a knife (of similar date?) from Tabor. And a re-examination of a tablet, probably of the 13th century, found long ago at Beth Shemesh, has indicated that it too represents an abecedary—this time, however, not according to the West Semitic tradition, but much closer to the South Semitic one! [229] The conclusion to be drawn from these new discoveries and new interpretations is that the order of the South Semitic alphabets (South Arabic and Ethiopic) is virtually as old as that of the West Semitic ones, and that in both cases it was a deliberate part of the new invention.

When we turn to the related question of the *names* of the letters, the situation has not been clarified to quite the same extent since 1958. My proposal was that, in addition to or even instead of the more or less meaningful letter-names of the later tradition derived from the oldest letter-forms by the so-called acrophonic principle, [230] there existed a system of letter-names which were inherently meaningless. They consisted, more like our own present-day letter-names, of a given consonant and an (arbitrary) vowel or diphthong. The earliest evidence for this type of system of letter-names comes from another sort of Ugaritic abecedary, one in which each successive letter of the Ugaritic letter-sequence is equated with a syllabic sign in Mesopotamian cuneiform of the form consonant-plus-vowel. [231] Later evidence was seen to be provided by at least four Hebrew letter-names: *waw* and *taw* which, so far from being named for the "hook" and "mark," respectively, which their pictograms allegedly represented, were in my opinion rather the origins of the semantic values

---

[227] For these and the following references see Dietrich and Loretz 1988, esp. pp. 206-258; *eidem*, 1989, esp. pp. 108f; cf. also Wilhelm 1973:284f.

[228] Lapp 1967, esp. pp. 19-21.

[229] Ryckmans 1988; cf. Loundine 1985; references courtesy Mark Smith.

[230] Above, n. 217.

[231] Hallo 1958:336.

secondarily assigned to these letter-names (much as in the case of "X-Beine" or "O-Beine" in German); and *ṣaw and qaw*, which occurred in Isaiah 28:9-13 in the context of a spelling-lesson sarcastically pictured as being administered by the prophet.

⸝ The response to these suggestions has not been resoundingly favorable. They had been anticipated to some extent by E.W. Heaton in 1956. [232] B.A. Levine speaks of "the rather imaginative interpretation of Isa. 28:9f. as representing infantile mimicry of the pronunciation of Hebrew letters." [233] And Daniel I. Block, among others, has offered a wholly different interpretation of the prophetic passage. [234] As far as the Ugaritic evidence is concerned, Frank Cross continues to insist that the Mesopotamian equivalents are themselves abbreviations of longer words, e.g. B=be=bet, Q=qu=qoph. [235] Yet many of the other Mesopotamian equivalents, as far as preserved, do not lend themselves so easily to this explanation. Their vocalization may diverge from that traditionally assigned to the Hebrew letter-names, e.g. in the Septuagint; [236] this is the case, e.g., with H = ú, which stands for *wo* according to Cross although we might rather expect *e*, or with P = pu, where we might expect *pi* (*pe*). In other cases, Cross must posit a totally different meaning for the reconstructed name, or an error of the Ugaritic scribe.

I will therefore confine myself to some of the arguments that have been advanced on both sides of the issue in the interim. The Isaiah passage itself has continued to elicit a variety of interpretations. That *ṣaw leṣaw, qaw leqaw* is nothing more than gibberish, an impenetrable prophetic utterance concealing or conveying God's plan [237] has been rightly questioned by J.M. Schmidt. [238] Little better is the suggestion that it reproduces the "shouts and cries of a party of drunkards," [239] although there is merit in linking the choice of exclamations to the "vomiting and excrement" (*qi' ṣo'ah*) of the immediately preceding verse (Isa. 28:8). [240] The notion of a functioning school-system in

---

[232] Heaton 1956:179f.
[233] Levine 1986.
[234] JBL 103 (1984) 331 n. 41. See also below at notes 237-244.
[235] Cross and Lambdin 1960; Cross 1967.
[236] Hallo 1958:331.
[237] A.F. Key, JBL 86 (1967) 203.
[238] VT 21 (1971) 69, n. 1.
[239] S.A. Hopkins *apud* Driver 1976:242.
[240] Cf. D.I. Block, JBL 103 (1984) 331, n. 41, and see already Coss and Lambdin 1960:24, n. 21.

Isaiah's time has been strengthened by several attempts at reconstructing such a system from the Biblical and comparative evidence, most notably by André Lemaire. [241] The excavation of "school texts" at Kadesh Barnea in the northeastern Sinai dating from the seventh century [242] lends further support to the notion of Isaiah as a teacher. Isaiah has even been regarded as the son of a scribe and himself a royal scribe who, when out of favor, became a "part-time" teacher. [243] And another "spelling-lesson" has been detected in Isaiah 10:19, regarded "as a passing reference to children learning their ABC" by E.W. Heaton. [244]

The notion that letter-names, even if inherently meaningless, can acquire the status of meaningful nouns or adjectives, can now be illustrated by numerous analogies from a variety of writing traditions. Such acquired meaning can be based on the shape of the letters, their pronunciation, or their place in a fixed mnemonic order. The shape of the archaic *tau*, for example, resembled a modern X; as such it came to mean not only "mark" in general, [245] but specifically "signature" since, then as now, an illiterate person would use X in that function. This is the meaning suggested for *tawi* ("my *taw*") in Job 31:35 already by the King James Version, and more recently by many commentators. [246] In the Talmud, the Greek letter-names *gamma* and *chi* (in the forms *gam* and *khi*) are used to describe certain configurations. [247] But already in pre-Biblical Mesopotamia, cuneiform signs, which had or eventually acquired their own names, [248] were early pressed into service to describe some of the endless configurations of entrails and other ominous phenomena. [249]

Cuneiform evidence also provides an intriguing case of a secondary meaning based, not on the shape, but on the (presumed) pronunciation of letter-names, in this case of West Semitic letter-names! It has long been a puzzle why, in addition to the standard Sumerian logogram for scribe in Akkadian, DUB.SAR, which passed into Ak-

---

[241] Lemaire 1981; cf. the review by Levine 1986.

[242] Lemaire and Vernus 1980.

[243] Anderson 1960.

[244] Heaton 1956:174.

[245] Hallo 1958:337.

[246] P. Hyatt, BA 6 (1943) 72; P. Hirsch, BAR 6/2 (1980) 50-52; M.H. Pope, *Job* (= AB 15, 1965, 1973) 238; *idem*, UF 13 (1981) 305 and n. 1.

[247] Fink 1935.

[248] Christian 1913.

[249] Kraus 1950, esp. p. 147 end.

kadian as *tupšarru* and into Hebrew as *tiphsar* (Jer. 51:27; Nah. 3:17), the later texts have a second logogram, (LÚ).A.BA, likewise translated by *tupšarru*, and often occurring in parallelism with it. [250] The answer seems to be that, while the traditional DUB.SAR continued to write with reed stylus in cuneiform on clay tablets, the (LÚ).A.BA was the scribe, often pictured by his side on Assyrian reliefs, who wrote in the newer and simpler West Semitic script, using pen and ink on parchment or papyrus. His name may therefore be interpreted as "the man of the alphabet," a suggestion first made in print by Simo Parpola [251] and by Karlheinz Deller citing Parpola [252] and, more recently, by S.J. Lieberman. [253]

If this etymology is correct, then the Assyrians apparently knew the first two letters of the Aramaic alphabet as *a* and *ba* in the early first millennium! They appear to have borrowed the term at least as early as the 11th century, to judge by colophons from the library of Tiglath-pileser I,[254] presumably from 13th century Ugarit, where it occurs both in a colophon [255] and, in the form AB.BA, in a lexical list. [256] We can therefore go further and say that already in Ugaritic the first two letter-names may have been pronounced thus. Since the "bilingual" abecedary from Ugarit [257] suggests rather that the second letter was called *be*, the new evidence merely underlines the probability that the vowel assigned to any given letter-name in this scheme was essentially arbitrary.

The last case illustrates a third manner of deriving new meanings from letter-names, namely according to their sequence in the traditional order. Thus we have what appears to be *a-ba* as the word for "alphabet" in the Akkadian of Ugarit and the neo-Assyrian period, just as we have "aleph-beit" as the name for the Hebrew alphabet from Middle Hebrew on, and the word "alphabet" in English based

---

[250] Cf. e.g. Postgate 1976:10.

[251] S. Parpola *apud* H. Tadmor, RAI 25 (1982) 459. Cf. also Greenfield 1991:176f.

[252] Deller, BaMi 13 (1982) 151f. For clay tablets inscribed entirely in Aramaic, see now E. Lipiński, "Aramaic clay tablets from the Gozan-Harran area," JEOL 33 (1995) 143-150.

[253] Mimeographed addenda to HUCA 58 (1987) 203. A forthcoming article on "The earliest name of the alphabet" was promised there but has not, to my knowledge, appeared.

[254] Deller, BaMi 13 1982:151; H. Hunger, AOAT 2 (1968)32, No. 51.

[255] J. Nougayrol, *Ugaritica* 5 (1968) 252.

[256] Nougayrol 1965:37.

[257] Above at n. 231.

on the Greek letter-names. Similarly, "abecedary" is readily derived from the Latin letter-names. But we can cite a further analogy. The second half of the alphabet begins with LMN, and this has been suggested as the origin of the Latin and English word "element," which otherwise has no satisfactory etymology, by M.D. Coogan. [258]

We can dispense with other legacies of the older scheme of West Semitic letter-names here proposed, including gnostic and mystic uses of the letters or of the Isaiah passage. [259] What is clear is that not only the order but also the names of the letters in our own modern alphabet have a lineal antecedent in the mid-second millennium invention of the West Semitic syllabary. [260]

Bibliographical References

Abusch, Tzvi, 1981: "Notes on a pair of matching texts: a shepherd's bulla and an owner's receipt," SCCNH 1:1-9.

Afanas'eva, V.K., 1987: "Das sumerische Sargon-Epos. Versuch einer Interpretation," AoF 14:237-246.

Albright, William F., 1966: *The Proto-Sinaitic Inscriptions and their Decipherment* (= HTS 22).

Alster, Bendt, 1987: "A note on the Uriah letter in the Sumerian Sargon legend," ZA 77:169-173.

————, 1990: "Lugalbanda and the early epic tradition in Mesopotamia," Moran AV 59-72.

Amiet, Pierre, 1972: *Glyptique Susienne* I (Paris, Geuthner).

Anderson, R.T., 1960: "Was Isaiah a scribe?" JBL 79:57f.

Bauer, Josef, 1971: "Altsumerische Beiträge. 3. Ein altsumerischer Brief," WO 6:151f.

Brandes, Mark, 1980: "Modelage et imprimerie aux débuts de l'écriture en Mésopotamie," *Akkadica* 18:1-30.

Christian, Viktor, 1913: *Die Namen der assyrisch-babylonischen Keilschriftzeichen* (= MVAG 18/1).

Coogan, M.D., 1974: "Alphabets and elements," BASOR 216:61-63.

Cooper, Jerrold M., 1993: "Paradigm and propaganda: the Dynasty of Akkade in the 21st century," in Liverani, *Akkad* 11-23.

———— and Wolfgang Heimpel, 1983: "The Sumerian Sargon legend," Kramer AV 2:67-82.

Cross, Frank M., Jr., 1967: "The origin and early evolution of the alphabet," EI 8:8*-24*.

————, 1980: "Newly Found Inscriptions in Old Canaanite and Early Phoenician Scripts", BASOR 238:1-20.

———— and Thomas O. Lambdin, 1960: "A Ugaritic abecedary and the origins of the proto-Canaanite alphabet," BASOR 160:21-26.

---

[258] Coogan 1974.

[259] Cf. e.g. Dupont-Sommer 1946.

[260] For other implications of the question, see Warner 1980.

Dalley, Stephanie, 1984: *Mari and Karana: Two Old Babylonian Cities* (London/New York, Longman).

Demsky, Aaron, 1977: "A proto-Canaanite abecedary dating from the period of the Judges," *Tel Aviv* 4:14-27.

—— and M. Kochavi, 1978: "An alphabet from the days of the Judges," BAR 4/3:22-30.

Dietrich, M. and O. Loretz, 1988: *Die Keilalphabete. Die phönizisch-kanaanäischen und altarabischen Alphabete in Ugarit* (= ALASP 1).

——, 1989: "The cuneiform alphabets of Ugarit," UF 21:101-112.

Driver, G.R., 1976: *Semitic Writing* (3rd ed., London/New York, Oxford U.P.).

Dupont-Sommer, A., 1946: *La Doctrine Gnostique de la Lettre "waw"* (= BAH 41).

Ebeling, Erich, 1938: "Briefe," RLA 2:65.

Englund, Robert K., 1993: review of Schmandt-Besserat 1992 in *Science* 260 (11 June 1993) 1670f.

—— and Hans J. Nissen, 1993: *Die lexikalischen Listen der archaischen Texte aus Uruk* (Berlin, Mann).

Falkenstein, Adam, 1936: *Archaische Texte aus Uruk* (= AUW 2).

Fink, E., 1935: "Schriftgeschichtliche Beobachtungen an den beiden griechischen Buchstaben G und X, deren sich der Talmud zur Bezeichnung von Gestalten bedient," HUCA 10:169-183.

Gelb, I.J., 1952: *A Study of Writing: The foundations of Grammatology* (1st ed.) (London, Routledge and Kegan Paul).

——, 1980: "Principles of writing systems within the frame of visual communication," *Processing of Visible Language* 2:7-24.

Green, Margaret W. and Hans J. Nissen, 1987: *Zeichenliste der Archaischen Texte aus Uruk* (Berlin, Mann).

Greenfield, Jonas C., 1991: "Of scribes, scripts and languages," in Cl. Baurain, C. Bonnet and V. Krings, eds., *Phoinikeia Grammata* (=Collection d'Études Classiques 6) (Liège/Namur, Société des Études Classiques) 173-185.

Gurney, Oliver, 1957: "A letter of Gilgamesh," AnSt 7:127-136.

Hallo, Rudolf, 1924: "Ausgrabungen am Sinai," *Jüdische Wochenzeitung* 1/31 (Dec. 23) cc. 4-7.

——, 1926: Die Schriftzeichen vom Sinai und das Problem der 'heiligen' Schrift," *Der Morgen* 2:82-96; 182-187; English translation by Gertrude Hallo (MS).

Hallo, William W., 1958: "Isaiah 28:9-13 and the Ugaritic abecedaries," JBL 77:324-338.

——, 1981: "Letters, prayers, and letter-prayers," PWCJS 7:17-27.

——, 1990: "Proverbs quoted in epic," Moran AV 203-217.

——, 1994: "The Context of Scripture: Ancient Near Eastern texts and their relevance for Biblical exegesis," PWCJS 11:9-15.

Heaton, E.W., 1956: *Everyday Life in Old Testament Times* (London, Batsford).

Kienast, Burkhart and Konrad Volk, 1995: *Die Sumerischen und Akkadischen Briefe des III. Jahrtausends* (= FAOS 19).

Klauber, Ernst, 1911: *Keilschriftbriefe: Staat und Gesellschaft in der babylonisch-assyrischen Briefliteratur* (= Der Alte Orient 12/2).

Kochavi, Moshe, 1977: "An ostracon of the period of the Judges from 'Izbet Sartah," *Tel Aviv* 4:1-13.

—— et al., 1978: *Aphek-Antipatris 1974-1977: The Inscriptions* (= Reprint Series No. 2) (Tel Aviv, Tel Aviv University).

—— and Aaron Demsky, 1978: "An Israelite village from the days of the Judges," BAR 4/3:19-21.

Komoróczy, Geza, 1975: "Zur Ätiologie der Schrifterfindung im Enmerkar-Epos," AoF 3:19-24.

Kramer, Samuel Noah, 1952: *Enmerkar and the Lord of Aratta: a Sumerian Epic Tale of Iraq and Iran* (= Museum Monographs) (Philadelphia, University Museum of the University of Pennsylvania).

Kraus, Fritz R., 1950: review of YOS 10 in JCS 4:141-154.

————, 1985: "Altbabylonische Briefe mit Siegelabrollungen," Birot AV 137-145.

Lapp, Paul W., 1967: "The 1966 excavations at Tell Ta'annek," BASOR 185:2-39.

Lemaire, André, 1981: *Les Écoles et la Formation de la Bible* (Fribourg, Editions Universitaires / Göttingen, Vandenhoeck & Ruprecht).

———— and P. Vernus, 1980: "Les ostraca paléo-hébreux de Qadesh-Barnea," Or. 49:341-345.

Levine, Baruch A., 1986: review of Lemaire 1981 in JNES 45:67-69.

Lieberman, Stephen J., 1980: "Of clay pebbles, hollow clay balls, and writing: a Sumerian view," AJA 84:351-358.

Loundine, A.G., 1985: "L'origine de l'alphabet," CILL 11/1-2:173-202.

Michalowski, Piotr, 1976: "Six neo-Sumerian Letter-orders," JCS 28: 160-168.

————, 1993: "Tokenism," *American Anthropologist* 95:996-999.

Millard, Alan R., 1995: "Strangers from Egypt and Greece–The signs for numbers in early Hebrew, "Lipiński AV 189-194.

Nougayrol, Jean, 1965: " 'Vocalises' et 'Syllabes en liberté à Ugarit," Landsberger AV 29-39.

Oppenheim, A. Leo, 1959: "An operational device in Mesopotamian bureaucracy," JNES 18 (1959) 121-128.

Postgate, J.N., 1976: *Fifty Neo-Assyrian Legal Documents* (Warminster, Aris and Phillips).

Powell, Marvin J., 1981: "Three problems in the history of writing: origins, direction of script, literacy," *Visible Language* 15:419-440.

————, 1994: review of Schmandt-Besserat 1992 in JAOS 114:96f.

Rainey, Anson F., 1975: "Notes on some proto-Sinaitic inscriptions," IEJ 25:106-116.

Ryckmans, Jacques, 1988: "A.G. Lundin's interpretation of the Beth Shemesh abecedary: a presentation and commentary," *Proceedings of the Seminar for Arabian Studies* 18:123-129.

Schmandt-Besserat, Denise, 1992: *Before Writing* (2 vv.) (Austin, University of Texas Press).

Shendge, Malati J., 1983: "The use of seals and the invention of writing," JESHO 26:113-136.

Sollberger, Edmond, 1966: *The Business and Administrative Correspondence under the Kings of Ur* (= TCS 1).

Tigay, Jeffrey H., 1974: "Moses' speech difficulty," *Gratz College Annual* 3:29-42.

————, 1978: "Heavy of mouth and heavy of tongue: on Moses' speech difficulty," BASOR 231:57-67.

Vanstiphout, H.L.J., 1986: "Some remarks on cuneiform *écritures*," Hospers AV 217-234.

Warner, Sean, 1980: "The alphabet: an innovation and its diffusion," VT 30:81-90.

Watt, W.C., 1987: "The Byblos matrix," JNES 46: 1-14.

Wilhelm, Gernot, 1973: "Eine Krughenkelinschrift aus Kamid el-Loz," UF 5:284f.

Zimansky, Paul, 1993: review of Schmandt-Besserat 1992 in *Journal of Field Archaeology* 20/4:513-517.

CHAPTER TWO

THE SECONDARY ASPECTS OF CIVILIZATION

If the three essentials of civilization were cities, capital formation and the invention of writing, they were followed almost immediately by certain secondary elements which they brought in their train. These may be identified as the beginnings of (bronze) metallurgy and with it the beginning of the Bronze Age, the emergence of kingship, the specialization of crafts and professions, and the employment of writing for monuments and canons, i.e. historiography and literature generally.[1] In what follows, some of these developments will be illustrated selectively, others more systematically.

1. MANUFACTURING

Textile-manufacture and metallurgy were the twin pillars of ancient Near Eastern industry in general, and of Mesopotamian industry in particular. [2] "Together with the surpluses of agriculture (they) provided the bulk of the native component in the balance of trade." [3] I will therefore concentrate on aspects of manufacturing (metallurgy and textile industry) and of agriculture (notably cereal culture and livestock husbandry), as well as on the role of the merchants who made it possible for Mesopotamia (and Syria) to turn the profits from these enterprises into what we might call "foreign exchange."

The foundation of Mesopotamian metallurgy was the alloying of copper with another metal intended to harden it. Initially arsenic or antimony were used for this purpose, as indicated by archaeological finds dating to the period of transition from Stone Age to Bronze Age, a period sometimes referred to as the Chalcolithic (i.e. metal-and-stone) Age. [4] But the noxious qualities of these alloys no doubt manifested themselves soon enough, and resort was had instead to tin, a metal found more sporadically and at greater distances, espe-

---

[1] ANEH 30-34; cf. also Hallo 1992.
[2] Yamauchi 1993. For leather manufacturing see below, ch. II 2 and nn. 170-176.
[3] Hallo 1979:8; cf. also BiOr 38 (1981) 276f.
[4] E.g. Salonen 1969.

cially from the sources of copper but, by way of compensation, required in much smaller proportions than copper. Sumer in lower Mesopotamia was in the happy position of lying conveniently athwart the crossroads of the overland routes to the sources of tin and the sea-borne routes to the sources of copper. This helps account for its early prominence in the new bronze metallurgy, as shown by J.D. Muhly. [5]

We may turn then, first, to the specific proportions in which these two ingredients were alloyed. In 1963 I defined it as "six parts copper to one part tin" in pre-Sargonic and neo-Sumerian texts; [6] in the intervening Sargonic period, the proportions were "eight parts of copper to one part of tin." [7] Since then, the discoveries at the great Syrian citadel of Ebla have revealed a flourishing economy there on the eve of the Sargonic period; here too the proportions were more nearly eight parts of copper to one part of tin. [8] At Old Babylonian Mari, the range was from six to eight. [9]

Such carefully calibrated calculations imply a refined system of weights and measures, and such was indeed available. Marvin Powell has devoted himself particularly to this phenomenon; among his many contributions, two on weights and measures may be cited here. [10] In addition, he is my authority for the fact that the "small pound" (ma-na-tur), already established as one-third of a shekel, [11] also occurs in this value at Susa. [12] The generalized Akkadian term for "measure" (mašhum) passed into Sumerian as a loanword for a container of standardized size. [13] Another container of this type was the (giš)-ba-rí-ga, Akkadian paršiktu, suggesting an rš phoneme in the original Sumerian (or substrate) word; [14] whether it had anything to do with ka-ba-rí-ga in the metal texts remains to be seen. It is now known to have represented a container of exactly 60 "liters" (sila₃) capacity. [15]

Again we can expand our horizons to include Ebla, noting an

---

[5] Cf. in detail Muhly 1973, 1976. Differently Moorey 1982.

[6] Hallo 1963:139 s.v. lal.

[7] Ibid. s.v. ma-na-tur.

[8] D.O. Edzard, ARET 2 (1981) 31:11.

[9] Limet 1985:203f.

[10] Powell 1987-90; 1992. Cf. also below, ch. II 2, n. 113.

[11] Hallo 1963:139.

[12] Personal communication.

[13] Hallo 1963:139; cf. now CAD M s.v. mašhu C.

[14] For this phoneme see von Soden 1959:52; Salonen 1969:317f.

[15] P. Steinkeller, ZA 69 (1979) 179f.; cf. J. van Dijk, Or. 52 (1983) 457.

equally elaborate, and in part divergent, system of weights and measures there. The weights have been studied by the current epigrapher of the expedition, Alfonso Archi, first in Italian [16] and then in English, [17] as well as by F. Pomponio. [18] The system of capacity-measures has been discussed by Pettinato, [19] and Archi has edited a fascinating Ebla "school-text" which calculates the amounts of grain-rations due varying numbers of laborers, and which incidentally enables us to confirm the relationship, established on the basis of archival texts, between the various units of capacity. [20] At least one of these units, the an-zam_x, is again clearly based on the name of a vessel, the Sumerian $a(n)$-zam, which passed into Eblaite as a-za-mu-mu, i.e. $azammu$ [21] into Akkadian as $assammu$ [22] and into Hebrew as '$asam$. [23]

Given the careful measures used to alloy the components of bronze in both Mesopotamia and Syria, it may be interesting to describe some of the procedures followed in the process of preparing the finished product. The main problem was to generate the necessary heat. The flat plains of lower Mesopotamia were notoriously poor in the kind of hills which could channel blasts of wind like so many natural bellows into a man-made furnace, as it is assumed was the case in the copper mines and smelters of Timna in the Arava valley between Israel and Jordan, once (erroneously) referred to as "King Solomon's mines." [24] Equally, Sumer was poor in lumber. Resort therefore tended to be had to three substitute fuels: coal, brushwood (kindling) and dung.

The last of these three fuels may perhaps be the first to receive notice here, since it is too often overlooked entirely. And yet it is the most important source, since it belongs to the realm of "replaceable assets" or "renewable resources," also regarded as part of the "secondary products revolution." [25] It was dealt with especially by Kilian Butz, [26] and is referred to in the texts as $\check{s}urim$ or, in Akkadian, as $putru$, $rub\d{s}u$ or $kab\hat{u}$.

---

[16] Archi 1980.
[17] Archi 1987.
[18] Pomponio 1980.
[19] AfO 25 (1974-7) 26.
[20] Archi 1989.
[21] G. Pettinato, MEE 2 (1980) 97 *ad* r. iv 1; MEE 4 (1982) 288:788.
[22] Cf. CAD A s.v.
[23] B.A. Levine and W.W. Hallo, HUCA 38 (1987) 51.
[24] Glueck 1959: 153-157; Rothenberg 1961, 1972.
[25] See below, ch. II 2.
[26] See the references *ibid.*, nn. 138-140.

Coal, Akkadian *pēntu*, Hebrew PHM, was previously identified with a Sumerian logogram of uncertain reading but with the component elements "block" and " fire" (LAGAB X IZI); [27] this is now seen to have further Sumerian equivalents: *(na₄)-pi-in-di* [28] *na₄-*^{d}ŠE.TIR, [29] and *na₄-izi* [30]. The first of these is clearly a loan-word from Akkadian; the second is literally "the grain-stone," and the last is literally "the fire-stone." Indeed it is rendered into Akkadian by *aban išati*, " fire-stone," as well as by *pentu*. Further literature on this and other kinds of coal is furnished by Salonen. [31]

As for brushwood, this consisted, in the absence of expendable trees, largely of dried out shrubbery in various guises. The relevant terminology has been studied at length by Salonen, [32] though it is possible to expand even his exhaustive list. So, for example, the translation "fuel-wood" has been proposed for Akkadian *kuzallu* [33] or *kuzullu*. [34] In common parlance, however, the Akkadian word for wood (*iṣu*) [35] and the Sumerian word for grass (*ú = šammu*) served as catch-all designations, [36] so notably in the personal name *Ú-šè-hé-gin*, "May he (my son) go after brushwood (for me)!," [37] an allusion to a " non-canonical" constituent of the "catalogue of filial duties" best preserved in the Ugaritic myth of Aqhat [38] and discussed by O. Eissfeldt [39] and, more recently, by M.J. Boda. [40]

Salonen has also provided us with the terminology of the ovens in which all this fuel was consumed. [41] Here too, out of a bewildering number of technical terms, it may suffice to highlight the one most familiar in common Akkadian parlance, *tinūru* or *tunūru*. [42] The Sumerian equivalents are legion, including some that sound like cog-

[27] Hallo 1963:139f.

[28] E.g. UET 5:292 ii 6, 558 rev. 8'; see the editions by Leemans 1960:28 and 30.

[29] MSL 10 (1970) 35 gap α.

[30] *Ibid.* 10:20 and 32:92.

[31] Salonen 1964:337f.

[32] Salonen 1964-65.

[33] J. Lewy, HUCA 17 (1943) 55-57 and n. 244..

[34] Cf. CAD s.v.

[35] Cf. CAD I 219 s.v. *iṣu* 2c.

[36] For *ú* in the sense of firewood, see already Gordon, SP 108 (4) and 140 (7) *ad* S.P. 1.126' and 1.186.

[37] *Ibid.* 332; cf. Falkenstein NG 2:2 *ad* 1:2.

[38] ANET 150:27-34, 45-48.

[39] Eissfeldt 1966.

[40] Boda 1993; cf. also Gudea Statue B vii 46, cited Krispijn 1982:92.

[41] Salonen 1964.

[42] *Ibid.* 101-103.

nates or loanwords: *(im)-du-ru-na, ti-nu-ur, tu-nu-ur, dile-en, dili-na* [43] as well as *(im)-tu-ru-na, (im)-durun-na, (im)-du$_5$-rí-na, (im)-šu-rin-na, du-ru-un, di-li-na,* and *di-li-im.* [44] The obvious uncertainty as to the precise pronunciation of the Sumerian word makes it a prime candidate for assignment to a substrate language, a point perhaps supported by the appearance of the same word, in the form tandoor, in India.[45]

The by-products of the smelting process were primarily slag, frit and glaze. For slag it had been suggested that the Sumerian word was *sù*-GAN and, although no Akkadian equivalent was proposed, the possibility of a connection with Hebrew *sigim* was entertained. [46] Meantime it has been suggested that *laga$_x$*, written LAGAB, and equated with Akkadian *laga'u,* identifies "slag from a kiln," [47] as well as such semantically related concepts as "dandruff," "dried phlegm," and "exudation (of ears.)" [48]

As for frit and glaze, they were tentatively identified with Sumerian *zab-zab-ga,* Akkadian *zabzabgû,* Ugaritic SPSG, Hittite *zapzagai-,* and Hebrew **saphsigim.* [49] The Hebrew cognate is based on an emendation of Proverbs 26:23, an emendation soundly rejected by M. Dietrich, O. Loretz and J. Sanmartin, who find it astonishing that it has now even found an echo in Sumerology. [50] They reject as well the appeal to the archaeological evidence from prehistoric Jericho, [51] and indeed its remoteness in time is daunting, but it needs to be pointed out that meantime the chronological gap has been considerably lessened by the discovery of a "human mask of glazed frit" in the tombs of the *èntu*-priestesses in the cemetery of the cloister *(gipāru)* at Ur. [52]

In addition to these visible by-products of the metallurgical processes, there was an inevitable loss in smelting as evidenced by the difference in weight between the original constituents and the finished alloy. This difference was in Sumerian tellingly described as

---

[43] *Ibid.*

[44] Civil 1973.

[45] J.S. Cooper, NY Times 2-8-77, editorial page (letter to the editor).

[46] Hallo 1963:140; cf. Abramski 1958.

[47] CAD L s.v.

[48] MSL 9:101.

[49] Hallo 1963:140, n. 66 and 142 (8).

[50] It is "erstaunlich" that the emendation "jetzt sogar in der Sumerologie Anklang findet": Dietrich, Loretz and Sanmartin 1976:39 and n.19.

[51] E.M. Good, JBL 77 (1958) 73; cf. Hallo 1963:140, n. 66.

[52] P. Weadock, *Iraq* 37 (1975) 110.

"what the fire consumed" (*izi-kú-(bi)*, [53] and in Akkadian as *imti*; [54] the former concept was extended as well to the manufacture of textiles. We may therefore turn to that aspect of the early Mesopotamian manufacturing economy, second only to metallurgy as a source of revenue and often enough, as in the Old Assyrian trade between Assur and Anatolia (Turkey), intimately connected with the former.

The textile industry at Ur under the last king of its Third Dynasty was studied in a pioneering article by Jacobsen in 1953, [55] and the broader range of the whole neo-Sumerian textile industry in a monograph by H. Waetzoldt in 1972. [56] In 1979, I offered an analysis of a particularly elaborate neo-Sumerian balanced account of the manufacture of textiles, and combined it with the evidence of literary and archival texts of the succeeding Old Babylonian period to round out the picture of the procedures involved. [57] The literary evidence had previously been treated by Kramer, [58] who returned to the subject in 1964. [59] A fascinating comparison has since been drawn between the Mesopotamian evidence and that of the Linear B texts from Mycenean Crete and Greece by J.L. Melena, albeit under the enigmatic title "On the Linear B ideogrammatic syllabogram *ze*"; I am not in a position to evaluate its results. [60]

On the basis of the Old Babylonian evidence, the process of turning wool into textiles can be summarized as follows: plucking, combing, spinning, braiding, warping, weaving, and cleaning. [61] Beyond the archival and literary sources used to reconstruct this process, the lexical evidence may now be invoked. In the great cuneiform "encyclopedia" called, after its ancient incipit, HAR-ra = *hubullu*, the section on wool includes in Tablet (=chapter) XIX the following entries: "plucked wool, spun wool, threaded(?) or knotted(?) wool, combed wool." [62]

The first of these steps, plucking, is called *peš*₅ in Sumerian, and

---

[53] Limet 1960:295 s.v. *ne-kú*.
[54] Limet 1985:202; cf. CAD s.v. *imtu* (pl.).
[55] Jacobsen 1953, repr. TIT 216-229 and 422-427.
[56] Waetzoldt 1972.
[57] Hallo 1979, esp. pp. 4-13.
[58] References in Hallo 1979:8f., n. 32.
[59] Kramer 1964.
[60] Melena 1987.
[61] Hallo 1979:9.
[62] MSL 10 (1976) 128:11, 15, 17, 18; cf. already Waetzoldt 1972:120.

napāšu in Akkadian; the next, combing, is *pusikku* in Akkadian [63] though *mašādu* for "to comb" and *mušṭu* [64] or, at Ebla, *musadu* [65] for "a comb" are also attested; [66] the last, cleaning, can best be read *dàn* = *zakû, zukkû.* [67] As for the "steeping" (*lubbukat*) reconstructed in the Old Babylonian archival text, it has now been suggested that it should be understood as another form of braiding or plaiting (reading *sub-bukat*). [68]

The by-product of the combing process was salvaged to provide the cheapest kind of wool and the cloth made from it, called *mug* = *mukku*; [69] the term passed into Syriac and into Talmudic Aramaic as *mokh*, "mean or thrown away wool," or the cheap cloth made from it, fit only for such menial tasks as wiping the vagina. [70] It figured prominently in some neo-Sumerian archival texts. [71]

A special branch of the textile industry was devoted to the manufacture of felt, and there was a professional specialist for making felt. [72] One of the principal uses to which the finished felt was put was the production of mattresses; as such felt formed a suitable adjunct to the making of beds, whose general appearance is well documented in the form of numerous clay models of beds which are thought to have served as illustrations of the sacred marriage or, alternatively, as inducements to human fertility. [73]

The ultimate source of Mesopotamia's successes in textile manufacture was its wealth in wool-bearing livestock—sheep in the first place, but also to a lesser extent goats, both raised in such superabundance in the mixed pastoral-agricultural economy of Sumer. But what was demonstrably true there at the turn from the third to the second millennia was equally true of the earlier situation in Syria, where the newly found documents from Ebla now reveal staggeringly large herds of sheep (and cattle), and thus account for the equally astounding numbers of finished cloth and garments registered as gifts,

---

[63] Cf. also M. Civil, JNES 26 (1967) 210f.
[64] CAD M s.vv.
[65] ARET 5 No.1 ii 1; equated with *giš-ríg* in VE 1359'; see MEE 4:337.
[66] CAD M s.vv.
[67] Civil *apud* Steinkeller 1980:83.
[68] CAD S s.v. *sabāku.*
[69] Hallo 1979:6.
[70] Stol 1983:18f.
[71] Curtis 1994:99.
[72] Steinkeller 1980.
[73] Salonen, 1963, esp. pp. 107-139 and pls. xvi-xix; Cholidis, 1992.

offerings, and exports in its great ledgers. To a lesser extent the same situation prevailed as well in Old Assyrian Assur early in the second millennium; we are not sure how much of its textile production was due to home-grown wool, but clearly it figured prominently in the overland trade with Anatolia, with "ingots" of tin typically wrapped in finished cloth before being loaded onto donkeys for the long journey northwestward across the Taurus Mountains. We will therefore turn next to agriculture, and particularly animal husbandry.

Bibliographical References

Abramski, S., 1958: " ' Slag' and 'tin' in the first chapter of Isaiah," EI 5:105-107 (in Hebrew; English summary p. 89*).

Archi, Alfonso, 1980: "Considerazioni sul sistema ponderale di Ebla," preprint, 29pp. + viii pls.

———, 1987: "Reflections on the system of weights from Ebla," *Eblaitica* 1:47-89.

———, 1989: "Table des comptes Eblaites," RA 83:1-6.

Boda, M.J., 1993: "Ideal sonship in Ugarit," UF 25:9-24.

Cholidis, Nadja, 1992: *Möbel in Ton* (= AVO 1).

Civil, Miguel, 1973: "Notes on Sumerian lexciography, II," JCS 25:21-25.

Curtis, John B., 1994: "Ur III Texts in the Bible Lands Museum," ASJ 16: 77-113.

Dietrich, M., O. Loretz and J. Sanmartin, 1976: "Die angebliche Ug.-He. Parallele *SPSG//SPS(J)G(JM)*," UF 8:37-40.

Eissfeldt, Otto, 1966: "Sohnespflichten im Alten Orient," *Syria* 43:39-47.

Glueck, Nelson, 1959: *Rivers in the Desert: a History of the Negev* (New York, Farrar, Straus and Cudahy).

Hallo, William W., 1963: "Lexical notes on the neo-Sumerian metal industry," BiOr 20:136-142.

———, 1979: " *Obiter dicta ad SET*," Jones AV:1-14.

———, 1992: "From Bronze Age to Iron Age in Western Asia: defining the problem," in Ward and Joukowsky 1992:1-9.

Jacobsen, Thorkild, 1953: "On the textile industry at Ur under Ibbi-Sin," Pedersen AV 172-187.

Kramer, Samuel Noah, 1964: "Sumerian literature and the history of technology," *Ithaca: Proceedings of the 10th International Congress of the History of Science* (Paris) 377-380.

Krispijn, H.J.Th., 1982: *De Tempelbouw van Gudea van Lagaš* (Leiden, Brill).

Leemans, W.F., 1960: *Foreign Trade in the Old Babylonan Period as revealed by texts from southern Mesopotamia* (= SD 6).

Limet, Henri, 1960: *Le Travail du Métal au Pays de Sumer au temps de la IIIe dynastie d' Ur* (Paris, Société d'Édition "Les Belles Lettres").

———, 1985: "La technique du bronze dans les archives de Mari," Birot AV 201-210.

Melena, J.L., 1987: "On the Linear B ideogrammatic syllabogram *ze*," *Minos* 20-22:389-457.

Moorey, P.R.S., 1982: "The archeological evidence for metallurgy and related technologies in Mesopotamia, c. 5500-2100 B.C.," *Iraq* 44: 13-38 and pl. 1.

Muhly, James D., 1973: *Copper and Tin: the Distribution of Mineral Resources and the Nature of the Metals Trade in the Bronze Age* (= TCAAS 43:155-535).

———, 1976: *Supplements to Copper and Tin* (=TCAAS 46:77-136).

Pomponio, F., 1980: "AO 7754 ed il sistema ponderale di Ebla," OA 19:171-186.

Powell, Marvin A., Jr., 1987-90: "Masse und Gewichte," RLA 7:457-517.
———, 1992: "Weights and measures," ABD 6:897-908.
Rothenberg, Benno, 1961: *God's Wilderness* (London, Thames and Hudson).
———, 1972: *Timna: Valley of the Biblical Copper Mines* (London, Thames and Hudson).
Salonen, Armas, 1963: *Die Möbel des alten Mesopotamien nach sumerisch-akkadischen Quellen* (= AASF 127).
———, 1964: "Die Öfen der alten Mesopotamier," BaMi 3:100-124 and pls. 19-28.
———, 1964-65: "Bemerkungen zur sumerisch-akkadischen Brennholzterminologie," JEOL 18:331-338.
———, 1969: "Zur Lautlehre der Khalkolithischen Substratsprache in Mesopotamien," BiOr 26:317f.
Steinkeller, Piotr, 1980: "Mattresses and felt in early Mesopotamia," OA 19:79-100.
Stol, Marten, 1983: *Zwangerschap en Geboorte bij de Babyloniërs en in de Bijbel* (Leiden, Ex Oriente Lux).
Von Soden, Wolfram, 1959: "Assyriologische Miszellen," WZKM 55:49-61.
Waetzold, Hartmut, 1972: *Untersuchungen zur neusumerischen Textilindustrie* (= Studi Economici e Technologici 1).
Ward, W.A. and M.S. Joukowsky, eds., 1992: *The Crisis Years: the 12th Century B.C. from beyond the Danube to the Tigris* (Dubuque, Kendall/Hunt).
Yamauchi, Edwin, 1993: "Metal sources and metallurgy in the Biblical world," *Perspectives on Science and Christian Faith* 45/4:252-259.

2. Agriculture [74]

The agricultural revolution marked the beginning of the neolithic period in the Near East and is thus sometimes referred to simply as the neolithic revolution. It involved the domestication of both plants and animals, [75] generally—dogs apart—in that order, [76] but not everywhere; in Anatolia, new evidence has been brought forward to suggest that, there at least, pigs may have been domesticated first of all. [77] In the dry-farming belt of adequate rainfall sometimes referred to as the Fertile Crescent, the first domesticates were identified as long ago as 1952 by Robert J. and Linda Braidwood; they consisted of six previously wild plant and animal species. [78] In lower Mesopotamia, the evolution of irrigation techniques increased agricultural productivity to the point that it generated an impressive wealth based equally on plants and animals. Barley and other cereals were fed not only to humans but also to large and small cattle. [79] Large cattle, initially domesticated for their meat, were eventually exploited to pull the plow and the cart and thus made larger-scale agriculture possible. This and associated developments are dated just before the urban revolution of the late fourth millennium, and probably helped to make it possible and necessary. They were therefore identified by Andrew Sheratt as a further revolution, a so-called "secondary products revolution." [80]

The primary goal of animal husbandry is the meat and other one-time products of the slaughtered animal, such as hide, horns, tail, carcass and entrails. The "secondary products" of animal husbandry are, in addition to draught power, also milk, wool and dung. They are thus secondary not only in the logical but in the historical sense, in that their exploitation began considerably later than that of the

---

[74] The substance of this chapter was presented to the 41st Rencontre Assyriologique Internationale, Berlin, 6 July, 1994, and will appear, in slightly altered form, in a forthcoming AV.

[75] Ucko and Dimbleby 1969; Zohary and Hopf 1988.

[76] ANEH 11-15; for a Biblical echo of the sequence, see above, ch. I 1, pp. 10f. *ad* Gen. 4:2.

[77] John Nobel Wilford, "First settlers domesticated pigs before crops," *New York Times*, May 31, 1994, C1:6, based on the excavations at Hallan Cemi in southeastern Turkey directed by Michael Rosenberg (University of Delaware).

[78] ANEH 15, n. 26.

[79] Cf. especially Maekawa 1983-1994.

[80] Sheratt 1981.

primary products. They may with equal justification be called "replaceable assets" [81] or "renewable resources." [82]

The designation as a renewable resource is particularly apt for wool, since the average sheep could be counted on for many years of shearing, and deaths in a herd would be naturally replaced by births. The latter was true as well of (large) cattle. Indeed, the "growth of a herd of cattle in ten years" on a tablet of neo-Sumerian date shows an increase from six to thirty-two heads of cattle in the decade, together with a steady annual income in butter and cheese. [83] The fact that the tablet is either a school text or "a theoretical, *ideal* model" [84] does not detract from its evidentiary value. It is almost as though, in modern terms, cattle—large and small—represented an investment that offered both income and capital appreciation, so to speak. No wonder that the very concept of capital is etymologically connected to cattle and chattel. [85]

The value placed on cattle in the ancient Near East may be gauged by the amount of attention devoted to them in the various collections of laws, loosely referred to as law codes. [86] In particular, it is oxen that provide type-cases for such legal concerns as rents [87] and negligence. [88] In the latter connection, even a dead ox invited the lawgivers' attention. The oldest Akkadian "code" of laws now known is that of the Old Babylonian kingdom of Eshnunna, discovered in two exemplars in the outskirts of Baghdad in 1948; [89] a partial duplicate was discovered in 1982. [90] In paragraph 53 of these laws we read: "If an ox has gored an(other) ox and caused its death, the owners of both oxen shall divide the price of the living ox and the flesh [91] of the dead ox." This provision is a parade example of "precedent law": an actual or putative judgment of such transcendent equitability that it deserved to become the model for all future judges. And

---

[81] Hallo, BiOr 38 (1981) 277.
[82] Hallo, BiOr 42 (1985) 637.
[83] Gelb 1967; Nissen, Damerow and Englund 1990:139-144; 1993:97-102.
[84] J. Friberg *apud* Hallo, BiOr 50 (1993) 164.
[85] See above, ch. I 2.
[86] On these "codes" see below, ch. VIII 1.
[87] See below, ch. VIII 1, n. 10.
[88] Finkelstein 1973, 1981; Jackson 1974.
[89] Goetze 1956.
[90] Roth 1990.
[91] So with the copies of both exemplars by Goetze (UZU = *šīru*, " flesh") *versus* his reading DAH = *taḫḫum* and his translation by "value" in the *editio princeps* (Goetze 1956:132) and by "equivalent" in ANET 163.

indeed, we have at least one attested court case involving the alleged goring of one ox by another; it comes from Nuzi on the northeastern periphery of the Babylonian world. [92]

The law of Eshnunna illustrates the judicial wisdom, or judiciousness, of such precedent law, and the essential link between law and wisdom familiar from the tale of Solomon's judgment between the two prostitutes claiming the same baby for their own (I Kings 3:16-28). But beyond this instance of "Solomonic judgment," the Bible preserves, in the Covenant Code of the Book of Exodus, a provision equally judicious and at the same time remarkably similar to that of Eshnunna: "If a man's ox collides with his fellow's ox and it (the latter) dies, they shall sell the living ox and divide its price, and the dead one they shall also divide" (Ex. 21:35). Since this particular provision recurs in no other ancient "law code," not even in the section on goring oxen in the more famous and longer-lived Laws of Hammurapi, it raises the interesting question whether the lawgivers of Eshnunna and Israel arrived independently at the same ingenious solution or, if not, how knowledge of the precedent passed from one to the other or, perhaps, from a common source to both. The last possibility should not be dismissed out of hand. To this day, oral law is widely shared by the Bedouin over the entire "Fertile Crescent," from the Sinai Peninsula to the Persian Gulf. [93] A comparable situation may have prevailed at the beginning of the second millennium B.C., when Amorite tribes spread over all parts of the same area.[94]

The importance thus imputed to domesticated animals in the laws can be documented textually as far back as the beginning of the Bronze Age and the invention of writing. [95] The archaic texts from Uruk, which are beginning to yield their secrets due largely to the efforts of Hans Nissen and his colleagues in Berlin, often deal with livestock. [96] The archives from Ebla attest to enormous herds of large and small cattle, sometimes driven over considerable distances. Giovanni Pettinato's synthesis of the evidence in 1979 already records as many as 80,000 sheep in a single tablet, [97] and his more recent

---

[92] Hallo, JAOS 87 (1967) 64 and n. 1; BP 139f.; Finkelstein 1981:21, n. 5.
[93] Bailey 1993:22.
[94] Hallo, BP 58.
[95] For the older secondary literature on animal husbandry in Mesopotamia see Foster 1982:163, n. 10.
[96] Nissen, Damerow and Englund 1990, 1993. See esp. 1990 ch. 14= 1993 ch. 12.
[97] Pettinato 1979; 1981:162. The reference is to TM.75.G.1582, published origi-

survey of 1986 includes a tablet with nearly 12,000 large cattle. [98]
Such numbers are also reflected and even exceeded in later literary
formulations. [99]

Impressive as they are, however, such early or creative statistics do
not furnish many details. For these, we are better served by the neo-
Sumerian archives, which exceed even the Ebla texts not only in
number but also in the meticulousness of their bookkeeping, their
explicitness, and—certainly for now—their intelligibility. In what follows, I propose to exploit these advantages in pursuit of two principal
lines of inquiry, first the nature of the renewable resources provided
by livestock, and second the nature of the products and by-products
of the slaughtering process. I will have recourse to all the relevant
archival texts, especially from the great cattle yards at Drehem, conveniently summarized in two recent studies by the Sumerian Agricultural Group [100] and Marcel Sigrist respectively. [101] But I will make
particular reference to the de Liagre Böhl Collection at Leiden, of
which I published 175 texts, mostly bearing on the neo-Sumerian
livestock industry, in handcopies in 1963-73; [102] I copied an additional 32 texts in 1991 for inclusion in my edition of all the texts
foreseen for a forthcoming volume of SLB. As usual, I will also invoke
Sumerian literary and lexical texts as well as occasional iconographic,
artifactual and anthropological evidence.

The capital represented or typified by domesticated animals comes
in two very different guises—living and dead. Only in the first of these
aspects can we speak, literally, of "livestock." But in this aspect, livestock is a parade example of what was referred to earlier as "secondary products" or "renewable resources." And among these, the most
fundamental, and certainly the most obviously renewable one is
draught power, more precisely the ability of large cattle to carry or
haul loads. Carrying involves in particular asses, and probably accounts for their considerable numbers and precise typology in the
neo-Sumerian texts, which even use different signs for male and fe-

---

nally by Archi 1980:21f. and pl. ix; republished Archi 1984:68f. and fig. 16. Cf. *ibid.*
for TM.75.G.1574 with 84,250 sheep.
   [98] Pettinato 1986:164 and 411f.: 1991:82 and 257f.
   [99] Cf. e.g. Hall 1986.
   [100] "Domestic animals of Mesopotamia," BSA 7 (1993) 8 (1995).
   [101] Sigrist 1992.
   [102] Hallo 1973. The first fascicle, consisting of 68 texts, appeared in 1963.

male asses in at least one Leiden text, [103] as well as for the existence of special donkey-herders (*sipa-anše-ama-gan* [104] or *sipa-anše-kunga₂* [105] for the different kinds of donkeys. [106]

Hauling includes onagers pulling chariots, but more often it involves oxen, and in two ways. One is in connection with the ox-cart which, in Sheratt's words, "opened up new possibilities for bulk transport and reduced the friction of distance." [107] The other is in connection with the heavy machinery required to produce the great surpluses in grain and other crops for which southern Mesopotamia became famous: the plow, the seeder-plow, the harrow and the threshing-sledge. [108] The operations which they performed—plowing, seeding, harrowing and threshing—are described, or rather *prescribed*, in detail in a Sumerian literary genre known as "Instructions," (Sumerian *na-ri-ga* or *na-de₅-ga*, Akkadian *aširtu*). Such instructions, typically collections of proverbial wisdom on a given topic, were also tradited in the name of the antediluvian king and flood-hero Shuruppak, and a king of Isin called Ur-Ninurta. But the "Instructions of Ninurta" are attributed in their concluding doxology to no less than the divine Ninurta, son of Enlil and his "trustworthy farmer." Their opening line (incipit) is more realistic: "In days of yore a farmer instructed his son," followed by more than a hundred lines of practical instructions on agricultural procedures. In modern treatments, they are therefore sometimes referred to as "The Farmer's Almanac." [109] Others call them the "Sumerian Georgica" for the precedent they provide for Vergil's *Georgica* and, incidentally, for Hesiod's *Works and Days*. [110] Under the title "The Farmer's Instructions," they are now conveniently available in the new edition by Miguel Civil. [111]

Lines 48-51 of these Instructions may be cited here by way of illustration. They show that the recommended rate of seeding was to

---

[103] TLB 3:192 (L.B. 566) appears to write GÌR x PA for males, GÌR x SAL for females. TLB 3:2 and 176 do not appear to make this orthographic distinction; 194 writes clearly GÌR + SAL. Cf. also Sigrist 1992:30f.

[104] E.g. TLB 3:176. Cf. *ibid.* 4: *sipa-am[a-g]an-na-ke₄-ne*; 194: *sipa-ama-gan*.

[105] Written ANŠE.BAR.AN; cf. e.g. TLB 3:177.

[106] For the much debated question of their zoological identity, see most recently von den Driesch 1993; for earlier literature see Foster 1982:163, n. 31.

[107] Sheratt 1981:262.

[108] Salonen 1968:375-398: "B. Tierkraft."

[109] Especially Kramer, HBS ch. 11.

[110] Walcot 1966.

[111] Civil 1994.

drop grain every two " fingers" of furrow. [112] A typical furrow of 360 " fingers" in length would thus require 180 grains, meaning that the seeder-plow had to be filled with that much seed-grain. The seed-grain required for an entire field was a function of this formula multiplied by the number of furrows. In actual practice the latter figure was expressed as the number of furrows per 360 " fingers" of width, since the distance between furrows was, within limits, a matter of local and individual preference. [113] A number of neo-Sumerian archival texts show, with mathematical precision, just how the "Farmer's Instructions" were carried out in practice in this instance. [114]

But they tell us more. Line 99 of the Instructions says: "When you are about to hitch the oxen (to the threshing sledge), let your men who 'open' the barley stand by with the oxen's food." This is a singularly "humane" provision, and a telling antecedent to the Biblical injunction "You shall not muzzle an ox while it is threshing" (Deut. 25:4) as noted long ago by Kramer. [115] But the Sumerian prescription was not merely a pious desideratum. It was actually carried out in practice as can be seen from texts in which fodder for the oxen is generously allotted by the side of the carefully calculated amount of seed-grain, and in almost the equivalent quantity [116] or, at Girsu/Lagash, in the ratio of 1:2. [117] Such fodder is called in Sumerian mur-gu_4, in Akkadian $imru$ and later $ballu$ ("mixture"), and it is an interesting commentary on its importance to the contemporary culture to note that the equation among the three terms became the first entry, and hence the incipit and title, of the canonical commentary series to the great cuneiform "encyclopedia" HAR-ra = $hubullu$. It is also worthy of note that the "plow-oxen" (gu_4-$apin$) of the temple of Shara at Umma had their own workmen ($erin_2$) assigned to them. [118]

In addition to all the agricultural duties already indicated, oxen (and occasionally asses) were also employed for turning the water

---

[112] Differently Salonen 1968:206f.; Civil 1994: 83f.

[113] Pettinato and Waetzoldt 1975; cf. Powell 1972:182f., 1984:51 and n. 63; Maekawa 1974:48-51.

[114] The classic example of this correspondence is the Nippur text BE 3/1:92, for which see most recently Maekawa 1981:46-48. A newer one is the Umma text MVN 1:86, for which see Hallo 1976.

[115] 1963:296f., 342.

[116] Hallo 1976:40; BP 98f. and 164.

[117] Maekawa 1995, esp. p. 176.

[118] Cf. e.g. TLB 3:71:15. This entry may be intended to subsume the previous two, and in turn is part of the total described as $erin_2$ $šu$-bar-ra $sukkal$-mah.

wheel, an essential mechanism in the process of irrigation wherever "wet farming" was practiced. [119]

Turning next to small cattle, their most important renewable resource was their wool (in the case of sheep) and their hair (in the case of goats). The word for both is the same in Sumerian and written with a sign—*sig*—which derives by gunification from the sign for cloth (*túg*), but is equated with two different words, *šipatu* and *šartu* respectively, in Akkadian. [120] Sheep's wool was spun into thread, and the thread was woven into cloth. Again the archival texts bear out the literary ones in documenting the procedures involved. They show that sheep-shearing took place once a year (for up to three months) [121] and that sheep with a full fleece (*udu-bar-gál*) were carefully distinguished from those ready for plucking (*udu-ur₄-ra*) [122] and from those with an "empty fleece" (Leerfliess, *udu-bar-su-ga*), i.e. shorn. [123] The Ur III texts even distinguish a category of "growing fleece" (*bar-mú*). [124] They document every step in the process from combing to washing to spinning to weaving and account for the use made of the by-products or the weight-loss suffered at every step of the process. [125]

The textile industry which developed under the Third Dynasty of Ur ended up by employing thousands of workers, mostly women, and rivalling the metallurgy industry in importance as it had earlier at Ebla. It served to convert the agricultural wealth as represented by sheep into manufactures with a market far beyond the borders of Sumer, and thus constituted an important factor in the balance of trade with other regions, by the side of raw wool, which was among the "exchangeable commodities" counted as assets by the merchants of the time and thus presumably serving as exports. [126]

Goat hair may have been in somewhat less demand, judging by its price, which was only one-half to one-fifth that of sheep's wool. [127]

Common to both large and small cattle, but less important eco-

---

[119] Salonen 1968:223-228.

[120] Deimel, ŠL II/4 (1933) 997f. In "gumification," part of a sign is emphasized by additional wedges (*gunû*).

[121] Waetzoldt 1972:10-16: " 'Schur' ."

[122] Snell 1986:137.

[123] Heimpel 1993:127f. PSDB 101 translates *bar-su-ga* by "plucked fleece."

[124] E.g. TLB 3:37 ii 18-20 (cited PSDB 101) and 140 i 8.

[125] See above, ch. II 1, nn. 53f.

[126] *Ibid.* and below, ch. II 3.

[127] 1.5 to 2 *shiqil* silver per pound, compared to 4 to 7.5 for wool according to Waetzoldt 1972:74f. Cf. Daniel C. Snell, *Ledgers and Prices* (= YNER 8, 1982) 178-181.

nomically than either draught power or wool, was their milk. [128] It is generally assumed that in Mesopotamia this derived from both cows and sheep or goats, largely on the basis of surviving usage in the modern Near East. [129] The texts do not specifically distinguish between cow's milk and goat's milk; while there are two terms in both Sumerian and Akkadian, these are thought to correlate with the quality of the milk (more or less creamlike) [130] or perhaps with the level of the idiom (more or less literary), rather than with its source. In fact *ga* = *šizbu* is the standard term, while *gara*$_x$ = *lišdu* occurs, so far, only in lexical lists; in two Old Babylonian bilingual literary contexts, *lišdu* (*lildu*) translates *ga*. [131]

Milk was further turned into butter (or ghee) and cheeses of several kinds with the help of a churn (*dug-šakir, šakirru*). In part perhaps because of its phallic symbolism, the churn became a metaphor for fertility and figures prominently in the poetry devoted to the cult of Dumuzi and Inanna. This is well exemplified by a portion of a Dumuzi lament studied by Thorkild Jacobsen, [132] and by the hymn Ishme-Dagan J, [133] edited by myself, [134] and newly reedited by Samuel Noah Kramer. [135]

Last but not least of the secondary products of animal husbandry is dung. [136] As fuel, building material, caulking material etc., it remains important to this day to the Marsh Arabs (Ma'dan) whose way of life, now sadly threatened with extinction, has been studied by Wilfred Thesiger, Gavin Young, Gavin Maxwell, S. Westphal-Hellbusch, Elizabeth Warnock Fernea, and others. [137] It was more often overlooked in Assyriological discussions, with the notable exception of D.O. Edzard, who recognized at least two terms for dung in their vocabulary. [138] R. Frankena made passing reference to the Akkadian

---

[128] Stol 1993:99-113; *idem*, forthcoming; Englund, forthcoming.

[129] For some textual evidence, cf. Jacobsen 1983 = 1984:198f. (u).

[130] Jacobsen, *ibid.*, suggests that the reference may be specifically to buffalo cream.

[131] Hallo, RAI 17 (1970) 128:52, cited CADL 215; Å. Sjöberg, JCS 26 (1974) 163:11 and 170 *ad loc.* Stol 1993:100, compares Hebrew *lāšād* (Num. 11:8, Ps. 32:4).

[132] Jacobsen 1993 = 1994:192-200.

[133] So labelled by Marie-Christine Ludwig, *Untersuchungen zu den Hymnen des Išme-Dagan von Isin* (= Santag 2, 1990) 11f.

[134] Hallo, "New hymns to the kings of Isin," BiOr 23 (1966) 239-247, esp. pp. 244f.

[135] Kramer 1989. Cf. also a partial translation by Jacobsen, JAOS 1983 = 1984:198 (t).

[136] See already above, ch. II 1.

[137] Cf. especially Maxwell 1957.

[138] Edzard 1967:312f. s.vv. *muṭāl, sirĝma*.

term *putru* (Sumerian *si-šurim*(GANAM)-*gu₄*) in 1978, and Kilian Butz dealt more systematically with the concept in 1979 and 1983. [139] Although the words for dung are, perhaps understandably, not often mentioned in the archival or literary texts, they are well represented in the lexical lists. [140]

So much for the renewable resources provided by animal husbandry. What then of the slaughtered animals? Here we begin with a minor crux interpetum. I have always held that the neo-Sumerian archival texts, especially from Drehem, drew a fundamental distinction between animals that were slaughtered (*ba-úš*) and those that died of "natural causes" (*ri-ri-ga* or *de₅-de₅-ga* [141] = *miqittu*, lit. "fallen (dead)"). [142] This view is not universally shared, [143] but finds some support in (a) a model court record from Nippur, [144] (b) the mention, in Ur texts, of a "knife for slaughtering (small) cattle," [145] and (c) the texts from Lagash conveniently collected by Daniel C. Snell in his study of "The rams of Lagash." [146] One group of these, dated Shulgi 47 and Amar-Suen 2, lists animals in the "fallen" category besides others that are routinely listed as present, absent, or in arrears. [147] Twelve of these texts are at Leiden, and three of them, dealing with small cattle, are balanced accounts inscribed on round tablets of the type otherwise usually reserved for surveys of agricultural land studied by Pettinato; parallels to this rarer usage are cited by him, [148] R. Kutscher, [149] and H. Waetzoldt. [150] One of the three Leiden texts actually employs the finite form of the verb, *bí-rí*, "they fell dead there," which so far is to my knowledge a unique occurrence. [151]

---

[139] See references in my review of RLA 6/5-6 and 7-8 in BiOr 42 (1985) 637.

[140] HAR-ra = *hubullu* II in MSL 5 (1957) 75f., lines 311-319.

[141] So according to M. Powell, OLZ 71 (1976) 462 and Sigrist 1981:147f., presumably on the basis of the entry (di-e = RI) = *mi-qit-tu* in MSL 3 (1955)57:3a; cf. MSL 14 (1979) 259:296f.; 297:22.

[142] Hallo, "Contributions to neo-Sumerian," HUCA 29 (1958) 81.

[143] Cf. e.g. the more nuanced view of Sigrist 1992:70f.

[144] T. Jacobsen, "An ancient Mesopotamian trial for homicide," *Analecta Biblica* 12 (1959) 134, line 7, reprinted in TIT 198f., line 7.

[145] H. Waetzoldt, BiOr 32 (1975) 384 (*ad* p. 223): *gír-udu-úš*.

[146] Snell 1986.

[147] Ibid. 138f.

[148] Pettinato 1969. See p. 6 n. 1 for possible parallels to the Leiden texts.

[149] *Wadsworth Atheneum Bulletin* Sixth Series 6/1-2 (1970) No. 1 and fig. 1.

[150] Review of preceding in BiOr 30 (1973) 431.

[151] TLB 3:87 ii 3. Cf. also the baffling *(šu-gíd udu) in-nu-ri* of Sigrist, *Tablettes du*

Whether such animals were considered unfit for human consumption may be left open here. But even duly slaughtered animals were not so considered without more ado. We have literary testimony to the belief, in Sumer as in later Israel, in an original vegetarian dispensation which was replaced by divine consent to human meat-eating only under certain conditions. Theoretically, eating meat involved primordial guilt feelings which could be assuaged only by sharing the meat with the deity through sacri-fice, thus literally "making holy" the essentially profane act. [152] In practice, it meant that meat-eating took place only in the context of sacrifice: the deity, in the form of its anthropomorphic or "basilomorphic" statue, partook of the meat first, and the priesthood and laity only ate what the deity deigned to leave over. [153] My interpretation of the literary evidence in this regard has received some endorsement from Claus Wilcke, [154] and support from an independent study by Henri Limet. [155]

The texts amply indicate the class-bound character of the Mesopotamian diet. Meat consumption in the context of sacrifice was primarily a privilege of royalty, including the queen, whether by title or name. Numerous texts specifically designate small cattle (and fowl) as "food for My Lady" (níg-kú nin-mà) in the translation of the CAD, [156] while others mention Shulgi-simtum as the object of deliveries (mu-DU);[157] according to Mark Cooper, the "Lady" in question is in fact invariably Queen Shulgi-simtum. [158] Foreign rulers like Tabban-darah of Simurrum also shared the privilege. [159] No doubt the elaborate Akkadian recipes of Old Babylonian date recently published from the Yale Babylonian Collection [160] were intended for such royal and aristocratic consumers. [161] Meat for the lower ranks of society was a rare treat, probably confined to the great religious festivals. As for the

---

Princeton Theological Seminary (= OPSNKF 10, 1990) 15:3; Sigrist (p. 38) takes it as straw ("paille").

[152] See below, ch. VII 1.

[153] *Ibid.*; cf. Hallo 1987 and Kutscher AV (1993) 20.

[154] RLA 7 (1987) 123.

[155] Limet 1989.

[156] E.g. TLB 3:13f., 196. For the translation cf. CADB 190bc

[157] E.g. TLB 3:198f; cf. 15.

[158] JCS 38 (1986) 124-126.

[159] E.g. TLB 3:15; on Tabban-darah cf. Hallo, "Simurrum and the Hurrian frontier," RAI 24 (= RHA 36, 1978) 71-83, esp. pp. 74-76.

[160] YOS 11 (1985) Nos. 25-27.

[161] Cf. below, ch. III 2.

semi-free classes, they rated a bare subsistence diet, as amply attested by the ration-lists of the "great organizations," and discussed in several studies by I.J. Gelb. [162]

Although not properly speaking domesticated animals, fish, fowl and venison may be mentioned here as supplements to the essentially meatless diet. The first two have been amply illuminated by Armas Salonen in separate monographs, [163] and the first furthermore by Robert Englund. [164] In several texts, fowl is part of the royal diet, [165] and some mention young gazelles as a delivery for(?) the king. [166] As for fish, it is worth reiterating that it consisted primarily of smoked fish, Sumerian *ku₆-izi* or *izi-ku₆* , Akkadian *nun išati*. [167] The notion that the Sumerian term should be read *ku₆-gibil*, "fresh (lit. new) fish," remains inherently implausible given the great quantities involved and the climate of lower Iraq. [168] Englund supports the translation "smoked fish," though proposing yet another reading, *ku₆-še₆* . [169]

The slaughtering process yielded a number of by-products of which hides were the most significant. The leather industry based on them continued without interruption into the Isin Dynasty, and has been studied by Crawford, [170] Fish, [171] Goetze, [172] Sigrist [173] and van de Mieroop; [174] the particular case of shoes has again been dealt with monographically by Salonen. [175] Other leather products included bags of many varieties. [176]

Carcasses [177] were also salvaged and fed to dogs by the dog-herd-

---

[162] E.g. Gelb 1985. Cf. most recently Redding 1993.

[163] Salonen 1970, 1973.

[164] Englund 1987; rep. 1990.

[165] E.g. TLB 3:13f. Cf. above.

[166] E.g. TLB 3:207: *mu-DU lugal*.

[167] J.J.A. van Dijk, *La Sagesse Suméro-Accadienne* (Leiden, Brill, 1953) 64 *ad* "Silver and Copper" line 71. Jean Bottéro, RLA 6 (1981) 194 holds that *nun išati* refers "à un mode de cuisson plutôt que de conservation."

[168] Salonen 1970:193f., citing Hallo, JAOS 87 (1967) 66; previously *idem*, HUCA 30 (1959) 111, n. 40.

[169] JESHO 31 (1988) 178; cf. *idem* 1987, 1990: 217-219.

[170] Crawford 1948.

[171] Fish 1951, 1955, 1956.

[172] Goetze 1955.

[173] Sigrist 1981.

[174] Van de Mieroop 1987.

[175] Salonen 1969.

[176] E.g. *(kuš) du-gan* in TLB 3:19. See Salonen 1965:163-195.

[177] Written *ád (adda₂)*, i.e. UDU x ÚŠ or *ad₆ (adda)*, i.e. LÚ (or LÚšeššig) x ÚŠ (Akkadian *pagru*).

ers (*sipa ur-ra* or *ur-gir$_x$-ra*); one Leiden text even mentions sheep and
goats slaughtered as "regular offerings" (*sá-du$_{10}$*) for dogs. [178] Others
were fed to exotic animals in what may have been primitive zoos. It
is characteristic of the meticulous bookkeeping of the neo-Sumerian
scribes that they tended to itemize carcasses separately from hides, as
though it were not obvious that slaughtered animals would normally
provide one of each; thus one Leiden text lists separately 150 (respectively 146) sheep carcasses and 150 (resp. 146) sheepskins. [179]

Other by-products of the slaughtering process included horns
(which served for needles and other uses), tails (of uncertain use), and
something called a yoke (*šudun* or *šu-dul$_9$*). According to Sigrist, the
reference is to real yokes, retained for their value after the oxen or
bullock bearing them had been slaughtered. [180] This seems reasonable
when the reference is to the yoke of an ox, as in a Leiden text which
he transliterates, [181] but less so when the "yoke" is that of a sheep, as
in another Leiden text which he does not cite. [182] Perhaps the reference is to a feature of the entrails called yoke (*nīru*) in Akkadian. [183]

That brings us finally to the entrails, last of the non-renewable
resources and, like dung among the renewable ones, often overlooked
in this connection. The Mesopotamian devotion to divination by the
entrails in general (extispicy) and the liver in particular (hepatoscopy)
goes back to Sumerian times; it is surely a function of two other characteristic traits: one the evident revulsion against eating the entrails,
and two the abhorrence of waste. Both problems were solved at one
stroke when, after the king had "commissioned appropriate animal
sacrifices to the gods and ... the priests (had) consumed the meat that
the deity (in the form of his statue) had ostensibly left uneaten, the
entrails were put to good use in the search for a favorable omen." [184]
So I put it more than twenty years ago and so I would continue to
argue today.

It was suggested at the outset that the domestication of plants may
have preceded the domestication of animals, and even helped make

---

[178] TLB 3:34 ii 9-12; similarly Sigrist, AUCT 1:224 (with *sipa-ur-gir$_x$-ra*).
[179] TLB 3:50.
[180] Sigirist 1981: 154 and n. 39.
[181] *Ibid.* 156; the text is TLB 3:51 (not 50). Note the omission of line 5 in his
transliteration (5 *àd-amar*).
[182] TLB 3:50(!), writing *šudun*.
[183] Nougayrol 1968:50; Starr 1993.
[184] ANEH 159.

the latter possible. But we have seen at every turn that, once domesticated, animals played a major role in the cultivation of plants, especially cereals. Thus we can be briefer in covering some aspects of
cereal agriculture not directly or exclusively related to draught power
or other animal input. Irrigation, which has already been mentioned
in connection with the water wheel, can no doubt be given the chief
credit for turning lower Mesopotamia into a fabulously abundant
source of agricultural surpluses, especially in the third millennium. [185]
By the early second millennium, salinization had begun to take its
toll, according to a theory of Jacobsen [186] which has both critics [187]
and defenders. [188] The actual yield of Old Babylonian times has been
estimated as 54-60 *gur* per *bur*. [189] But for all the vagaries to which
irrigation was exposed by changing technologies and political conditions, [190] lower Mesopotamia was still the bread-basket of the ancient
world as late as Achaemenid and Seleucid times. And where irrigation was not possible or necessary, high yields could be registered by
means of "dry farming" techniques which depended on adequate
rainfall. [191]

Bibliographical References

Archi, Alfonso, 1980: "Allevamento e distribuzione del bestiame a Ebla," *Annali di
Ebla* 1:1-33 and 12 pls.; rep. in StEb 7 (1984) 45-81 and figs. 3-20.
Artzy, Michal and D. Hillel, 1988: "A defense of the theory of progressive soil salini-
zation in ancient southern Mesopotamia," *Geoarchaeology* 3:235-238.
Bailey, Clinton, 1993: "The role of rhyme and maxim in Bedouin law," *New Arabian
Studies* 1:21-35.
Civil, Miguel, 1994: *The Farmer's Instructions: a Sumerian Agricultural Manual* (Barcelona,
Editorial Aula).
Crawford, Vaughn, 1948: *Terminology of the Leather Industry in Late Sumerian Times* (Ph.D.
Thesis, Yale).
Edzard, Dietz O., 1967: "Zum Vokabular der Maʿdān-Araber im südlichen Iraq,"
Eilers AV 305-317.
Englund, Robert K., 1987: *Organisation und Verwaltung der Ur-III Fischerei* (Ph.D. Thesis,
Munich; rep. as BBVO 10, 1990).
———, forthcoming: "Regulating dairy productivity in the Ur III period."

---

[185] Turner 1981; Postgate 1984.
[186] Jacobsen 1982, esp. p. 39.
[187] Powell 1985, esp. pp. 30-32.
[188] Artzy and Hillel 1988.
[189] W.F. Leemans, JESHO 18 (1975) 141; 21 (1978) 197.
[190] See BSA 4-5 for a whole double-issue devoted to "Irrigation and cultivation in
Mesopotamia."
[191] Weiss 1986.

Finkelstein, Jacob J., 1973: "The goring ox," *Temple Law Quarterly* 46/2:169-290.

———, 1981: *The Ox That Gored* (= TAPhS 71/2).

Fish, T., 1951: "New KUŠ texts," MCS 1: 50-55.

———, 1955: "KUŠ texts of the Isin period," MCS 5:115-124.

———, 1956: "Umma tablets concerning KUŠ," MCS 6:22-54; "Lagash tablets concerning KUŠ," *ib.* 55-77; "Drehem tablets concerning KUŠ," *ib.* 85-103.

Foster, Benjamin R., 1982: *Umma in the Sargonic Period* (= MCAAS 20).

Gelb, I.J., 1967: "Growth of a herd of cattle in ten years," JCS 21:64-69.

———, 1985: "The ancient Mesopotamian ration system," JNES 24:230-243.

Goetze, Albrecht, 1955: "A Drehem tablet dealing with leather objects," JCS 9:19-21.

———, 1956: *The Laws of Eshnunna* (= AASOR 31).

Hall, Mark G., 1986: "A hymn to the moon-god, Nanna," JCS 38:152-166.

Hallo, William W., 1973: *Sumerian Archival Texts* (= TLB 3).

———, 1976: review of MVN 1 in BiOr 33:38-40.

———, 1987: "The origins of the sacrificial cult: new evidence from Mesopotamia and Israel," Cross AV 3-13.

Heimpel, Wolfgang, 1993: "Zu den Bezeichnungen von Schafen und Ziegen in den Drehem- und Ummatexten," BSA 7:115-160.

Jackson, Bernard S., 1974: "The goring ox again," JJP 18:55-93.

Jacobsen, Thorkild, 1982: *Salinity and Irrigation Agriculture in Antiquity* (= BM 14).

———, 1983: "Lad in the desert," JAOS 103:192-200, rep. Kramer AV 2 (1984) 192-200.

Kramer, Samuel Noah, 1963: *The Sumerians: their History, Culture, and Character* (Chicago, University of Chicago Press).

———, 1989: "The churns' sweet sound: a Sumerian bucolic poem," EI 20:113*-117*.

Limet, Henri, 1989: "La mort du mouton de sacrifice," *Anthropozoologica* (3me. numero special) 59-68.

Liverani, Mario and Wolfgang Heimpel, 1995: "Observations on livestock management in Babylonia," ASJ 17:127-144.

Maekawa, Kazuya, 1974: "Agricultural production in ancient Sumer," *Zinbun* 13:1-60.

———, 1981: "The agricultural texts of Ur III Lagash in the British Museum (I)," ASJ 3:37-61.

———, 1983-94: "The management of fatted sheep (udu-niga) in Ur III Girsu/Lagash," ASJ 5 (1983) 81-111, 6 (1984) 55-63, 16 (1994) 165-176.

———, 1995: "The agricultural texts of Ur III Lagash of the British Museum (X)," ASJ 17:175-231.

Maxwell, Gavin, 1957: *A Reed Shaken by the Wind* (London, Longmans Green).

Nissen, Hans, Peter Damerow, and Robert K. Englund, 1990: *Frühe Schrift und Techniken der Wirtschaftsverwaltung im alten Vordern Orient* (Bad Salzdetfurth, Franzbecker).

———, 1993: *Archaic Bookkeeping: Writing and Techniques of Economic Administration in the Ancient Near East* (Chicago, University of Chicago Press).

Nougayrol, Jean, 1968: "Le foie 'd'orientation' BM 50494," RA 62:31-50.

Pettinato, Giovannni, 1969: *Texte zur Verwaltung der Landwirtschaft in der Ur-III Zeit: "Die runden Tafeln"* (= AnOr 45).

———, 1979: *Ebla: un impero inciso nell'argila* (Milan, Editore S.p.A.).

———, 1981: *The Archives of Ebla: an Empire Inscribed in Clay* (Garden City, Doubleday).

———, 1986: *Ebla: nuovi orizzonti della storia* (Milan, Rusconi), tr. by C. Faith Richardson as *Ebla: a New Look at History* (Baltimore, Johns Hopkins U.P., 1991).

——— and Hartmut Waetzoldt, 1975: "Saatgut und Furchenabstand beim Getreideanbau," Salonen AV 259-290.

Postgate, J. N., 1984: "The problem of yield in cuneiform texts," BSA 1:97-102, 111-113.

Powell, Marvin A., Jr., 1972: "Sumerian area measures and the alleged decimal substratum," ZA 62:165-221.

———, 1984: "Late Babylonian surface mensuration: a contribution to the history of Babylonian agriculture and arithmetic," AfO 31:32-66.

———, 1985: "Salt, seed, and yields in Sumerian agriculture. A critique of the theory of progressive salinization," ZA 75:7-38.

Redding, Richard W., 1993: "Subsistence security as a selecive pressure favoring increasing cultural complexity," BAS 7:77-98.

Roth, Martha, 1980: "The scholastic exercise 'Laws about rented oxen'," JCS 32:127-146.

Salonen, Armas, 1965: Die Hausgeräte der alten Mesopotamier (Teil I) (= AASF 139).

———, 1968: Agricultura Mesopotamica (= AASF 149).

———, 1969: Die Fussbekleidung der alten Mesopotamier (= AASF 157).

———, 1970: Die Fischerei im alten Mesopotamien (= AASF 166).

———, 1973: Vögel und Vogelfang im alten Mesopotamien (= AASF 180).

Sheratt, Andrew, 1981: "Plough and pastoralism: aspects of the secondary products revolution," Clarke AV 261-305.

Sigrist, Marcel, 1981: "Le travail des cuirs et peaux à Umma sous la dynastie d'Ur," JCS 33:141-190.

———, 1992: Drehem (Bethesda, CDL Press).

Snell, Daniel C., 1986: "The rams of Lagash," ASJ 8:133-217.

Starr, Ivan, 1993: "A new omen text concerning the 'yoke' (nīru) of the liver," Hallo AV 230-235.

Stol, Marten, 1993: "Milk, butter, and cheese," BSA 7:99-113.

———, forthcoming: "Milch und Milchprodukte," RLA 8.

Turner, John W., 1981: Early Mesopotamian Agriculture: a Quantitative Model for Ur III Umma (Ph.D. Dissertation, Yale University).

Ucko, Peter J. and G.W. Dimbleby, 1969: The Domestication and Exploitation of Plants and Animals (London, Duckworth).

Van de Mieroop, Marc, 1987: Crafts in the Early Isin Period (= OLA 24).

Von den Driesch, Angela, 1993: "'Hausesel contra Hausonager.' Eine kritische Bemerkung ... über die Equiden Vorderasiens," ZA 83:258-267.

Waetzoldt, Hartmut, 1972: Untersuchungen zur neusumerischen Textilindustrie (= Studi Economici e Tecnologici 1).

Walcot, P., 1966: Hesiod and the Near East (Cardiff, University of Wales Press).

Weiss, Harvey, ed., 1986: The Origins of Cities in Dry-Farming Syria and Mesopotamia in the Third Millennium B.C. (Guilford, CT, Four Quarters Publishing).

Zohary, Daniel and Maria Hopf, 1988: Domestication of Plants in the Old World (Oxford, Clarendon Press).

3. Trade and Traders [192]

All the wealth thus accumulated by the surpluses generated from manufacturing and agriculture would not have availed the ancient Mesopotamian and Syrian economies much without a mechanism for exchanging it for wares lacking in the lands under their control and which thus had to be imported from beyond their borders. We have already seen, in connection with silver as money, how the merchant provided this essential mechanism, even acquiring a less than savory reputation in the process. [193] But the role of the merchant underwent a number of transformations in spite of the perennial character of the needs that he met. In what follows I wish to sum up the native views of trade and traders as recovered from the texts, chiefly lexical and literary, and to raise the question whether the textual evidence suffices to propose a historical paradigm for the evolution of trade and the profession of traders.

Previous studies of trade—and there has been no lack of them lately—have surveyed the subject from mostly other perspectives. An entire Rencontre Assyriologique was devoted to the subject of "Trade in the Ancient Near East," [194] but only a few of the contributions placed major emphasis on the native evidence; those by Samuel Noah Kramer on the testimony of the Sumerian literary sources and by Gerd Steiner on the language(s) of the traders may be singled out from this point of view. [195] A slightly earlier compendium, *Ancient Civilization and Trade,* used mainly archeological and anthropological approaches and arrived at a useful interregional overview. [196] Under the title of "explaining trade in ancient western Asia," Norman Yoffee provided an extensive review article on both of these collective works. [197] A third one, *Ancient Economy in Mythology,* aims at a considerably wider coverage. [198] Among monographic treatments, one may point to Hans Neumann's study of the Ur III evidence, W.F. Leeman's clas-

---

[192] Portions of this chapter were presented to the XXXVIIIème Rencontre Assyriologique Internationale, Paris, July 8, 1991, and appear in its Comptes Rendus as Hallo 1992.

[193] Above, ch. I 2.

[194] RAI 23, published first in *Iraq* 39 (1977) 1-231, and then as Hawkins 1977.

[195] Kramer 1977; Steiner 1977.

[196] Sabloff and Lamberg-Karlovsky 1975.

[197] Yoffee 1981.

[198] Silver 1991.

sic treatments of the Old Babylonian material, and Horst Klengel on the Hittites. [199] The first millennium evidence has been sifted by A.L. Oppenheim and, more recently, by M. Elat. [200] In distinction from all these studies, my point of departure will be the Sumerian terms which, at one time or another, were equated with Akkadian *tamkāru*. [201] I will not concern myself with the *ummânu* and his Sumerian equivalents, whose function in connection with trading ventures can better be translated by our "capitalist" or "entrepreneur" or "silent partner".

In a sense, the earliest lexically attested term for merchant is *ibira* or *tibira*, equated with Akkadian *tamkāru* in the basic lexical series *ea=A=naqu*. [202] The alternation between a vocalic onset and an initial *t*- marks this term as a substrate word. [203] But the same term is also equated with *gurgurru*, "craftsman," [204] and this may be its earlier meaning. What the nature of the craft may have been is suggested by the fact that it is occasionally written with the logogram for metal-worker, URUDU.NAGAR. [205] This implies an early association of trading with itinerant metal-workers, a situation familiar, for example, from the Irish tin-smiths or tinkers of later European history. [206]

Another term for trader with a possible substrate origin may be *dam-gàr*, here presumed to be the source of Akkadian *tamkāru*. [207] We may ignore attempts to find a Semitic etymology for the term, although *makāru* means "to do business, to use (silver, etc.) in business transactions" in Old Assyrian, [208] and even "to trade" in two passages in the late compendium of legal terminology known by its incipit as

---

[199] Neumann 1979; Leemans 1950, 1960 (cf. the review of the latter by Hallo 1963); Klengel 1979.

[200] Oppenheim 1967; Elat 1987, 1993.

[201] To the exclusion, e.g., of the designation LÚ.KAR which is supposed to mean "merchant" at Ebla, though equated with "runaway, fugitive" in the lexical texts such as MSL 14:141, 169; cf. Steinkeller, Hallo AV 243, n. 30.

[202] B. Landsberger, JAOS 88 (= Speiser AV, 1968) 133-147, esp. p. 139 line 126, and Landsberger's comments *ad loc.*, p. 146; cf. now MSL 14 (1979) 308:126.

[203] Landsberger and K. Balkan, *Belleten* 14 (1950) 238.

[204] MSL 12:103:231 and CAD G *s.v.*

[205] Landsberger, JAOS 88 (= Speiser AV, 1968) 146 *ad* 126; elsewhere KA x KIB: Ea III 126 and MSL 12:137:263; 16:87:270. For *tibira* in the meaning "metal-worker" see also *idem* 1974:11.

[206] Cf. John M. Synge, "The Tinker's Wedding," in *The Complete Works* (New York, Random House, 1935) 175-209.

[207] Landsberger 1974:12.

[208] CAD M/1 *s.v.*; the two references from Ugarit listed there may reflect West Semitic influence.

ana ittišu. [209] Oppenheim suggested that "the old problem of the relationship between *makāru* and *tamkāru* might require some rethink-
ing." [210] But Landsberger's "skepticism" on this point remains
valid, [211] and CAD's derivation of *tamkāru* from *makāru*, as indicated
s.v. makāru, remains to be justified *s.v. tamkāru.*

Salonen may be on the right track in associating the term with the
earliest stratum of professional designations characterized by two syllables and the ending *-ar*, as in *nagar (nangar), bahar, engar, kapar, arar*
and *ušbar (ešbar).*[212] Often, too, these and "later" substrate nouns
(dated by Salonen to the later Chalcolithic, ca. 5000-3500 B.C.) have
a cluster of two medial consonants, one of which tends to be a liquid,
as in *agrig, ašlag, (t)ensi(g), bur-gul, šandan*, to stay with the professional
names. [213] In Salonen's scheme, substrate nouns in *-ar* (including
dam-gàr) date from what he calls the late Neolithic or early Chalcolithic period (ca. 5500—5000 B.C.). [214] F.R. Kraus, too, proposes a
substrate origin for both Sumerian *dam-gàr* and Akkadian *tamkāru.* [215]

Such an origin need not, however, rule out a Sumerian etymology,
at least a popular etymology, for the term. For it is never written
with a single sign, or logographically, but invariably with the two
signs *dam* and *gàr*, which either represent a kind of syllabic writing
or, more likely, an attempt to suggest a Sumerian meaning for the
term. In the latter case, I would propose to understand it as "spouse
of the purse," since *dam* = "wife" or "husband" and *gàr* = "pocket"
or the like, as in the term *a-gàr*, "water pocket, polder, irrigation dis-
trict" (Akkadian *ugāru*). [216] Indeed the pictogram for *gàr* most likely
represents a pouch, perhaps of leather, pulled shut by a drawstring
around its neck. If all this is granted, the trader's function had passed,
already in prehistoric times, from the itinerant tinker to the emerging

---

[209] *kù-bal-šè-ak* and *kù šu-bal-ak* in Sumerian; cf. CAD M/1 126d and Lipiński
1988.
[210] Oppenheim 1974, esp. p. 237, n. 17.
[211] Landsberger 1967.
[212] Salonen 1969, esp. p. 109.
[213] For a somewhat analogous phonological phenomenon in Hebrew quadriliter-
als, see Meir Fraenkel, "Das 'reš' als Dehnzeichen in den Quaternärstämmen,"
HUCA 31 (1960) 72-102.
[214] Salonen 1969, esp. p. 118.
[215] Kraus 1973:111.
[216] Hallo, JCS 23 (1970) 58f. This term also has a much debated etymology; see
most recently W. van Soldt, BSA 4 (1988) 107.

professional, wedded to his money-bag. We shall presently see ample testimony to this perception of matters in later Sumerian literature.

The earliest contextual attestation of the trader is older than any of these lexical entries. It dates from the very beginning of the historic period, and employs the term *šab-gal*, which is equated with *tamkāru* in the Group Vocabulary, [217] admittedly a late lexical source. Falkenstein and Vaiman [218] and more recently Englund [219] have identified this professional name in archival texts of the Jemdet Nasr Period (ca. 3100-2900 B.C.). Given the probable provenience of these texts from temples or palaces, Powell concluded from this fact that "one can therefore suppose that the symbiosis of the merchant with the temple and palace economy which was typical of a later period already existed at this time." [220] If he is correct, this represents the early institutionalization of what had heretofore been perhaps a strictly individual enterprise.

Again we may venture an etymology. *šab-gal* means literally "big pot," and in later literary allusions is typically paired with *šab-tur*, or "little pot." Long ago I claimed these expressions for a kind of "colloquial" Sumerian, i.e. one which used terms in a mildly facetious rather than a strictly literal sense. [221] In the present instance, the allusion may be to the merchant's air of self-importance, or perhaps to his large fund of capital. The latter seems likelier in light of the Akkadian equivalent of *šab-tur*, which is itself a loanword from a Sumerian word meaning literally "the purse carrier." [222] Once again, the merchant seems to be identified in the popular imagination, and in popular etymology, with money.

If we have so far dealt with what appears to have been overland trade, we can next turn to overseas and long-range traffic. The Sumerian term for traders so engaged seems to have been *ga-raš* or

---

[217] W.G. Lambert, JCS 41 (1989) 4, citing V R 16:22gh; previously Hallo 1965:199, n. 5a and 1979:165 n. 55.

[218] See the references in Hallo 1979:165, n. 55, and add Vaiman in *Wirtschaft und Gesellschaft im Alten Vorderasien*, ed. by J. Harmatta and G. Komoroczy (Budapest, Akademiae Kiado, 1976) (repr. from Acta Antiqua Academiae Scientiarum Hungaricae 22, 1974) 20.

[219] Englund 1988:154; cf. also Vaiman, BaMi 21 (1990) 98 and 101 *ad* PI 100.

[220] Powell 1978:140 and n. 37. (Translation mine.)

[221] Hallo 1979, esp. p. 165, n. 55; 1985. The concept of "colloquial Sumerian" has meantime been applied by Jacob Klein to "Enlil and Namzitarra" (ASJ 12, 1990, 57).

[222] Cf. below at nn. 260-264.

ga-eš₈, more specifically *ga-eš₈-a-ab-ba*, " *kaeššu* of the sea," [223] from which the Akkadian *kaeššu* was derived as a loanword, but which was also, if less often, equated with *tamkāru* in the lexical lists. [224]

The first literary allusion to this kind of trade, or *nam-garaš*, is a negative one. The epic of Enmerkar and the Lord of Aratta, [225] best described as a veritable aetiology of long-distance trade, shows how, in return for lapis lazuli and other semi-precious stones as well as precious metals from Aratta, a city and land perhaps as far away as Afghanistan, [226] Sumer furnished grain, fruit, reed and livestock in a classic case of low-weight, high-value luxury items traded for agricultural surpluses. When the epic begins, such trade did not yet exist, [227] while by its end, it seems to describe Uruk's imports of light but costly objects from Aratta as tribute due from this defeated rival, and Uruk's export of its agricultural surplus as tokens of Enmerkar's magnanimity in victory. [228] Since Enmerkar dates to the Second Early Dynastic Period, and his epic with some probability to the neo-Sumerian period, this aetiology, like many others in the Enmerkar-Lugalbanda cycle, reveals the view which 21st century Sumer had, however anachronistically, of its 26th century past. [229]

But we need only move to the Third Early Dynastic Period for a literary work that is actually contemporary with the situation it describes. Like "Enmerkar and the Lord of Aratta" it describes the trader as a *garaš*. This time, however, it is not a Sumerian but an Akkadian composition; indeed, W.G. Lambert has aptly described it as "a work of the most ancient Semitic literature" in the first attempt at a connected translation of the text. [230] It is known in an exemplar from Abu Salabikh published by R.D. Biggs [231] and later seen, not only to join another text from there, [232] but also to have a duplicate from Ebla. D.O. Edzard, who published the Ebla exemplar, [233] called

---

[223] Cf. Oppenheim 1954, esp. pp. 14f. and n. 22.

[224] CAD K *s.v.* cites Diri VI D 17, as restored.

[225] Latest translation by Jacobsen, *Harps* 275-319.

[226] Hansman 1972:118, n. 97; 1978; differently Majidzadeh 1976.

[227] Line 17: *nam-garaš nu-un-ak*. Cf. Kramer 1977:61 and n. 10.

[228] See esp. ll. 595 - end.

[229] Cf. above, ch. I 3 for some of these aetiologies.

[230] Lambert 1989.

[231] R.D. Biggs, *Inscriptions from Abu Ṣalābīkh* (OIP 99, 1974) No. 326.

[232] *Ibid.*, No. 342.

[233] D.O. Edzard, ARET 5 (1984) No. 6; cf. M. Civil, ZA 74 (1984) 163, n. 8.

it a hymn to Shamash, the sun-god, [234] while Alfonso Archi referred to it as an epic. [235] Lambert characterized the text as an "Old Akkadian work of mythology (whose) most frequently appearing divine name is that of the sun god." [236] In 1989, he translated it, in part, as follows: "Foreign trade (garaš₄) he gave to the traders. [237] The lands [238] yielded lapis and silver, sissoo wood, cedar, cypress, juniper ... perfumed oil, vegetable oil, honey ... the property of the traders." [239] This list looks strikingly like that of the purchases of the neo-Sumerian merchants which in their turn can best be described as imports. [240] In 1992, Lambert restudied the text in depth; the list of "imports" remains as before. [241]

For the sake of completeness we may also mention one further piece of evidence from Ebla. A peculiar logogram written MÁ.HU[242] and thought to stand for Sumerian u_5, usually rendered by Akkadian rakkābu, "rider," [243] is translated by Archi variously as "commerçant" [244] and as "messager." [245] Lambert, in his new study of the Shamash text, continues to render it unambiguously as "trader." [246] Perhaps it was simply in the nature of early international travel that its two main functions, communication and trade, were often enough combined in the same person(s).

I would like now briefly to pursue some of the themes already struck, and to do so, again, primarily through the native literary sources. To begin with the association of the merchant with silver, this approaches the character of a cliché in the Sumerian proverbs. We have cited them at length to this effect in the discussion of silver as money. [247] The merchant's proverbial obsession with money may

---

[234] ARET 5 p. 30, followed by Th.J. Krispijn, JEOL 32 (1991-2) 18 and n. 16 ("an Akkadian hymn").

[235] Archi 1987.

[236] Lambert 1989:3.

[237] Written GARAŠ over GARAŠ at Ebla.

[238] I would say "foreign lands" (KUR.KUR).

[239] Lambert 1989:33.

[240] Curtis and Hallo 1959, esp. pp. 111f.; Hallo 1963. Cf. already A.L. Oppenheim, AOS 32 (1948) 137 (end).

[241] Lambert 1992.

[242] Or sometimes MÁ.SI, according to Lambert 1992:61.

[243] P. Steinkeller, Or. Ant. 23 (1984) 34, n.8.

[244] A. Archi, Kupper AV 197, n. 4.

[245] Ibid., 200 (top).

[246] Lambert 1992:59.

[247] Above, ch. I 2.

well have led to his unpopularity. In the process of providing the essential mechanism for trade, he may have acquired a reputation for
sharp practices.

Perhaps this reputation is the reason why it was thought necessary
or prudent to entrust the merchant to the special supervision of deities charged with administering justice.   In the Sumerian tradition—where Enlil himself could be pictured as a merchant [248]—this
was the goddess Nanshe, and the great hymn in her honor condemns
the merchant who, in Kramer's translation, "substitutes the small
weight for the large weight, the small measure for the large measure." [249] The late incantation-and-ritual Shurpu still speaks of the
"curse of paying by the small measure and buying by the large measure," [250] or of "giving (a loan) according to the lesser mina (but)
collecting (it) according to the larger mina." [251] Similar sentiments
can be found in Egyptian and Biblical literature. [252] In the Bible,
dishonesty in the matter of weights and measures is more frequently
condemned as a veritable "abomination of the Lord" than any other
offense. [253] At least once such dishonesty is imputed specifically to a
merchant, referred to elsewhere as "one who circulates" (sôḥēr) [254] but
here as a "Canaan(ite) in whose hands are false scales" (Hos 12:8). [255]
The heavy Canaanite involvement in maritime trade is reason
enough for the ethnic label to have become a generic term for the
profession of merchant. [256] The Canaanites themselves are thought to
have called their traders bidaluma, though this translation has been
questioned. [257]

In the Akkadian tradition, it was Shamash who was particularly
charged with administering justice, and the all-seeing Sun was relied
on to catch out the dishonest merchant, whether at home or on the
road far from home. We have already seen that the Old Akkadian
myth about or hymn to this deity was much concerned with trade
and traders. The great preceptive hymn to Shamash, parts of which,

---

[248] Civil 1976.
[249] Kramer, HBS 265, ll. 142f.; cf. Heimpel 1981 ad loc.
[250] Erica Reiner, Šurpu (AfO Beiheft 11, 1958) 42, line 64.
[251] CAD M/1:220d.
[252] Hallo, BP 69.
[253] Hallo 1985a:36f.
[254] Landsberger 1967.
[255] Elat 1979:529.
[256] Sasson 1966.
[257] Lipiński 1988.

if not all of it, may well go back to Old Babylonian times, has him deeply involved with what I. Nakata has called the "Mesopotamian merchants and their ethos." [258] In the translation by Lambert, [259] it again contrasts "the merchant who practices trickery as he holds the balance, who uses two sets of weights" with "the honest merchant who holds the balances and gives good weight" or "the merchant ... who weighs out loans (of corn) by the minimum standard but requires a large quantity in repayment" with "the honest merchant who weighs out loans (of corn) by the maximum standard, thus multiplying kindness." It invokes Shamash as both the protector and the critical observer of the entrepreneur (*ummānu*), the travelling merchant (*tamkāru*) and his apprentice (the *šamallû*). [260]

The last two professions are even represented in the heavenly court of Shamash himself. The "two apprentice-(merchants) of Ebabbar" are identified in the great god-list An=Anum as the divine *šab-gal* and the divine *šab-sir*, translated by Lambert as "Senior Trader" and "Junior Trader" respectively. [261] As we have seen, the human equivalent of the first occurs already in the Jemdet Nasr texts. [262] That of the second is *šab-tur*, equated in the Group Vocabulary with *šamallû* [263]. The latter concept deserves some further attention.

"Apprentice" is actually not so much the translation of the Akkadian term *šamallû* as of the Akkadian loanword borrowed from it into Aramaic *šewaliya* and Mandaic *ašwaliya* and *šulyta*. The Akkadian term itself is a loanword from Sumerian *šaman-lá (šagan-lá)*, literally the "purse carrier." And indeed it is not the merchant but his apprentice who is described in Akkadian as the purse carrier (*naš kīsi*) in the Shamash hymn. [264]

Such purse carriers were also significantly involved in the machinations imputed to the Kassites by Tukulti-Ninurta I of Assyria in his epic. They are alleged to have served as secret emissaries to potential allies in the Kassite war against the Assyrians. [265] More recently it has

---

[258] Nakata 1970-71.

[259] *Babylonian Wisdom Literature* (Oxford, 1960) 133.

[260] *Ibid.*, esp. ll. 65-70, 103-121, 138f.

[261] Lambert 1989:4.

[262] Above, notes 218f.

[263] Lambert, JCS 41 (1989) 4; cf. already Hallo 1965:199, n. 5a.

[264] Line 139, and at least one exemplar of l. 69 according to the restoration proposed by Nakata 1970-71:91, n. 3.

[265] P.B. Machinist, *The Epic of Tukulti-Ninurta* (Ph.D. Thesis, Yale, 1978) 227-229 *ad* II A 9'.

been remarked that "the connection of the merchants and messengers with treaty provisions is inferred from their prominence in the narrative (i.e., the epic) but not explicitly stated." [266] However, if we recall the ambiguity surrounding the Eblaite u_5 (merchant or messenger), [267] and the alleged absence of the trader in the epic of "Enmerkar and the Lord of Aratta," where the mediating role was instead assigned to the emissary or messenger (kin-gi_4-a, [268] we may suggest an ultimate convergence of the two functions: that of the travelling merchant and that of the emissary or messenger or even international spy. Jacobsen may therefore be on the right track in suggesting that the "Sitz im Leben" of "Enmerkar and the Lord of Aratta" (and other Sumerian epics) was the royal court of Ur which wished, by the performance of such epics, to entertain and flatter the many foreign emissaries who paid court to the neo-Sumerian kings in their palaces, and that the real hero (or "anti-hero") of these epics is the messenger even when the ostensible subject is trade! [269]

This rapid survey of some of the ancient Near Eastern evidence for trade and traders, mostly in lexical or literary form, has suggested reasons for associating the trader in turn with itinerant metal-work, with silver as money and with other early types of capital formation, with the "great organizations" of temple and palace economy, and with diplomacy. Whether these associations define successive stages in the trader's profession or all co-existed at the same time must be left for future investigation.

Bibliographical References

Archi, Alfonso, 1987: "More on Ebla and Kish," *Eblaitica* 1:126-140.
Civil, Miguel, 1976: "Enlil, the merchant: notes to CT 15:10," JCS 28:72-81.
Curtis, John B. and William W. Hallo, 1959: "Money and merchants in Ur III," HUCA 30:103-139.
Elat, Moshe, 1979: "The monarchy and the development of trade in ancient Israel," in Lipiński, STE 2:527-546.
———, 1987: "Der *tamkāru* im neuassyrischen Reich," JESHO 30:233-254.
———, 1993: "International trade and its merchants in the Assyrian Empire," Malamat AV 12-17 (in Hebrew; English summary p. 231*).

---

[266] J.A. Brinkman, "Political covenants, treaties, and loyalty oaths in Babylonia...," in *I Trattati nel mondo antico*, ed. by Luciano Canfora *et al.* (1990) 81-112, esp. p. 91, n. 39.

[267] Above, notes 242-246.

[268] Above, notes 227f.

[269] Jacobsen, "The royal court at Ur III," lecture, Yale, Feb. 26, 1976; *Harps* 277.

Englund, Robert K., 1988: "Administrative timekeeping in ancient Mesopotamia," JESHO 31:121-185.

Hallo, William W., 1963: review of Leemans 1960 in JCS 17:59f.

————, 1965: "A mercantile agreement from the reign of Gungunum of Larsa," Landsberger AV 199-203.

————, 1979: "Nungal in the egal: an introduction to colloquial Sumerian?" JCS 31:161-165.

————, 1985: "Back to the Big House: colloquial Sumerian, continued," Or. 54: 56-64.

————, 1985a: "Biblical abominations and Sumerian taboos," JQR 76:21-40.

————, 1992: "Trade and traders in the ancient Near East: some new perspectives," RAI 38:351-356.

Hansman, J., 1972: "Elamites, Achaemenians and Anshan," Iran 10:101-125.

————, 1978: "The question of Aratta," JNES 37:331-336.

Hawkins, J.D., ed., 1977: Trade in the Ancient Near East (London, British School of Archaeology in Iraq).

Heimpel, Wolfgang, 1981: "The Nanshe Hymn," JCS 33:65-139.

Klengel, Horst, 1979: "Handel und Kaufleute im hethitischen Reich," AoF 6:69-80.

Kramer, Samuel Noah, 1977: "Commerce and trade: gleanings from Sumerian literature," Iraq 39:59-66.

Kraus, F.R., 1973: Vom mesopotamischen Menschen ... (=MKNAWL n.r. 36/6).

Lambert, W.G., 1989: "Notes on a work of the most ancient Semitic literature," JCS 41:1-33.

————, 1992: "The language of ARET V 6 and 7," Quaderni di Semitistica 18:41-62.

Landsberger, Benno, 1967: "Akkadisch-hebräische Wortgleichungen I. Akk. sāhiru = hebr. sōḥēr 'Kaufmann'," Baumgartner AV 176-190.

————, 1974: "Three essays on the Sumerians," MANE 1/2.

Leemans, W.F., 1950: The Old Babylonian Merchant (= SD 3).

————, 1960: Foreign Trade in the Old Babylonian Period as revealed by texts from Southern Mesopotamia (= SD 6).

Lipiński, Edward, 1988: "š u - b a l a - a k a and badalum," in Waetzoldt and Hauptmann 1988:257-260.

Majidzadeh, Yousef, 1976: "The land of Aratta," JNES 35:105-113.

Nakata, I., 1970-71: "Mesopotamian merchants and their ethos," JANES 3:90-101.

Neumann, Hans, 1979: "Handel und Händler in der Zeit der III. Dynastie von Ur," AoF 6:15-52.

Oppenheim, A. Leo, 1954: "The seafaring merchants of Ur," JAOS 74:6-17.

————, 1967: "An essay on overland trade in the first millennium BC," JCS 21:236-254.

————, 1974: "Old Assyrian magaru or makaru?" Güterbock AV 229-237.

Powell, Marvin A., Jr., 1978: "Götter, Könige und 'Kapitalisten' im Mesopotamien des 3. Jahrtausends v.u.Z.," Oikumene 2:127-144.

Sabloff, J.A. and C.C. Lamberg-Karlovsky, eds., 1975: Ancient Civilization and Trade (Albuquerque, University of New Mexico Press).

Salonen, Armas, 1969: "Die ältesten Berufe und Erzeugnisse des Vorderen Orients," in Die Fussbekleidung der alten Mesopotamier (= AASF 157) 97-119.

Sasson, Jack M., 1966: "Canaanite maritime involvement in the second millennium B.C.," JAOS 86:126-138.

Silver, Morris, ed., 1991: Ancient Economy in Mythology (Savage, MD, Rowman and Littlefield).

Steiner, Gerd, 1977: "Kaufmanns- und Handelssprachen im Alten Orient," Iraq 39:11-17.

Waetzoldt, Hartmut and Harald Hauptmann, eds., Wirtschaft und Gesellschaft von Ebla (= HSAO 2).

Yoffee, Norman, 1981: "Explaining trade in ancient western Asia," MANE 2:21-60.

CHAPTER THREE

THE REFINEMENTS OF CIVILIZATION

As the essentials of civilization brought certain secondary aspects almost inevitably in their train, so these secondary aspects in their turn encouraged and facilitated tertiary developments which advanced culture beyond the stage of bare subsistence to the level of refinement and even enjoyment of some of the luxuries of life. We have already seen that among the imports of the merchants were many low-weight, high value items that can be regarded as luxuries—spices, aromatic woods, precious metals and semi-precious stones among many other things. In what follows, a small number of more specialized refinements of early civilization will be considered, notably in the areas of travel, culinary arts, and games.

1. TRAVEL AND GEOGRAPHICAL KNOWLEDGE

Travel was resorted to by merchants, emissaries, armies, and kings. In the case of kings, it could even be undertaken for pleasure, as when Hammurapi, king of Yamhad with its capital at Halab (Aleppo), wrote to Zimri-Lim, king of Mari: "The man (i.e., king) of Ugarit wrote me as follows, saying: 'Show me the house (i.e., palace) of Zimri-Lim. I would see it!' So now, I have sent a man (of?) his son to you (to inspect it)." [1] Conversely, a king of Mari made a trip to Ugarit. [2]

Travel could proceed at a leisurely pace or by forced marches. In the third and second millennia, a daily march of 25-30 km was not unusual. [3] In the first millennium, the neo-Assyrian armies could cover from 20-40 km per day. [4] According to the neo-Assyrian version of the Gilgamesh Epic, a normal rate of travel was 150 *bēru* in 45 days, or about 3 *bēru* per day; since the *bēru* is a little over 10 km, [5]

---

[1] Malamat 1989:25f. and pl. IIa.
[2] Villard 1986.
[3] Hallo 1964:63.
[4] Kühne 1980, esp. p. 69.
[5] CAD s.v.

that would mean approximately 30 km per day. Gilgamesh and En-kidu, however, managed to cover fifty *bēru* or over 500 km per day, if we are to believe the Epic (IV i 1-4; 44'f.); [6] the restoration of the relevant passage as proposed long ago by E.A. Speiser [7] has since been confirmed by the discovery of a new fragment, [8] and is adopted by the latest translations. [9]

Even this mythical speed (if granted) was not unique. King Shulgi of Ur (ca. 2093-2046 B.C.) boasted of having run from his capital city of Ur to the religious capital at Nippur and back again in a single day in order to celebrate the lunar festival in both cities on a single day. The distance in question is 15 *bēru* or ca. 150 km each way, and 300 km for the round trip! That distance, if not the feat itself, is confirmed by a contemporaneous archival text. [10] The feat was considered so significant that it inspired a date formula of the king (his seventh), allusions in at least two royal hymns (Hymns C and a newly publish-ed fragment) [11] as well as a detailed description in a special hymn entirely devoted to it (Hymn A). This hymn was, to judge by the many duplicates preserved of it, one of the most popular in the ex-tensive repertoire of royal hymns glorifying Shulgi; its most recent translations by Samuel Noah Kramer [12] and Jacob Klein [13] are ap-propriately entitled or subtitled "The king of the road." In the hymn, the run begins and ends at Nippur, but there is little doubt that both sources allude to the same event, and indeed well illustrate the prin-ciple that "there are striking and sometimes even literal parallels ... between the date formulas and the royal hymns," [14] a thesis that was elaborately defended by Douglas Frayne both in general and with respect to this instance. [15]

The achievement of Shulgi, whether credible or not, still resonated under the First Dynasty of Isin which succeeded the Third Dynasty

---

[6] Cf. also iv 9'-11' according to the neo-Babylonian text LKU 40.

[7] ANET 1950, 1955:82.

[8] CT 46:21.

[9] Bottero, Gilgamesh, 98f.; Tournay and Shaffer, *Gilgamesh* 106f.; for a different translation see Tigay, *Evolution* 8 and n. 18.

[10] Hallo, VTS 40 (1988) 61, n. 45; R.K. Englund, JESHO 31 (1986) 167f. and n. 40.

[11] Klein 1993 (ii 10'-11').

[12] ANET 584-586.

[13] Klein 1981:167-217.

[14] Hallo, RAI 17:118f.; cf. below, ch. VI 1.

[15] Frayne 1981, esp. pp. 187-191; 1983.

of Ur in the hegemony of Sumer. Ishme-Dagan of Isin, whose repertoire of royal hymns is second only to Shulgi's in extent, and who
modeled himself in many respects on the earlier ruler, [16] gave us two
texts on one tablet of which the first is, in the opinion of Klein, "a
copy of an inscription of a royal statue, on which Šulgi was probably
represented in a position of running toward Nippur" and the second
"a copy of an inscription of an Išmedagan statue, which represented
this king in a similar posture." [17] If Klein is correct, then there is here
confirmation of the rest of the thesis correlating not only date formulas and royal hymns, but both with royal inscriptions and perhaps
even with royal statues. [18] It may be noted, however, that Ishme-Dagan has scaled down his claim: he ran only one way! The rate of 15
double-hours per day implied by this feat is the same claimed for
Gilgamesh and Enkidu on their return trip to Uruk (XI 301). [19]

Shulgi's achievement has been interpreted as "a kind of publicity
stunt to commemorate the activities of year six" when, according to
the relevant date formula, he put the road to Nippur in order. [20] As
amplified in his Hymn A, this involved determining the length of the
bēru, i.e., presumably "dividing the roads into equal sections and establishing 'road stations'(Sum. é-danna, Akk. *bît bēri*." [21] These "road-
stations" or caravanserais, literally " *bēru*-houses," were presumably
placed, at least theoretically, at one *bēru* intervals; in each were built
bivouacs called *é-gal*, literally "big house, palace." [22] These featured
such amenities as gardens and rest-places (Hymn A line 30). As a
result of all this royal solicitude, the wayfarer could expect to find rest
and refreshment there as in a well-built city (Hymn A 31-35) according to a cliché also found in other contexts (Pickaxe and Plow ll. 156-
8). [23]

Other kings also displayed solicitude for roads and travelers.
Shulgi's father Ur-Nammu made similar if more modest claims both
in the date formula of his fourth year [24] and in a royal hymn, and

---

[16] Klein 1990.
[17] Klein 1985, esp. p. 9*; cf. also Frayne 1983.
[18] Hallo, VTS 40 (1988) 61.
[19] Cf. Tournay and Shaffer, *Gilgamesh* 246f.
[20] Frayne 1981:187.
[21] Klein 1981: 207 *ad* l. 29; cf. CAD s.v. *bēru* A.
[22] For this meaning see Hallo, JCS 31 (1979) 162 and n. 17; Or. 54 (1985) 64 and
n. 32.
[23] Cf. Vanstiphout 1984:246 and n. 31.
[24] So Waetzoldt 1990.

perhaps even in a royal inscription, according to Frayne. [25] And Gungunum, effectively the first king of the Larsa dynasty, claimed the foundation of caravanserais (*é-danna* or *é-kas*$_4$) [26] as well as the dredging of rivers in the date formula of his 19th year; [27] it is less likely that *é-danna* here refers to a toponym [28] such as is attested lexically. [29]

Given the importance thus attached to overland travel, it should not come as a total surprise that geographical knowledge was prized, organized and disseminated at an early date. In 1964, I summarized "the scope of Babylonian geography" under four headings: maps, geographical-name lists, cadastres and itineraries. [30] Since then, some or all of this ground has been traversed again by a number of other scholars. In 1967, E. Heinrich and U. Seidl surveyed 'groundplans from the ancient Near East,' asserting that some of these drawings had occasionally been dealt with, but that a systematic survey didn't exist yet. [31] In 1978, J.D. Muhly again reviewed much of the same material in a study of "Ancient Cartography," [32] as did R. North in 1979, [33] K.R. Nemet-Nejat in 1982, [34] W. Röllig in 1983 [35] and A.R. Millard in 1987. [36] Clearly the emphasis in all these more recent studies is on cartography, and this aspect may well begin our update of ancient geographical knowledge.

It has been suggested in the past that primitive attempts at cartography may be detected among the "Ritzzeichnungen" or drawings scratched on the reverse of Early Dynastic lexical and literary texts from Fara (Shuruppak) and Abu Salabikh. [37] The examples from Abu Salabikh are now available in the publications by R.D. Biggs. [38] The

---

[25] Frayne 1981:106-111.
[26] So W. Sallaberger, ZA 82 (1992) 139.
[27] Edzard, ZZB 55, n. 250; 102 and n. 492.
[28] So M.B. Rowton, JCS 21 (1967) 273, n. 29; cf. also RG 2 and 3 s.v.
[29] MSL 11:14:6; 62:17; 102:211.
[30] Hallo 1964:57-63.
[31] Heinrich and Seidl 1967, esp. p. 24: "Einige diesser (alten Grundriss-)Zeichnungen wurden zwar gelegentlich behandelt, jedoch eine zusammenfassende Darstellung gibt es noch nicht."
[32] Muhly 1978.
[33] North 1979, esp. pp. 13-23.
[34] Nemet-Nejat 1982, ch. 1: "History of Babylonian cartography."
[35] Röllig 1983.
[36] *Apud* Harley and Woodward 1987:107-116.
[37] Hallo 1964:57, nn. 4f.
[38] Biggs 1966:82f.; 1974:30f. and Nos. 2, 47, 60 and 281.

discovery of the archives of Ebla has meantime turned up similar evidence from that site from only a little later. [39]

True cartography, it is often assumed, began with the Egyptians. Denis Wood, for example, author of a standard history of the discipline, [40] states: "Cartography was created by Egyptian surveyors seeking to recover land boundaries after the cyclical flooding of the Nile." [41] But while this practical impetus may account for Egypt's priority in the field of geometry, the earliest Egyptian map dates from the fourteenth century, and even after that the genre does not become plentiful. The first unquestionable maps from Mesopotamia date from the Sargonic period, and are almost a millennium older. They picture territories near Gasur (the later Nuzi) and Lagash respectively. [42] This is also the time and provenience of the oldest architectural groundplans of buildings, [43] including temples. [44]

Both territorial maps and architectural plans came into their own in neo-Sumerian times. In addition to the examples listed in 1964, [45] attention may be called to the earlier survey by Trevor Donald [46] and the subsequent ones by Muhly, Nemet-Nejat, Röllig and others. [47] Among other additions to the corpus may be noted a map of the *gu₄-mul* field; [48] fields of this name are known in both Umma and Lagash. [49] As a matter of historical interest, it may be added that as early as 1896, one of the neo-Sumerian field plans from Lagash (RTC 416) was already made the subject of a short monograph by A. Eisenlohr. [50]

The long interval from neo-Sumerian to neo-Babylonian times is more sporadically attested in the history of Mesopotamian cartography, [51] though passing mention may perhaps be made of the "Graffiti and drawings on the cuneiform tablets from Bogazköy-Hattusha" presented by A. Ünal to the 35th Rencontre Assyriologique Interna-

---

[39] G. Pettinato, MEE 3 (1981) 244 No. 59; cf. the photograph pl. xxxiii b.
[40] Wood 1992.
[41] *Apud* Hitt 1995:33.
[42] Hallo 1964:57, nn. 7f.; cf. below, n. 62.
[43] *Ibid.* 61, n. 25.
[44] Lenzen 1955, esp. pp. 24f. *ad* RTC 66; add OIC 19:3.
[45] Hallo 1964:57, n. 10; 61, n. 26.
[46] Donald 1962.
[47] See above, notes 31-36.
[48] D.I. Owen, JCS 24 (1972) 149:1.
[49] Pettinato 1967:270f.
[50] Eisenlohr 1896.
[51] Hallo 1964:57, nn. 12-17; 61, n. 27.

tionale (Philadelphia, 1988), and of the ground-plan of a temple dated to Kassite times by D.J. Wiseman. [52] Wiseman has also published an elevation of a ziggurrat (stepped temple tower) from neo-Babylonian times. [53] The neo-Babylonian field plans were discussed in a preliminary study by K.R. Nemet-Nejat and then in her definitive volume. [54] The famous neo-Babylonian *mappa mundi* [55] has been reedited by W. Horowitz [56] and discussed by M. Stol. [57]

A subsidiary question of cartography may be raised here, and that is the matter of "orientation." The very word, by its etymology, implies facing east, and that is indeed what Jews do to this day when praying—at least those who live to the west of Jerusalem—as indicated in the synagogue by a sign called or inscribed with the word *mizrach*, "east, place of sunrise." (Moslems by contrast face Mecca.) A similar presumption underlies the etymology of the southern country of Yemen—this time in Arabic as well as Hebrew (*teyman*): it is the land lying on the right from the point of view of a Near Easterner living to the north of Yemen (as most do) and facing the sunrise. Similarly, the country of Sam'al, even in the records of the Assyrian (who lived east of it), is that country which lies to the left of those living south of it (as most do) and facing the sunrise. [58]

This usage of the first millennium B.C. can be traced back to the late third millennium by a revealing passage in the Cycle of Temple Hymns collected by Enheduanna, daughter of Sargon of Akkad. [59] Speaking of Nippur in the second of these hymns (line 28), she says: " (Oh Nippur,) your right and your left hand are Sumer and Akkad (respectively)," i.e., Sumer lies to the right of Nippur and Akkad to the left. [60] Strictly speaking, we could say that Sumer lay to the southeast of Nippur and Akkad to its northeast, but the meaning seems clear: right is south, left is north, and orientation is indeed to the east.

How does this toponymic and literary evidence compare with the

---

[52] Wiseman 1972, esp. fig. 4; cf. fig. 3a for another Middle Babylonian (?) ground plan.

[53] *Ibid.* figs. 1f.

[54] Nemet-Nejat 1975, 1982.

[55] Hallo 1964:61, n. 24.

[56] Horowitz 1988.

[57] Stol 1988-89.

[58] But cf. now a Shim'al in Arabia (Ras-al-Khaimah)! Vogt and Franke-Vogt 1987.

[59] Cf. below, chs. V 3 and VIII 3.

[60] For the ideological implications of this passage, see Hallo, Kutscher AV (1993) 26.

actual maps recovered from ancient Mesopotamia? Eckhard Unger was sure that he had the answer as early as 1935 when he began his survey of "ancient Babylonian maps and plans" [61] with the Old Akkadian map from Nuzi (Gasur) published by T.J. Meek the same year. [62] On that oldest of all the world's known maps, east was clearly on the "top" of the tablet—at least if the tablet was held in such a way that the lines of cuneiform ran from left to right. But that writing direction only became standard half a millennium later! [63] If the lines are read from top to bottom, as they no doubt were in Sargonic times, then north is at the top of the tablet.

The question of the orientation of maps cannot be divorced from that of the orientation of buildings, especially temples. G. Martiny devoted an entire monograph to the subject in 1932, [64] but more recent researchers have tended to deal more cursorily with it, notably J. Margueron and E. Heinrich who each contributed two massive volumes to the history of monumental architecture in Mesopotamia. [65] Here the initial question is whether such buildings are oriented to the points of the compass or to the midpoints between these points. Beyond that, it is a question whether temples are meant to face the rising or setting sun and to catch its rays at certain times of the day or year. The most daring hypothesis in this regard may well be the old one of Julian Morgenstern, according to whom the Temple of Solomon in Jerusalem, perhaps after the fashion of its Near Eastern prototypes, was so oriented that the rising sun cast its light between the pillars called Jachin and Boaz and into the Holy of Holies, the innermost cella, on just two days of the solar year, namely the vernal and autumnal equinoxes, approximately marked by the festivals of Passover and Tabernacles respectively in the luni-solar calendar. [66]

On balance it appears that there is some evidence for orientation to the east, and that this orientation also applied to some if not all early cuneiform maps. If so, it is a convention *not* bequeathed to the West. Instead, according to Boorstin, Ptolemy, the "indisputable father of modern geography," [67] "established the convention, second

---

[61] Unger 1935.

[62] HSS 10 No. 1; cf. above, n. 42.

[63] Cf. Hallo, JCS 34 (1982) 114f.

[64] Martiny 1932; cf. *idem* 1940; for a related study of his, see JKF 3 (1959) 235-235, cited Hallo, HUCA 33 (1962) 11, n. 79.

[65] Margueron 1982, esp. p. 170 and n. 7; Heinrich 1982, 1984.

[66] Morgenstern 1960, esp. pp. 165, 178f.

[67] Boorstin, *Discoverers* 97.

nature to us today, of orienting maps with the north at the top and the east at the right." [68] Christian maps from A.D. 600 to 1300, however, ignored Ptolemy's convention, [69] and the word "orientation," if not its current meaning, remind us of the older Near Eastern convention.

A second repository of Mesopotamian geographical knowledge was represented by lists of geographical names.   The organization of knowledge in lists was a characteristic medium for Mesopotamian learning from the beginning, and helped propagate and perpetuate the invention of written Sumerian in which all received wisdom was believed to be contained. Typically such lists were carefully organized to reflect, by their inclusions and exclusions, what native thought conceptualized as belonging to a given semantic field and, by their taxonomy, the way native thinkers classified the world about them as they observed it. Only later was the "science of list-making" (Listenwissenschaft) adapted to a specifically lexical purpose by adding additional columns which contained such information as: the meaning of the (Sumerian) term in Akkadian, or the meaning of the dialectal, archaic or obscure Akkadian term in simpler or contemporary Akkadian (commentaries to HAR-ra = *hubullu* and the so-called synonym lists); the pronunciation of the Sumerian term; the " name" of the sign (in the case of syllabaries); the equivalent word in dialectal Sumerian ("Eme-sal vocabulary"); and, on the Mesopotamian periphery, the translation or even mistranslation of the Sumerian and Akkadian entries into the local language(s). [70]

Lists of this sort featuring geographical names have long been known from Old Babylonian times on. [71] What is new is the discovery that they form part of the learned literature already of the third millennium! This literature includes, in addition to a few mathematical exercises, lists of professional names, animals names, plant and tree names, metals, textiles and vessels according to a preliminary survey by H.J. Nissen. [72] And it features prominently three lists of place names.

---

[68] *Ibid.* 98.

[69] *Ibid.* 101f.

[70] Von Soden 1985, 1994, ch. 11, with earlier literature, to which add von Soden 1974.

[71] Hallo 1964:61, with nn. 30-41.

[72] Nissen 1981, esp. pp. 106f..

The first of these is a straightforward list of place names with some 290 entries. It begins with two obscure place-names (HA.GIDIM, Antu) before passing on to a series of more than twenty toponyms of recognizably or at least arguably trans-Tigridian location. [73] The Ugarat of line 5 is not to be confused with Ugarit, the famous city on the Syrian coast. [74] Nothing suggests that the list was at home in Syria even though its best preserved exemplar comes from Ebla. [75] It has even been proposed that it contains two extensive sections of Palestinian place names. [76] But the text has numerous fragmentary duplicates from Abu Salabikh in Mesopotamia that antedate the Ebla exemplar by at least a century, [77] and the combined edition of the Mesopotamian and Syrian exemplars by G. Pettinato [78] shows an almost total congruity. Perhaps the most that can be said at this time is that the list may have originated in northern Babylonia, specifically perhaps Kish, as first proposed by Piotr Steinkeller. [79] He is followed in this opinion by Douglas Frayne in his extensive analysis of the text [80] in which he shows that it consists of two groups of routes: one along the water-courses of northern Babylonia from Sippar in the northwest to Kisurra in the southeast, and the other along or across the Tigris. [81]

The second archaic geographical list has an even greater antiquity, as well as a greater longevity. It is also more complex, for while it begins with place names, it continues with other toponyms (names and designations of property and buildings), then professional names, and finally divine names. It is first attested in at least four and possibly more discrete exemplars from the Jemdet Nasr level at Uruk, and indeed Uruk is among its opening entries. In fact it begins with Ur, Nippur, Larsa, Uruk, Kesh, and Zabalam, all prominent Sumerian cities. [82] It is next attested among the archaic texts from

---

[73] Frayne 1992:72-81; for the latest edition and discussion of the neo-Assyrian parallels, see Levine 1989.

[74] See above, at notes 1f. and ch. I 3.

[75] G. Pettinato, MEE 3 No. 56.

[76] Shea 1983 *ad* ll. 91-140 and 188-219..

[77] Biggs 1974: 71-78.

[78] Pettinato 1978; MEE 3:227-241; cf. Pomponio 1983:285-290.

[79] Steinkeller 1986:32.

[80] Frayne 1992:88.

[81] Cf. the summary *ibid.* 88.

[82] Green 1977.

Ur, [83] Fara, [84] and Abu Salabikh, [85] and then is heard of no more until the second millennium, when a single Old Babylonian exemplar turned up recently among the texts discovered at Ur. [86] This list, then, seems most at home in southern Mesopotamia.

The third archaic geographical list is perhaps the most intriguing of all. It is sometimes referred to as the "Names and Professions List," but in fact it includes toponyms as a characteristic third element and can better be described as a "Name, Profession, and Toponym List." [87] Its structure is such that each of its first twelve sections lists by name and profession the leading officials of as many different Sumerian cities. These are, in order: Sippar, Akshak, Badar or Matar, A-LAK 527, Adab, Uruk(?), Za-ki-x, Ishkar, Durum, A'ur or Awur, Urua, AB and x. [88] The thirteenth section is by far the longest; it ends, surprisingly enough, with the entry "Divine Zababa, king of Kish, praise!" It would therefore appear that this list, like the first, originated in Kish.

This third list was first identified among the texts from Abu Salabikh by Biggs who offered a preliminary edition. [89] A single Ebla duplicate was recognized and published by Pettinato in 1981. [90] In the same year, A. Archi joined five other fragments to the Ebla exemplar and published a new edition of the entire text, together with its Abu Salabikh parallel. [91] Three years later he was able to join three more fragments, though having to eliminate two of the earlier ones. [92] Meantime, F.M. Fales and T.J.H. Krispijn discovered "An early Ur III copy of the Abū Salābikh 'Names and Professions' list," [93] thus showing that the text survived to the end of the third millennium, although now the concluding doxology was addressed to Nisaba, patron-goddess of scholars.

Despite its scholarly character, however, this third list with its specific personal names and titles seems more like a one-time compila-

---

[83] UET 2:283 (+262?) according to Nissen 1981:106.
[84] SF 23f.
[85] Biggs 1974, Nos. 21f.
[86] O.R. Gurney, UET 7 No. 80.
[87] Fales and Krispijn 1979-80:41.
[88] Hallo, BM 25 (1992) 74 and n. 47. For Matar see Steinkeller 1986.
[89] Biggs 1974:62-71 and Nos. 61-81.
[90] MEE 3, No. 43; cf. already Pettinato, JCS 31 (1979) 116f.
[91] Archi 1981.
[92] Archi 1984.
[93] Fales and Krispijn 1979-80.

tion or census. It has in fact been described as "some form of model cadastre or census within the scholarly production from Tell Abu Salabikh." [94] We know from later (Old Babylonian) times of model court cases, model contracts, and model letters, all of which employed real names and reflected real situations in order to train student scribes in the requirements of their craft. As likely as not, such later model texts were copied from authentic originals on deposit in royal or other archives. But once entered into the scribal curriculum, they were thereafter copied by successive generations of scribal students in different locations as assiduously as any scholarly lexical list or creative literary composition. Let us turn, then, to the cadastres properly speaking.

The earliest candidates for the genre are the archaic "boundary-stones" which detail the boundaries, size and ownership of real estate. [95] The Sumerian examples of these texts have been edited by D. O. Edzard in the context of Sumerian legal documents of the third millennium B.C. [96] The entire corpus, including the Akkadian examples, is now available in a monumental edition by I.J. Gelb, P. Steinkeller and R.M. Whiting in the context of the pre-Sargonic and Sargonic stone monuments. [97] There is also the special case of "The Frontier of Shara," inscribed on a most unusual medium: a clay vase. [98] The discovery of partial duplicates on a clay tablet from Adab [99] and on a stone tablet of unknown provenience in the Yale Babylonian Collection [100] seems to suggest that this text belongs more properly in the category of canonical or literary compositions. [101]

That is certainly the case with the treatise known as the "Empire of Sargon of Akkad." [102] Although it purports to describe the provinces of the great Sargonic realm, it is almost certainly the product of a literary renaissance of neo-Assyrian times, perhaps inspired by Sargon's neo-Assyrian namesake, Sargon II of Assyria (721-705 B.C.),

---

[94] *Ibid.* 41.
[95] Hallo 1964:62, n. 42.
[96] Edzard 1968.
[97] Gelb, Steinkeller and Whiting 1991.
[98] Hallo 1964:62, n. 43.
[99] On this duplicate see most recently Zhi 1988:15 and n. 57; 1989:17 and n. 31.
[100] Hallo, RAI 17 (1970) 121.
[101] See the translation based on all three duplicates in IRSA 91-93; for the translation of line 7 see M. Lambert, RA 70 (1976) 95f.
[102] Hallo 1964:62, n. 44.

like certain other literary works glorifying the older king, including the "Sargon Birth Legend." [103] A new edition of the text has been provided by A.K Grayson. [104]

But there are also genuine pre-Sargonic and Sargonic texts which have been claimed for the genre. Thus the text DP 613, dated to the fourth year of Urukagina (Uruinimgina) of Lagash, [105] is described by M. Lambert as a cadastre of the uru_2-quarter of Lagash dedicated to the cult of deceased royalty and grandees, while HSS 3:42 is described as a draft (*brouillon*) of the same text. [106] B.R. Foster has described as cadastres the late Sargonic texts from Umma which result from the surveys by the recorder of deeds (sag-sug_5) and his surveyor (gu-$šur$). [107]

The neo-Sumerian period is represented by the official cadastre of the provinces of Ur-Nammu, the founder of the Third Dynasty of Ur. This is preserved not only on the clay tablet versions which represent the archival or, more likely, the canonical copies of the text [108] but also, it appears, by fragments of the original stone monument(s) from which the later copies were copied. This had already been intimated by F.R. Kraus in his edition of the copies [109] on the basis of stone fragments from Nippur with similar though not identical entries. It has now been raised to the level of virtual certainty by the discovery of a stone fragment in the Metropolitan Museum of Art which, while it does not duplicate the Kraus copies either, complements them with a description of the area of Umma which accords perfectly with the prologue of the Laws generally attributed to Ur-Nammu. [110] The conversion from "monument to canon" illustrated by the Ur III cadastre has wider implications for the origins of canonical literature. [111]

The connection between cadastres and "law codes" is not merely coincidental. Rather, it seems conceivable that cadastres and laws

---

[103] On this see most recently Longman, FAA 53-60, 215f.; Hallo, BP 47f., 130.
[104] Grayson 1974-77.
[105] For the reading of his name, see below, ch. VIII 1, n.12.
[106] Lambert 1957:132.
[107] Foster 1982:82-89; 1982a:69-84.
[108] Hallo 1964:61, n. 45.
[109] Kraus 1955, esp. p. 67; cf. Hallo 1964:61, n. 46.
[110] Frayne and Hallo, forthcoming.
[111] Cf. already Hallo, RAI 17 (1970) 121; more recently Klein 1986.

(and perhaps a concluding hymn) originally formed a unit, if J. Klima is correct in seeing the framework of the codes as juridically integral parts of the proclamation detailing, as it were, the extent of the empire for which the laws were operative. [112]

For the sake of completeness, we may note what are sometimes considered cadastral texts in Hittite. [113] Finally, the question may be raised whether the concept was represented lexically in antiquity. A leading candidate is *(im)-mu-da-sa₄* = *mudasû*, [114] a "list (of persons to whom fields are distributed." [115]

A native designation may also be proposed for the last geographical genre to be considered, the itinerary. According to A.L. Oppenheim, it is *mardītu* in neo-Assyrian, [116] although this term is more often translated simply as "road, course, way" or "stage, distance between stopping places," [117] or by "Marschabschnitt, Ruhetag, Station." [118]

Itineraries are in some ways the most interesting geographical texts of all; certainly they are the most informative, at least potentially. They record the successive stations along the route of a journey or march. Such stations may be major cities, small villages, or mere caravanserais; the record may be prescriptive or descriptive; the stations may or may not be exhaustively listed; they may or may not be equidistant from each other in mileage or elapsed time. All these variables notwithstanding, itineraries are the nearest ancient equivalents to modern maps and our best source for plotting on a map the innumerable geographical names revealed by other texts.

The notion that the "Eblaite Geographical Atlas" (above) already represents a kind of itinerary [119] has not found much favor. Thus the oldest example of the genre generally now recognized is contained in a letter of Old Assyrian date found at Shemshara. [120] It was published by J. Laessoe, [121] and was commented on by M.C. Astour. [122] There

---

[112] Klima 1974, esp. p. 150; 1975, esp. pp. 578f.
[113] H.A. Hoffner, Jr., AOS 55 (1974) 54 and n. 21.
[114] Von Soden, Or. 20 (1951) 164f.
[115] CAD M s.v.
[116] Oppenheim, *Ancient Mesopotamia* 119.
[117] CAD M s.v.; cf. Levine 1989:90: "stage in a journey or activities connected with a stage in a journey"; cf. *ibid.*, p. 81.
[118] Weidner 1966:43 and n. 22.
[119] Shea 1983:595, 602.
[120] Hallo 1964:62, n. 51.
[121] Laessoe 1971.
[122] Astour 1987:44-46. Cf. also Joannès 1992 for an Old Babylonian example.

are also Hittite examples of the genre [123] and especially neo-Assyrian ones. [124] The latter have meantime been studied by E.F. Weidner, [125] Edzard, [126] and L.D. Levine, [127] and augmented by a recent find from Dur-Katlimu published by W. Röllig. [128]

But by far the most significant example of the genre is represented by the Old Babylonian text variously known as "An Old Babylonian Itinerary" [129] or "The Road to Emar." [130] This text is known in three duplicates, sufficiently different from each other so that the question can be raised whether they represent the identical textual tradition. [131] More likely, however, both the existence of the parallel texts and the variations among them can better be explained on the assumption "that the Itinerary is part of a royal campaign which was on the way to becoming a piece of literature." [132]

Since the publication of the Yale duplicate in 1964, the Old Babylonian itinerary has been the subject of innumerable studies, both in the aggregate and in detail. Its specific geographical identifications have generally been confirmed, although the location of three important sites, Mankisum, Tuttul and Urkish, have had to be modified. [133]

A mere glance at the Old Babylonian volume of the *Répertoire Géographique des Textes Cunéiformes* [134] will indicate the extent to which the historical geography of the period is indebted to the Itinerary: of some sixty ancient names of cities and towns localized provisionally or definitively on its map, fifteen recur in the itinerary. Some fifty others can be localized with its help. It is thus somewhat gratuitous to assert, in this connection, that "Spaziergänge auf den Landkarten unterschiedlicher Verlässlichkeit, häufig ohne sich in eigener Anschauung ein Bild von den geographischen Verhältnissen gemacht zu haben, führen immer zu spekulativen und nur in seltenen Fällen

---

[123] Frantz-Sabo 1970.
[124] Hallo 1964:62, nn. 49f.
[125] Weidner 1966.
[126] Edzard 1977:218f.
[127] Levine 1989.
[128] Röllig 1983a.
[129] Goetze 1953.
[130] Hallo 1964.
[131] Edzard 1977:217f.
[132] Hallo 1964:84 and n. 4.
[133] Goetze 1964; Beitzel 1978. Urkish = Tell Mozan according to G. Buccellati as quoted in the New York Times, Nov. 21, 1995 C1,5.
[134] Groneberg 1980.

wahrscheinlichen Lokalisierungen. Das ist aber der methodische An-
satz vieler älterer Lokalisierungsvorschläge und findet sich auch noch
in jüngeren Publikationen," [135] or to illustrate this assertion by adding: "An jüngeren Publikationen sind die beiden Aufsätze von A.
Goetze ... und von W.W. Hallo ... zu nennen, die ausgehend von
einer Tagesstrecke von 25-30 km, mit dem Zirkel auf Landkarten
Lokalisierungen vornehmen." [136]

Suffice it to say here that two of the most important localizations
proposed or validated on the basis of the itinerary have meantime
been amply confirmed by subsequent excavations: that of Shubat-Enlil at Tell Leilan [137] and of Emar itself at (Eski-)Meskene. [138] A third
one, that of Ekallatum at Hakal (Haichal), [139] while not yet confirmed
by excavations, seems supported by a Mari text subsequently published by M. Birot [140] and also won the endorsement of J. Laessøe. [141]
Since Laessøe's comments are in Danish, and not generally available,
they are offered here in translation by Ulla Kasten.

> Ekallâtum (Akkadian "the palace"), a city on the left (eastern) bank of
> the Tigris, north of the lower Zab. Ekallâtum has not yet been finally
> identified with a specific site. Most Assyriologists have wanted to place
> Ekallâtum at a point of the Tigris south of Assur; but various considera-
> tions in placing it (lastly in an itinerary text in the Yale Babylonian
> Collection [YBC 4499] published by W.W. Hallo in connection with his
> article "The Road to Emar," JCS 18 [1964] 57-88) have made it nec-
> essary to seek the ruins of Ekallâtum *north* of Assur. Hallo (op. cit.,
> 72) has discussed the position of the city based on text material and has
> shown that a number of maps of the area show a site "variously spelled
> Hakal, Haichal or Hekat" 25 km north of Qal'at Shirqat (near the
> ruins of Assur), on the left bank.
>
> In 1964 and 1965 the author of this article had the opportunity to
> travel in the region around Assur, both west and east of the Tigris, with
> station in the village of Isdîra Wasta east of the Tigris across from Jirnâf.
> The site of Tulûl el-Haikal which is the place Hallo mentions, is situ-
> ated a few kilometers north of here. The "Bagdad" map, Series 1301,

---

[135] *Ibid.* xv.
[136] *Ibid.* xix, n. 32.
[137] Hallo 1964:73f.; cf. more recently Weiss 1985; Charpin 1987.
[138] Hallo 1964:81; see e.g. Beyer 1982.
[139] Hallo 1964:72.
[140] *Syria* 50 (1973) 4f.
[141] J. Laessøe, *Det Forste Assyriske Imperium* (Copenhagen University, 1966) 32f.,
n. 25.

Sheet N 1-38, Edition 7-GSGS (Director of Military Service, War Office, London, 1962 [World 1:1,000,000]) where the three Isdîra-villages are found under the name "Sudairah," provides a note: "Haichat" (Ruined) (-t being an obvious typographical error for -l) about the area called Tulûl el-Haikal ("haikal" is locally often pronounced "haičal") by the local population. Tulûl el-Haikal, "the Haikal-hills" (*tulûl*, plural of Arabic *tell* "ruin-mound") cannot linguistically be separated from Akkadian *ekallâtum*, "palaces," plural of *ekallum*, one of the few Sumerian loanwords (Sumerian é-gal, "large house"), which has survived in Hebrew *hêkhal*, "royal palace; temple," Biblical Aramaic *hêkhal* and Egyptian Aramaic *haikhělâ* (same meaning); Akkadian *ekallum* has thus survived—through Aramaic or Syriac to Arabic, and it is therefore very likely that an ancient place name like Ekallâtum would have survived in the form Haikal. Tulûl el-Haikal is an extensive ruin-site (4-6 km^2) with many low mounds/hills (tell's), but without any one prominent elevation which would indicate the presence of a zikkurat or suggest long-term habitation. This circumstance can be said to complicate the identification of Tulûl el-Haikal as Ekallâtum, since this ancient city already existed before the time of Shamshi-Adad—he conquered it—and is mentioned in texts from the later Assyrian period. (See, e.g., A.T. Olmstead, *History of Assyria* [1923], 66, 268; and Leroy Waterman, *Royal Correspondence of the Assyrian Empire*, Vol. 4 [1936], Index p. 152 s.v. Ekallâte, and E. Unger in RLA 2, 319f. s.v. Ekallâte.)

Note, however, 1) that this city may have been inhabited only during shorter periods of time, and uninhabited during long intervals, which would explain that the various habitation-levels and destruction-levels have not raised the niveau of the site considerably higher than the surrounding country, and 2) that the considerable irrigation projects about 20 years ago may have influenced the stratification of the ruins and the outline of the area. Sd. Muhammad Ali Mustafa (Department of Antiquities, Government of the Republic of Iraq) kindly informed me that archeological sampling before the above mentioned irrigation projects provided evidence of the presence of considerable Islamic settlements (the size of Samarra!) and, under that, large areas of Assyrian remnants of buildings. Surface findings included a wealth of potsherds originating from Assyrian ceramic industry. Sd. Fuad Safar (same department) kindly informed me that a trench in the western edge of the site, possibly at the ancient Tigris bank, brought forth a brick stamped with Salmanassar III's name and titles, which indicates that the city was inhabited, and that construction took place during his reign (858 - 824 B.C.).

The surface findings in 1964 and 1965 consisted of sherds of post-Assyrian, mainly Parthian pottery. Everything considered, it is very likely that Ekallâtum's ruins are hidden under the low hills of Tulûl el-Haikal. The apex of the zikkurat in Kâr-Tukulti-Ninurta (now: Tulül

el-ʿAqr) is within sight; on the opposite bank of the river to the south-
west one can see the vast ruins of Assur, and directly across from Haikal, the ruins of the Assyrian Ubâse (now: Huwaish) which in
neo-Assyrian texts have to be associated with Ekallâtum.

Certainly the location of Ekallatum *upstream* from Assur (and probably
on the opposite—left-bank of the Tigris) has revolutionized the understanding of the Assyrian King List and of Old Assyrian [142] and Middle Assyrian history. [143] Whether it was called Mashkan-kallatum in
neo-Sumerian times [144] remains to be seen, but the analogy of
Shubat-Enlil shows that we do have to reckon with the possibility of
name-changes, sometimes at frequent intervals. [145]

The possible implications of the itinerary for Biblical studies, especially Genesis 14, [146] have also received some attention, especially by
N.-E.A. Andreasen and C. Cohen. [147] And L.D. Levine has given us
a new edition of the "Zamua itinerary." [148]

Summing up, we can confidently state that the theoretical knowledge of geography matched the far-flung travels of merchants, emissaries and armies in the Ancient Near East.

---

[142] Cf. e.g. Beitzel 1984.
[143] Cf. e.g. Longman, FAA 155-157.
[144] D.I. Owen, ASJ 3 (1981) 66f.
[145] I.e. Shechna: Charpin 1987a.
[146] Hallo 1964:86.
[147] Andreasen 1980; Cohen 1991.
[148] Levine 1989.

Bibliographical References

Andreasen, N.-E.A., 1980: "Genesis 14 in its Near Eastern context," SIC 1:59-77.

Archi, Alfonso, 1981: "La 'Lista di Nomi e Professioni' ad Ebla," SEb 4:177-204.

———, 1984: "The 'Names and Professions List': more fragments from Ebla," RA 78:171-174.

Astour, Michael C., 1987: "Semites and Hurrians in Northern Transtigris," SCCNH 2:3-68.

Beitzel, B.J., 1978: "From Harran to Imar along the Old Babylonian itinerary: the evidence from the *Archives Royales de Mari*," LeSor AV 209-219.

———, 1984: "Ishme-Dagan's military actions in the Jezirah: a geographical study," *Iraq* 46:29-42.

Beyer, Dominique, ed., 1982: *Meskéné-Emar: dix ans de travaux 1972-1982* (Paris, Editions Recherche sur les Civilisations).

Biggs, Robert D., 1966: "The Abū Ṣalābīkh tablets: a preliminary survey," JCS 20:73-78.

———, 1974: *Inscriptions from Tell Abū Ṣalābīkh* (= OIP 99).

Charpin, D., 1987: "Shubat-Enlil et le pays d'Apum," M.A.R.I. 5:129-140.

———, 1987a: "L'autre nom de Shubat-Enlil," M.A.R.I. 5:130-132.

Cohen, Chaim, 1991: "Genesis 14:1-11—an early Israelite chronographic source," SIC 4:67-107.

Donald, Trevor, 1962: "A Sumerian plan in the John Rylands Library," JSS 7:184-190.

Edzard, Dietz O., 1968: *Sumerische Rechtsurkunden des III. Jahrtausends aus der Zeit vor der III. Dynastie von Ur* (= VKEK A 4).

———, 1977: "Itinerare," RLA 5:216-220.

Eisenlohr, August, 1896: *Ein altbabylonischer Felderplan* (16 pp. + iii pls.) (Leipzig).

Fales, F.M. and Th.J.H. Krispijn, 1979-80: "An early Ur III copy of the Abu Salabikh 'Names and Professions' list," JEOL 26:39-46 and pl. iii.

Foster, Benjamin R., 1982: *Umma in the Sargonic Period* (= MCAAS 20).

———, 1982a: *Administration and Use of Institutional Land in Sargonic Sumer* (= Mesopotamia 9).

Frantz-Sabo, G., 1970: "Itinerare ... bei den Hethitern," RLA 5:220.

Frayne, Douglas R., 1981: *The Historical Correlations of the Sumerian Royal Hymns (2400-1900 B.C.)* (Ann Arbor, University Microfilms).

———, 1983: "Šulgi the runner," JAOS 103:739-748.

———, 1992: *The Early Dynastic List of Geographical Names* (= AOS 74).

——— and W.W. Hallo, forthcoming: "New texts from the reign of Ur-Nammu."

Gelb, I.J., Piotr Steinkeller and R.M. Whiting, 1991: *Earliest Land Tenure Systems in the Near East* (2 vv.) (= OIP 104).

Goetze, Albrecht, 1953: "An Old Babylonian itinerary," JCS 7:51-72.

———, 1964: "Remarks on the Old Babylonian itinerary," JCS 18:114-118.

Grayson, A.K., 1974-77: "The empire of Sargon of Akkad," AfO 25:56-64 and pls. i-ii.

Green, Margaret W., 1977: "A note on an archaic period geographical list from Warka," JNES 36:293f.

Groneberg, Brigitte, 1980: *Die Orts- und Gewässernamen der altbabylonischen Zeit* (= RG 3).

Hallo, William W., 1964: "The road to Emar," JCS 18:57-88.

Harley, J.B. and D. Woodward, 1987: *The History of Cartography*, vol. 1 (Chicago, University of Chicago Press).

Heinrich, Ernst, 1982: *Die Tempel und Heiligtümer im alten Mesopotamien* (Berlin, de Gruyter).

———, 1984: *Die Paläste im alten Mesopotamien* (Berlin, de Gruyter).

———— and Ursula Seidl, 1967: Grundrisszeichnungen aus dem alten Orient," MDOG 98:24-45.

Hitt, Jack, 1995: "Atlas shrugged: the new face of maps," *Lingua Franca* 5/5:24-33.

Horowitz, W., 1988: "The Babylonian Map of the World," *Iraq* 50:147-165 and pl. x.

Joannès, Francis, 1992: "Un mission secrète à Ešnunna," RAI 38: 185-193.

Klein, Jacob, 1981: *Three Šulgi Hymns* (Ramat-Gan, Bar-Ilan University Press).

————, 1985: " Šulgi and Išmedagan: runners in the service of the gods (SRT 13)," *Beer-Sheva* 2:7*-38*.

————, 1986: "On writing monumental inscriptions in Ur III scribal curriculum," RA 80:1-7.

————, 1990: "Šulgi and Išmedagan: originality and dependence in Sumerian royal hymnology," Artzi AV 65-136.

————, 1993: "A self-laudatory Šulgi hymn fragment from Nippur," Hallo AV 124-131.

Klíma, J., 1974: "Die juristischen Gegebenheiten in den Prologen und Epilogen der mesopotamischen Gesetzeswerke," Beek AV 146-169.

————, 1975: Les données juridiques dans les prologues et épilogues des lois mésopotamiennes," RHDFE 53:575-595.

Kraus, Fritz R., 1955: "Provinzen des neusumerischen Reiches von Ur," ZA 51:45-75.

Kühne, H., 1980: "Zur Rekonstruktion der Feldzüge ... im Habur-Gebiet," BaMi 11:44-70.

Laessøe, Jorgen, 1971: "An aspect of Assyrian archaeology," Unger AV 189-195.

Lambert, Maurice, 1957: "Le quartier de Lagash," RSO 32:123-143.

Lenzen, H.J., 1955: "Mesopotamische Tempelanlagen von der Frühzeit bis zum zweiten Jahrtausend," ZA 51:1-36.

Levine, Louis D., 1989: "K. 4675+—the Zamua itinerary," SAAB 3:75-92.

Malamat, Abraham, 1989: *Mari and the Early Israelite Experience* (= The Schweich Lectures ... 1984).

Margueron, J., 1982: *Recherches sur les Palais Mesopotamiens* ... (2 vv.) (Paris, Geuthner).

Martiny, Günter, 1932: *Die Kultrichtung in Mesopotamien* (Berlin, Hans Schoetz).

————, 1940: "The orientation of the Gimilsin temple and the palace chapel," OIP 43:92-96.

Morgenstern, Julian, 1960: "The King-God among the Western Semites," VT 10:138-197.

Muhly, James D., 1978: "Ancient cartography," *Expedition* 20/2:26-31.

Nemet-Nejat, Karen, 1975: "A Late Babylonian field plan," JANES 7:95-101.

————, 1982: *Late Babylonian Field Plans in the British Museum* (= StPSM 2).

Nissen, Hans J., 1981: "Bemerkungen zur Listenliteratur Vorderasiens im 3. Jahrtausend," in Luigi Cagni, ed., *La Lingua di Ebla* (= IUONsm 14) 99-108.

North, R., 1979: *A History of Biblical Map-Making* (=Beihefte zum TAVO, Reihe B).

Pettinato, Giovanni, 1967: *Untersuchungen zur neusumerischen Landwirtschaft* 1/1 (= Richerche 2).

————, 1978: "L'Atlante Geografico del Vicino Oriente attestato ad Ebla e Abū Salābīkh (I)," Or. 47:50-73 and pls. vii-xii.

Pomponio, F., 1983: "Notes on the lexical texts from Abū Ṣalābīkh and Ebla," JNES 42:285-290.

Röllig, Wolfgang, 1983: "Landkarten," RLA 6:464-467.

————, 1983a: "Ein Itinerar aus Dur-Katlimu," *Damaszener Mitteilungen* 1:279-284.

Shea, William H., 1983: "Two Palestinian segments from the Eblaite Geographical Atlas," Freedman AV 589-612.

Steinkeller, Piotr, 1986: "Seal of Išma-ilum, son of the governor of Matar," *Vicino Oriente* 6:27-40.

Stol, Marten, 1988-89: "De babylonische wereldkaart," *Phoenix* 34/2:29-35.

Unger, Eckhard, 1935: "Ancient Babylonian maps and plans," *Antiquity* 9:311-322.

Vanstiphout, Herman L.J., 1984: "On the Sumerian disputation between the hoe and the plough," *Aula Orientalis* 2:239-251.

Villard, P., 1986: "Un roi de Mari à Ugarit," UF 18:387-412.

Vogt, Burkhard and Ute Franke-Vogt, 1987: *Shimal 1985/1986: Excavations of the German Archaeological Mission in Ras Al-Khaimah, U.A.E.* (=BBVO 8).

Von Soden, Wolfram, 1974: *Sprache, Denken und Begriffbildung im Alten Orient* (= AWLM AGSK 1973:6).

———, 1985: *Einführung in die Altorientalistik* (Darmstadt, Wissenschaftliche Buchgesellschaft), tr. by Donald G. Schley as *The Ancient Orient: an Introduction to the Study of the Ancient Near East* (Grand Rapids, Eerdmans, 1994).

Waetzoldt, Hartmut, 1990: "Zu einigen Jahresdaten Urnammus," N.A.B.U. 1990:4 No. 6.

Weidner, Ernst F., 1966: "Assyrische Itinerare," AfO 21:42-46 and pl. viii.

Weiss, Harvey, 1985: "Tell Leilan and Shubat-Enlil," M.A.R.I. 4:269-292.

Wiseman, Donald J., 1972: "A Babylonian architect?" AnSt 22:141-147.

Wood, Denis, 1992: *The Power of Maps* (New York, Guilford Press).

Yang Zhi, 1988: "The excavation of Adab," JAC 3:1-21.

———, 1989: *Sargonic Inscriptions from Adab* (= Periodic Publications on Ancient Civilizations 1) (Changchung, The Institute for the History of Ancient Civilizations).

2. Culinary Arts

When Abraham was visited by the three messengers who were to announce the forthcoming birth of his beloved son Isaac, he demonstrated his hospitality by inviting the messengers to a meal before ever learning what was their mission. "Let me fetch a morsel of bread that you may refresh yourselves" he said with modest understatement (Gen. 18:5) before proceeding to entertain them with a feast fit for kings. For in the same breath he instructed Sarah: "Quick, three measures of choice flour! Knead and make cakes!" while he himself "ran to the herd, took a calf, tender and choice, and gave it to the servant-boy, who hastened to prepare it. He took curds and milk and the calf that had been prepared, and set these before them; and he waited on them under the tree as they ate" (ib.7f.). [149]

This familiar passage is probably the nearest thing in the Bible to a description of culinary methods! (Cf. also I Sam. 28: 24.) For all its intense preoccupation with food, the Hebrew Bible concerns itself very little with its preparation. What it provides in abundance is dietary laws, blessings of fertility or curses of infertility laid on field and barn, sacrificial regulations, narratives of provisioning in the wilderness, of feast and famine, of Jonah's gourd and Esther's banquets—but nary a word about what might be called the ancient Israelite "cuisine," i.e., that combination of ingredients and their preparation which went into the making of a meal. Even so authoritative a volume as Roland de Vaux's *Ancient Israel: Its Life and Institutions* has nothing to say about the subject in the nearly 600 pages in which it covers every other aspect of Israel's family, civil, military and religious institutions. [150]

We need not, however, be daunted by this silence of the Biblical text, for we have other sources at our disposal to fill in the lacunae of the Biblical record, notably the findings of Biblical archaeology, both artifactual and textual. Among the latter, the ancient Near East is particularly rich in "archival" documents, those records of daily life which are conspicuously lacking from the literary, or "canonical," writings of which the Hebrew Bible is exclusively made up. Such

---

[149] The mingling of milk and meat in apparent violation of the (later) dietary laws exercised Rabbinic exegesis less than the anomaly of the three divine messengers having to eat (or consenting to eat). See Plaut, *Torah* 122.

[150] De Vaux 1961.

archival documents provide us with extensive information about ancient food production and consumption. They are known, for example, from Egypt, and have been combed for the light they shed on food in all its manifestations in two volumes entitled *Food: the Gift of Osiris*. [151] For ancient Turkey, the Hittite texts, though relatively poor in archives, are rich in ritual prescriptions and other evidence of food production and preparation, all conveniently assembled in a volume entitled *Alimenta Hethaeorum*. [152] But the most abundant documentation comes, as so often, from ancient Mesopotamia, the bread-basket of the ancient world, where the fertility of the rivers, fields and stables was matched by the prolixity of the scribes who, beginning before the end of the fourth millennium B.C., left us countless clay tablets inscribed in cuneiform with every detail of food production, preparation and consumption. [153]

This assertion can be illustrated with a kind of "recipe" text from the time of Hammurapi, king of Babylon (1792-1750 B.C., according to the "middle chronology"). The present text is, in fact, dated to his 35th year, i.e. 1758 B.C., and was excavated at Nippur, the great religious capital of Sumer and Akkad. It was rejoined from two fragments, and is still not completely restored, but sufficient remains for its general sense to be clear. As reconstructed by Marcel Sigrist, [154] it constitutes the record of offerings to various deities at the temple of Nusku in Nippur during the course of one lunar year of 354 days (6x30 + 6x29). And it includes, in the meticulous bookkeeping for which the Mesopotamian scribes are noted, the daily amounts needed for what A. L. Oppenheim described as "the care and feeding of the gods." [155] Thanks to this fastidious record-keeping, we know that they consumed, or at least were offered, one boiled pasture-fed sheep and one "good fish" daily, [156] along with a variety of more complicated dishes whose ingredients are listed before the dishes themselves are named. This provides us, in effect, with recipes of sorts for the respective foods. Thus the fine or thin bread [157] is made of two kinds

---

[151] Darby 1977.
[152] Hoffner 1974.
[153] For a glossary of culinary equivalents in Sumerian, Akkadian and English, see Limet 1987:144-147.
[154] Sigrist 1977.
[155] Oppenheim, *Ancient Mesopotamia*, 183-198.
[156] *1 udu-ú síl-qum,1 ku₆ sig₅*.
[157] *ninda-sal-la* (= *akalu ruqqu?*).

of flour, "quality flour" and finely ground flour; [158] the product is
probably equivalent to the "thin loaves" which Hittite temple officials
were required to provide for their deities, [159] and to the "thin cakes of
unleavened bread" (NJV: "unleavened wafers") mentioned in the Bible (Lev. 2:4) as an offering to God. [160] There follows a coarse kind of
bread, the so-called large loaves or breads, [161] six of which require 12
liters of coarse flour, [162] and in addition call for small but specific
amounts of spices and other additives to provide, one presumes, the
desired flavoring. These additives include emmer or groats, [163] a variety of different herbs and, finally, a tiny amount of salt—one-twelfth
of a liter to be exact—[164] in order to allow the dough to rise or, literally, to ferment. [165] The verb, which occurs here for the first time in
this sense in any cuneiform text, is related to the common Akkadian
noun for sour-(dough) (*emṣu*) and thus to Hebrew *chameṣ*, the leavened
bread familiar from the laws of the Passover holiday.

    Next comes a concoction made of finely ground flour, ordinary
dates and dates from Tilmun in the Persian Gulf, butter, [166] cheese, [167]
a kind of wine, apples and figs, the whole mixture described as a kind
of sweet roll [168] or "marmalade," [169] and served up, in part on golden
vessels or spoons, in part on assorted ordinary dishes.

    This and similar texts [170] are intended, not as recipes for the cooks
and bakers, but as records of expenditures carefully kept by the
scribes in charge of temple kitchens against the possibility of a future
audit by some higher authority. Because they are at home in the
temples, they may be described as ritual texts, but unlike most of the
ritual texts of the Bible, they are not prescriptions for actions to be
taken in the future but descriptive of actions already completed in the

---

[158] *zì-sag* (= *qēmu rēši*), *zì-kum* (= *isqūqu*).

[159] CoS 1:114:52, 116:11; cf. Hoffner 1974 s.v. NINDA.SIG = *akalu qatnu*.

[160] Levine and Hallo 1967:45 and 57 s.v. *ninda-sal-la*.

[161] *ninda-gal*.

[162] *zì-sig₁₅* = *hišlētu*.

[163] *eša* = *sasqû*.

[164] 15 *gín*.

[165] *ana emmuṣu*.

[166] *i-nun* = *himētu*; cf. the *nim-i-nun-na* = *zumbi himēti*, literally the "butter-fly."

[167] *ga-har* = *eqīdu*; cf. *ga-har-ag* = *gubnatu*, Hittite *gabban*, Heb. *gebina*, for which see
Hoffner 1966.

[168] *ninda i-dé-a* = *mersu*.

[169] So Kingsbury 1963:4-9, ll. 4, 33, 62; he reads *níg-i-dé-a*.

[170] Cf. especially Kingsbury 1963; new edition by A. Westenholtz in preparation.
See also below, at nn. 173-183.

past. They can therefore better be labelled "descriptive rituals," and examples of this genre have been identified by Baruch Levine in the Pentateuch [171] and among the texts from Ugarit. [172] But they are once more most commonly found in Mesopotamia, and may be illustrated by two lengthy examples of the genre, one dated just three years before the text with which we began, the other broken where the date should have been but probably of about the same time, and both found, this time, not at Nippur but at Ur. Both texts are concerned with "offerings to the temple gates of Ur," but I will cite only the dated one, because it illustrates another crucial component of the Mesopotamian cuisine, namely beer. [173]

Wine grew on the hilly flanks of the Zagros in the northern part of Mesopotamia, mainly Assyria, but in the south, or Babylonia, dates or, more often and more particularly, barley was available in such abundance that it was the preferred ingredient in a beer that was mass-produced by the simple device of putting barley-bread into a vat of water, adding malt, and letting the mixture stand until it had fermented. [174] Sometimes one did not even bother to pour the finished drink out of the vat but drank it through long straws while standing or seated at the vat—a practice amply illustrated in the contemporary art. [175]

There were, however, many different qualities of beer thus produced, and the descriptive rituals (as well as other account texts) were careful to specify the qualities involved. The tablet from Ur lists no less than five varieties. The best kind was a dark beer further specified as " 2:1 beer," [176] meaning that it required two times its volume in barley to produce a given volume of beer. There were also two kinds of beer specified as 1.5 : 1, one a " fine beer" [177] and one mixed with wine to judge by its name. [178] Finally there were two kinds of beer specified as 1:1. One was made from emmer rather than barley, [179] the other was simply called " 1:1 beer." [180] The Akkadian name of

---

[171] Levine 1965; cf. Rainey 1970.
[172] Levine 1963; 1983.
[173] Levine and Hallo 1967 (Text B = UET 5:507).
[174] Civil 1964.
[175] Cf. e.g. Buchanan 1965:207 and nn. 20f. and pl. xvi.
[176] *kaš-lul-a-2-ta*; cf. *kaš-lù-lù-a = šikaru dalhu*.
[177] *kaš-sig₅*.
[178] *kurun* (written KAŠ.DIN) = *karānu, kurunnu, šikaru, šību*.
[179] *ulušin* (written KAŠ.ZÍZ.ÀM) = *ulušinnu*.
[180] *kaš-1-ta = malmalu*. Cf. Levine and Hallo 1967:54 s.v. *kaš-diš-ta-àm*.

the latter means literally " (beer made) of equal parts," as has long
been known from lexical texts where it occurs together with "double
strength beer" and "triple strength beer," [181] but it is only our text
that provides the clinching argument for these translations, since it
adds the handy information as to how much grain [182] went into the
production of each kind of beer. Specifically, 12 liters of dark 2:1 beer
required 24 liters of barley; 62 liters of fine 1.5 : 1 beer required 93
liters of barley; 122 liters of 1:1 beer required 122 liters of barley and
so on. [183]

So much for the evidence of the descriptive rituals of Hammurapi's time. Not all delicacies, however, were reserved for the gods of
Babylonia. In the first place, the gods were represented in effigy, i.e.,
in the form of statues, and the dainties, as well as the meat offerings
(of which more later), [184] were fed to them in their guise as statues,
seated at the "table of the god," [185] not unlike the Biblical "table of
the Lord" (Malachi 1:7,12). What they deigned to leave over was,
after a suitable interval, distributed to the clergy and, at their discre-
tion, to the faithful masses waiting patiently outside the sacred pre-
cincts.

In the second place, we have secular texts galore in which spices,
condiments and all manner of other comestibles were catalogued as
being in the possession of private entrepreneurs or otherwise involved
in a variety of transactions. One text dated to the reign of Amar-
Suen of Ur, almost 300 years before Hammurapi, will suffice to show
that culinary delicacies were not confined to the tables of the gods but
could equally adorn the table of the king—perhaps even of lesser mortals. This text tells us what went into a royal banquet. It reads in
part: "Six pigs, their daily fodder being three liters each, for three
months and 17 days, from month IX (day 1) to month XII day 17.
Their barley is 1926 liters; fodder for the pigs for the royal banquet." [186] King Amar-Suen, it appears, was a veritable glutton.

Until recently, only a handful of isolated cuneiform texts could

---

[181] šikaru šinnu, šikaru šullušu; cf. CAD s.v. malmalu.

[182] še-bi, literally: "its barley."

[183] Levine and Hallo 1967 figs. 3f. (middle columns); cf. now also Charpin
1986:309f.

[184] See below, ch. VII 1.

[185] banšur dingir = paššur ili; cf. e.g. Šurpu V 76 and PSD s.vv. banšur dingir-e-ne,
banšur DN.

[186] Sigrist 1990 No. 177.

claim to be true recipes. One is an Old Babylonian recipe for making beer. [187] A neo-Babylonian text [188] was edited by E. Ebeling as "a recipe for spicing meat," [189] and described by A.L.Oppenheim as "a recipe for the preparation of a hot and pungent sauce." [190] According to Oppenheim it belongs to the broader class of "procedural instructions" [191] which also includes mathematical, ritual, medical, chemical and alchemical texts, notably instructions for preparing perfumes and for making glass. All feature "the use of the second person singular, and the tendency to restrict the vocabulary to technical terms which refer unequivocally to specific actions." [192]

In 1985, however, three clay tablets of unknown provenience from the Yale Babylonian Collection changed all this. These three tablets can indeed be regarded, not just as recipes, but as whole collections of recipes, in other words, as cookbooks. In fact they constitute, as of now, the world's oldest cookbooks. At first the three tablets were published only in the form of cuneiform copies, prepared many years earlier by Mary Inda Hussey, an Assyriologist who died in 1952. These copies were included in a volume otherwise devoted for the most part to rituals and incantations in Sumerian, Akkadian, Subarian-Hurrian, Elamite and an unknown or secret language. The volume, edited by Jan van Dijk, was accordingly entitled *Early Mesopotamian Incantations and Rituals*, hardly a title calculated to call attention to cookbooks. [193] The catalogue of the volume described the three texts, which were obviously neither incantations nor rituals, simply as "Akkadian recipes." And van Dijk's introduction did not enlarge very much on this laconic description, though it did call attention to some recently published remarks on the texts by Jean Bottéro, and to his forthcoming translation of them.

The recipe texts were assigned to Bottéro for editing, and indeed he is the ideal person for the task. He is not only one of the world's leading Assyriologists, but well known among his colleagues and

---

[187] J. van Dijk, *Sumer* 13 (1957) 113, pl. 23A, republished as TIM 9:52; cf. also *Sumer* 13:115, pl. 24 = TIM 9:51. For alleged pre-Sargonic beer recipes, cf. Stol 1987-90:326.
[188] GCCI 2:394.
[189] Ebeling 1949; cf. also CAD Q 68b.
[190] A.L. Oppenheim, *Glass and Glassmaking in Ancient Mesopotamia* (Corning, The Corning Museum of Glass Press, 1970) 5, n. 6.
[191] *Ibid.* 4.
[192] *Ibid.* 5; cf. also Borger, HKL 3:116f. s.vv. "Chemie, Rezepte."
[193] YOS 11 Nos. 25-27.

friends as a devoted gourmet cook. He has combined these talents to provide some preliminary glimpses into the Yale texts, both in learned [194] and more popular format. [195] His definitive edition of the texts has just appeared. [196] While the results are in many respects fascinating, they fail to meet Professor Bottéro's own exacting gastronomic standards. In a letter to an American colleague, he confessed that "he would not wish such meals (as described in these texts) on his worst enemies." [197]

But his colleagues at Yale were not so easily discouraged. Hosting the American Oriental Society meeting in 1986, they took the occasion to invite some 150 members to sample one of the more elaborate recipes in the Yale cookbooks, prepared according to their best understanding of the text by Alexandra H. Hicks, editor of the Herb Society of America and a food historian at the University of Michigan, who flew to New Haven for the occasion with spices and other ingredients gathered from as far away as Italy. Everyone survived the experience and indeed pronounced the result a resounding success. [198]

Here follows one of the simpler recipes based on Bottéro's preliminary translation. "Meat Stew. Take some meat. Prepare water, throw fat into it, then add [...], leek and garlic, all crushed together, an equal amount (? - *mehru*), and some plain *šuhutinnû*." Leek and garlic, the principal identifiable ingredients added to this dish by way of spicing it up, were already familiar from Sumerian mythology [199] and proverbs. [200] These two items, together with fish, appear as staples of the normal diet which, because of their smell, were to be avoided by cultically clean persons. [201] This recipe just happens to be the first one in the first of the three Yale tablets, cited as A by Bottéro. [202] That tablet has in all 25 recipes, summarized at the end as "21 meat dishes and 4 vegetarian dishes." But in fact three of the so-called vegetarian dishes also have meat added to them. [203]

---

[194] Bottéro 1981; 1987.
[195] Bottéro 1982; translated as Bottéro 1985.
[196] Bottéro 1995.
[197] Bottéro 1987:19.
[198] Hallo 1993:29f.; cf. now J.S. Cooper *apud* Bottéro 1995:8, n. 8.
[199] Alster 1972:16f., 42, 64-67, and 105f. *ad* ll. 110-118.
[200] Civil 1987:30f.
[201] Hallo, JQR 76 (1985) 32f.
[202] YOS 11:25:1f. For "meat stew" or "broth" (*mê širim*) in context, see Rimah 150:13.
[203] Specifically leg of mutton according to Bottéro 1987:12, n. 6.

Each of the 25 dishes dealt with on this particular tablet is identified by name at the outset, thus providing us with what is in effect a
virtual table of contents, making allowance for the fact that some of
the names still elude identification or translation. The first is the simple "meat stew" already cited. This is followed by a dish called
"Assyrian" —somewhat surprising in a text dating, to judge by script
and language, to the time of Hammurapi or his immediate successors,
when Assyria was far from prominent in Babylonian affairs. Next
come two dishes called red and "bright" or "clear" respectively. Then
we get three meat stews named respectively for the deer, gazelle, and
(nanny)-goat stock that is their chief ingredient. After three somewhat obscure entries, we get ten more stews named for cassia, lamb,
spleen, pigeon, mutton, vinegar or salt water, and wild dove, as well
as an Elamite stew, and three uncertain concoctions. So much for the
"meat stews." The so-called vegetable dishes include one apparently
made of left-overs, [204] one from an herb of uncertain identification,
and one made from an unidentified vegetable, perhaps a kind of turnip. The tablet ends with the only truly vegetarian dish, the "choice"
or "cultivated" turnip.

Here is how the leftovers are prepared on the basis of Bottéro's
translation (though he thinks the recipe is named for an as yet
unidentified ingredient). "There must also be the meat from a leg of
lamb. Prepare the water, add fat,[...], vinegar, beer, onions, (an herb
called) spiney, [205] coriander, *samidu*, cumin (a spice name that has retained its Sumerian and Akkadian guise to this day), [206] and beetroot
(possibly named for the crab, to which it may bear a resemblance) to
throw into the pot (no equivalent in the text!). Then crush garlic and
leeks, and add them (break in text!). Let the whole cook into a
mash, [207] onto which you sprinkle coriander and *šuhutinnû*." If this
isn't a recipe for leftovers, it should be!

But numerous as they are, these 25 recipes are still tantalizingly
brief. Even when we can identify —and obtain—all or most of the
ingredients, we remain in doubt about many steps in the procedure
which are left to the imagination, or rather, more likely, to an oral

---

[204] *tu-úh-ú.*

[205] *egigirum*; elsewhere (in recipe 24) *egengirum*, i.e., "rocket," a plant used in Europe
as a salad; cf. CAD s.v.

[206] *gamun* = *kamūnu*; here written Ú.DIN.TIR as if "the Babylonian herb," instead of
the earlier Ú.TIR.

[207] *šipku*; cf. Bottéro 1987:11, n. 2.

tradition that probably accompanied these written instructions. Most notably we are left in the dark as to the quantities of any ingredient to be furnished, or the yields to be expected. Perhaps like some modern cooks, you just added a pinch of this and a smidgeon of that. Even the longest recipes are silent on this point, as on the time taken to cook anything. But they do furnish additional and intriguing glimpses of Old Babylonian culinary techniques. For this purpose we need to turn to the second of the Yale cookbooks, tablet B in Bottéro's presentation. [208].

Tablet B is bigger than tablet A by a good 40% (165 x 225 mm to 118 x 164 mm). It contained at least 245 lines of text (more—according to Bottéro 260—when complete) compared to only 75 for tablet A. It is inscribed in two columns on each face. If for all that it contains only seven recipes, that is because each of them is written out in much more lavish detail. All of them seem to deal with one sort of fowl or another, including the unidentified *kippu* served at Yale. *If* the word is a loanword from Sumerian *kib*, it could be a seagull, or a swallow, [209] or even a cormorant. [210] We solved the problem at Yale by substituting chicken for the uncertain *kippu* of the recipe—perhaps in the silent hope that we could compare the Dutch word for chicken which is kip! And perhaps we chose this recipe because it is the shortest in this otherwise prolix tablet—so I will confine my citations from this tablet to this recipe. In Bottéro's translation then:

> If you want to cook *kippu* in a stew, then prepare them as you would *agarukku*. First, clean them and rinse them in cold water and place them in an open pot. Then put the pot back on the flame and add some cold water to it and flavor it with vinegar. Next, crush together mint and salt and rub the *kippu* with the mixture. After this, strain (?) the liquid in the kettle and add mint to this sauce. Place the *kippu* back into it. Finally, add a bit more cold water and turn the entire mixture into a pot. To be presented and then dished out. [211]

The third Yale tablet, tablet C, is the smallest and most fragmentary of the three and has the least to add to our knowledge.

---

[208] YOS 11:26.

[209] *kib-su = sinuntu.*

[210] *kib-ᵈnin-kilim-ma*, "mongoose-*kib*; cf. Wilcke, *Lugalbanda* 177f. *ad* 1.159.

[211] Literally: "before the knife" (*meher naglabi*).

For whom were these recipes written and who dined on such elaborate fare in the age of Hammurapi? It was hardly the common man, who barely eked out a subsistence level of nutrition to judge from the abundant indication of the ration lists, nor yet the priesthood, for the accounts of sacrificial offerings such as those with which we began are far more modest. Perhaps it was a wedding party, for the groom was required by law and custom to rival the dowry provided by the father of the bride with the ingredients for the marriage banquet. [212] More likely it was the aristocracy, or even the king himself. For we know of royal repasts which were little short of astounding in the quantity if not also the quality of the comestibles consumed. Here for example is the menu for a royal banquet tendered by Yasmah-Addu of Mari, a contemporary of Hammurapi:

" 900 litres of KUM-bread, 60 litres of bread made with *sammidatum*-flour; 2,020 litres of sour *emsum*-bread made of *burrum*-cereal, 950 litres of cake, 2,185 litres of 'sour' *emsum*-bread made of barley, 940 litres of *alappanum*-mead, 100 litres of chick-peas, 11 litres of *isququm*-flour, 6 litres of *sasqum*-semolina, 3 litres of *sammidatum*-flour, 70 litres of (linseed)-oil, 3 litres of honey (or date-syrup), 4 litres of linseed, 5 litres of dates—meal of the king and his men in Mari on the fourth day of the eleventh month (*kiskisum*)." [213]

This record of gluttony could be matched nearly a millennium later at the dedication of the palace of Assurnasirpal (883-859 B.C.) in the capital city of Kalah (Nimrud) in 879 B.C. The details of the menu can be found readily enough in Sir Max L. Mallowan's *Nimrud and its Remains.* [214] It included 10,000 doves, and an equal numbers of turtledoves, other small birds, fish, gerbils, eggs, loaves of bread, measures of beer and skins of wine, to mention only part of the menu. Two centuries later, the last great king of Assyria, Assurbanipal (668-627 B.C.), decorated the walls of his palace at Nineveh with scenes of the royal cuisine—both the service at the royal table and the preparations in the royal kitchens. Such scenes even inspired the Italian filmmaker

[212] Westbrook 1988 s.vv. *biblum, zubullum;* Greengus 1966.

[213] S. Dalley, *Mari and Karana* (London/New York, Longman, 1984), 78-80, based on ARMT 11:1.

[214] M.E.L. Mallowan, *Nimrud and Its Remains* (New York, Dodd Mead, 1966) vol. 1:69f.; cf. also ANET 560.

Giovanni Pastrone (1882-1959), who liked to fill the background of his movies with scenes taken from or redolent of antiquity. [215]

Such scenes lend at least a semblance of plausibility to the Biblical assertion that "Solomon's daily provisions consisted of 30 *kors* of semolina, and 60 *kors* of [ordinary] flour, 10 fattened oxen, 20 pasture-fed oxen, and 100 sheep and goats, besides deer and gazelles, roebucks and fatted geese" (I Kings 5:2f.). And so our path has ended where it stated—with the Hebrew Bible. Along the way we have sampled the cuisine of ancient Sumer, Babylonia and Assyria, and I hope that you have found it to your taste.

Bibliographical References

Alster, Bendt, 1972: *Dumuzi's Dream: Aspects of Oral Poetry in a Sumerian Myth* (= Mesopotamia 1).

Bottéro, Jean, 1981: "Küche," RLA 6:277-298.

———, 1982: "La plus vieille cuisine de monde," *L'Histoire* 49 (October, 1982) 72-82.

———, 1985: "The cuisine of ancient Mesopotamia," BA 48/1:36-47.

———, 1987: "The culinary tablets at Yale," JAOS 107:11-19.

———, 1995: *Textes culinaires Mesopotamiens: Mesopotamian Culinary Texts* (= Mesopotamian Civilizations 6).

Buchanan, Briggs, 1965: "A dated 'Persian Gulf' seal and its implications," Landsberger AV 204-209 and pl. xvi.

Charpin, Dominique, 1986: *Le clergé d'Ur au siècle d'Hammurabi (XIXe - XVIIIe siècles av. J.-C.)* (Geneva/Paris, Droz).

Civil, Miguel, 1964: "A hymn to the beer goddess," Oppenheim AV 67-89.

———, 1987: "Sumerian riddles: a corpus," *Aula Orientalis* 5:17-37.

Darby, William J. et al., 1977: *Food: the Gift of Osiris* (2 vv.) (London/New York, Academic Press).

De Vaux, Roland, 1961: *Ancient Israel: its Life and Institutions* (New York, McGraw Hill).

Ebeling, Erich, 1949: "Ein Rezept zum Würzen von Fleisch," Or. 18:171f.

Greengus, Samuel, 1966: "Old Babylonian marriage ceremonies and rites," JCS 20:55-72.

Hallo, William W., 1993: "The oldest cookbooks in the world," BR 9/4 (August 1993) 26-31, 56.

Hoffner, Harry A., Jr., 1966: "A native Akkadian cognate to West Semitic *GBN 'cheese'?" JAOS 86:27-31.

———, 1974: *Alimenta Hethaeorum* (= AOS 55).

Kingsbury, Edwin C., 1963: "A seven day ritual in the Old Babylonian cult at Larsa," HUCA 34:1-34.

Levine, Baruch A., 1963: "Ugaritic descriptive rituals," JCS 17:105-111.

———, 1965: "The descriptive ritual texts of the Pentateuch," JAOS 85:307-318.

---

[215] Cf. his *Cabiria: Visione Storica del III secolo a.C.* (Turin, Museo Nazionale del Cinema, 1977), esp. figs. 311, 393, etc. (I am grateful to Angela Della Vacche for giving me a copy of this book.)

———, 1983: "The descriptive ritual texts from Ugarit: some formal and functional features of the genre," Freedman AV 467-475.

——— and William W. Hallo, 1967: "Offerings to the temple gates at Ur," HUCA 38:17-58.

Limet, Henri, 1987: "The cuisine of ancient Sumer," BA 50/3:132-147.

Rainey, Anson F., 1970: "The order of sacrifices in Old Testament ritual texts," *Biblica* 51:485-498.

Sigrist, Marcel, 1977: "Offrandes dans le temple de Nusku à Nippur," JCS 29:169-183.

———, 1990: *Tablettes du Princeton Theological Seminary* (= OPSNKF 10).

Stol, Marten, 1987-90: "Malz," RLA 7:322-329.

Westbrook, Raymond, 1988: *Old Babylonian Marriage Law* (= AfO Beiheft 23).

3. GAMES

"All work and no play makes Jack a dull boy" applied in the ancient world as well as today. [216] The typical Mesopotamian lunar month had twenty-nine days if "hollow," thirty if "full," and six of these days were set aside as holidays: three for lunar festivals [217] and three for vacation days or rest days. [218] Among the former was almost certainly the day of the full moon (the 15th or sometimes the 14th of the month) to judge by a fragmentary tablet from the temple of Inanna at Nippur detailing work due the temple from the ninth to the 17th(?) day of a month and conspicuously skipping the 14th. [219] There may even have been seven days off in some months. [220] The monthly lunar festivals and the great annual festivals were the occasion for sacrifices and rites, [221] but also for much play and entertainment. [222]

B. Landsberger has discussed the evidence for *passu* = doll and other Akkadian designations for playing and toys, [223] including the jump-rope (*keppû*), the knuckle-bone or astragal (*kiṣallu*), and the famous *pukku* and *mekkû* for which Gilgamesh was prepared to go to the netherworld; Landsberger here equates them with hoop and driving-stick, [224] though others continue to use his older rendering of drum and drumstick. [225] More recent suggestions include other toys like "a kidney-shaped wooden puck ... which was driven with a hockey-stick," [226] or a ball and mallet, [227] or "a large, solid wood ball and a long wood stick ... [a] game played in connection with weddings," [228] or a scraper and its stick. [229] There is even a proposal to see *pukku* and

---

[216] This is a revised version of Hallo 1993. Some of the same ground was gone over at the same time by Kilmer 1993.

[217] *ezen-aš-aš* =(?) *eššeššu*.

[218] *u₄-duₐ-a*; cf. Hallo 1977:12; Englund 1988: 172, n. 46.

[219] Civil 1980:230-232. The other text cited ib. (p. 229) likewise appears to deal with work for a temple at Nippur.

[220] *ib-tag₄ u₄ 7* [...]; *ibid.* 229. For "time off" in general see Englund 1991.

[221] Sallaberger 1993, esp. ch. 2.

[222] Cf. especially Dossin 1938:7 and 11, ll. 18-23 as interpreted by CAD H 235c and 240b; K 182d; N/1:17a.

[223] Landsberger 1960; 1961.

[224] "Reifen und Treibstecken"; cf. Landsberger 1960:124-126; 1961:23; CAD M/2 s.v. *mekkû*.

[225] ANET 507; for the "shamanistic" significance of this rendering cf. Hallo, Sarna AV 184 and n. 3.

[226] T. Jacobsen, Moran AV (1990) 234, n. 7.

[227] "Boule et maillet": Tournay and Shaffer, *Gilgamesh* 254-257.

[228] Kilmer 1982: 129f.

[229] Duchesne-Guillemin 1983.

mekkû, as well as the terms for wrestling, [230] as designating different kinds of boardgames. [231]

I.J. Gelb has discussed the whole phenomenon of "homo ludens in early Mesopotamia," dealing especially with such professions as singers, musicians, snake-charmers and bear-wards, all of whom were active at festivals. [232] The last mentioned, called *ud-da-tuš* in Sumerian, is particularly noteworthy, given the prominence of bear-baiting and the like in Russia and other cultures to this very day. It is equated with Akkadian *aluzinnu*, variously regarded as a jester or buffoon, prankster or trickster, to whom a whole literary text is devoted. [233] The theme, if not the profession, recurs in Biblical literature, more prominently than is sometimes realized. [234] In what follows, simpler pastimes will be reviewed, notably dice, board-games, and "tops."

At first sight it may seem odd that so specific a phenomenon as dice should have its origin in antiquity, and yet that is true not only of the concept but of the precise form. The earliest dice now known come, it is true, not from the Near East but from India or rather from prehistoric Pakistan, home of the Indus Valley culture. From Alamgirpur and Harappa at its northern end to Lothal on the Arabian Sea, G.F. Dales reports finds of such dice. [235] They differ from our own dice only in the arrangement of the dots on the six sides. Modern dice arrange the dots in such a way that opposite sides always add up to seven: 1+6, 2+5, and 3+4. The Indus Valley dice most often have opposite sides numbered consecutively, i.e. 1+2, 3+4, and 5+6, although there are also four examples of a different arrangement (1+2, 3+5, 4+6) and one each of other arrangements (1+3, 2+4, 5+6; 1+2, 3+6, 4+5; 1+3, 2+5, 4+blank; and even 1+6, 2+5, 3+4 as in modern dice). [236]

The date of these finds depends on the dates assigned to the Indus Valley culture as a whole, but it seems reasonable to place its *floruit*, in Mesopotamian terms, between the Third Early Dynastic period (ca. 2500-2300 B.C.) and the reign of Gungunum of Larsa (ca. 1932-

---

[230] Sumerian *lirum* and *gešpu*, Akkadian *umāšu* and *abāru*.
[231] Vermaak, RAI 41. See generally Edzard 1993.
[232] Gelb 1975.
[233] Foster 1974:74-79; 1992; *idem*, BM 824-826, FDD 365-367..
[234] Niditch 1987.
[235] Dales 1968:18f.
[236] *Ibid.*

1906 B.C.), when a precise synchronism has been established between the "Persian Gulf seals" known from Lothal at the end of the
Indus Valley period and Mesopotamian chronology on the basis of
the impression of such a seal on a dated tablet in the Yale Babylonian
Collection. [237] The implications of the Yale seal impression have been
recognized by E. Porada, [238] and underscored by a similar find, likewise dated to the early Isin-Larsa period, though less precisely than
the Yale example, among the tablets of Susa. [239]

If we may date the Indus Valley dice to the beginning of the Indus
Valley culture as suggested above, then we may indeed look "to South
Asia and to the Harappan period for the possible origin of the cubical
type of dice," as proposed by Dales. [240] Their next attested stop on
the way westward would then be at Shahr-i Sokhta in northeastern
Iran just inside its border with Afghanistan. Here were found a gam-
ing board together with an intact set of "men" and dice in a grave
(No. 713) dating from approximately 2300 B.C. [241] Admittedly, the
four dice in question differ from their Indus Valley counterparts: they
are made of wood, not terracotta, stone or faience; though square in
section, they are rectangular rather than cubical; instead of six numbered sides, they have only four; and instead of by dots, the numbers
are indicated by "thin rings of ivory and mother-of-pearl inlaid into
the wood" or, in one case, "by a series of finely incised rhombs and
triangles." [242] The fact that these dice were designed for a specific
board game may account for these differences.

In Mesopotamia itself, at any rate, the earliest dice are clay or
terracotta cubes and generally resemble their Indus Valley counterparts. Tell Chuera in the north has yielded one example from the
Early Dynastic III period in which the opposite sides are intended to
add up to 7. [243] Dales noted examples from the Royal Cemetery at
Ur, [244] from Tepe Gawra and Tell Asmar (Eshnunna) in the Akkadian

---

[237] Hallo and Buchanan 1965.
[238] E.g. in Porada 1971.
[239] Lambert 1976.
[240] Dales 1968:18.
[241] Tosi 1982:65.
[242] Piperno and Salvatori 1982:80 and pl. xxii.
[243] U. Moortgat-Correns, AfO 35 (1988) 161f.
[244] One of these dates to the First Dynasty of Ur (which Dales equates with Early
Dynastic III, others with Early Dynastic II), the other was found loose and "could
date from anytime from" ED III to Ur III. See also below, note 261.

period, and from Nippur in the Kassite period. [245] The second die from Ur and that from Nippur have an arrangement of the dots reflecting one of those popular among the Indus Valley examples (1+2, 3+6, 4+5); the one from Tepe Gawra has yet another arrangement (2+3, 4+5, 6+1). [246] Later examples of Mesopotamian dice are known from Assur, where they have been studied by E. Klengel-Brandt, [247] and from Babylon, where there is even a die made of glass. [248]

Continuing our journey westward, we next find dice attested in Palestinian excavations dating to the early second millennium, for example at Gaza [249] and Tell Beit Mirsim. [250] These dice again differ from the standard cubes: they are shaped like truncated four-sided pyramids and numbered with from one to four dots only, plus one dot on the top face. W.F. Albright derived this form from Egypt, whence he thought it was presumably borrowed also into Greece, [251] but Dales notes that, in Egypt, (cubical) dice "were not common until Graeco-Roman times, though isolated examples have been found at Thebes and Amarna dating to the New Kingdom (mid-16th century B.C.) at the earliest." [252] Recently a bone die has been found at Ashkelon with a "modern" arrangement of the dots. [253]

The Greeks themselves were divided in their opinion on the inventors of dice, variously crediting (or blaming?) the Egyptian god Toth (to whom they also attributed the invention of the alphabet) or the Phoenician Palamedes son of Naupolis; they themselves have even left us the first discussion of loaded dice; and they furnished Mishnaic (post-Biblical) Hebrew with its various words for dice, and perhaps the very idea itself. [254] Certainly the Rabbis preferred to see gambling with dice as a foreign vice and even found a Psalm passage to back up their condemnation of such gambling, though they never outlawed it. [255] The final step in the development of the die with its

---

[245] Dales 1968:18.
[246] See the illustration in Hallo 1983:22.
[247] Klengel-Brandt 1980.
[248] R. Borger *et al.*, eds., *Die Welt des alten Orients: Keilschrift—Grabungen—Gelehrte* (1975) No. 177; cf. the illustration in Hallo 1983:20.
[249] *Ibid.* 22 and the illustration p. 23.
[250] *Ibid.* 22 and n. 8.
[251] *Ibid.*
[252] Dales 1968:18, n. 29.
[253] Wapnish 1991:57; see the illustration in Hallo 1993:84*.
[254] Hallo 1983:22f.
[255] *Ibid.* and n. 12.

modern arrangement of the dots dates to early Islamic times at the latest. [256]

Some of the dice and die-like objects were found, as we have seen, in association with board games, and these too have a hoary antiquity. Without attempting a complete survey here, a sampling of representative types may be offered. There are principally three of these. The simplest game board consists of a surface with a number of holes, typically 58 in all, disposed in four lines, such that two outer lines have 19 holes each and two central lines ten each. There may also be up to four larger holes at the ends of these lines. This game no doubt required counters, to be moved into or across the holes according to the rules of the game.

Such boards are first attested in IXth Dynasty Egypt (ca. 2100 B.C.) and there and in Palestine are made of wood or ivory, elsewhere of stone or clay. Examples of the latter are known from Ras el Ayin and Tell Ajlun in Syria, [257] from Mesopotamia, [258] and from Susa in Elam. [259] Some examples even come from the palace of Esarhaddon and bear his royal inscription. [260] They date from all periods; indeed, their modern counterparts are in use in the Near East to this day.

A more sophisticated board-game came to light with the excavations of the Royal Graves at Ur, now generally dated to the beginning of the Early Dynastic III period. [261] Here was found an elaborate game magnificently inlaid with shell and lapis lazuli truly fit for a king—or queen—such as buried there. The surface of the board is divided into twenty (square) fields, disposed in such a way that two rows of three squares at one end are connected to (or separated from) four rows of three squares at the other end by two rows of one square each. Each square is elaborately decorated in one of seven patterns of which two occur once each, two twice each, one four times, and two five times. [262] This "royal game of Ur" has even inspired a modern replica. Until very recently, the rules of the game were unknown,

---

[256] *Ibid.*
[257] Nougayrol 1947; Moortgat-Correns 1959.
[258] Ellis and Buchanan 1966; see the illustration in Hallo 1993:85*.
[259] De Mecquenem 1905:103-106 and figs. 340-349.
[260] Gadd 1934; cf. Borger 1956:69, par. 31.
[261] H.J. Nissen, *Zur Datierung des Königsfriedhofes von Ur* (Bonn, Habelt, 1966).
[262] Woolley 1934:274-279 and pls. 95-99; see the illustration in Hallo 1993:86* (left).

though it was a safe assumption that it was played with counters or "men" such as are found with other board games; that it was played by two contending parties; and that the players moved the counters from field to field in such a way as to end up with particular counters in particular fields.

The somewhat later wooden gameboard from Shahr-i Sokhta (above) has the same arrangement as the game from Ur, and was found together with a bag for pieces. [263] Interestingly, it is in the form of a snake. [264] There is also a broken gameboard from Mohenjo Daro. [265]

Later variations on the royal game of Ur have the twenty squares disposed in such a way that, after the first four rows of three squares each, the other eight squares either follow the middle tier of four squares in one long line, [266] or else follow two of the tiers in lines of four rows of two squares each. [267] When the end of the board is broken off, it is uncertain which of the dispositions is followed. [268]

A curious descendant of the 20-field game from Ur has been discovered in the excavations at Kamid el-Loz (Kumidi) in Lebanon: at least ostensibly, it doubled as a liver-model for divination purposes. [269] More distant cousins of the Ur game may be represented by the Egyptian *senet*-game with (usually) thirty squares, [270] often arranged to resemble a snake, [271] and the gameboard with 18 fields (circles) from Knossos on Crete. [272] In the Ramesside period (XIXth and XXth dynasties), the Egyptian game frequently illustrates the Book of the Dead (ch. 17) and its thirty squares are interpreted as regions in the realm of the dead. [273]

A third type of gameboard is represented by two Mesopotamian

---

[263] Piperno and Salvatori 1982, pl. xxi; see the illustration in Hallo 1993:86* (right).

[264] Cf. below, note 271.

[265] I.L. Finkel, lecture presented at the Rencontre Assyriologique Internationale XXXVIII (Paris, 1991).

[266] Harrak 1987.

[267] Douglas van Buren 1937.

[268] De Kainlis 1942-44.

[269] Meyer 1982, with a complete survey of the various genres of boardgames; cf. the review by M. Gorg, ZA 76 (1986) 306-309, esp. pp. 307f.

[270] Pusch 1979; cf. the review by V.L. Davis, JAOS 102 (1982) 174f.; Needler 1953.

[271] Ranke 1928.

[272] Brumbaugh 1975.

[273] Milde 1988.

exemplars divided into eighty-four fields by horizontal, vertical and diagonal lines. One of them is provided with an Akkadian set of rules of a sort, the other seems to proclaim that its rules(?) are not written down (*nu-sar-meš*), though it adds the ancient name of the game: "pack of dogs" (*illat kalbē*). [274] Both were published, as chance would have it, in the same volume, an anniversary volume dedicated to C. Virolleaud, the former by E.F. Weidner, [275] the latter by J. Bottéro. [276] Weidner thought of his exemplar as a "Losbuch," a form of divination in which one arrives at a designated oracular utterance by throwing a die or an astragal or undertaking some other manipulation leading to a number which directs one further. [277] M. Riemschneider even developed a theory of fate-determination in the guise of a board-game. [278]

Because his exemplar was dated to 177/6 B.C. in the Hellenistic period, more specifically in the Parthian or Arsacid period of Mesopotamian history, Weidner was inclined to derive it from Greek precedent, where such "Losbücher" were well known. But the simultaneous publication of Bottéro's exemplar, dated by its editor to the neo-Babylonian period, suggested a native origin for both exemplars, [279] and the very notion that they represent "Losbücher" was disputed by Landsberger, who preferred to regard them as outright game-boards. [280]

In 1990, the British Museum convened the first academic colloquium on "Board Games of the Ancient World," and here Irving Finkel of the Museum's Department of Western Asiatic Antiquities took matters one step further. He considered the rules inscribed on the reverse of the Parthian game-board not only to apply to the 84-square game on its obverse, but also to hold the clue to the twenty-square game from the Royal Graves of Ur, albeit dating nearly 2500 years later. According to the late text, "two players use five pieces, which are named after birds (Raven, Rooster, Swallow, Eagle and an

---

[274] Landsberger 1960:126-129.
[275] Weidner 1956.
[276] Bottéro 1956.
[277] Weidner 1956, following G. Weil.
[278] Riemschneider 1953:157-173: "Die Schicksalsbestimmung als Brettspiel"; cf. *ibid.* 174-193: "Die Ausdrücke für das Spielbrett und seine Teile," and 194-211: "Spieltechnik und Spielgott."
[279] Weidner 1956:182f.
[280] Landsberger 1960:127f.

unidentified bird). The pieces are moved after a dice, made from an animal knucklebone, is thrown." [281]

But the story does not end there. A modern survival of one or both of these games has been recognized by Finkel in a board game called Asha that was known in the Jewish community of Cochin in southern India. According to the recollections of an aged member of this community, the game was still played by two players, each using five pieces. It was played only by women, and even by them only once a year, during the fast-day of the Ninth of Av which commemorates the destruction of the First and Second Temples in Jerusalem. [282]

All such Near Eastern dice and board games may thus be said to be ancestral to their European successors, and this may also be true of the simple top. [283] But there is one kind of top whose travels may have gone in the opposite direction. That is the "teetotum," described in the *Oxford Universal Dictionary* (1955) as "A small four-sided disk or die having an initial letter inscribed on each of its sides, and a spindle passing down through it by which it could be twirled or spun with the fingers like a small top, the letter which lay uppermost, when it fell, deciding the fortune of the player....The letters were originally the initials of Latin words, viz. T *totum*, A *aufer*, D *depone*, N *nihil* (i.e.,' all, take away, pay, nothing'). Later they were the initials of English words, T take-all, H half, N nothing, P put down." [284] The English word can be traced back to 1753 or 1720, but the device itself is likely to go back much further.

It does not take much imagination to see it as the lineal antecedent of the popular Jewish top known as the *dreidel*, employed at the festival of Chanukka for playing innocent games of chance. The four sides of this top are inscribed with the Hebrew letters N,G,H and Sh, interpreted as an acronym for Hebrew *nes gadol haya sham*, "a great miracle happened there," an allusion to the miracle of the oil which Chanukka commemorates. But the real significance of the letters is in Yiddish, where they stand for *nichts* or *nimm*, *ganz* or *gib*, *halb*, and *shtell* or *shenk*, i.e. " nothing (or take), all (or pay), half, and pay up," [285]

---

[281] M. Bailey, *London Observer*, September 23, 1990, p. 3; cf. already Weidner 1956:177.

[282] *Ibid.* At the Rencontre Internationale Assyriologique XXXVIII (Paris, 1991), Finkel enlarged on these matters; his publication is eagerly awaited.

[283] Van Beek 1989.

[284] Cited Hallo 1983:23.

[285] *Ibid.*

or in German, where "the original medieval dice used ... by gamblers was inscribed with the four letters: *N,G,H,* and *S.*" [286] In sum, the simpler the game, the more likely it is to cross geographical and chronological boundaries and delight ever new generations in diverse cultures.

Bibliographical References

Borger, R., 1956: *Die Inschriften Asarhaddons Königs von Assyrien* (= AfO Beiheft 9).

Bottéro, Jean, 1956: "Deux curiosités assyriologiques," *Syria* 33:17-35.

Brumbaugh, Robert S., 1975: "The Knossos game board," AJA 79:135-137.

Civil, Miguel, 1980: "Daily chores in Nippur," JCS 32:229-232.

Dales, George F., 1968: "Of dice and men," JAOS 88 (= Speiser AV) 14-23.

De Kainlis, A., 1942-44: "Un jeu assyrien du Musée du Louvre," RA 39:19-234.

De Mecquenem, R., 1905: "Offrandes de fondation du Temple de Chouchinak," MDP 7:61-130.

Dossin, Georges, 1938: "Un rituel du culte d'Ištar provenant de Mari," RA 35:1-13.

Douglas van Buren, E., 1937: "A gaming-board from Tall Halaf," *Iraq* 4:11-15 and pl. vi.

Duchesne-Guillemin, Marcelle, 1983: "Pukku and mekkû," *Iraq* 45:151-156.

Edzard, Dietz O., 1993: " *mekkû, pukku* und," RLA 8:34.

Ellis, Richard S. and Briggs Buchanan, 1966: "An Old Babylonian gameboard with sculptured decoration," JNES 25:192-201 and pl. xvii.

Englund, Robert K., 1988: "Administrative timekeeping in ancient Mesopotamia," JESHO 31:121-185.

———, 1991: "Hard work—where will it get you? Labor management in Ur III Mesopotamia," JNES 50:255-280.

Foster, Benjamin R., 1974: "Humor and cuneiform literature," JANES 6:69-85.

———, 1992: "Humor and wit—Mesopotamia," ABD 3:328-330.

Gadd, C.J., 1934: "An Egyptian game in Assyria," *Iraq* 1:45-50.

Gelb, I.J., 1975: "Homo ludens in early Mesopotamia," Salonen AV 43-76.

Hallo, William W., 1977: "New moons and sabbaths," HUCA 48:1-18.

———, 1983: "The First Purim," BA 46: 19-29.

———, 1993: "Games in the Biblical world," *Eretz-Israel* 24 (Malamat Volume) 83*-88*.

——— and Briggs Buchanan, 1965: "A 'Persian Gulf' seal on an Old Babylonian mercantile agreement," Landsberger AV 199-209.

Harrak, A., 1987: "Another specimen of an Assyrian game," AfO 34:56f.

Kilmer, Anne D., 1982: "A note on an overlooked word-play in the Akkadian Gilgamesh," Kraus AV 128-132.

———, 1993: "Games and toys in ancient Mesopotamia," *Actes du XIIe Congres International des Sciences Préhistoriques et Protohistoriques* (Bratislava) 359-364.

Klengel-Brandt, E., 1980: "Spielbretter und Würfel aus Assur," AoF 7:119-126 and pls. xiiif.

Lambert, Maurice, 1976: "Tablette de Suse avec cachet du Golfe," RA 70:71f.

Landsberger, Benno, 1960, 1961: " *passu* = 'Puppe' und andere Bezeichnungen für 'spielen' und 'Spielzeug'," WZKM 56:117-129; 57:22f.

---

[286] Noy 1971:c. 1393.

Meyer, J.W., 1982: "Lebermodell oder Spielbrett," in R. Hachmann *et al.*, *Bericht über die Ergebnisse der Ausgrabungen in Kamid el-Loz* (= SBA 32) 53-79.

Milde, H., 1988: "It is all in the game," Heerma van Vos AV 89-95.

Moortgat-Correns, Ursula, 1959: "Ein Spielbrett von Tell Ailun (?)," Friedrich AV 339-345 and (6) pls.

Needler, W., 1953: "A thirty-square draught-board in the Royal Ontario Museum," JEA 39:60-75 and pl.iv.

Niditch, Susan, 1987: *Underdogs and Tricksters: a Prelude to Biblical Folklore* (San Francisco, Harper and Row).

Nougayrol, Jean, 1947: "Un 'jeu' de Ras el Ain," RA 41:46-49.

Noy, Dov, 1971: "Folklore," EJ 6:1374-1410.

Piperno, M. and S. Salvatori, 1982: "Evidence of western cultural connections from a Phase 3 group of graves at Shahr-i Sokhta," RAI 25:79-85 and pls. xix-xxv.

Porada, Edith, 1971: "Remarks on seals found in the Gulf states," *Artibus Asiae* 33:331-337.

Pusch, E.B., 1979: *Das Senet-Brettspiel im alten Ägypten* I (= Münchner Ägyptologische Studien 38).

Ranke, Herrmann, 1920: *Das altägyptische Schlangenspiel* (= SHAW 1920/4).

Riemschneider, Margarete, 1953: *Augengottheit und Heilige Hochzeit*. (Leipzig, Koehler and Amelang).

Sallaberger, Walter, 1993: *Der kultische Kalender der Ur III-Zeit* (2 vols. = UAVA 7).

Tosi, M., 1982: "The development of urban societies in Turan and Mesopotamian trade with the east: the evidence from Shahr-i Sokhta," RAI 25:57-77.

Van Beek, Gus, 1989: "The Buzz: a simple toy from antiquity," BASOR 275: 53-58.

Wapnish, Paula, 1991: "Beauty and utility in bone: new light on bone crafting," BAR 17/4:54-57 and 72; reprinted in L.E. Stager, *Ashkelon Discovered* (Washington, Biblical Archaeology Society 1991) 61.

Weidner, Ernst F., 1956: "Ein Losbuch in Keilschrift aus der Seleukidenzeit," *Syria* 33:175-183 and pl. vii.

Woolley, C. Leonard, 1934: *The Royal Cemetery* (= Ur Excavations 2) (2 vols., London, The British Museum).

CHAPTER FOUR

THE CALENDAR

Of all human institutions, the calendar is one of the most culture-bound and yet at the same time one of those most likely to travel across cultural boundaries. Next to the alphabet, the calendar may well be, in some of its aspects, the most obvious legacy of the Ancient Near East to the modern world. Not all of these aspects will, however, be considered here. They can be divided broadly speaking into two categories, time-units based on natural phenomena, and such as are purely human inventions. Only the latter lend themselves readily to a comparative and historical approach. The former are too universal for facile assertions of inter-cultural dependence; they include the day, the month, the seasons and the year.

The day is based on the regular alternation of sunrise and sunset, and the lunar month, directly or ultimately, on the reappearance of the new moon at 29 or 30-day intervals, both observations of such obvious simplicity that they could well have been made independently in many parts of the world and at all times. The seasons are not quite as universal or universally identical as the day and the (lunar) month, and deserve study for each culture in its own terms, [1] but neither are they man-made. The divine promise to Noah surely resonates in all cultures: "So long as the earth endures, seedtime and harvest, cold and heat, summer and winter, day and night shall not cease" (Gen 8:22).

The solar year is based on the annual recurrence of the seasons or of certain seasonal factors. In Egypt, the annual inundation of the Nile was the principal constant governing the economic well-being of the country, not only in ancient times but almost to the present, i.e. until the construction of the high dam at Aswan in the 1960's. It is caused by the melting of the snows of the East African highlands, and the resultant excess of water carried downstream; it normally recurs, or recurred, at such regular intervals that the Egyptians very early on

---

[1] Cf. e.g. Landsberger 1949.

calculated the year as consisting of 365 days. They thus added to the older calendar based on lunar months (which was retained for ritual purposes) a civil calendar which divided the solar year into twelve months of thirty days each with a five-day festival at the end to make up the difference. [2]

In Mesopotamia, there was no equally regular recurrence of annual natural phenomena; instead the month of twenty-nine or thirty days, based on the observation of the new moon, served as the basic unit of time. It was learned early on that a cycle of twelve or thirteen such months saw the recurrence of the same seasonal (solar) phenomena, giving rise to a year which was a compromise between lunar and solar considerations and which is best described as a luni-solar year. As eventually regularized, it provided for a thirteenth (intercalary) month in seven out of every nineteen years. This system, with minor adjustments, was subsequently taken over by the Jews together with the Babylonian month names and serves as the basis for the Jewish religious calendar to this day. [3]

At third millennium Ebla in Syria, open as it was to both Mesopotamian and Egyptian influences, a year of 364 days was, it has been suggested, employed at least for purposes of calculations. [4]

But there are also time-units which are largely or wholly independent of natural phenomena, including the hour (and its subdivisions), the week, and the era. From the historian's point of view, these are much likelier threads for pursuing cultural interconnections, and it is their origins that will be investigated here.

1. The Hour

The division of the (solar) day into twenty-four hours is neither God-given nor dictated by nature; rather it is an invention of the Egyptians which can be traced back at least as far as 1300 B.C. [5] But these Egyptian hours were "seasonal" hours, i.e. they varied in length according to the season of the year, each representing one twelfth of the time between sunrise and sunset or sunset and sunrise respectively. (Strictly speaking, the night was divided into twelve hours and the

---

[2] Cf. e.g. Neugebauer 1962:80-82; Spalinger 1995.
[3] Wacholder and Weisberg 1971.
[4] Archi 1989:2.
[5] Neugebauer 1962:85f.

day into ten, and there were two twilight hours). [6] They were "replaced by 'equinoctial hours' of constant length only in theoretical works of Hellenistic astronomy." [7] Recently, however, it has been tentatively suggested that "a comparable system was in use in Ugarit around 1200 B.C." [8]

The Mesopotamians originally employed an archaic division of the 24-hour day into four six-hour periods. [9] But they too learned to operate with seasonal hours. According to a new interpretation of the evidence, they called these hours *simānu*, hitherto thought of as a general term for "time" or "season." But the evidence of the horoscopes, in particular, shows that an expression such as "day 22 in the 11th *si-man*, the child was born" refers to the eleventh seasonal hour after sunrise. When a child was born at night, the horoscopes refer to the time, not by seasonal hours, but by watches of the night, probably because the determination of the exact seasonal hour was dependent on the use of a sundial, attested in Babylonia since the end of the second millennium—and obviously useless at night. Since there were twelve seasonal hours of daylight (and twelve between sunset and sunrise), the highest number occurring with *simānu* is twelve. [10] As late as the middle of the seventh century B.C., a text still "records the length of seasonal hours for every fifteenth day of an 'ideal' solar year." [11]

The seasonal hour was well suited to the earliest equipment for keeping time, the sundial and gnomon, the latter being the Greek name for the pole which, by the shadow it cast on the dial, indicated the time of day. The Sumerian term for gnomon was established as *u₄-sakar* by A. Sachs who found "the incipit of ... two curious and difficult tablets ... to be translated ... 'if you want to construct a gnomon' " among his *Late Babylonian Astronomical and Related Texts*; [12] according to A.L. Oppenheim, the tablets belong to the genre of "procedural instructions." [13] Sachs subsequently joined an additional fragment to one of the tablets and, though both remain fragmentary,

---

[6] *Ibid.*
[7] *Ibid.* 81.
[8] De Jong and van Soldt 1989:75.
[9] Englund 1988:168.
[10] Rochberg-Halton 1989.
[11] Pingree and Reiner 1974-77.
[12] Sachs 1955 xxxiv.
[13] See above, ch. III 2, n. 191.

their evidence has yielded important information on the Babylonian sundial. [14]

The Akkadian equivalent of Sumerian u_4-*sakar* is *uskaru* or *askaru*, a loanword from the Sumerian term, with many different if related meanings including lunar crescent, ornamental or votive moon-disc, a part of the wheel or the door, a crescent-shaped area in a mathematical problem-text, a crescent-shaped formation in the liver of a sacrificial sheep [15] and a semicircle. [16] The fact that some typical sundials actually consist of a semicircle and a pole lends additional support to Sachs' hypothesis.

Sundials of such type have long been known from Egypt, and one such, made of ivory, and dated to the reign of Merneptah at the end of the Bronze Age, [17] was found in Gezer, an Egyptian outpost in Palestine until it was given to King Solomon as part of the dowry of the Pharaoh's daughter whom he married (I Kings 9:16). There was also a quite different type, in which the shadow of the sun was not cast by a pole on a semicircular surface, but by two walls on two flights of steps. Such a sundial or better perhaps sunstaircase is preserved in a model in the Cairo Museum. It provides the prototype for the famous "sundial" of Ahaz, king of Judah which figured prominently in the story of the illness of his successor Hezekiah (II Kings 20:9-11 = Isaiah 38:7-8). With the help of this Egyptian parallel, and of an improved reading of the Biblical passage provided by the Isaiah Scroll from Qumran, it is possible to preserve the "sunstaircase" of the Israelite tradition [18] even if the "sundial" has to go. [19]

As stated, the seasonal hour was well suited to such devices, which divided the hours of daylight into segments that equalled each other but varied in absolute length according to the time of the year. But it was quite *unsuited* to the more sophisticated time-piece known as the water-clock. This device measured time segments of equal length as determined by the time it took the water to run out of predetermined portions of a vessel. The Greeks knew such a clock as a "clepsydra," literally "water-thief," and used it, among other things, to keep their

---

[14] Rochberg-Halton 1989:162-165.
[15] Hallo, HUCA 48 (1977): 4.
[16] J. van Dijk, Falkenstein AV (1967) 248-250; Cl. Wilcke, *Kollationen* (1976) 29 (116); for the reading see M. Civil, RA 60 (1966) 92.
[17] For his significance in Israelite history see below, ch. IX 2.
[18] Yadin 1958.
[19] Iwry 1957.

orators from exceeding their time-limits in the law-courts. The most
elaborate clepsydra was in the "Tower of the Winds" built in the Roman agora of Athens ca. 75 B.C. [20]

Long before the Greeks, however, the Mesopotamians knew such
clocks. They called them *giš-dib-dib, giš-lidda₂, giš-níg-ninda₂ or giš-*KAB-
az in Sumerian and *dibdibbu* or *maltaktu* in Akkadian. The last term
reflects the root meaning of *latāku,* i.e. "examine carefully, measure
out exactly," as in *litiktu,* "true measure." [21] These waterclocks measured time not by distance but by weight, i.e. the weight in *ma-na* or
"pounds" of water that had flowed out of them. [22] They are known
as early as Old Babylonian times from lexical [23] and mathematical
texts, [24] and even the Old Babylonian story of the flood invoked the
water-clock to announce the coming of the flood. [25] The water clock
also became a staple of Babylonian (and Egyptian) astronomy. [26]

Under such circumstances, it was inevitable that the seasonal hour
be eventually replaced by the "equinoctial" hour, "a constant unit of
time" and one "independent of the seasonal variation in length of
daylight." [27] According to O. Neugebauer, this change took place in
the first part of the first millennium. [28] Perhaps it can be attributed
to King Nabonassar of Babylon and his astronomers, who introduced
so many innovations into calendaric, chronographic and astronomic
traditions after 747 B.C. [29]

This equinoctial hour was called *danna* in Sumerian, *bēru* in Akkadian; since there were twelve such units in a twenty-four hour day,
the term is usually translated into English as "double-hour." The native term is based on a unit of distance (ca. 10 km), ostensibly that
covered on foot in two hours. [30] As we have seen, however, travel
proceeded at a rate of anywhere from 20-40 km per day, with 30 km,
or about 3 *bēru* per day being the ideal average. [31] So the equation

---

[20] Noble and de Solla Price 1968; cf. de Solla Price 1975 ch. 2 *et passim.*
[21] Hallo, JQR 76 (1985) 26, n. 24; Civil 1994:153-163.
[22] Rochberg-Halton 1989:150.
[23] CAD D and M s.vv.; MSL 5 (1957) 151:6-10; 6 (1958) 156:198f.
[24] Nemet-Nejat 1988:295 and nn. 105f.; 1993:70-72.
[25] Lambert and Millard 1969:90f., l. 36.
[26] Neugebauer 1947; repr. 1983:239--245; Sambin 1988; Spalinger 1993:178f.
[27] Rochberg-Halton 1989:147.
[28] *Ibid.*
[29] Hallo 1988.
[30] Rochberg-Halton 1989:147.
[31] See above, ch. III 1.

can at best be based on the shortest day of the year, the winter sol-stice, when eight hours (four double-hours) was conventionally taken to be the length of daylight [32] and hence presumably the time avail-able for travel. More often, however, it was the longest day that was involved in calculations based on the equinoctial hour. [33]

Such an assumption is, moreover, contradicted by the habit of avoiding travel and military campaigns in the winter and launching them instead in the spring, the time of the vernal equinox, i.e. after the rainy season and if possible before the first harvest. This usage was well attested in Assyrian records [34] and the Bible, [35] where we read of "the turn of the year, the season when kings go out (to bat-tle)" (II Samuel 11:1 = I Chronicles 20:1). It thus seems more prob-able that the conversion of the concept of *bēru* from a measure of distance to one of time was of a piece with other semantic shifts in the field of metrology, e.g. with respect to volume measures.

One more step had to be taken before the twelve equinoctial dou-ble-hours could be converted into the twenty-four equinoctial hours in use to this day. This step took place outside of Mesopotamia in the Hellenistic astronomical schools. According to F. Rochberg-Halton, it reflected "the combination of Egyptian seasonal hours with the sexagesimal reckoning of Babylonian time." [36] The same Babylonian sexagesimal reckoning is ultimately responsible for the division of the equinoctial hour into sixty minutes and the minute into sixty sec-onds, [37] as well as of the circle into 360 degrees. A dissent is regis-tered by Boorstin, who dates the introduction of the system of 24 equinoctial hours to the 14th century A.D., and derives the 360 de-grees of the circle from the Egyptian year (see above). [38] He also notes that "until 1873 the Japanese retained the 'natural' sunlight day di-vided into 6 equal hours between sunrise and sunset. Their 'hour' still varied from day to day." [39]

---

[32] Rochberg-Halton 1989:151.

[33] Gehlken 1991.

[34] Meissner, BuA I 106f.

[35] De Vaux, *Ancient Israel* 251.

[36] Rochberg-Halton 1989:147.

[37] Note, however, that the second is today said to be "based on the oscillation of a cesium atom," according to Alexandra Bandon, *The New York Times Magazine* (July 30, 1995) 12.

[38] Boorstin, *Discoverers* 39-42.

[39] *Ibid.* 78.

Bibliographical References

Archi, Alfonso, 1989: "Table des comptes Eblaites," RA 83:1-6.

Civil, Miguel, 1994: *The Farmer's Instructions: a Sumerian Agricultural Manual* (Barcelona, Editorial Aula).

De Jong, T. and W.H. van Soldt, 1989: "Redating an early solar eclipse record (KTU 1.78): implications for the Ugaritic calendar and for the secular accelerations of the earth and moon," JEOL 30:65-77.

De Solla Price, Derek J., 1975: *Science Since Babylon* (2nd ed.) (New Haven/London, Yale U.P.).

Englund, Robert K., 1988: "Administrative timekeeping in ancient Mesopotamia," JESHO 31:121-185.

Gehlken, E., 1991: "Der längste Tag in Babylon (MUL.APIN und die Wasseruhr)," N.A.B.U. 1991/4:65f., No. 95.

Hallo, William W., 1988: "The Nabonassar Era and other epochs in Mesopotamian chronology and chronography," Sachs AV 175-190.

Iwry, Samuel, 1957: "The Qumran Isaiah and the end of the dial of Ahaz," BASOR 147:27-33.

Lambert, W.G. and A.R. Millard, 1969: *Atra-ḫasīs: the Babylonian Story of the Flood* (Oxford, Clarendon).

Landsberger , Benno, 1949: "Jahreszeiten im Sumerisch-Akkadischen," JNES 8:248-297.

Nemet-Nejat, Karen R., 1988: "Cuneiform mathematical texts as training for scribal professions," Sachs AV 285-300.

————, 1993: *Cuneiform Mathematical Texts as a Reflection of Everyday Life in Mesopotamia* (= AOS 75).

Neugebauer, Otto, 1947: "Studies in ancient astronomy. VIII. The water clock in Babylonian astronomy," *Isis* 37:37-43. Reprinted in Neugebauer 1983:239-245.

————, 1962: *The Exact Sciences in Antiquity* (2nd ed.) (Providence, Brown U.P.)

————, 1983: *Astronomy and History: Selected Essays* (New York etc., Springer).

Noble, J.V. and Derek J. de Sola Price, 1968: "The water clock in the Tower of the Winds," AJA 72:345-355.

Pingree, David and Erica Reiner, 1974-77: "A neo-Babylonian report on seasonal hours," AfO 25:50-55.

Rochberg-Halton, Francesca, 1989: "Babylonian seasonal hours," *Centaurus* 32:146-170.

Sachs, Abraham J., 1955: *Late Babylonian Astronomical and Related Texts* (Providence, Brown U.P.).

Sambin, Chantal, 1988: *L'Offrande de la soi-disant 'clepsydre'* (Budapest, Chaire d'Egyptologie).

Spalinger, Anthony J., 1993: "A religious calendar year in the Mut Temple at Karnak," *Revue d'Egyptologie* 161-184.

————, ed., 1995: *Revolutions in Time: Studies in Ancient Egyptian Calendrics* (San Antonio, TX, Van Siclen Books).

Wacholder, Ben Zion and David B. Weisberg, 1971: "Visibility of the new moon in cuneiform and rabbinic sources," HUCA 42:227-242.

Yadin, Yigael, 1958: "The dial of Ahaz," *Eretz-Israel* 5:91-96 and pl. xxx (in Hebrew; English summary pp. 88* f.).

2. The Week

If the twenty-four hour day is a legacy of Egypt and Mesopotamia, the seven-day week is definitely independent of both these ancient cultures, although they have never ceased to be searched for the roots of this crucial modern institution that now enjoys global acceptance. The origins of the seven-day week have to be sought, instead, in ancient Israel. It remains true now, as it did in 1977, that "the uniquely biblical conception of the week and the sabbatical cycle stands out equally by virtue of its pervasiveness in biblical laws and letters, as by its absence from the surrounding Near East." [40] In what follows, the arguments assembled in my earlier study will be presupposed, and confronted with the subsequent discussion of the theme.

In insisting that the Biblical concept of the week is independent of any natural phenomena including the phases of the moon, there was no intention to deny the possible evolution of that concept out of an earlier lunar cycle. The very title of my study, "new moons and sabbaths," alluded to this Biblical phrase used by the early prophets Hosea and Isaiah in a sense very close to the sense of "new moon and full moon" admitted for Psalm 81:4. [41] In the latter passage, the term for full moon is *kese*, but a comparable sense has since been defended at length by M. Fishbane for *shabbat* in the prophetic passages, [42] largely on the basis of the equation of that term with Akkadian *šapattu*, for which the meaning "full moon" is not in doubt, [43] although the equation itself has been long debated. [44]

It is, then, conceivable that the Biblical term, like its putative Akkadian cognate, *originally* designated a phase of the moon; but if so its meaning was incontestably altered when the term was applied to the novel concept of the weekly rest day. In fact, as U. Cassuto argued long ago, it is possible that "the Israelite Sabbath was instituted in *opposition* to the Mesopotamian system.... Israel's Sabbath day shall not be as the Sabbath of the heathen nations; it shall not be the day of the full moon, or any other day connected with the phases of the moon and linked, in consequence, with the worship of the moon, but

---

[40] Hallo 1977:15.
[41] *Ibid.* 9 and nn. 41f.
[42] Fishbane 1984:149f. and nn. 18-21.
[43] Hallo 1977:8 and n. 36.
[44] Cf. e.g. Tur-Sinai 1951.

it shall be the *seventh day...*, the seventh in *perpetual* order, independent and free from any association with the sign of the heavens and any astrological concept." [45]

Just when did this transformation in the meaning of the Biblical Sabbath take place? According to A. Lemaire, [46] it should be dated to the return from the Babylonian exile after 538 B.C., inspired in part by the reform of the calendar under Babylonian influence, and partly by the experience of the Babylonian *dies nefas* or unfavorable days, an idea which goes back at least to Friedrich Delitzsch. [47] N.-E.A. Andreasen, on the contrary, argues that "that Levitical and priestly circles were responsible for resurrecting, reformulating, and reinterpreting the Sabbath traditions before the exile. It was from the fund of traditions preserved by these circles that H, Ezekiel, and P drew their Sabbath material. In it we find commands to keep the Sabbath, prohibitions of work on it, the Sabbath formula, characterization of the seventh day as Yahweh's day, the creation Sabbath, and the Sabbath as a sign and a covenant." [48] The question still awaits a clear answer.

Meantime the search for a Babylonian week has not abated. It should be obvious by now that a mere seven-day period, no matter how institutionalized, bears no comparison with the Biblical week when it occurs in isolation rather than in inviolate sequence. That is the case with the seven-day festival celebrating the dedication of the temple of Nin-Girsu at Girsu by Gudea of Lagash as commemorated in his famous Cylinder Inscriptions, [49] or the seven-day ritual in the Old Babylonian cult at Larsa, [50] or the sacred-marriage rite at Emar [51] now available in no less than three different editions, [52] or even the newest and most intriguing discovery of all: a seven-day period of mourning for the deceased king Shulgi of Ur! [53]

The last mentioned "week" has a possible precedent in the tradi-

---

[45] Cassuto 1961:68.

[46] Lemaire 1973.

[47] Cf. Finkelstein 1958:432f.

[48] Andreasen 1972:259.

[49] Sauren 1975; latest translation by Jacobsen, *Harps* 386-444; exhaustive comparative study by Hurowitz 1992.

[50] Kingsbury 1963; new edition by A. Westenholtz in preparation.

[51] Hallo 1977:17, n. 83.

[52] Arnaud, *Emar* 6/3:326-337, No. 369; Dietrich 1989; Fleming 1992.

[53] Hallo, Tadmor AV (1991) 158f. and nn. 87-94, with previous literature; 1991:180f. and nn. 58-60. Cf. also below, ch. VII 2, n. 81.

tions surrounding Naram-Sin of Akkad as preserved in "The Curse of Agade" which depicts "the survivors of the Gutian devastation performing a seven-day lamentation ceremony in Nippur to pacify Enlil" [54] or, alternatively, describes "in a certain sense the reversal of a ceremony for dedicating a new temple" where "Enlil is audience to seven days of lamentation." [55] It also provides a remote antecedent for the seven days of mourning attested for Adad-guppi, mother of the last Babylonian king, [56] as well as the seven days of mourning mentioned in various passages in the Bible, [57] the Apocrypha, [58] and the Midrash. [59]

Mention may also be made of the royal benediction which concludes the Sumerian composition known today as "Nanna-Suen's Journey to Nippur." [60] Based on the translation by Edzard, this reads "Oh my king, on your throne, Enlil's, you have verily accomplished (this) in seven days. On your holy throne, that of the great mother Ninlil(?), oh lord Ashimbabbar, you have verily accomplished (this) in seven days." [61] What the mysterious "(this)" is that took seven days to complete is indicated neither here nor in the similar translation by Wilcke. [62] But in light of the parallels which this passage displays with the royal hymn in honor of "The Coronation of Ur-Nammu," [63] and of additional, still unpublished parallels, D.R. Frayne has plausibly argued that the benediction alludes to the coronation of a king of Ur in Nippur, symbolized by the journey of the chief deity of Ur to the chief deity of Nippur. [64]

The most persistent candidate for the title of "the Babylonian Sabbath" is the neo-Babylonian institution first given that designation by A.T. Clay in 1915. [65] It is, however, entirely dependent on the lunar month. The half dozen texts of a certain characteristic type which Clay published to illustrate this phenomenon listed the sheep sac-

---

[54] Cooper 1983:251f. *ad* ll. 196-206; cf. Hallo 1991:181, n. 61.
[55] A.(V.) Hurowitz, Kutscher AV (1993) 40.
[56] Hallo 1991:180 and n. 57.
[57] *Ibid.* 180 and nn. 53-55. Hallo 1977:10, n. 49, should be corrected accordingly.
[58] Hallo 1991:180, n. 56.
[59] Hallo 1991:179f. and nn. 47-52.
[60] Ferrara 1973:106, ll. 349-352.
[61] D.O. Edzard, ZA 63 (1973) 300.
[62] Cl. Wilcke, RAI 19 (1974) 187. Cf. PSDB 134c.
[63] See below, ch. VI 2.
[64] Frayne 1981:115-120.
[65] YOS 1 pp. 75-81; cf. Hallo 1977:8f.

rificed on each day of the month, with special offerings (*hitpu*) indicated for certain days of the month, most often the 7th, 14th, 21st and 28th. But the corpus of such texts, published and unpublished, has now grown to over forty; they date from the last year of Nabonidus to the sixth year of Cambyses; and a forthcoming study of the entire corpus by Ellen Robbins will show that the special offerings diverge from the " norm" by one or two days as often as not. They may have some tenuous connection to the phases of the moon, but are unlikely models for the Israelite Sabbath.

More interesting is the designation of the special offerings, *hitpu*. In 1977, I stated:[66]

> The root *ḫtp* is familiar in Arabic, Hebrew and Aramaic in connection with slaughtering or hunting and occurs already in a Ugaritic text in the specific context of a sacrifice. We read, in a prayer to Ba'al, "A bull, oh Ba'al, we consecrate (to you), a votive offering, oh Ba'al, we dedicate (to you), the first fruits, oh Ba'al, we consecrate (to you), the booty, oh Ba'al, we offer (to you), a tithe, oh Ba'al, we tithe (to you)." The word translated "booty" here is *ḫtp*, comparable to the *ḥetep* ("prey") of Proverbs 23:28. Given the context, however, the word may already foreshadow the connotation of a kind of sacrifice. That is surely the meaning of Akkadian *hitpu* which occurs in monthly sacrificial lists of the late first millennium.

The Ugaritic text in question is RS 24:266 = KTU 1.119, cited then from the partial edition by A. Herdner. [67] In an addendum, [68] I noted a new study of the text by A. Spalinger, and a proposed Egyptian cognate in the approximate sense of " (food) offering." [69] Since then, several new attempts have been made to explain the Ugaritic text.

Herdner herself published the full text in 1978 [70] after it had already been included in the authoritative compendium of Ugaritic texts of 1976; [71] it reappears in the second edition of 1995.[72] P. Xella dealt with it in 1978 and 1981. [73]

Yitzhak Avishur translated the text into Hebrew and provided a

---

[66] Hallo 1977:8.
[67] Herdner 1972:694.
[68] Hallo 1977:17f.
[69] Spalinger 1978.
[70] Herdner 1978.
[71] KTU 123f., showing the *p* of *ḫtp* damaged.
[72] KTU (2nd ed.) 133f.
[73] Xella 1978; 1981:25-34.

new commentary. He rendered Ugaritic *ḥtp* by Hebrew *qorban*, "offering," on the basis of Akkadian *ḥitpu*, rejecting an emendation to *ḥtk* proposed by Baruch Margalit (below). He compared the five synonyms for offering found in the Ugaritic text to the five or six such terms found in Deut. 12:6 where, by a kind of process of elimination, the Ugaritic *ḥtp* corresponds to Hebrew *zbḥ*, "sacrifice." [74] Margalit dealt with *ḥtp* and the problem of equating it with *ḥitpu*. His proposal to emend the text to *ḥtk*, "son," rests in part on the assumed parallel with *bkr*, "first-born," in the preceding line, in part on the orthographic similarity between the Ugaritic signs for P and K. [75]

J.C. de Moor included the composition in his selection of liturgical texts from Ugarit and translated the crucial word into Dutch as "de *ḥitpu*-verplichtingen," the hitpu-obligations. [76]

Jack M. Sasson took issue with Margalit's emendation and with other elements of his proposal, paraphrasing the passage as follows: [77]

> We shall sacrifice a bull//We shall fulfill a pledge
> We shall sacrifice a (?)*kr*//We shall fulfill a *ḥtp*
> We shall (therefore/furthermore) pay a tithe.

The Egyptian reliefs adduced by Spalinger in connection with the Ugaritic prayer have also come in for renewed attention. L.E. Stager identified the relief in Spalinger's fig. 2 as a stele of Merneptah, not of Ramses II, and as picturing the Egyptian siege of Ashkelon, with the king of Ashkelon sacrificing his own son in a gesture of ultimate desperation. [78] Stager was basing himself on the work of Frank J. Yurco, who has since given his own reasons for assigning the stele to Merneptah, and reproduced the relief showing the siege of Ashkelon. [79]

Spalinger had noted three children shown in three different positions on the relief. James K. Hoffmeier added the interesting suggestion that "these depictions represent a sequence of events. A child is shown to the besiegers, it is slain in full view, and then the corpse is

---

[74] Avishur 1978-79.
[75] Margalit 1981, esp. pp. 76f., 83 .
[76] De Moor 1983:251f.
[77] J.M. Sasson, BAR 12/3 (1987) 60.
[78] Stager 1985, esp. p. 57*.
[79] Yurco 1990, esp. pp. 28f.

thrown down for the enemy to see." [80] Spalinger had sought to but-
tress his arguments by appeal to II Kings 3:26-27a:

> Seeing that the battle was going against him, the king of Moab led an
> attempt of seven hundred swordsmen to break through to the king of
> Edom; but they failed. So he took his firstborn son, who was to succeed
> him as king, and offered him up on the wall as a burnt offering.

In this he was preceded by Ph. Derchain, [81] and followed by Margalit. [82] But it is worth noting the Rabbinic view (Kimhi, Gersonides,
Abarbanel) according to which the Biblical passage means that Mesha
sacrificed, not his own son, but the son of the king of Edom whom he
had previously captured; this would justify the prophetic condemnation of Moab as the one who "burned the bones of the king of Edom
to lime" (Amos 2:1). [83] The resultant "great wrath ... upon Israel" (II
Kings 3:27b) has also been variously interpreted and attributed. [84]

Finally, Spalinger had called attention to a possible Egyptian cognate, *htp(w)*. This word occurs in the "cuneiform vocabulary of Egyptian words" from El Amarna first published in 1925 by S. Smith and
C.J. Gadd. [85], and now numbered EA 368 by A.F. Rainey. [86] This
lexical text has been described by P. Artzi as a "practical vocabulary" [87] dealing (in lines 5-11) with "the (royal) house and its furni-
ture." [88] In line 11, Egyptian *ha-tà*(DA)-*pu* is equated with Sumerian
giš-banšur, "table." An offering table may well be implied. [89]

To the extent that these parallels, both Egyptian and Biblical, truly
illustrate a situation as described in the Ugaritic prayer, they may be
said to lend support to Margalit's reading of the latter text. But its
context, both the wider one and the immediate one, militates against
the emendation. The rest of the text deals in ordinary, rather than
extraordinary sacrifices, and even the poem which concludes the text
concerns the not overly uncommon contingency of a siege. Moreover

---

[80] BAR 13/2 (1987) 60f.
[81] Derchain 1970.
[82] Margalit 1981; 1986.
[83] Cf. Cogan and Tadmor 1988:47f.; Bradley Aaronson, BAR 16/3 (1990) 62, 67.
[84] Cogan and Tadmor 1988:47f.; J.J.M. Roberts in Finkelstein AV (1977) 184f.,
n. 25.
[85] Smith and Gadd 1925.
[86] Rainey 1970:34f.
[87] RAI 30 (1986) 211.
[88] Artzi 1990:141f.
[89] Cf. von Soden, AHw s.v. *paššuru* (3), PSD B s.v. *banšur* (2.1), and above, ch. III
2.

the strict parallelism of the verbs suggests a rough equivalence of the first image with the third and of the second with the fourth, as in Sasson's paraphrase (above), not of the first with the second and the third with the fourth as in Margalit's translation.   One does not "pay" a son as one would a vow, yet that is the sense of *ml'* in the second and fourth images, comparable to Hebrew *šlm* used of paying vows. And if the " firstborn" of the third image is parallel to the "bull" of the first, then it is a firstling of the flock more likely than of a human being.   Finally, moving from bull to vow to (first-born) son, the fifth image would be anticlimactic, even if we understood it, with Margalit, as "a tenth (of our wealth)." Thus it is not surprising that the consensus of Ugaritic scholarship accepts the reading *ḥtp* and the comparison with Akkadian *ḥiṭpu*.

One question that has barely been addressed in all these discussions is the phonemic one. Only Margalit pointed out that "attempts to interpret Ugaritic Ḥ-T-P as the equivalent of Akkadian H-T-P are highly improbable on purely phonological grounds," [90] and Xella noted the difficulties involved. [91] These difficulties may be stated simply.   Normally, Ugaritic (and proto-Semitic) Ḫ is reflected by Akkadian H, while Ugaritic Ḥ is reflected by Akkadian zero or, more precisely, by an Ablaut *e* for original *a* and, in Assyrian, also for original *i*. This is particularly evident in initial position. So, for example, Ugaritic *ḥdw* corresponds to Akkadian *hadû*, "to rejoice," while Ugaritic *ḥbr* corresponds to Akkadian *ibru* (Assyrian *ebru*), "friend." But there are also occasionally examples of a correspondence between Ugaritic Ḥ and Akkadian H, as in *ḥwš* for *hiāšu*, "hurry," or in *rḥṣ*, "wash" for *rahāṣu*, " flood." [92] In the case of *ḥkm* for *hakāmu* and *ḥrm* for *harāmu*, the possibility of Amorite influence has been suggested. [93] There is also the possibility of a late or learned loan-word from West Semitic into Akkadian. The existence of an Akkadian root *hatāpu* in Old Babylonian texts from Elam makes this a less likely solution.

A subsidiary question is that of the second root letter. Several Semitic languages have a root *ḥtp* with a meaning close to that of *ḥṭp*. If the root with emphatic dental is original, the loss of this emphatic

---

[90] Margalit 1986:76, n.3; cf. 1981:76f. and 83, n. 4.

[91] Xella 1978:135. Cf. now also Tropper 1995 who, however, does not include *ḥiṭpu* among more than forty examples of proto-Semitic Ḫ realized as Akkadian H.

[92] P. Fronzaroli, *La Fonetica Ugaritica* (1955) 18; M. Held, JBL 84 (1967) 277, n. 26; refs. courtesy M.S. Smith.

[93] W.G. Lambert in Haas 1992:138; cf. Stern 1991 ch. 1.

may represent a special case of "Geer's Law," according to which Akkadian and, to some extent, other Semitic languages do not tolerate two emphatics in one root.[94] All in all, the existence of a Ugaritic *ḥṭp*, and its possible relationship to (late) Akkadian *hiṭpu*, remain somewhat uncertain.

With that we return to our main theme and repeat that all efforts to find a pre-Israelite origin for the seven-day week have remained fruitless. On the other hand the growth of the sabbatical idea has been enormous, first within Judaism and then beyond. As a basic ideology of periodic rest, it extended beyond the week to the sabbatical year and the jubilee, and beyond Israel to most of the world.

Bibliographical References

Andreasen, N.-E. A, 1972: *Rest and Redemption : a Study of the Biblical Sabbath* (Berrien Springs, MI, Andrews U.P.).

Artzi, Pinhas, 1990: "Studies in the library of the Amarna archive," Artzi AV 139-156.

Avishur, Yitzhak, 1978-79: "Prayer to Baal," *Shnaton* 3:254-262 (in Hebrew, English summary pp. xxvf.).

Cassuto, Umberto, 1961: *A Commentary on the Book of Genesis Part One: From Adam to Noah* (tr. from the Hebrew ed. of 1944) (Jerusalem, Magnes Press).

Cogan, Mordechai and Hayim Tadmor, 1988: *II Kings* (= AB 11).

Cooper, Jerrold S., 1983: *The Curse of Agade* (= The Johns Hopkins Near Eastern Studies [13]).

De Moor, J.C., 1983: "Enkele liturgische teksten uit Ugarit," in K.R. Veenhof, ed., *Schrijvend Verleden* (Leiden, Ex Oriente Lux) 247-252.

Derchain, Ph., 1970: "Les plus anciens témoignages de sacrifices d'enfants chez les Sémites occidentaux," VT 20:351-355.

Dietrich, Manfried, 1989: "Das Einsetzungsritual der Entu von Emar," UF 21:47-100.

Ferrara, A.J., 1973: *Nanna-Suen's Journey to Nippur* (StPSM 2).

Finkelstein, Jacob J., 1958: "Bible and Babel," *Commentary Magazine* 26: 431-444.

Fishbane, Michael A., 1984: *Biblical Interpretation in Ancient Israel* (Oxford, Clarendon Press).

Fleming, Daniel E., 1992: *The Installation of Baal's High Priestess at Emar: a Window on Ancient Syrian Religion* (= HSS 42).

Frayne, Douglas R., 1981: *The Historical Correlations of the Sumerian Royal Hymns* (Ann Arbor, University Microfilms).

Geers, Frederick W., 1945: "The treatment of emphatics in Akkadian," JNES 4:65-67.

Greenspahn, Frederik E., ed., 1991: *Essential Papers on Israel and the Ancient Near East* (New York/London, New York University Press).

Haas, Volkert, ed., 1992: *Aussenreiter und Randgruppen: Beiträge zu einer Sozialgeschicchte des Alten Orients* (= Xenia 32).

---

[94] Geers 1945; Knudsen 1961.

Hallo, William W., 1977: "New moons and sabbaths: a case-study in the contrastive approach," HUCA 48:1-18. Reprinted in Greenspahn 1991: 313-332.

———, 1991: "Information from before the flood: antediluvian notes from Babylonia and Israel," *Maarav* 7 (Gevirtz AV) 173-181.

Herdner, A., 1972: "Une prière à Baal des Ugaritains en danger," CRAIBL 1972:693-703.

———, 1978: "Nouveaux textes alphabétiques de Ras Shamra," *Ugaritica* 7:31-39.

Hurowitz, Victor (Avigdor), 1992: *I Have Built You an Exalted House: Temple Building in the Bible in Light of Mesopotamian and Northwest Semitic Writings* (= JSOTS 115).

Kingsbury, Edwin C., 1963: "A seven day ritual in the Old Babylonian cult at Larsa," HUCA 34:1-34.

Knudsen, Ebbe E., 1961: "Cases of free variants in the Akkadian *q* phoneme," JCS 15:84-90.

Lemaire, A., 1973: "Le Sabbat à l'époque royale israélite," RB 80:161-185.

Margalit, Baruch, 1981: "A Ugaritic prayer for a city under siege," PWCJS 7:63-83 (in Hebrew).

———, 1986: "Why King Mesha of Moab sacrificed his oldest son," BAR 12/6:62-64, 76.

Rainey, Anson F., 1970: *El Amarna Tablets 359-379* (= AOAT 8).

Sauren, Herbert, 1975: "Die Einweihung des Eninnu," RAI 20:95-103.

Smith, Sidney and Cyril J. Gadd, 1925: "A cuneiform vocabulary of Egyptian words," JEA 11:230-239.

Spalinger, Anthony J., 1978: "A Canaanite ritual found in Egyptian reliefs," *Society for the Study of Egyptian Antiquities* 8:47-60.

Stager, Lawrence E., 1985: "Merenptah, Israel and Sea Peoples: new light on an old relief," *Eretz-Israel* 18:56*-64*.

Stern, Philip D., 1991: *The Biblical* Herem (= Brown Judaic Studies 211).

Tropper, Josef, 1995: "Akkadisch *nuḫḫutu* und die Repräsentierung des Phonems /ḥ/ im Akkadischen," ZA 85:58-66.

Tur-Sinai, N.H., 1951: "I. Der angebliche babylonische Ursprung des biblischen Sabbat. II. Hamushtu. III. Shapattu und Sabbat," Bi.Or. 8:14-24.

Xella, Paolo, 1978: Un testo ugaritico recente (RS 24.266, Verso, 9-19) e il 'sacrificio dei primi nati'," RSF 6:127-136.

———, 1981: *I Testi Rituali di Ugarit I* (= Studi Semitici 54).

Yurco, Frank J., 1990: " 3200-year-old picture of Israelites found in Egypt," BAR 16/5:20-38.

3. THE ERA

Let us pause a moment to review the two basic kinds of calendar features which we have delineated. On the one hand there are the natural divisions of time, notably the day, the month, and the year, i.e., those dictated by the rhythms of nature. Since these rhythms are identical the world around, they are likely to have inspired very similar time divisions everywhere on earth. Such similarities, then, are poor indicators of cultural borrowing.

On the other hand there are the artificial divisions of time, notably the hour and its subdivisions, and the week. We have seen that these conventions began in the Near East and spread from there around the globe. But they are not alone in this regard. For practical purposes the largest calendaric unit of all is the era, and this is definitely in the artificial category. In two previous studies, I have traced the history of this institution, indicating first what earlier systems of dating it replaced [95] and then how the specific system still in use today came to replace these earlier systems. [96] Let me review the evidence assembled in those articles while adding some new insights achieved in the relatively short time span since they appeared.

First we need a working definition of the era. I use the term to describe a convention whereby the designations of successive years are, by common consent, arranged in sequence. The convention in almost universal use today is the Christian Era, or "Common Era," in which each successive year is assigned a consecutive number according to its putative distance from the birth of Jesus Christ, i.e., *ab anno domini* , or A.D. Retroactively, years before this event are similarly designated as dating so many years "before Christ" (B.C.) or "before the Common Era" (B.C.E.).

It is now generally argued that the event itself took place in or shortly before 4. B.C., since it is said to have occurred in the reign of Herod the Great, who died in that year, a year marked by an eclipse of the moon. The discrepancy can be explained by the relatively late date at which the Christian Era was introduced. It was not until the early sixth century that a Syrian monk, Dionysius Exiguus, calculated the date of the birth of Jesus—and erred slightly in his calculations.

---

[95] Hallo 1984-85.
[96] Hallo 1988; previously Hallo 1983.

But that detail is of no concern from a calendaric point of view; it is the putative date of Christ's birth that serves as the "epoch" or starting point of the era based on it.

The system is of such obvious utility and such consummate simplicity that it directly inspired, in short order, the Islamic era of the seventh century of our era, and the Jewish era first attested in texts and tombstones of the eighth and ninth centuries. Between them, these three eras have by now conquered most of the world. We enjoy their convenience without normally giving a thought to what life would be like without them—or what it may have been like before they were invented. For there certainly was such a time! For thousands of years, humanity made do with a variety of systems which changed, not only with each reign or administration, but with each city or state. Elaborate lists were required to calculate the distance from one year date to another, and to correlate contemporary year dates in different polities. What were some of these earlier, and more cumbersome, systems?

The earliest system, first known from Egypt since the very beginning of its historic period, was that of naming each year, or every other year, by royal decree according to an outstanding event of the preceding year, or biennium, and then compiling long lists of these names for reference. The system was adopted in Mesopotamia only toward the very end of the Early Dynastic Period, in the 24th century B.C. By then it was being replaced in Egypt by an annual cattle-census which served indirectly as a count of the regnal years of each pharaoh.

A second system was that of naming each year after an individual, usually a high official, either in an order determined by lot or according to a predetermined sequence. Such a system was in use in Assyria from the beginning of the second millennium on, and in Greece during its classical phase. The official who gave his name to the year, as well as the year named after him, was called *limu* in Akkadian and eponym in Greek, the Greek term often being applied to the Assyrian phenomenon as well. Lists of eponyms provided means of counting the intervals between given years; some of the lists added brief designations of the main event(s) of the year in the manner of the Babylonian year names. Recent progress in the publication of the archives from Mari have added significantly to the oldest lists of Assyrian eponyms. [97]

Cumbersome though they appear to us, both of these older systems of year-names provide an inestimable fringe-benefit for the modern historian: a running record of the important events of each year in the estimation of the contemporaries.

It was only gradually that a third system was devised which dispensed with year names altogether and resorted instead to what appears to us as an obvious and practical scheme: numbering the years. There were brief experiments in this direction in the third millennium at Lagash under its first Dynasty and at Umma in the Sargonic Period, [98] and again in the 18th century under Rim-Sin of Larsa and Hammurapi of Babylon, [99] but the older system of year-names persisted into the beginnings of Kassite rule and the Middle Babylonian period. It was not until the history of Babylonia had run half its course that it occurred to one of its Kassite kings, probably Kadashman-Enlil I or Burnaburiash II early in the fourteenth century, to number the years of his reign from his accession on. [100] The new system had a limited appeal, however, since each king began a new era with his own accession, and each dynasty dated by its own rulers. It also sacrificed the historical information enshrined in the older year-name system.

The first efforts to devise a more universal system of dating had to wait another millennium, and the impulse may have come from the world of learning rather than from any direct royal initiative. In particular, it was astronomy that demanded a more continuous and less cumbersome system of counting years for its calculations of long-term trends and of foreseeable astronomical phenomena such as eclipses. Babylonian astronomy made great progress in the first millennium, and this progress depended less on observation than on calculation. [101] These calculations were made possible by the superb tradition of Babylonian mathematics which in turn rested on a convenient system of written number symbols and the use of the eminently serviceable base sixty. The Greek achievement in mathematical astronomy is associated with the likes of Hipparchus (ca. 181-126 B.C.) and other figures of the Hellenistic period as summarized and preserved

---

[97] Birot 1985; Veenhof 1985.
[98] Foster 1982: 2-7.
[99] Hallo 1988:177 and n. 22.
[100] Brinkman 1976:402.
[101] Rochberg-Halton 1991.

in Ptolemy (ca. A.D. 100-178); it is the direct heir of the Babylonian legacy. [102]

The late Babylonian priest Berossos (ca. 350-275 B.C.), writing in Greek for Antiochus I (281-261 B.C.) and a Hellenistic audience, attributed the beginnings of the new astronomy and historiography to an otherwise undistinguished Babylonian king Nabonassar (Nabunasir), who came to the throne in 747 B.C., and Ptolemy himself operated with a "Nabonassar Era" beginning in that year. [103] It is conceivable that such an era was merely a construct designed to facilitate Ptolemy's own calculations, for it was quite customary to project the "epochs" or starting dates of Hellenistic eras far into the past, in particular, it seems, into the 8th century B.C., as was the case, for example, with the Olympic Era and the Era of the Founding of Rome (*ab urbe condita*), both constructs of the 3rd century B.C.—a coincidence not, perhaps, entirely due to chance.[104]

Alternatively, however, it is not entirely excluded that Ptolemy preserved an authentic tradition. Nabonassar's accession seems to have been marked by upheavals both terrestrial and celestial, [105] including as it now appears an eclipse, [106] and inspired by these or other portents, he may have introduced, or attempted to introduce, a new era of dating by numbered years independent of any single reign and intended to embrace, at a minimum, all the rulers of Babylon who succeeded him. For according to Berossos, he collected together the records of the kings before him and either destroyed or hid or simply summarized them "in order that the list of Chaldean kings might begin with him." And we can argue that he, or the astronomers of his court, introduced numerous other calendaric and historiographic innovations. These probably included the so-called Metonic cycle of seven intercalations of an entire month in nineteen years. It was intended to reconcile the luni-solar calendar with the progression of the seasons, and was traditionally credited to the Athenian Meton late in the fifth century. But the principle was clearly recognized in Babylo-

---

[102] Neugebauer 1962, ch. 6; Toomer 1988.

[103] Burstein 1978.

[104] But cf. W. Burkert, Homo Necans (1983) 94: "It is probably just chance that the list of [Olympic] victors begins in the year 776, for it was about then that the Greek alphabet was introduced."

[105] Hallo 1988:186.

[106] Rochberg-Halton 1991a:324f.; Beaulieu and Britton 1994:79.

nia well before that, and Meton's debt to Babylonian precedent is
now harder than ever to deny. [107]

Nabonassar may also have been responsible for two compilations
which appear to end precisely with his accession in 747, the "Chronicle of Market Prices" and the "Synchronistic History," and he may
have inaugurated four others which began with it. These are the
semi-annual "astronomical diaries," the "Babylonian Chronicle," the
"Dynastic Prophecy" and the Uruk King List. [108] It is less certain that
this was true also of a fifth one, the " 18-year cycle texts," also known
as the "Saros texts," but these have meantime also received renewed
attention, with Rochberg-Halton [109] and other experts now inclined
to trace them back to Nabonassar. [110] As to whether the diaries were
meant to serve as the "data base" for a new omen corpus, as I have
long held, the experts differ. [111] Aaboe agrees that "The diaries can
be viewed as collections of raw materials for omens," [112] while
Rochberg-Halton sees " no evidence that the intent was to produce a
new compendium of celestial omens based on the updated observations of phenomena." [113]

We have long known of the document described in modern terms
as a "Synchronistic History," since it correlates the major events of
Babylonian and Assyrian history during the long centuries when
those two kingdoms existed side by side. The document has sometimes been compared to the Biblical Book of Kings, which includes
the complicated history of the Divided Monarchy, carefully dating
the accession of each king of Israel by the reign of his contemporary
in Judah, and vice versa. Within cuneiform literature, the document
has been compared to the well attested genre of chronicles, since it
summarizes and dates events in typical chronographic fashion. Its
most recent edition, in fact, is in A.K. Grayson's volume on "Assyrian

---

[107] Bowen and Goldstein 1988; Toomer 1988:353.

[108] Hallo 1988:187-189.

[109] Rochberg-Halton 1991a:324, but correct "Nabonassar year 7 (-548)" to
"Nabonidus year 7" and "The text is preserved only from year 7 of Nabonassar, but
Kugler has suggested that the list could have begun with the first year of the reign"
to "The text is preserved only from year 7 of Nabonidus but Kugler has suggested
that the list could have begun with the first year of the reign of Nabonassar."

[110] Beaulieu and Britton 1994; cf. Bowen and Goldstein 1988:50 and n. 52.

[111] Hallo 1983:16; 1988:188.

[112] CAH (2nd ed.) III/2 (1991) 278.

[113] Rochberg-Halton 1991a:330.

and Babylonian Chronicles," where it appears as Chronicle 21. Grayson, like earlier interpreters, regarded the composition as thoroughly biased history, biased, that is, in favor of Assyria, which seemed to get the best of Babylonia in every encounter even when other sources cast doubt on such an outcome. He was therefore sure that the document emanated from an Assyrian source, presumably an Assyrian court. [114]

A new study of the evidence by J.A. Brinkman permits a more nuanced assessment. He finds enough traces of Babylonian triumphs, or of Assyrian failures, to allow for the possibility of several sources, at least some of which could be Babylonian. In addition he notes that the record stops with Nabonassar's immediate predecessor, himself emerging gradually from obscurity. [115] I would therefore be prepared to take matters one step further and suggest that the Synchronistic History, or one of its sources, is yet one more effort by the scribes of Nabonassar's court to sum up all previous history, and one more possible argument for the reality of a Nabonassar Era.

But whether the Nabonassar Era was a creation of Nabonassar or of Hipparchus or of Ptolemy is not crucial to our purpose for, in any case, it was not directly ancestral to our own. That distinction belongs rather to the Seleucid Era, another product of the 3rd century B.C. It reflects a true blending of Greek and Near Eastern elements. So appealing was its simplicity that it crossed borders of space and time and was widely adopted for centuries, and in parts of the Near East continued in use to our own day. And yet it started as just another regnal year system for just another single dynasty. How then did it achieve its wide appeal?

The answer seems to be that the Seleucid Era began more by accident than by design. Certainly it did not begin in 312 B.C. when Seleucus I captured Babylon from his rival, though that was later made into its epoch, or starting date. Nor did it begin to serve as an era in 304, when the first cuneiform texts from Babylonia were dated to his reign, by then in its eighth year. [116] Rather, we may reconstruct the following scenario. [117]

---

[114] Grayson 1975:50-56.

[115] Brinkman 1990; 1990a:74f.

[116] Hallo 1984-85:145 and n. 21; see now McEwan 1985 (appeared 1986); for a text dated just nine days later (I/12) see now Beaulieu 1994:73 *sub* 11545.

[117] Hallo, 1984-85; cf. now also van der Spek 1992.

The Seleucid rulers of Mesopotamia, like some of their contemporary Greek dynasts elsewhere in the Near East, favored dynastic royal names, with every king called Seleucus or Antiochus, or Ptolemy in Egypt or Mithridates in Pontus or Attalus in Pergamon. A cognomen or second name served to distinguish the successive bearers of these dynastic names. In addition, it became customary for each of these rulers to associate a designated successor, usually a son, with them as co-regents in their lifetime, no doubt in hopes of securing a smooth succession upon their own demise. Such co-regencies had been in use in the Near East in previous dynasties, but never so systematically.

Whether one or both of these factors contributed to the development is not clear, but it appears that Seleucus I died in his 31st year (281 B.C.) and his son Antiochus I succeeded him as sole ruler (or as co-regent with his son) after a co-regency of 12 years (292-281). At that point, instead of calling the year either his 13th or his first, he chose instead to call it the 31st of Antiochus and *his* son Seleucus—or authorized his scribes to do so. [118] When his successors followed his example, the way was finally cleared for replacing regnal years with dynastic years.

The Seleucid Empire fell on hard times before long, and by the first century B.C. bowed to the superior might of Rome. But its dating system expanded even as its own borders contracted, perhaps even because of that, and it survived the fall of the whole house of Seleucus to become widely accepted in the Greek-speaking parts of the Near East, where it generally became known as the "Era of the Greeks." As such it provided the model for the Christian, Moslem and Jewish Eras another millennium later. The origins of one of the most practical calendar conventions of the modern world can thus be traced back to the dynastic politics of the Greek rulers of Mesopotamia. But if the mysteries of these origins are thereby cleared up, it remains a bigger mystery why it took so long for such a useful innovation to emerge.

---

[118] On the question of Antiochus' co-regent(s) see Hallo 1984-85:146 with nn. 34f.; Renger 1985:258 and n. 9.

Bibliographical References

Beaulieu, Paul-Alain, 1994: *Late Babylonian Texts in the Nies Babylonian Collection* (= Catalogue of the Babylonian Collections at Yale 1) (Bethesda, CDL Press).

——— and J.P. Britten, " Rituals for an eclipse possibility in the 8th year of Cyprus," JCS 46:73-86.

Birot, Maurice, 1985: "Les chroniques 'assyriennes' de Mari," M.A.R.I. 4:219-242.

Bowen, Alan C. and Bernard R. Goldstein, 1988: "Meton of Athens and astronomy in the late fifth century B.C.," Sachs AV 39-81.

Brinkman, John A., 1976: *Materials and Studies for Kassite History, vol. I* (Chicago, Oriental Institute of the University of Chicago).

———, 1990: Political covenants, treaties, and loyalty oaths in Babylonia and between Assyria and Babylonia," in Canfora et al., 1990:81-112.

———, 1990a: "The Babylonian Chronicle Revisited," Moran AV 73-104.

Burstein, Stanley M., 1978: "The *Babyloniaca* of Berossus," SANE 1:141-181.

Canfora, Luciano *et al.*, eds., 1990: *I trattati nel mondo antico. Forma, ideologia, funzione* (Rome, "L'Erma" di Brettschneider).

Foster, Benjamin R., 1982: *Umma in the Sargonic Period* (= MCAAS 20) (Hamden, CT, Archon Books).

Grayson, A.K., 1975: *Assyrian and Babylonian Chronicles* (= TCS 5).

Hallo, William W., 1983: "Dating the Mesopotamian past: the concept of eras from Sargon to Nabonassar," *Bulletin of the Society for Mesopotamian Studies* 6:7-18.

———, 1984-85: "The concept of eras from Nabonassar to Seleucus," JANES 16-17:143-151.

———, 1988: "The Nabonassar Era and other epochs in Mesopotamian chronology and chronography," Sachs AV 175-190.

McEwan, G.J.P., 1985: "The first Seleucid document from Babylonia," JCS 30:169-180.

Neugebauer, Otto, 1962: *The Exact Sciences in Antiquity* (New York, Harper & Brothers).

Renger, Johannes, 1985: "Ein seleukidischer Ehrentitel in keilschriftlicher Überlieferung," Or. 54:257-259.

Rochberg-Halton, Francesca, 1991: "Between observation and theory in Babylonian astronomical texts," JNES 50:107-120.

———, 1991a: "The Babylonian Astronomical Diaries," JAOS 111:323-332.

Toomer, G.J., 1988: "Hipparchus and Babylonian astronomy," Sachs AV 353-362.

Van der Spek, R.J., 1992: review of Hammond, *The Macedonian State* in BiOr 49:286-289.

Veenhof, Klaas R., 1985: "Eponyms of the 'later old Assyrian period' and Mari chronology," M.A.R.I. 4:191-218.

CHAPTER FIVE

LITERATURE

1. Creativity, Genre and Canon

As with the calendar, there are two kinds of issues at stake here. We cannot simply trace the modern Western concept of literature back to the ancient Near East, for the creative impulse is well-nigh universal. All cultures seem to find ways to record their impressions of the world about them in verbal form, whether oral or written. Yet there are certain conventions of the literary process that are not universal but particular to given cultures, and some of these show a remarkable degree of continuity. One of these is the question of authorship. [1]

In the usual sense of the modern word, authorship is by no means as universal as might at first seem to be the case. Modern readers expect to attribute every piece of literature to a given author or, to put it another way, to consider it the creation—indeed the intellectual property—of a given author, and they are prepared to pay the author accordingly. But in many cultures, authorship in this sense is irrelevant. It may be attributed to a fictitious person, or to a figure out of the remote past, whether historical or legendary, or it may be waived in favor of anonymity. The literary work may be considered the property, not of an author, but rather of the performer who recites it, or of the scribe who copies it, or of the patron who commissioned it, and they may be rewarded accordingly. The very word author (Latin *auctor*) may carry with it overtones of authority (Latin *auctoritas*)—both derived from the same root—and such authority (and authenticity) may be thought better conveyed by a pseudonymous or pseudepigraphic attribution, i.e., to a fictitious author or to a real person other than the author respectively, than by one to the actual but obscure creator.

It is thus, for example, that the earliest Egyptian literature is attributed to Im-hotep, the wise man of the Old Kingdom who was also

---

[1] For an early and programmatic discussion of creativity and canonization in cuneiform see Hallo 1962.

credited with designing the great pyramid of Djoser and otherwise so distinguishing himself that he was eventually assigned divine status. Similar attributions are known from ancient Mesopotamia, where Enki, the Sumerian god of wisdom, or his Akkadian counterpart Ea, is regarded as author of such works of literature as the astrological omen series *enuma Anu Enlil*. [2] In another tradition, the same omen corpus is identified with Oannes-Adapa, the first of the seven wise *apkallu*'s, semi-divine beings from before the Flood who brought culture to Sumer. [3] In Rabbinic tradition, similarly, Enoch is identified with Oannes-Adapa and endowed with special wisdom.[4]

But Mesopotamia also presents us with examples of authorship in the modern sense of the term, though not in the manner of the modern title-page. The ancient Mesopotamian equivalent of the title-page comes at the end of a literary text; it is generally referred to as a "colophon" on the basis of the comparable Greek phenomenon, which in turn took its name from the Greek colony of Colophon on the Eastern shore of the Aegean. In Mesopotamia it furnishes, at various periods, one or more of the following particulars: the title of the composition, its length, its position in a larger sequence of compositions, the name of the scribe who made the copy, the date when he made it, the source of the copy, the name of the patron who commissioned the copy, and a prayer for its safe preservation—everything, in short, but the name of the author! [5] Instead, that information has to be gleaned, if it is available at all, from other sources. Such sources are of three kinds, two extrinsic to the text, the other intrinsic.

The first two are by far the commoner sources of our information. Sometimes the detective work of modern archaeology and philology may combine to suggest the likely scribe—and hence, on occasion, author—of literary compositions found in a given house. More often, our evidence consists of lists of literary compositions with the authors to whom they are attributed. These have been recovered and studied by W.G.Lambert in particular. [6] Of interest is the fact that authorship in these catalogues is indicated by the phrase "of the mouth of NN,"

---

[2] Cf. in general Kramer and Maier 1989:18, 195, and the review article by Hallo, in press.

[3] Hallo 1963:176 and nn. 79-85; 1977:4 and n. 9. In the meantime van Dijk 1980:20 *ad* no. 90 has also come around to this point of view.

[4] Wacholder 1963.

[5] Leichty 1964; Hunger 1968.

[6] Lambert 1957, 1962, 1976.

while the phrase "hand of NN" in the colophons identifies the scribe who made a given copy.

More complex, and in some ways more interesting, are the rarer indications of authorship incorporated in the texts themselves. Sometimes they are implicit, as in the genre of literary autobiography, that is to say of first-person accounts. I refer here not to royal inscriptions, which are historical rather than literary in character, and which were composed for the king by his court scribes as was no doubt obvious to all who read or rather heard them. In literary autobiography, by contrast, the fiction that the subject was the author may have carried some conviction. In Sumerian we may cite such examples as royal hymns by King Shulgi of Ur in which he details his educational and other attainments, insisting on his personal authorship of the songs in his honor. [7] In Akkadian there is a long tradition of fictional autobiography, from the self-same Shulgi to Adad-guppi, queen-mother of Nabonidus, the last Babylonian king. [8]

Even where the intrinsic indications of authorship are explicit, they may be concealed rather than revealed in the body of the text. This is the case with the so-called "Babylonian Theodicy," a "wisdom" text so forthright in its challenge to conventional morality that its author felt constrained to defend himself as " (loyal) servant of god and king" and to hide his name, together with this disclaimer, in an acrostic. [9] A similar precaution is displayed by two short prayers on a single tablet, but here the name of the author (or suppliant?) is revealed in the body of each prayer as well. [10] Acrostics are messages contained or concealed within the initial (and, in the preceding case, also the final) syllables of the successive lines or stanzas of a poem; they are attested in first millennium texts in Akkadian and Egyptian and, in the form of alphabetic acrostics, in Biblical Hebrew; in post-Biblical Hebrew, they are also frequently employed to indicate authorship or for other purposes. [11]

In the Bible, all the "literary prophets," from Amos and Hoseah to Haggai, Zechariah and Malachi, may be said to be the avowed authors of the prophetic books that bear their names. And in the

[7] Castellino 1972:51 line 197; 251, lines 35-39; Jacobsen 1982.
[8] Longman 1991.
[9] Lambert 1960: ch. 3.
[10] Sweet 1969; latest translation by Foster, BM 2:620f.
[11] Brug 1990.

case of Jeremiah, the text informs us in addition of the name of his scribe, Baruch son of Neriyah, and the circumstances under which he copied and recopied the prophet's words. That very Baruch, along with Jerahmeel the king's son who is also mentioned in the autobiographical portions of the book, have become substantially more palpable figures by the discovery—albeit in unprovenanced context—of seal impressions of both men. [12]

In cuneiform literature, only a few compositions incorporate an intrinsic indication of authorship that is at once explicit and overt. By far the earliest example, indeed the earliest case of non-anonymous authorship in all of world literature, is represented by the princess Enheduanna and some of her female successors, of whom more below. [13] Here I only wish to call attention to the epic of the deity of pestilence or scorched earth called Erra. [14] According to its own denouement, the text of this epic was vouchsafed to one Kabti-ilani-Marduk in a dream and set down by him upon awaking without so much as a word added to or subtracted from his nocturnal revelation or inspiration. Whether this represents a claim to authorship or on the contrary its denial remains open to question. A "third work of Babylonian literature that bears its author's name" is the Gula hymn of Bullutsa-rabi. [15] There is also the possibility that the great wisdom composition known by its incipit as *Ludlul bel nemeqi*, "let me praise the lord of wisdom," is the work of Shubshi-meshre-Shakkan, who appears in it in the first person. [16]

Thus authorship seems to have played no more than a marginal role in Mesopotamian literature. Much the same could be said about other cuneiform literatures. In Hittite, certain rituals are ascribed to authors, both male and female, but mainly, it seems, to enhance their fame and efficacy. Such is, for example, the case of the ritual of Anniwiyanni against impotence. [17] In Ugaritic, where the corpus of literary compositions is more limited, the sole bibliographic indications are the occasional laconic superscripts of the form L'QHT, literally

---

[12] Avigad 1978, 1979. Cf. below, ch. VIII 3 p. 268.
[13] Ch. VIII 3.
[14] Latest translations by Foster BM 2:771-805, FDD 132-163.
[15] Lambert 1967:107; latest translations by Foster, BM 2:491-499, FDD 229-237.
[16] Latest translations by Foster, BM 1:308-325, FDD 298-316; for the personal name see O.R. Gurney, RA 80 (1986) 190.
[17] See below, ch. VIII 3, n. 123.

"to (or for) Aqhat." But so far from ascribing the composition that follows to an author named Aqhat, the clear intention is to *describe* it as being *about* Aqhat. This usage raises problems for the Biblical Psalter, whose frequent superscripts of the form LDWD, LShLMH, L'SPh and so forth have usually been translated as "by David, Solomon, Asaf" etc., but which may need to be understood, at least in some instances, as "about David, Solomon" etc.

The reason for all this marginality of value placed on authorship can be sought in a related phenomenon: the relatively low esteem accorded to originality. Contrary to ourselves, ancient readers or audiences—perhaps because they were typically audiences—seem to have prized adherence to familiar norms far above originality. Or, to put it another way, originality had to be achieved by new and possibly minor variations within familiar norms. The few exceptions to this rule strike us as the random musings of a bored scribe, or the disjointed doodles of an inattentive pupil—for example the unique exemplar of the composition which Martha Roth has edited under the title of "The Slave and the Scoundrel." [18]

Even parody, which among other humorous categories is relatively well represented in cuneiform literature, makes its point by lampooning traditional literary conventions but has to do so precisely by following, or seeming to follow, those norms. [19] (It may be well, in this connection, to remember that the Greek term *par-ode* derives from *ode*, "song," like other discrete literary genres such as tragedy, comedy, threnody and rhapsody, and like melody and prosody with which it also shares a common root.) A possible example is "The Hymn to the Pickaxe (or Hoe)," whose popularity can be argued by the numerous duplicate exemplars and multiple provenances in which it is attested. It is such a mixture of serious and frivolous passages that modern interpreters have assigned it to a variety of genres.

A clearer example of parody is "The Message of Lu-dingirra to his Mother," which constitutes a *reductio ad absurdum* of the genre of literary letter or letter-prayer, expanding the elaborate salutations of the genre until they occupy nearly the entire text, and reducing the message proper to a meaningless single concluding line: "Your beloved

---

[18] Roth 1983; for a new rendering see Alster 1992.

[19] Foster 1974. For additions to the dossier of humorous texts, see below, ch. V 3 and Scurlock 1993.

son Lu-dingirra greets you!" [20] A Biblical analogy of sorts is the Book of Jonah, cast in the traditional genre of prophecy, though it basically has no prophetic message, instead ending in a one-line anticlimax about "Nineveh, that great city, in which dwell more than 120,000 souls who know not their right hand form their left, and also much cattle." [21]

In saying this, we have inevitably identified one of the principal vehicles for the transmission of and adherence to literary norms in cuneiform, namely genre. The importance of genre was recognized early in the study of Mesopotamia literature, because Akkadian and especially Sumerian or bilingual compositions very often carried their own generic labels; eventually whole catalogues of literary catalogues were discovered which grouped compositions by genre. [22] And these genres were not merely the broad, vague categories familiar in modern prose, such as the novel, novella, essay or biography. Rather they were more akin to the precise categories of poetry, such as epic, lyric, ode or sonnet, and shared with these the double determination of form and function.

It was in fact the discovery of cuneiform genres that led to a modern revolution in Biblical scholarship by Hermann Gunkel and others. They developed a method of genre research (Gattungsforschung) which initially served as a key to the Hebrew Psalter, and subsequently inspired a school of "form criticism" that extended to the entire Biblical corpus. [23] Ironically, the same methodology was largely neglected in cuneiform studies for the better part of a century. Only recently have the virtues of this approach been recognized there. [24] Such native categories as laments (*balag, ér-šèm-ma*), royal hymns (*adab, tigi*), antiphonal (love-)songs (*bal-bal-e*), disputations (*a-da-man-du₁₁-ga*) or even proverbs and riddles (*i-bi-lu-du₁₁-ga*) have yielded up their secrets precisely because they have been studied as variations within predetermined generic norms. [25]

But if there was adherence to these norms, that is not to imply that

---

[20] Civil 1964; for analogies of the composition to the Biblical Song of Songs see Cooper 1971.

[21] Orth 1990; Trible 1994.

[22] See the examples listed by Hallo 1975 and add van Dijk 1989; J.A. Black, AfO 36-7 (1989-90) 125 (noting 9 fragments of *ér-šèm-ma* catalogues).

[23] Hallo 1968:71-73. For a recent survey see Tucker 1971.

[24] See especially e.g. Vanstiphout 1986.

[25] Cf. also the disputations, for which see below, ch. V 3.

it was slavish or blind. There was no "gattungsgesetzliche Polizei" to enforce it. [26] In the millennial course of literary history, there were bound to be transformations and, though they supposedly took place within the existing norms, their cumulative effect was considerable. The dialectic between ostensible adherence to the generic norms and the actual departures therefrom form the proper object of "genre-history," the attempt to trace the evolution not only of individual compositions but of whole *genres* over time. Sometimes the evolution is fairly obvious, as for example in the case of the traditions about Gilgamesh. Here, indeed, is a parade example of literary evolution, unrivalled in the ancient world, perhaps even in the modern world, for the evolution of the Gilgamesh Epic can be traced across a span of more than two millennia.[27]

Genre-history, however, traces not only the evolution of individual literary entities, but also and more particularly, as its name implies, of whole genres. Sometimes the successive stages remain within a single genre, or family of genres. This can be illustrated by the case of the city-laments or what may be called, by analogy to the comparable Biblical genre, congregational laments. In Mesopotamia, these continued to be known by the same native genre-names in spite of the gradual but fundamental transformations that they underwent over time. Beginning as ritual apologies to the deity for the apparent sacrilege involved in razing the remains of specific ruined temples as a necessary precondition to their reconstruction, they ended as generalized liturgical litanies recited at predetermined times in the cultic calendar without reference to any one specific temple or city or to any real historical event. [28]

At other times, the successive stages of genre-history involve a change or changes in genre, and it is only the analysis of the successive stages that permits us to connect them. Such is the case with individual prayer or, to revert to Biblical terminology, with the individual lament. Beginning as a prayer in letter-form, or letter-prayer, it ended as a so-called *ér-šà-hun-gá*, a "lament for appeasing the heart (i.e., of the angry deity)." [29]

But form-criticism and genre-history have a larger significance

---

[26] Hallo 1992.
[27] See below, ch. V 3.
[28] See below, ch. VII 2.
[29] See below, ch. VII 3.

than only revealing the norms to which Near Eastern literature was subject in successive periods. They imply in their turn, and contribute to, a conception of literature which at any one time admitted only certain works as meeting these norms, in other words as canonical. It may well be argued whether there is a canon of literature today and, if so, what works belong to it. [30] It may even be argued whether the Greek word (*kanon*) is best suited to describe the ancient Near Eastern phenomenon before and beyond the strictly religious sense in which it is applied to the Biblical corpus—though I have strenuously defended this usage. [31] But there can be little doubt that the ancient Near East had a clear conception of what constituted the proper corpus of literary texts.

In Mesopotamia, these were the texts included in the curriculum of the scribal schools. They were not necessarily "literary" in the strict, modern sense of edifying or entertaining belletristic; the criterion for inclusion was rather that they served to train scribes in the "script and language of the Chaldaeans" as it was still expressed in the Bible when the use and knowledge of both had almost run their course (Daniel 1:4). They are thus better referred to as canonical than as literary texts. They are well known to us from model texts and student extracts emanating from the schools, from catalogues listing and classifying them, from colophons which indicate the sequence of compositions in the corpus, and from collective tablets which enter successive compositions in the prescribed order and in abbreviated form. In addition, there is a whole apparatus of scholarly devices designed to preserve and transmit the correct text of the accepted corpus, including the counting of lines, the insertion of inadvertently omitted lines, the indications of breaks in the prototype or of variant readings and the reconciliation of such variants, glosses on difficult words and commentaries made up of such glosses, among other devices. [32]

Again, the existence of a canon does not necessarily imply a static situation. On the contrary, just as genres had their history, so did the canon. Over the course of the millennia, it changed by jettisoning old components and introducing new ones. Sometimes these changes were gradual and piecemeal, sometimes sudden and wholesale. In

---

[30] Hallo 1990.
[31] Hallo 1991.
[32] Ibid.

every case, however, they emerged in response to the changing cultural and political scene in the country. The scribal schools were not ivory towers. They existed under royal or priestly auspices and served the needs of palace and temple. They thus responded to changes in the cultural climate—political or religious—or what we might call ideology. [33]

To cite just one example, the notion of divine kingship, perhaps imported from Egypt, had a limited appeal in Mesopotamia, but for some five hundred years of its long history it prevailed there (ca. 2250-1750 B.C.). This same half millennium was also a period of intense literary productivity, and major genres, including certain kinds of royal hymns and sacred marriage texts, evolved to reflect and propagate the royal assertion of divine status. Indeed the whole canon of that period served, in part, that purpose. It may be described as the neo-Sumerian canon, in distinction to its predecessor, the Old Sumerian canon. By the end of Hammurapi's reign, the ideology of divine kingship was being abandoned, and with it this canon; at the same time Akkadian literature evolved into a canon of its own under Babylonian auspices. Subsequently a fourth canon, characterized by bilingual Sumero-Akkadian texts, can be identified. [34]

While the details of these developments remain to be investigated, the legacy to our own concept of literature is clear. Then as now, creativity and canonization, originality and adherence to traditional norms were in tension with each other, but the tension itself was a creative one. The balance which was struck, though very different from our own, has bequeathed to us a rich legacy worth the effort of its rediscovery.

Bibliographical References

Alster, Bendt, 1990: "Sumerian literary dialogues and debates and their place in ancient Near Eastern literature," Lokkegaard AV 1-16.
————, 1992: "Two Sumerian short tales reconsidered," ZA 82:186-201.
Avigad, Nahman, 1978: "Baruch the scribe and Jerahmeel the king's son," IEJ 28:52-56 and pl. 15.
————, 1979: "Jerahmeel and Baruch, king's son and scribe," BA 42:114-118.
Brug, John F., 1990: "Biblical acrostics and their relationship to other ancient Near Eastern acrostics," SIC 3:283-304.

---

[33] Hallo 1975a.
[34] Ibid.

Castellino, Giorgio R., 1972: *Two Šulgi Hymns (BC)* (= Studi Semitici 42).

Civil, Miguel, 1964: "The 'message of Ludingirra to his mother' and a group of Akkado-Hittite 'proverbs'," JNES 23:1-11.

Cooper, Jerrold S., 1971: "New cuneiform parallels to the Songs of Songs," JBL 90:157-162.

Foster, Benjamin R., 1974: "Humor and cuneiform literature," JANES 6:69-85.

Hallo, William W., 1962: "New viewpoints on cuneiform literature," IEJ 12:13-26.

———, 1963: "On the antiquity of Sumerian literature," JAOS 83:167-176.

———, 1968: "Individual prayer in Sumerian: the continuity of a tradition," Speiser AV 71-89.

———, 1975: "Another Sumerian literary catalogue?" StOr 46:77-80; 48/3:3.

———, 1975a: "Toward a history of Sumerian literature," Jacobsen AV:181-203.

———, 1977: "New moons and sabbaths: a case-study in the contrastive approach," HUCA 48:1-18.

———, 1990: "Assyriology and the canon," *The American Scholar* 59:105-108.

———, 1991: "The concept of canonicity in cuneiform and Biblical literature: a comparative appraisal," SIC 4:1-19.

———, 1992: review of Maul, *"Herzberuhigungsklagen"* in BiOr 49:777-780.

———, in press: "The Theology of Eridu," JAOS (review article on Kramer and Maier 1989).

Hunger, Hermann, 1968: *Babylonische und assyrische Kolophone* (= AOAT 2).

Jacobsen, Thorkild, 1982: "Oral to written," Diakonoff AV 129-137.

Kramer, Samuel Noah and John Maier, 1989: *Myths of Enki, the Crafty God* (New York/Oxford, Oxford U.P.).

Lambert, W.G., 1957: "Ancestors, authors, and canonicity," JCS 11:1-14.

———, 1960: *Babylonian Wisdom Literature* (Oxford, Clarendon).

———, 1962: "A catalogue of texts and authors," JCS 16:59-77.

———, 1967: "The Gula hymn of Bullutsa-rabi," Or. 36:105-132 and pls. viii-xxiii.

———, 1976: "A late Assyrian catalogue of literary and scholarly texts," Kramer AV 313-318.

Leichty, Erle, 1964: "The colophon," Oppenheim AV 147-154.

Longman, Tremper III, 1991: *Fictional Akkadian Autobiography: a Generic and Comparative Study* (Winona Lake, IN, Eisenbrauns).

Orth, Michael, 1990: "The effects of parody in the Book of Jonah," SIC 3:257-281.

Roth, Martha T., 1983: "The slave and the scoundrel: CBS 10467, a Sumerian morality tale?" JAOS 103:275-282 (rep. as Kramer AV 2:275-282).

Scurlock, JoAnn, 1993: "Real estate for the birds: a few suggestions on ADD 469," N.A.B.U. 1993/1:11f. No. 17.

Sweet, Ronald F.G., 1969: "A pair of double acrostics in Akkadian," Or. 38:459f.

Trible, Phyllis, 1994: *Rhetorical Criticism: Context, Method, and the Book of Jonah* (Minneapolis, Fortress).

Tucker, Gene M., 1971: *Form Criticism of the Old Testament* (Philadelphia, Fortress).

Van Dijk, J.J.A., 1980: *Texte aus dem Reš-Heiligtum in Uruk-Warka* (= BaMi Beiheft 2).

———, 1989: "Ein spätbabylonischer Katalog einer Sammlung sumerischer Briefe," Or. 58:441-452.

Vanstiphout, Herman L.J., 1986: "Some thoughts on genre in Mesopotamian literature," RAI 32:1-11.

Wacholder, Ben Zion, 1963: "Pseudo-Eupolemus' two Greek fragments on the life of Abraham," HUCA 34:83-113

2. Bilingualism and the Beginnings of Translation

"And all the earth was (of) one tongue and (of) uniform speech" or—in the rather free translation of the New English Bible—"Once upon a time all the world spoke a single language and used the same (or: few) words" (Gen. 11:1). Thus begins the tale (in the NEB version, we might almost say, the fairy-tale) of "the confusion of tongues" and, we should add, the dispersion of peoples from their original home in lower Mesopotamia. The tale is found near the end of the primeval history that makes up the first eleven chapters of Genesis—set between the so-called Table of Nations (Gen. 10) and the "line of Shem" (Gen. 11:10-26). It is a *locus classicus* for an early awareness of linguistic issues, albeit an ambiguous one, given the problem of translating the plural of the numeral one, which recurs only four times in the Bible, mostly in the plain sense of "a few (days)," [35] and which is translated above variously by "uniform, same, or few."

In an unpublished paper, [36] Aaron Shaffer has suggested a novel understanding of the passage as referring more specifically to the Mesopotamian situation where, by the beginning of the second millennium, all were of one tongue but of two written languages, Sumerian and Akkadian, with each word in the vernacular Akkadian corresponding to one in the learned Sumerian. These correspondences were eventually fixed in long lexical texts. Shaffer accordingly proposed to translate the Genesis passage: "All the earth was of one speech and corresponding words."

This situation was also presumably described in a Sumerian epic known by its modern title as "Enmerkar and the Lord of Aratta." [37] Although ostensibly concerned with more or less historic events, the epic also includes an aetiology on the confusion of tongues in the guise of a "spell (*nam-šub*) of Nudimmud (Enki)." [38] The proper translation of this pericope is almost as widely debated as that of the Biblical passage. [39] In line 142, for example, the initial *eme-ha-mun*,

---

[35] So in Gen. 27:44a, 29:20b, and Dan. 11:20b. For Ezek. 37:17b, NEB has: "then they will be a folding tablet (L'HDYM) in your hand."

[36] Delivered in New Haven (and elsewhere), November 1977; but see the quotation of the relevant portion in Staal 1979:5.

[37] Latest translation by Jacobsen, *Harps* 275-319.

[38] Jacobsen 1992; previously *idem, Harps* 288-290, lines 135-156; Talmon AV 403-416. Nudimmud is a deity equated with Enki.

[39] See especially Kramer 1943 and 1968, Van Dijk 1970, Alster 1973, Gurney 1974-7, and Kramer and Maier 1989:88f.

equated with Akkadian *lišān mithurti* in later lexical and bilingual texts,[40] was regarded by W. von Soden as designating Sumerian and Akkadian, those "languages of symmetry" which were attuned to each other by tradition and bilingual lists and which coexisted already at the time of the Enmerkar Epic.[41] Other translations proposed include "harmony-tongued(?)," [42] " (of) mutually opposed tongues," [43] " (of) different tongue," [44] "whose languages (originally) were opposed (to that of Sumer)," [45] "contrasting tongues," and most recently even "bilingual" or "polyglot." [46]

But what is *not* in dispute is that Mesopotamia is a parade example—and the earliest one documented anywhere—of "languages in contact" [47] or bilingualism. [48] It is literally the land between the rivers (originally within the great bend of the Euphrates; Greek *meso-potamia* is a loan-translation from Akkadian *birīt nārim*) [49], or the land of the two rivers (Egyptian *naharina*, Hebrew (Aram) Naharayim) meaning, originally, Euphrates and Balih or Euphrates and Habur and later Euphrates and Tigris, but figuratively it is the land of two linguistic and cultural streams, the older Sumerian one and the younger Semitic one—whether in Akkadian guise, or Amorite or Aramaic or ultimately Arabic.

It is not for nothing that modern examples of linguistic and cultural symbiosis have appealed to Mesopotamian precedent—as when Franz Rosenzweig entitled his essays on German Jewry (too optimistically as it turned out) "Zweistromland." [50] The allusion to this renowned theologian (1886-1929) is not coincidental, for he is one of the first systematic writers on the subject, not only of bilingualism, but of translation, as was duly noted by George Steiner's more recent

---

[40] Cf. CAD M/2:137.
[41] Von Soden 1959:132, cited by Sjöberg 1969:83.
[42] Kramer 1944:107; cf. Kramer 1968:109.
[43] Jacobsen 1946:147f., note 32 = TIT 364f., note 32.
[44] Sjöberg 1969:83.
[45] Alster 1973:103 with note 2.
[46] Jacobsen 1987:289 (in Talmon AV 406, he reverts to "of opposite persuasions"); Kramer and Maier 1989:88; Vanstiphout 1994: 148.
[47] Weinreich 1962; Haayer 1986.
[48] See especially von Soden 1960. For more recent treatments see Pedersén 1989 and Krispijn 1990. For the related phenomenon of diglossia (two socially distinct dialects), see Mausero 1993.
[49] Finkelstein 1962; originally "that territory surrounded on three sides by the great bend of the Euphrates "(*ibid.* 82).
[50] Hallo 1989.

classic on the theory of translation. [51] I have dealt elsewhere with this aspect of Rosenzweig's work, [52] and will forego reviewing his theories of translation, or the problems posed by applying them to his own writings. Instead, I will address some questions of translation in the context of ancient Near Eastern bilingualism.

My survey begins, not in Mesopotamia proper (in any of its senses), but in western Syria, where the Italian excavations at Ebla have revealed the existence of a prosperous and literate culture that owed much to Mesopotamia, and to Egypt as well, but that had developed along lines of its own to a degree previously unsuspected—and this as early as the third quarter of the third millennium. [53] The native language of Ebla was a form of Semitic—indeed the earliest form now known—combining features of grammar and lexicon later divided between East Semitic and (North)west Semitic and therefore best described as "North Semitic." [54] But the thousands of large-sized and well preserved tablets recovered from its royal archives and library employed the cuneiform of lower Mesopotamia which was primarily designed to write Sumerian. As a result, the bulk of each tablet, perhaps as much as 90%, was simply written in Sumerian, with only an occasional word or morpheme from the native Semitic language written in syllabic script, together with a large number of native personal and other proper names. [55]

Whether the Sumerian portions of the texts were read off in Sumerian or Semitic is not entirely clear. [56] What is clear is that the native scribes mastered the foreign script and language with the help of very extensive lexical lists in which the basic stock of Sumerian words was listed in a fixed sequence, with or without translations into the native Eblaite equivalents. [57] Where the equivalents are given, we thus have bilingual lexical lists which provide the first examples in history of systematic translation. Most notable in this regard is the

[51] Steiner 1975.

[52] Hallo 1982, 1988.

[53] For the latest discussion of Ebla chronology, see Astour 1992. For my own view see Hallo 1992:70.

[54] Von Soden 1981. For the even newer concept of "Central Semitic "see Voigt 1987. See now also Lambert 1992.

[55] For the personal names, see Archi 1988 and Krebernik 1988; for geographical names see Astour 1988; for divine names see Pomponio 1983.

[56] Civil 1984:75f.

[57] Hallo 1992:74-76 with notes 44-68. Previously Nissen 1981.

text which has been suitably given the modern title of "The Vocabulary of Ebla (VE)." [58] It includes nearly 1500 entries, represented by as many as nine different exemplars each, [59] which often enough exhibit variant spellings or translations, and together provide a substantial data-base. [60] Let me illustrate.

VE 572	balag	=	gi-na-ru₁₂-um	(kinārum)
			gi-na-rum	,,
			gi-na-lum	,,
VE 531a	šu-šu-ra	=	ma-ha-ṣi i-da	(mahāṣ idān)
(0411)			ṭa-ba-um	(ṭabāhum)
VE 179	eme-bal	=	a-ba-lu-um	(appālum)
(079)			a-ba-um	,,
			a-bí-lu-um	(āpilum)
			tá-da-bí-lu	(tatappilu)

The first two examples help illustrate the lexical affinities of Eblaite to both (North)west Semitic [61] and East Semitic, [62] an impression confirmed by the morphology. And the third example testifies to the existence of a professional translator at Ebla, his role sufficiently important or institutionalized to enter the "Vocabulary of Ebla" [63] as well as the standard unilingual list of professions (EDLuE) which Ebla shared with contemporary Mesopotamia, [64] where unilingual lists of Sumerian words and toponyms go back to the very beginnings of writing at the end of the fourth millennium. [65]

Ebla was visited and probably destroyed by Sargon. The great conqueror was at pains to unite the disparate parts of his growing

---

[58] Pettinato 1981 and 1982:115-343.

[59] E.g. VE 118 and 126 in Pettinato 1982:210f.

[60] Cagni 1984.

[61] Sumerian balag, "lyre "or "harp, " translated in Akkadian by the Sumerian loanword balaggu, is rendered in Eblaite by a cognate of Hebrew kinnôr.

[62] Sumerian šu-šu-ra, literally "strike the (two) hands, "is rendered in Eblaite by a cognate of Akkadian "striking (of) the two hands "and, alternatively, by a cognate of "to slaughter "occurring equally in Akkadian and (North)west Semitic.

[63] Fronzaroli 1980, esp. p. 92; Archi 1980, esp. p. 88. For the form of the last entry, see Hecker 1984, esp. p. 217; Kienast 1984, esp. p. 228.

[64] Pettinato 1981a:27 No.6:11, 30 No. 7:11, compared with Civil 1969:17 No. 1.53:11.

[65] Nissen 1981; cf. esp. the table on pp. 106f. Of the earliest (Uruk) lexical texts, some 10% go back to Uruk IV date, the rest are of Jemdet Nasr date (ibid. 101).

empire. His daughter Enheduanna used her outstanding command of Sumerian, probably literally her mother-tongue, to create a body of poetry intended to celebrate her father's achievements and make them theologically acceptable to the Sumerian speaking South. [66] He himself raised Akkadian to the status of an official court language, and had his royal inscriptions composed in Akkadian. But in at least two cases he provided them with translations into Sumerian; [67] they are known to us from parallel versions copied in Old Babylonian times by the scribes and student scribes of Nippur and Ur, who apparently made " field trips" to the open spaces before the palaces and temples of those cities, [68] where the original monuments were then still in place. [69] Together with a comparable inscription by Sargon's son and successor Rimush, [70] these early Sargonic royal inscriptions constitute the first true bilinguals known from Mesopotamia proper.

The Sargonic period also provides the first evidence of the existence of professional translators outside the lexical lists. [71] They were still designated by the Sumerian term *eme-bal,* literally "language-turner" (as at Ebla), or its later replacement *inim-bal,* literally "word-turner," [72] but the latter was eventually equated with an Akkadian term *targumannu* (or *turgumannu*), of uncertain origin but fist attested in Old Assyrian and perhaps derived from Hittite *tarkummai-*, "to announce, interpret, translate." [73] (Cf. Hebrew *meturgeman,* English dragoman.) The meticulous bookkeeping of the outgoing third millennium informs us of specialists in "turning the languages" of the Gutians and of Meluhha (the Indus Valley ?) during the Sargonic period, and of Marhashi (in Iran) and Amurru (in Syria) in the subsequent Ur III period, when there was also a "travelling interpreter" (*eme-bal kaskal-la*) for good measure. [74]

---

[66] Hallo and van Dijk 1968, esp. ch. 1; Chatzē 1988; Westenholz 1989.

[67] Hirsch 1963:34-39; Gelb and Kienast 1990:157-167; Frayne 1993:9-12, 27-29.

[68] For such " field trips "as part of the curriculum of the Old Babylonian scribal schools, see Sjöberg 1976, esp. p. 166 and nn. 26f.; Klein 1986 with the reservations of Yoshikawa 1989.

[69] Buccellati 1993.

[70] Hirsch 1963:68f.; Gelb and Kienast 1990:215-217; Frayne 1993:67-69.

[71] Above, notes 63f.

[72] Sjöberg 1975:152-156. The replacement occurs after Ur III times: *ibid.* 153 n. 4.

[73] Gelb 1968, esp. pp. 101f.; cf. Lambert 1987:410f.; Starke 1993.

[74] Sjöberg 1975:153, n. 4. Cf. Lambert 1987:409f.

By the beginning of the second millennium, Sumerian was ceasing to serve as a spoken language anywhere except perhaps near the head of the Persian Gulf. Monumental texts continued to employ it, but true bilinguals, in the sense of a single monument bearing both Sumerian and Akkadian versions, were confined to stone statues or steles with narratives extolling royal triumphs, [75] or what may be called "triumphal inscriptions," [76] and then only from the time of Hammurapi on. True bilinguals are also represented in what may be called "date-formula proclamations" or "promulgations" of the Hammurapi dynasty. [77]

But Sumerian continued to function as the language of learning and liturgy. In scribal schools and temples, it thus survived for another two millennia, much like Latin in post-classical Europe. The unilingual lists of words and names [78] were gradually provided with one or more explanatory columns which exploited to the full the technique of organizing knowledge in lists, a technique that was characteristic of Mesopotamian learning, its so-called "Listenwissenschaft." [79] Ordinarily, the explanatory column involved translation into Akkadian, but other equivalences were also introduced as the genre evolved, e.g., syllabic spellings to indicate the exact pronunciation of the Sumerian lemma written logographically, or a dialectal equivalent in Sumerian or, where divine names were concerned, a description of the deity's function, relationship to other deities etc.

Like these lexical lists, bilingual literary texts sometimes employed the column format. This was true of a letter-prayer from Old Babylonian Mari, [80] some mid-second millennium texts from the Hittite capital at Hattusha [81] and some slightly later texts from Assur, such as the great prayer of Tukulti-Ninurta I. [82] But other formats were also experimented with, at least initially, so for example occasional glosses above or more often below the Sumerian line, [83] enclosing

---

[75] Frayne 1991:407 and note 157. For an analysis of these texts see Krispijn 1982.

[76] Van Driel 1973.

[77] M.J.A. Horsnell, JNES 36 (1977) 283f., n. 40, with the additions of Hallo, Sachs AV (1988) 176, n. 33. For Mari letters discussing possible year names (in Akkadian), see ARMT 13:27, 47, and cf. Dalley 1984:69f.

[78] Above, notes 57, 65.

[79] Von Soden 1936, esp. p. 425 = 1965:35.

[80] Charpin 1985.

[81] Cooper 1971-2:6 and 11 (No. 7). Three columns were used for trilinguals (Sumerian-Akkadian-Hittite): ibid. 8f. (Nos. 1 and 2).

[82] KAR 128f. Cf. Hallo 1977, esp. p. 585. Cf. also KAR 97, a hymn to Ningirsu/Ninurta.

both versions in a single case, [84] or separating them by a "Glossenkeil," with the Akkadian in the middle between two half-lines of Sumerian. [85] There were even two instances of putting the Sumerian on the obverse and the Akkadian on the reverse. [86] By the first millennium, however, one format became almost universally favored for literary bilinguals, and that was the interlinear one, in which each Sumerian line was followed by its literal translation into Akkadian. [87]

One format that is conspicuous by its rarity is the case of straight translation into Akkadian in the *absence* of the Sumerian original. [88] Apart from some proverbs, this case is most notably illustrated by the twelfth tablet of the canonical Gilgamesh Epic, which has long been recognized as a late addition to the epic [89] based on the second half of the Sumerian composition variously known as "Gilgamesh, Enkidu and the Netherworld" or "Gilgamesh and the *huluppu*-tree." [90] But whatever the format, the bilingual tradition in Mesopotamia was characterized by a slavish fidelity to the received Sumerian text and a literalness of translation into Akkadian which extended to every morpheme and sometimes actually did violence to the meaning of the original—or what we today regard as its intended meaning. This characterization applies in the first place to the literary texts, but could be extended as well to the lexical texts and is perhaps best illustrated by a genre occupying a position in some sense midway between the two, the Old Babylonian grammatical texts. [91]

The Old Babylonian grammatical texts graphically illustrate the list-system of organizing knowledge in cuneiform. They are arranged in double columns, and each entry registers a Sumerian form in the left column, its Akkadian equivalent in the right column. Horizontal

---

[83] E.g. Wilcke 1970.

[84] E.g. Civil and Biggs 1966.

[85] E.g. CT:13:35-38, "The founding of Eridu. " Translation in A. Heidel, *The Baby-lonian Genesis* (1942) 49-52; (2nd ed., 1951) 60-63.

[86] Scheil 1927 (translation by van Dijk 1953:90-97) and F.E. Peiser, *Urkunden* (1905) 4f. (a prayer in the form of a school-text). For all the preceding see Cooper 1969.

[87] Krecher 1976.

[88] Hallo 1993:183f., note 5, with previous literature; cf. Krecher 1978:102.

[89] For dissenting opinions see now S. Parpola, JNES 52 (1993) 192-196 and below, n. 197.

[90] Hallo 1993:183f., with previous literature.

[91] Edzard 1971; Jacobsen 1974; Black 1984; for additions to the corpus see especially Gurney 1974:Nos. 97-102 (Old Babylonian). For unilingual forerunners dating back to Early Dynastic times, see Krispijn 1991-2:19f. *ad* SF 42, BM 3:29 and examples from Ebla. For the last, see also D'Agostino 1991.

dividing lines group the entries in a strict taxonomy according to person, number, mood and other considerations. The paradigm of the verb "to go" alone runs to over 300 entries. And while it is the longest of the paradigms, it is by no means the only one, as it only illustrates one verbal type, the simple intransitive verb. There are at least three others almost as long for other sorts of verbs, and other grammatical texts as well. What they all have in common is the careful grouping and ordering of the entries, the desire to enter every possible form, whether attested in the literature or made up on the basis of analogy, and finally the morpheme-for-morpheme equation with Akkadian forms.

Our survey of Ancient Near Eastern translation takes us next back to the "periphery"—that great swatch of the Fertile Crescent which surrounds the core area of the Sumero-Akkadian homeland of the cuneiform traditions. By the second half of the second millennium, Akkadian was becoming the lingua franca of the Near East, especially for diplomatic purposes, and scribal schools on the Mesopotamian pattern sprang up in a great arc from Amarna in Egypt, via Ugarit and other cities of the Levant, to Hattusha the Hittite capital in Anatolia. (In Susa, the Elamite metropolis of southwestern Iran, they had existed for some time already.) West of the Jordan, cuneiform texts have been found at Hazor, Megiddo, Taanach, Shechem, Aphek and Gezer, and invariably included among the finds were school-texts; the lone exception is Hebron. Along the Euphrates, the city of Emar yielded remarkable numbers of traditional Sumero-Akkadian canonical texts in native versions, often expanding on the received texts with sentiments borrowed from a more western tradition. Another innovation of these western texts is their tendency to add additional translations into the local vernacular—at Hattusha Hittite, and at Ugarit Hurrian or Ugaritic (if we may regard the abecedary in Ugaritic with Akkadian pronunciation in this light). The "message of Lu-dingirra to his mother" will illustrate this feature; though found at Ugarit, it clearly derives from Hattusha, for it comes in no less than four versions: Sumerian, syllabic Sumerian, Akkadian and Hittite, all written in parallel columns. [92]

Not all this translation activity in the west was confined to the schools. Here, as in Mesopotamia, the schools stood under the pa-

---

[92] For all the preceding, see Hallo 1979-80; 1992:80-86, with full documentation.

tronage of church and state, or rather temple and palace, and their alumni served these patrons. Thus we encounter the phenomenon of bilingualism on the highest levels, as, for example, in the drawing up of international treaties, a common enough requirement in the era of internationalism and cosmopolitanism known as the Amarna Age (ca. 1350-1275). Among the numerous treaties preserved from this age there are some in Hittite with more or less verbatim equivalents in Egyptian or Akkadian which, although recovered in separate documents from Egypt and Hattusha respectively, nevertheless qualify as bilinguals of sorts. [93] Much the same could already be said of the "Annals of Hattushili I" (ca. 1640), preserved on separate tablets, in Akkadian and Hittite respectively, from Hattusha. [94]

The balance of power characteristic of the outgoing Bronze Age came to a precipitous end under the onslaught of the great migrations of the 13th century. But bilingualism survived into the Iron Age that dawned in the 12th century. Indeed it was encouraged by the attendant relocation of whole ethnic entities. Thus, for example, the collapse of the Hittite empire in Anatolia drove the surviving speakers of Hittite across the Taurus into Cilicia and northern Syria, where they came in contact with speakers of Aramaic, themselves perhaps newly arrived from the Syrian desert. Together these totally unrelated ethnic groups evolved a so-called Aramaeo-Hittite or Syro-Hittite symbiosis among whose distinctive features was a reliance on writing systems derived either from Hittite or from the newer "alphabetic" script of the Phoenicians. A parade example is the royal inscription of Azitawadda, king of the neo-Hittite Danunites (Danaoi?), discovered in 1946-7 in Karatepe (Cilicia) on the Ceyhan river. This monumental inscription was recorded at least four times on the statues, orthostats, and gateway of the citadel and city of Azitawadda—three times in Phoenician and once in Luwian, a dialect of Hittite written in the Hittite Hieroglyphic script. [95]

From the same approximate time (i.e. the late 9th century) though much further east and hence closer to Assyria comes a more recently discovered bilingual monument, that of Tell Fekherye, ancient Sikannu, in northern Syria. The double inscription was discovered on the statue of a king or governor (MLK/ *šaknu*) of ancient Guzana, the

---

[93] ANET 199-205, 529f.
[94] Melchert 1978.
[95] ANET 653f.

Biblical Gozan, and is written once in Aramaic and once in the neo-Assyrian dialect of Akkadian. The Akkadian text is written vertically on the skirt of the statue, instead of horizontally in the manner adopted for cuneiform, even of the monumental sort, almost a millennium earlier (and for cursive canons and archives probably well before that). This was then a deliberate case of archaism, perhaps based on the notion that alphabetic script was expected to run perpendicular to the traditional cuneiform script. [96]

Returning to the core area of Assyria and Babylonia, it is enough to characterize the bilinguals of the first millennium in two broad strokes: (1) they settled on the interlinear format as the preferred method of presentation and (2) they adopted an almost slavish literalism in translation from Sumerian to Akkadian. The latter characterization could apply equally well to certain ancient versions of the Bible, especially some of the translations into Aramaic. [97] The Bible is no doubt the most translated book of all time, but not, as the foregoing has amply demonstrated, the first, though both superlatives have sometimes been claimed for it in the same breath even by such an authority as Rosenzweig. [98]

Nor, by the same token, is the Greek version of Aquila the first example of literal translation, though no less a scholar than James Barr makes that claim for it, and even suggests, as a reason, that Aquila's attention to the text's Hebraic properties is distinctively Jewish. [99] At most we can, following Edward Greenstein, consider the *meturgeman* the first practitioner of "simultaneous translation," and hold him responsible for the resultant literalism of some of the Targumim. [100] (His European namesake, the dragoman, would be a later example of the same tradition.) [101]

Finally, we must reject the claim that the concept of an "interlinear version" is original with Bible translation—even though it has been put forward by none other than Johann Wolfgang von Goethe, often regarded as the first systematic modern theoretician of translation, as well as a life-long practitioner of the art. [102] In the *Noten und Abhand-*

---

[96] Kaufman 1977:124, n. 44; 1982; Hallo 1982a:114.
[97] Levine 1988.
[98] Hallo 1988:293 with note 14; previously 1982:103* with note 30.
[99] Barr 1979:46 as paraphrased by Greenstein 1983:19.
[100] Greenstein 1983:20.
[101] Gelb 1968.
[102] Steiner 1977:256-260

lungen to his *West-östlicher Divan* (1819), [103] he briefly sketched out a tripartite typology of translation according to whether the source language is simply transferred into the target language, or whether the source language is transformed into the target language, or whether the source language and target language are somehow made equivalent. The first approach does violence to the target language, the second to the source language. Only the third can claim true fidelity to both, and only it therefore qualifies for the designation of interlinearity. [104]

Goethe described the second and third of these types of translation as "parodistic" and "metamorphic" in the etymologic sense of these words—and perhaps could have characterized the first as "metathesis" since simply to "transfer" from source to target language is literally to "translate," the older English rendering of the Greek *metathein* [105] in connection with Enoch in Septuagint (Gen. 5:24), Apocrypha (Sir. 44:16) and New Testament (Heb. 11:5). [106]

In his praise of the "interlinear version" of translation, Goethe was rejected a century later by Franz Rosenzweig, [107] but followed about the same time by Walter Benjamin, whose one brief essay on translation has had an impact far beyond its size. "Die Aufgabe des Übersetzers" ("The task of the translator") was originally prefaced to his translation of Baudelaire's *Tableaux Parisiens* of 1923, but frequently reissued [108] and translated. [109] According to Benjamin, "in some degree, all great writings, but the Scriptures in the highest degree, contain between the lines their virtual translation. The interlinear version of the Scriptures is the archetype or ideal of all translation." [110]

Goethe was preceded by Dryden (1631-1700), who preferred "paraphrase" to either "metaphrase" or "imitation" in translation. [111] In another sense, however, he was already anticipated by the Tannaim and Amoraim of the Rabbinic tradition. Rosenzweig had ar-

---

[103] Goethe 1981 II 255-258: "Übersetzungen. " Translated in Goethe 1968.

[104] Steiner 1977:256-260. For the concepts of source and target language see Hallo 1982:101*, 1988:289.

[105] Admittedly, Latin transfero/-ferre/-tuli/-latus is the calque of Greek *metapherein*; cf. Steiner 1977:77.

[106] Hallo 1982:103*f.

[107] See Hallo 1982:103* with note 27 for his "subtle polemic against Goethe."

[108] Benjamin 1955:40-54; 1961:56-69; 1977:50-62.

[109] Benjamin 1968 (cf. Steiner 1977:63, note 1); 1968a, 1969, 1973.

[110] Benjamin 1955:54; 1968:88; cf. Steiner 1975:62; 1977:65, 308.

[111] Dryden 1968; cf. Steiner 1977:253-256.

gued that "the Bible must surely be the first book to be translated and then held equal to the original text in the translation." [112] On the contrary, Etan Levine points out that, according to the Rabbis, the Targum (Aramaic translation) was *not* held equal to the Torah. Moreover, "The *meturgeman* [113] was expected to exercise caution in not misleading the assembled populace, either by verbatim literalism which would distort the sense of scripture, or by free paraphrase which would be blasphemous." [114] As Rabbi Judah said, "He who translates a verse according to its form—this one is a fabricator. And he who adds to it—this one deforms and diminishes it." [115] Or in the words of the Talmud, "He who translates a verse verbatim is a liar! And he who alters it is a villain and a heretic!" [116] By implication, only a third alternative, like Goethe's, can avoid both pitfalls.

Perhaps the typology is inherent in the enterprise of translation. In the very latest statement of the case, Nicholas de Lange speaks of the translator as either a copyist, a servant, or a creative artist, leaving no doubt that he prefers the last characterization. [117] Indeed he "would liken the translator to a performing musician," [118] though one might prefer Steiner's analogy with the composer putting a poem or narrative to music. [119]

To sum up: many cultures know of a Babel, a legend about the pristine unity of human speech, of the first confusion of languages and dispersion of peoples over the earth. [120] But only on the soil of Babylonia itself, and of the surrounding countries exposed to its influence, can we document the historic efforts to deal with bilingualism or multilingualism by means of translation.

---

[112] Cited Hallo 1982:103*; 1988:293.

[113] Translator; cf. above on Akkadian *targumannu/turgumannu*.

[114] Levine 1988:11 and notes 18f.

[115] Tosefta Megilla 4:41. Cf. Michael Klein 1976:519f.

[116] Talmud Bavli Qiddushin 49a, cited Levine 1988:11, note 21. Cf. also Greenstein 1983:20.

[117] De Lange 1993.

[118] De Lange 1993:6.

[119] Steiner 1977:416-424. For Steiner as a music critic, see his review of Charles Rosen, *The Romantic Generation* in *The New Yorker* (July 24, 1995) 85-88.

[120] Borst 1957-63.

Bibliographical References

Alster, Bendt, 1973: "An aspect of 'Enmerkar and the Lord of Aratta'," RA 67:101-110.

Archi, Alfonso, 1980: "Les textes lexicaux bilingues d'Ebla," SEb 2:81-89.

———, ed., 1988: *Eblaite Personal Names and Semitic Name-Giving* (= Archivi Reali di Ebla—Studi 1).

Astour, Michael C., 1988: "Toponymy of Ebla and ethnohistory of Northern Syria," JAOS 108:545-555.

———, 1992: "The date of the destruction of Palace G at Ebla" in Chavalas and Hayes 1992: 23-39.

Barr, James, 1979: *The Typology of Literalism in Ancient Biblical Translations* (= Mitteilungen des Septuaginta-Unternehmens 15, Göttingen).

Benjamin, Walter, 1955, 1961, 1971, 1977: *Schriften*; rep. as *Illuminationen: Ausgewählte Schriften* (Frankfurt a/M, Suhrkamp).

———, 1968: "The task of the translator," *Delos, a Journal on and of Translation* 2:76-99.

———, 1968a, 1969, 1973: "The task of the translator," in *Illuminations*, ed. by Hannah Arendt (New York, Harcourt Brace and World; rep. by Schocken).

Black, Jeremy A., 1984: *Sumerian Grammar in Babylonian Theory* (=StPSM 12).

Borst, Arno, 1957-63: *Der Turmbau von Babel: Geschichte der Meinungen über Ursprung und Vielfalt der Sprachen und Völker* (5 vols.). Vol. 1: *Fundamente und Aufbau* (Stuttgart, A. Hiersemann).

Buccellati, Giorgio, 1993: "Through a glass darkly: a reconstruction of Old Akkadian monuments described in Old Babylonian copies," Hallo AV 58-71.

Cagni, Luigi, ed., 1981: *La Lingua di Ebla* (= Istituto Universitario Orientale, Napoli, series minor 14).

———, 1984: *Il Bilinguismo a Ebla* (= Istituto Universitario Orientale, Napoli, series minor 22).

Charpin, Dominique, 1985: "Les malheurs d'un scribe ou de l'inutilité du Sumérien loin de Nippur," Sjöberg AV 7-27.

Chatzē, Tasia, 1988: *Enchentouanna: hē epochē, hē zōē, kai to ergo tēs* (Athens, Odysseas).

Chavalas, Mark W. and John L. Hayes, eds., 1992: *New Horizons in the Study of Ancient Syria* (= BM 25).

Civil, Miguel, 1969: *The Series lú = ša and Related Texts* (= MSL 12).

———, 1984: "Bilingualism in logographically written languages: Sumerian in Ebla," in Cagni 1984:75-97.

——— and Biggs, 1966: "Notes sur les textes sumériens archaïques," RA 60:1-16.

Cooper, Jerrold S., 1969: *Sumero-Akkadian Bilingualism* (Dissertation, Chicago).

———, 1971-2: "Bilinguals from Boghazköi," ZA 61: 1-22, 62:62 - 81.

D'Agostino, Franco, 1991: "The study of Sumerian grammar at Ebla, Part I," ASJ 13:157-180.

Dalley, Stephanie, 1984: *Mari and Karana: Two Old Babylonian Cities* (London/New York, Longman).

De Lange, Nicholas, 1993: *Reflections of a Translator* (= University of Cincinnati, Rabbi Louis Feinberg Memorial Lecture in Judaic Studies 16).

Dryden, John, 1968: "Three kinds of translation," *Delos* 2:167 - 170.

Edzard, Dietz Otto, 1971: "Grammatik," RLA 3:610-616.

Finkelstein, J.J., 1962: "Mesopotamia," JNES 21:73-92.

Frayne, Douglas R., 1991: "Historical texts in Haifa: notes on R. Kutscher' 'Brockmon Tablets'," BiOr 48:378-409.

———, 1993: *Sargonic and Gutian Periods (2334-2113 B.C.)* (= RIME 2).

Fronzaroli, Pelio, 1980: "Gli equivalenti di eme-bal nelle liste lessicali eblaite," SEb 2:91-95.

Gelb, I.J., 1968: "The word for dragoman in the Ancient Near East," *Glossa* 2:92-103.

———— and B. Kienast, 1990: *Die altakkadischen Königsinschriften* (= FAOS 7).

Goethe, Johann Wolfgang von, 1968: "Three types of translation," *Delos* 1:188-190.

————, 1981: *Sämtliche Werke* (Hamburger Ausgabe 1949-67, 12th ed.).

Greenstein, Edward L., 1983: "Theories of modern Bible translation," *Prooftexts* 3:9-39.

Gurney, Oliver, 1974: *Middle Babylonian Legal Documents and Other Texts* (= UET 7).

————, 1974-77: "A note on 'the Babel of Tongues'," AfO 25:170f.

Haayer, G., 1986: "Languages in contact: the case of Akkadian and Sumerian," Hospers AV 77-84.

Hallo, William W., 1977: Review of Marie-Joseph Seux, *Hymnes et Prières aux Dieux de Babylonie et d'Assyrie* in JAOS 97:582-585.

————, 1979-80: "The expansion of cuneiform literature," PAAJR 46-47:307-322.

————, 1982: "Notes on translation," *Eretz-Israel* 16 (H.M. Orlinsky Volume) 99*-102*.

————, 1982a: Review of C.B.F. Walker, *Cuneiform Brick Inscriptions* in JCS 34:112-117.

————, 1988: "Franz Rosenzweig übersetzt," in Wolfdietrich Schmied-Kowarzik, ed., *Der Philosoph Franz Rosenzweig (1886 1929)* (Freiburg/München, Karl Alber) vol. 1:287-300.

————, 1989: "German and Jewish culture: a land of two rivers?" *Shofar* 7/4:1-10.

————, 1992: "The Syrian contribution to cuneiform literature and learning," in Chavalas and Hayes 1992:69-88.

————, 1993: "Disturbing the dead," Sarna AV 183-192.

———— and J.J.A. van Dijk, 1968: *The Exaltation of Inanna* (= YNER 3).

Hecker, Karl, 1984: "Doppelt erweiterte Formen oder: der eblaitische Infinitiv," in Cagni 1984:205-223.

Hirsch, Hans, 1963: "Die Inschriften der Könige von Agade," AfO 20:1-82.

Jacobsen, Thorkild, 1946: "Sumerian Mythology: a review article," JNES 5:128-152; reprinted in Jacobsen TIT 104-131, 353-365.

————, 1974: "Very ancient texts: Babylonian grammatical texts," in Dell Hymes, ed., *Studies in the History of Linguistics: Traditions and Paradigms* (= Indiana University Studies in the History and Theory of Linguistics) 41-62.

————, 1992: "The spell of Nudimmud," Talmon AV 403-416.

Kaufman, Stephen A., 1977: "An Assyro-Aramaic *egirtu ša šulmu*," Finkelstein AV 119-127.

————, 1982: "Reflections on the Assyrian-Aramaic bilingual from Tell Fakhariyeh," *Maarav* 3:137-175.

Kienast, Burkhart, 1984: "Nomina mit t-Präfix und t-Infix in der Sprache von Ebla und ihre sumerischen Äquivalente," in Cagni 1984:225-255.

Klein, Jacob, 1986: "On writing monumental inscriptions in Ur III scribal curriculum," RA 80:1-7.

Klein, Michael, 1976: "Converse translation: a targumic technique," *Biblica* 57:515-537.

Kramer, Samuel Noah, 1943: "Man's golden age: a Sumerian parallel to Genesis 11:1," JAOS 63:191-194.

————, 1944: *Sumerian Mythology* (= Memoirs of the American Philosophical Society 21).

————, 1968: " 'The Babel of Tongues': a Sumerian version," JAOS 88:108-111; also published in Speiser AV 108-11.

———— and John Maier, 1989: *Myths of Enki, the Crafty God* (New York/Oxford, Oxford U.P.).

Krebernik, Manfred, 1988: *Die Personennamen von Ebla: eine Zwischenbilanz* (= BBVO 7).

Krecher, Joachim, 1976: "Interlinearbilinguen," RLA 5:124-128.

———, 1978: "Sumerische Literatur," in W. Röllig, ed., *Altorientalische Literaturen* (= Neues Handbuch der Literaturwissenschaft 1) 100-150.

Krispijn, Th.J.H., 1982: "Das Verb in den zweisprachigen Inschriften der Hammurabi-Dynastie," *Kraus AV* 145-162.

———, 1990: "Tweetalige teksten in de oudere Mesopotamische Literatuur," in W.J. Boot, ed., *Literatuur en Tweetaligheid: 22-23 Januari 1990* (Leiden, Rijksuniversiteit).

———, 1991-2: "The early Mesopotamian lexical lists and the dawn of linguistics," JEOL 32:12-22.

Lambert, W.G., 1987: "A vocabulary of an unknown language," M.A.R.I 5:409-413.

———, 1992: "The language of ARET V 6 and 7," *Quaderni di Semitistica* 18: 41-62.

Levine, Etan, 1988: *The Aramaic Version of the Bible: Contents and Context* (= ZATW Beiheft 174).

Mausero, Fernandez, 1993: *Diglossia: a Comprehensive Bibliography, 1960-1990 and Supplements* (Amsterdam/Philadelphia, J. Benjamins).

Melchert, H. Craig, 1978: "The Acts of Hattušili I," JNES 37:1-22.

Nissen, H.-J., 1981: "Bemerkungen zur Listenliteratur Vorderasiens im 3. Jahrtausend," in Cagni 1981:99-108.

Pedersén, Olof, 1989: "Some morphological aspects of Sumerian and Akkadian linguistic areas," Sjöberg AV 429-438.

Pettinato, Giovanni, 1981: "I vocabolari bilingui di Ebla," in Cagni 1981: 241-277 and pls. 1f.

———, 1981a: *Testi lessicali monolingui della Biblioteca L. 2769* (= MEE 3).

———, 1982: *Testi lessicali bilingui della Biblioteca L. 2769* (= MEE 4).

Pomponio, F., 1983: "I nomi divini nei testi di Ebla," UF 15:141-156.

Scheil, Vincent, 1927: "Contraste féminin," RA 24:34-37.

Sjöberg, Åke W., 1969: *The Collection of the Sumerian Temple Hymns* (= TCS 3).

———, 1975: "Der Examenstext A," ZA 64:137-176.

———, 1976: "The Old Babylonian Eduba," Jacobsen AV 159-179.

Staal, Frits, 1979: "Oriental ideas on the origin of language," JAOS 99:1-14.

Starke, Frank, 1993: "Zur Herkunft von akkad. ta/urgumannu(m) 'Dolmetscher'," WO 24:20-38.

Steiner, George, 1975: *After Babel: Aspects of Language and Translation* (New York/London, Oxford U.P.). Cited from paperback reprint, 1977.

Van Dijk, J., 1953: *La Sagesse Suméro-Accadienne* (Leiden, Brill).

———, 1970: "La 'confusion des langues': note sur le lexique et sur la morphoplogie d'Enmerkar, 147-155," Or. 39:302-310.

Van Driel, G., 1973: "On 'standard' and 'triumphal' inscriptions," Böhl AV 99-106.

Vanstiphout, H.L.J. 1994: "Another attempt at the 'spell of Nudimmud'," RA 88: 135-154.

Voigt, Rainer M., 1987: "The classification of Central Semitic," JSS 32:1-21.

Von Soden, Wolfram, 1936: "Leistung und Grenze sumerischer und babylonischer Wissenschaft," *Die Welt als Geschichte* 2:411-464 and 509-557; reprinted with Benno Landsberger, *Die Eigenbegrifflichkeit der babylonischen Welt* (Darmstadt, Wissenschaftliche Buchgesellschaft, 1965:21-133) (with additions).

———, 1959: Review of Borst 1957 in BiOr 16:129-132.

———, 1960: *Zweisprachigkeit in der geistigen Kultur Babyloniens* (= Österreichische Akademie der Wissenschaften, phil.-hist. Klasse, Sitzungsberichte 235/1).

———, 1981: "Das Nordsemitische in Babylonien und Syrien," in Cagni 1981:355-361.

Weinreich, Uriel, 1962: *Languages in Contact* (The Hague, Mouton).

Westenholz, Joan Goodnick, 1989: "Enḫeduanna, En-Priestess, Hen of Nanna, Spouse of Nanna," Sjöberg AV 539-556.

Wilcke, Claus, 1970: "Die akkadischen Glossen in TMH NF 3 Nr. 25 ...," AfO 23:84-87.

Yoshikawa, Mamoru, 1989: "m a š - d à r a and s a g - t a g," ASJ 11:353-355.

3. THE BIRTH OF RHETORIC [121]

A curious object turned up on the antiquities market in 1972. It was acquired by the Hamburg Museum of Arts and Crafts in 1983 and published in the Annual of the Museum in 1985. [122] In 1993 it was discussed by Michael Heltzer, to whom I owe my acquaintance with this curiosity. [123] The object is made of clay, in the shape of the lower half of a human leg, an unusual medium, to say the least. [124] It is inscribed in cuneiform script and in the Assyrian dialect of Akkadian. The text may be translated as follows:

> A woman called Pagti-remini, servant-girl of the woman Kursibtu, queen-consort of Assur-iddin, who had lifted Naru-eriba, the monkey-man, out of the river: she has continuously raised him up! Anyone who brings a lawsuit concerning him will pay 7(!) [125] sons; he will cause him to come forth. By order of the gods, they shall not kidnap the monkey-(-man?). Month Shabatu, day one, year of the eponymy of Adad-resh-ishi. Before Sin, before Shamash, before Ishtar, before Gula.

That this unique document is fictional was noted by the original editors ("eine fiktive Urkunde") as well as by Heltzer ("a fictive legal text"). We know all the kings of Assyria by name, and there is no Assur-iddin among them, although the name is common enough in the Middle Assyrian period to which the text may be dated on orthographic grounds. [126] The queen-consort's name means "butterfly," and her servant-girl's name invokes an otherwise unknown divinity. Her foundling-son has the tell-tale name "the river has compensated," presumably for a previous son lost in childbirth. And the four witnesses are all great gods: sun, moon, Venus-star and the healing goddess. The foundling is described as a monkey-man (*pagû*), his mother's name is based on the fictional divine name Pagti, and all are

---

[121] Presented to the First African Symposium on Rhetoric: Persuasion and Power, Cape Town, July 12, 1994.

[122] Franke and Wilhelm 1985.

[123] Heltzer 1993.

[124] For another cuneiform legal text inscribed on an unusually shaped clay surface, in this case resembling the axe-head of the deity by which the oath was administered, cf. Streck 1993.

[125] The text has 6. For the poetic idiom "seven sons "cf. esp. the song of Hannah (I Sam. 2:5), though in fact Hannah had only six children (ib. 21).

[126] Cf. Claudio Saporetti, *Onomastica Medio-Assira* (Studia Pohl 6, 1970) vol. 1:114-116.

enjoined from kidnapping him (*la ipûgu*). Far from recording a real court case, the object and its text seem rather to be an elaborate joke, complete with plays on words, fictional royalty, divine witnesses, and a unique writing surface. [127] The medium fits the message, and both belong more in the realm of fiction than of fact.

Therewith I hope to have alerted you to some basic problems besetting a rhetorical approach to cuneiform literature: how to distinguish fiction from non-fiction, how to identify a usually unknown author, how to divine his (or her!) intention, how to assess the impact on a presumed audience. [128] Cuneiform literature does not, as in the case of classical literature, provide us with a neatly prepackaged corpus of theoretical prescriptions or practical illustrations of the art of persuasion in public speaking. It does not, as in the case of Biblical prophecy, preserve impassioned orations inspired by firm belief, addressed to the innermost circles of power, and transmitted in virtually stenographic transcripts by secretaries such as Baruch son of Neriyah, whose seal impression, recently recovered (albeit from unprovenanced context), lends new historicity and authenticity to Jeremiah's words. [129] The preserved literature of Sumer and Akkad would not yield readily to the pioneering analyses of the prophetic art of persuasion by our host Professor Gitay, [130] nor to the whole line of Biblical exegesis that goes by the name of rhetorical criticism, [131] and that has most recently been conveniently surveyed by Watson and Hauser. [132] It would not answer to "a forensic understanding" such as newly and effectively applied by Edward Greenstein to the Book of Job, [133] or to the narratological analyses advanced by him [134] and such other literary critics as Adele Berlin. [135] It would not resonate to the combination of narratology and rhetorical analysis championed by Meir Sternberg [136] and Mary Savage, [137] nor yet to a novel thesis on the

---

[127] The nearest equivalent from the real world of cuneiform texts may be the inscribed footprints used to identify new-born triplets at contemporary Emar; cf. Erle Leichty, "Feet of clay, " *Sjöberg AV* (1989) 349-56.

[128] See below at notes 161f.

[129] Cf. above, n. 12.

[130] Gitay 1981; 1991.

[131] Dozeman and Fiore 1992. Add especially Jackson and Kessler 1974.

[132] Watson and Hauser 1993.

[133] Greenstein 1996.

[134] Cf. e.g. Greenstein 1981; 1982.

[135] See e.g. Berlin 1986; 1994.

[136] Sternberg 1983; cf. *ibid.* 47f., n. 1 for a summary of his earlier analysis of "the rhetoric of the narrative text "in the story of Dinah; cf. also *idem* 1985.

[137] Savage 1980.

"power of the word" that has just appeared posthumously from the pen of the late Isaac Rabinowitz. [138]

The reasons for these negative assessments are inherent in the nature of the cuneiform evidence, which differs fundamentally from both the Classical and the Biblical models. Whether we look at the literature in Sumerian and Akkadian as I intend to do, or in Hittite and in Ugaritic, each follows its own canons—and forms its own canons, as we shall see. For all that, some tentative efforts have been made, in the fairly recent past, to subject portions of the cuneiform canons to rhetorical analysis. I will review them here briefly, before attempting a programmatic statement of further possibilities.

It will not, I trust, be considered unduly immodest if I begin the survey with myself! [139] In 1968, in collaboration with J.J.A. van Dijk, I published a first critical edition of a Sumerian poem which we entitled "The Exaltation of Inanna." [140] It is expressly attributed to the first non-anonymous author in Mesopotamian history, perhaps in all of history: the princess Enheduanna (ca. 2285-2250 B.C.), known also by other poetic works and by monumental remains. [141] The poem's division into 153 lines represents an original feature of the composition, for these line divisions agree in all of its numerous exemplars, and the total is carefully counted in the colophon of at least one complete recension. [142] In our edition, we grouped these lines into 18 stanzas and three "rhetorical" parts and defended these groupings in a literary analysis without claiming that they too necessarily represented "original feature(s) of the composition." [143] The rhetorical parts we called "exordium" (or "proemium"), [144] "the argument," and "peroration" respectively and equated them with stanzas i-viii (lines 1-65), ix-xv (lines 66-135) and xvi-xviii (lines 136-153). Fifteen years later, I

---

[138] Rabinowitz 1993.

[139] Or if I cite an unpublished paper by a Yale undergraduate entitled "Rhetorical, linguistic and grammatological perspectives on comparatavism from the work of William W. Hallo "by Edward Robert O'Neill (1986?).

[140] Hallo and van Dijk 1968. A year later, the same composition was translated by Samuel Noah Kramer under the title of "Hymnal prayer of Enheduanna: the adoration of Inanna in Ur, " ANET 579-82.

[141] Hallo and van Dijk, 1968, ch. 1: "Enheduanna: her life and works. "See in detail below, ch. VIII 3.

[142] *Ibid.*, 35.

[143] *Ibid.*, 45.

[144] *Ibid.*, 53.

applied a similar rhetorical analysis to the first Epic of Lugalbanda ("Lugalbanda in the cave of the mountain"). [145]

While these examples have not been widely followed, it is at least worth noting that the term "proem" has been used to describe the first two stanzas of another Sumerian hymn to the goddess Inanna in its latest translation by Thorkild Jacobsen [146] and the first three lines of an Akkadian prayer to the god Nanna as translated by William Moran. [147] And at the sixth biennial conference of the Rhetoric Society of America held in May 1994 at Old Dominion University in Norfolk, Virginia, a paper was presented on "Enheduanna's 'The Exaltation of Inanna': toward a feminist rhetoric." [148] The author of the paper, Roberta Binkley, plans to make this the subject of her doctoral dissertation at the University of Arizona.

To return to my survey, in 1978 Adele Berlin explored "shared rhetorical features in Biblical and Sumerian literature." [149] She was not concerned with any one composition or genre, but with the whole gamut of Sumerian poetry, and particularly with a feature it shares with Biblical poetry, namely parallelism. Within this broader technique, she noted especially two rhetorical features, one "the particularizing stanza" and the other an ABAB word order pattern.

In his 1980 dissertation, Robert Falkowitz chose to define rhetoric still more widely. Rather than the prevalent classical definition of rhetoric as the art of persuasion in oratory, he prefers the medieval conception in which rhetoric formed a trivium, with grammar and dialectic, within the seven liberal arts, and as such applied to poetry and epistolography as well as to preaching. It was, in short, intended to inculcate the ability to communicate in a lofty idiom distinct from common parlance, let alone colloquialism, [150] and was, therefore, a proper subject of instruction in the schools. By this criterion, the curriculum of the scribal schools of Old Babylonian Mesopotamia could likewise be described as an exercise in rhetoric. That curriculum first

---

[145] Hallo 1983:165, 170.

[146] Jacobsen, Harps 113.

[147] Moran 1993:117; cf. below, at note 155.

[148] The paper was listed under the title "Foreshadowing rhetoric: 'The Exhaltation (sic) of Inanna'," in the section on "Early receptions of ancient Greek rhetoric." I am grateful to the author for giving me a copy of her paper.

[149] Berlin 1978.

[150] See below at notes 156-159 and 229.

required the Akkadian-speaking students to master the intricacies of cuneiform writing and the basic vocabulary of Sumerian by means of primers constituting syllabaries and vocabularies. But it then went on to connected texts in Sumerian and these typically began with the proverb collections, which Falkowitz accordingly renamed "The Sumerian Rhetoric Collections." [151]

Historians of Mesopotamian art have expanded the definition even more, freeing rhetoric of its verbal associations entirely—for better or worse—and extending it to the realm of non-verbal communication. [152]

More recent studies have tended to return to a narrower definition of rhetoric. Thus Richard Hess has studied the longest of the many letters sent by the Egyptian pharaoh at Amarna to his restless vassals in Asia during the Amarna period. He concludes that its elaborate argument and stylistic sophistication constitute "a creative use of rhetorical persuasion in order to counter the arguments of a vassal and set forth the pharaoh's case." [153] Piotr Michalowski uses rhetoric almost synonymously with stylistics in discussing negation as "a rhetorical and stylistic device." [154]

Returning to a stricter sense of rhetoric, Moran documents the classical preference for "the plain style" or what in Greek is called *ho ischnos charactēr* and in Latin *subtilis oratio* or *genus tenue* to signal its use in an Old Babylonian prayer to the moon-god. [155] This plain style should not, however, be confused with colloquialism. Moran regards the justly famous letter of a schoolboy to his mother (Zinu) as probably showing "colloquial speech" in Akkadian. [156] It has also been detected in Sumerian, both in wisdom literature [157] and in an incantation, [158] and in Biblical Hebrew. [159]

The most recent attempt to apply the canons of classical rhetoric

---

[151] Falkowitz 1982.

[152] Cf. especially Winter 1981.

[153] Hess 1990; cf. *ibid.* 148, n. 23 for his forthcoming "Rhetorical forms in the Amarna correspondence from Jerusalem."

[154] Michalowski 1991:134.

[155] Moran 1993. For another translation of the same text which appeared at the same time see Foster, BM 1:154f., FDD 293f.

[156] ANET 629.

[157] Hallo 1979; J. Klein, ASJ 12 (1990) 57 (Enlil and Namzitarra).

[158] Hallo 1985. For a "colloquial "morpheme (infixed -a-) see M. Yoshikawa, Or. 46 (1977) 461, rep. *idem*, ASSS 1 (1993) 266.

[159] Below, n. 229.

to cuneiform literature is also the most massive one. In a doctoral dissertation written at the Hebrew University of Jerusalem under the direction of Aaron Shaffer, Nathan Wasserstein has discussed *Syntactic and Rhetorical Patterns in Non-epic Old-Babylonian Literary Texts* (1993). Although I have not seen the thesis, I have its table of contents through the courtesy of the author. In nine chapters, he treats in detail the techniques of merismus, hendiadys, geminatio, zeugma, extraposition, hypallage, gradatio and enumeratio, rhyming couplets and the hysteron-proteron sequence.

One should also take note of some recent studies which investigate essentially rhetorical aspects of cuneiform literature without actually using the term. Thus Dietz Edzard has dealt with monologues in Akkadian literature. [160] Laurie Pearce has addressed the question of auctorial(?) intention, or "why the scribes wrote." [161] In an as yet unpublished paper, Barbara Porter has raised the issue of "impact on a presumed audience" with respect to neo-Assyrian royal inscriptions. [162]

Even this hasty survey, which has undoubtedly sinned by omission, suggests that there are, after all, some potential insights to be gained by a rhetorical approach to cuneiform literature. In what follows, I will attempt to identify some others which may serve to outline further directions that this approach might usefully take. I will not stop to dwell on the peculiarities of cuneiform literature, except to emphasize at the outset what is meant by that literature. It is emphatically not that vast corpus of accounts, contracts, letters and other documents of daily life which numbers in the hundreds of thousands and which constitutes some 80% of the surviving documentation. Although playing a crucial role in the reconstruction of ancient society and of the wellsprings of our own contemporary institutions, these documents are sometimes disparagingly referred to by Assyriologists as "laundry lists." I prefer to designate them as "archival." Secondly, cuneiform literature does not mean that smaller corpus of royal and other inscriptions which serves us as building blocks in the reconstruction of ancient history. Such texts are rather to be regarded as "monumental." The distinguishing hallmark of cuneiform literature

---

[160] Edzard 1990.
[161] Pearce 1993.
[162] Porter MS. My thanks to Dr. Porter for showing me her paper in advance of publication.

in the narrower sense, then, is its place in the formal curriculum of the scribal schools where, after the primers and the proverbs referred to earlier, the students learned to read and copy out the entire received canon of Sumerian (and later Akkadian) texts of diverse genres which creatively captured the whole range of human experience and the reaction of human beings to the world about them. These texts were literary in the narrower sense but not by any means always belletristic, for they included religious, scientific, philological and other genres not intended simply to edify or to entertain but first of all to educate. Since the curriculum embodied at any given time all those texts—and only those texts—which were thought necessary and proper to this pedagogic end, I have argued long and hard in favor of labelling these texts as "canonical" and their totality at any given period of history as the canon of that era. [163] I would now be prepared to suggest that they might equally well be labelled "rhetorical," using that term in the broader, medieval connotation cited earlier, but extending it far beyond only the proverb collections that stand near the beginning of the school curriculum.

Proverbs are only one genre among several that are collectively referred to, on the analogy of the Biblical example, as "wisdom literature." That literature was concerned with common mortals, not with gods or kings, and it often offered practical instructions in agriculture and other common human pursuits. Much of it is clearly oral in origin, and intended for oral delivery. Among the wisdom genres that would particularly lend themselves to a rhetorical analysis are three that are usually classified by Assyriologists as dialogues, diatribes, and disputations respectively. [164] Dialogues tend to take place between scribes or between scribal students and their masters or parents; [165] diatribes may involve men or women of various walks of life outdoing each other in inventive invective. [166] (Some scholars consider dialogues and diatribes a single genre.) [167] Disputations are the most artful of the three genres, and the only one identified as such in the

---

[163] For details see above, ch. V 1, esp. at note 31.

[164] For a general survey, see Alster 1990, esp. p. 7 for his sub-division of the genres into four according to their "content matter."

[165] See for example Sjöberg 1973.

[166] See for example Sjöberg 1971-72.

[167] E.g. Vanstiphout 1991:24 and n. 4.

native terminology; the term (*a-da-man* = *teṣîtu* or *dāṣātu*) recurs in cultic and archival texts which indicate the occasions when the disputations were performed. [168]

The disputations pit two parties against each other in formal debate. [169] The parties are typically antithetical phenomena from the natural or social environment—summer and winter, bird and fish, silver and copper, pickaxe and plow, for example. Each party rehearses its advantages first and then the shortcomings of the antagonist, in a series of arguments and rebuttals that may reach three or more "rounds" before the final judgment is rendered by the deity or, occasionally, the king, depending apparently on whether the setting of the disputation was conceived of as the scribal school attached to the temple or as the palace. [170] Typically (though not invariably) the palm goes to the party that, at the outset, might have appeared the weaker, as if in recognition of the persuasiveness of its argumentation. Thus the lowly pickaxe triumphs over the lordly plow, perhaps even receiving a token gift for his pains in what van Dijk has described as an anticipation of the enigmatic *kesiṭa* and gold rings awarded to Job at the end of his disputation. [171]

It seems, then, that the disputations have a stronger claim than the proverbs to be regarded as true exercises in rhetoric. In the view of H.L.J. Vanstiphout, one of their principal current interpreters, they "developed out of the abstract and neutral 'debate situation' primarily as an exercise in 'rhetorical skill' .... the debate, as a literary and rhetorical form, is in itself and as such the primary reason for being." [172] And "in most cases the victor wins on *rhetorical* points: he is the cleverest debater." [173] Hypothetically, we can reconstruct a kind of dramatic presentation in which two speakers (or actors or rhetors) assumed the respective roles. The preserved texts represent the libretti; their contents consist almost entirely of spoken parts, and the narrative interpolations constitute little more than "stage directions."

---

[168] Hallo *apud* Alster 1990:13, citing S.T. Kang, *Sumerian and Akkadian Cuneiform Texts* 1:155 and 190; add M. Sigrist, *Andrews University Cuneiform Texts* 1:794.

[169] See in detail Vanstiphout 1990, 1992.

[170] For the palace in this role, see already Hallo, HUCA 33 (1962) 29, n. 214, and JCS 24 (1971) 39, n. 2.

[171] Job 47:11. Cf. van Dijk 1957.

[172] Vanstiphout 1991:24, n. 5.

[173] Vanstiphout 1990:280.

Much the same could be said of some of the other genres which followed the wisdom literature in the scribal curriculum and which, unlike that, focused on kings and gods. What then are some of the rhetorical and stylistic devices that can be detected in these genres? I will confine myself to epic (including myth), not only because it is evidently omitted from Wasserstein's aforementioned thesis, but also because, of all cuneiform genres, this is the one which, even in translation, continues to have the widest appeal. [174] Who has not heard of the Epic of Gilgamesh?

What is perhaps less familiar is that to this day we still do not have any complete recension of the epic! Its discovery began in 1872 with the publication of *The Chaldaean Genesis* by George Smith, which included much of the story of the Flood in what proved to be Tablet XI of the epic; it created so much excitement in England that the *Daily Telegraph* supplied Smith with the funds to return to Kuyunjik (which turned out to be a part of ancient Nineveh) and find many more fragments of the epic. But in spite of more than 120 years of additional discoveries, the epic remains fragmentary. Even its very first line is broken and subject to different restorations and translations. I would venture to render it thus: "Of him who saw everything let me inform the country." [175] The audience is being invited to listen and here and in the next four lines is tempted by the inducement of sharing in the knowledge of someone who had travelled widely in the world and experienced much—like Odysseus "*polutropon hos mala polla ....*" In the next line, this geographical breadth is matched by chronological depth for Gilgamesh is said to have "brought back information from before the flood." [176]

But Gilgamesh is not alone among Akkadian epics in thus anticipating classical epic by attempting to attract the attention of a pre-

---

[174] Admittedly, there is no native genre corresponding to "epic "or "myth "even in Sumerian, which is rich in generic terminology, let alone in Akkadian, which is not. But there is a subset of "hymns" in honor of certain mortal heroes or, in the case of "myths," in honor of given deities.

[175] Cf. CAD N/1 111: "Let me proclaim to the land him who has seen everything(?)." Tigay, *Evolution* 141: "Him who saw everything, let me make known to the land." E.A. Speiser, ANET (1955) 73: "He who saw everything to the ends of the land." W. von Soden, UF 14 (1982) 236: "der alles gesehen hatte, (gleichwohl auch) das (eigene) Land regierte." John Gardner and John Maier, *Gilgamesh* (New York, Knopf, 1984) 57: "The one who saw the abyss I will make the land know." Tournay and Shaffer, Gilgamesh 38: "Celui qui a tout vu, célèbre-le, ô mon pays! "

[176] Hallo 1991.

sumed audience at the outset. Claus Wilcke has studied the exordia of Akkadian epics, and identified at least four other examples in which the poet steps forward to announce in the first person (typically in the cohortative mood) his intention to sing of a certain subject—a veritable *arma virumque cano*—often followed by exhortations to the audience to listen. [177] Among them are Old Babylonian examples thought to be hymnic-epic celebrations of Hammurapi's campaigns against the north [178] and the south, [179] and a hymn to Ishtar as Agushaya, "the mad dancer in battle." [180] Only one example dates from the late period, namely the canonical Anzu Epic [181].

Still others of the later compositions substitute for this exordium a circumstantial temporal clause which sets the stage for the narrative to follow, a kind of fairy-tale beginning with "once upon a time." The Akkadian conjunction is *enuma/inuma/inumi*, "when," which breaks down etymologically into *in umi*, "on the day that," and as such is a throwback to the Sumerian *u₄-...a-a*, "on the day that, when," which is such a standard incipit of Sumerian epic and other genres that it became the preferred form of the personal names which identified the antediluvian sages with the works of literature attributed to them. [182] In its Akkadian form it is most familiar from the incipit of the so-called "Epic of Creation," *enuma elish*. [183] Other examples include the much debated incipit of the (Late) Old Babylonian flood story of Atar-hasis, [184] and the Middle Babylonian myth of Nergal and Ereshkigal. [185]

A third rhetorical solution to introducing epic is to begin with a hymnic apostrophe to the royal or divine protagonist—a useful re-

---

[177] Wilcke 1977.

[178] Wilcke 1977:153-5 = CT 15:1-2, edited by Römer 1968.

[179] Wilcke 1977:179f. = CT 15:3-4, ed. by Römer 1967.

[180] Wilcke 1977:181-186 = VS 10:214 and RA 15:174-82, edited by B. Groneberg, RA 75 (1984) 107-34; latest translation by Foster, BM 1:78-88.

[181] Wilcke 1977:175-9, most recently edited by Hallo and Moran 1979; latest translations by Foster, BM 1:469-485, FDD 115-131.

[182] Hallo 1963:175f. Admittedly, the names lack the explicit preposition of the Akkadian and postposition of the Sumerian incipits.

[183] Wilcke 1977:163-75; latest translation by Foster, BM 1:351-402.

[184] Wilcke 1977:160-63; Foster, BM 1:158-83; cf. also a Middle Babylonian version from Ugarit, *ibid.* 195. For the incipit see i.a. W. von Soden, Or. 38 (1969) 415-432; UF 14 (1982) 235f.; Lambert, Or. 38 (1969) 533-8; J.J.A. van Dijk, RLA 3 (1969) 538; T. Jacobsen, Finkelstein AV (1977) 113-17; M.-J. Seux, RA 75 (1981) 190f.

[185] Wilcke 1977:159; Foster, BM 1:410-16, FDD 85-96.

minder that myth and epic do not constitute separate genres in cuneiform but only a subset of hymns to kings or gods. With Wolfram
von Soden (inspired by Benno Landsberger), it has therefore become
customary to describe the Akkadian of early examples of the subset
as the "hymnic-epic dialect." [186] The Epic of Erra and Ishum, for
example, begins with a hymnic apostrophe to Ishum. [187]

Rarest of all is the epic which begins *in medias res*, as in the case of
the story of Etana, both in its Old Babylonian and its late recensions. [188]

But enough of the proems of Akkadian epics. Let us look also at
their perorations, and let us begin once more with the epic of Gilgamesh. It has twelve chapters, or tablets, a pleasingly round number
in Mesopotamian tradition. Perhaps that is why a twelfth chapter was
added to the epic, for length of composition, whether in terms of
chapters or of lines, was a significant factor in cuneiform poetry. Not
only was it one of the few data regularly recorded in the otherwise
laconic colophons, [189] but compositional lengths of 200, 480 and 1080
lines may not be wholly accidental. [190]

In fact the twelfth tablet is "an inorganic appendage to the epic
proper" as E.A. Speiser put it. [191] C.J. Gadd [192] and S.N. Kramer [193]
had recognized it long ago as the straightforward translation of a
Sumerian original, a virtually unique occurrence in the long history
of Sumero-Akkadian bilingualism. Shaffer's edition [194] shows, in detail, how its 151 lines correspond to the second half of the Sumerian
epic of "Gilgamesh, Enkidu and the Netherworld." [195] This second
half, as we now know, is represented by two exemplars newly excavated in the Jebel Hamrin area, one of which ends with the incipit of

[186] Von Soden 1932, 1933; Groneberg 1971, and above, notes 178-180.
[187] Wilcke 1977:191-200; edited by Cagni 1969; latest translations by Foster, BM
2:771-805, FDD 132-163.
[188] Wilcke 1977:156-59, 211-14; edited by Kinnier Wilson 1985. Latest translations by Foster, BM 1:437-60, FDD 102-114.
[189] See above, note 142, for an example; Hunger 1968:1f.; Vanstiphout, Hospers
AV 220f.
[190] Hallo, BiOr 46 (1989) 347f. (Correct 250 to 200 in the case of the Shamash
hymn).
[191] ANET (1969) 97.
[192] Gadd 1933:134.
[193] Kramer 1944.
[194] Shaffer 1963.
[195] See on this epic most recently Hallo 1993.

another Sumerian Gilgamesh episode, namely Gilgamesh and
Huwawa (Gilgamesh and the Land of the Living). [196]
The latest study on the subject argues otherwise, contending that
the twelfth tablet is an organic part of the epic, a "necessary epilogue ..., and a final affirmation of the truth of what has been revealed," i.e. Gilgamesh's essential humanity. [197] But this study fails on
at least two counts. For one, it overlooks the fact that, outside the epic
if not within it, Gilgamesh does achieve a measure of immortality,
albeit as god of the netherworld. As Tzvi Abusch has shown, the
twelfth tablet (along with the sixth), was added to the epic precisely
to make that point. [198] Moreover, there is ample and incontrovertible
evidence for the gradual growth of the epic over time.

In point of fact the Gilgamesh epic in the final form which is the
basis of most modern translations is the product of a millennial evolution, an evolution which has been conveniently traced by Jeffrey
Tigay. [199] At an earlier stage, it undoubtedly concluded with Tablet
XI for, to quote Speiser again, "the last lines of Tablet XI are the
same as the final lines of the introduction of the entire work (I, i
16-19)." [200] The effect is one of "framing" the entire composition with
an invitation to inspect the great walls of Uruk built, as we know from
elsewhere, by Gilgamesh himself. [201] Such a framing effect, or *inclusio*,
familiar in the Bible from the Book of Job (and elsewhere), is lost by
the addition of Tablet XII. [202]

But the frame is not an original part of the epic either! The incipit
of its Old Babylonian recension is "supreme above kings" (*šūtur eli
šarri*) as should long have been seen from the colophon of Tablet II
but in fact was not until the discovery of a new fragment of Tablet I
at Kalah and its publication by Donald Wiseman. [203] There, as noted
by Shaffer, the words in question occur at the beginning of line 27 of
the first column. [204] That implies that the first 26 lines of the canoni-

---

[196] Cavigneaux and al-Rawi 1993:93f.
[197] Vulpe 1994. For a partial dissent see Kilmer 1982. Cf. above, note 89.
[198] Abusch 1986.
[199] Tigay, *Evolution*.
[200] ANET 97.
[201] Ilmari Kärki, *Studia Orientalia* 49 (1980) 190 *sub* Anam 1; D.R. Frayne, RIME
4:474f.; cf. R.J. Tournay, Albright AV (1971) 453-57.
[202] *Inclusio* frequently operates on the level of much smaller units. Cf. e.g. Job's
first speech as reconstructed by Greenstein 1996:258 (Job 3:3-end, 4:12-21).
[203] Wiseman 1975.
[204] *Ibid.* 158 n. 22; cf. also C.B.F. Walker, JCS 33 (1981) 194.

cal recension, including the entire passage about the walls of Uruk, were not originally part of the proemium—nor, probably, of the peroration. The oldest recoverable recension of the Akkadian epic began, not with the bard speaking in the first person and addressing the audience in the second, but with a standard hymnic introduction of the protagonist in the third. This hymnic introduction typically begins with epithets and keeps the audience in supposed suspense before revealing the hero by his proper name. It is, thus, an example of that rhetorical device which we noted earlier and to which Berlin has given the label of "particularizing parallelism." [205] It is a device much favored at the beginning of Akkadian and especially of Sumerian poems.

What this rapid survey of the evolution of the Akkadian Gilgamesh Epic suggests is that it involved such essentially rhetorical devices as self-introduction of the "speaker," invitation to the audience, hymnic apostrophe to the protagonist, partial repetition of the proemium to achieve a frame effect and closure, and mechanical addition of an extraneous addendum to arrive at a preferred length. The evolution of the composition thus proceeded, at least in part, by successive expansions at its borders. This is a process with possible analogues in the evolution of the Biblical corpus, notably in the case of literary prophecy as proposed by David Noel Freedman. [206] I have similarly advanced the notion of "a central core of Deuteronomy which gradually grew by accretion at both ends in what can almost be described as concentric circles." [207] Of course it was not the only means of expansion. A comparison of Old Babylonian and Neo-Assyrian recensions of Gilgamesh and other compositions shows expansion likewise in the interior —not always with an equally happy result from a modern esthetic point of view [208]— as well as juxtaposition of originally discrete compositions to form a greater whole. [209]

But we have not yet traced the evolution of the Gilgamesh Epic back to its earliest stages. In fact, the unified epic was preceded by a series of discrete, episodic tales not, as yet, organized around the cen-

[205] Above, note 149.

[206] *The Unity of the Hebrew Bible* (Ann Arbor, U. of Michigan, 1991), esp. pp. 57f.; *idem*, 1994.

[207] Hallo, BP 90.

[208] Cooper 1977.

[209] See especially Abusch 1995 and his previous studies on the series *Maqlu*, cited *ibid.*, 468f., nn. 2f.

tral theme of human mortality. Whether these discrete episodes were already unified in the earliest Akkadian recension remains a matter of debate, with Tigay favoring this view of matters [210] and Hope Nash Wolff questioning it. [211] What has hitherto been beyond dispute is that the earlier Sumerian episodic tales were *not* integrated. The new evidence from Me-Turan raises the possibility that they were beginning to be. [212] We have already encountered one half of one of them pressed into service for Tablet XII of the Akkadian epic. [213] But with the exception of "Gilgamesh and Agga" and "The Death of Gilgamesh," [214] the others, too, were bequeathed to the Akkadian poet, not in the form of mechanical or slavish translations but creatively adapted to fashion an entirely new composition.

The technique of blending discrete compositions into a larger cycle did not necessarily involve adaptation of a Sumerian original in a new Akkadian context, nor did it begin with Gilgamesh—though it is easier to recognize it there. But let us return where we began, to the princess-poetess Enheduanna. She is said to be the author of, among other compositions, [215] at least three hymns to the goddess Inanna, each with its own theme. We have already encountered "The Exaltation of Inanna" which commemorates the earthly triumphs of her father Sargon over his enemies within Sumer and Akkad, and sublimates them into cosmic terms. The poem "Inanna and Ebih" does the same for Sargonic triumphs over enemies on the northeastern frontier as symbolized by Mount Ebih (= Jebel Hamrin). [216] Finally, the poem "Stout-hearted lady" (*in-nin šà-gur₄-ra*) tells of the submission of the whole world to Sargonic hegemony as symbolized by its acknowledgement of Inanna's supremacy in every field of endeavor. [217] In this sequence, we move from Sumer and Akkad to the frontier and thence to the whole world. If we reverse the sequence, we can see the action coming ever closer to home, in a manner worthy of an

---

[210] Tigay 1977.

[211] Wolff 1969.

[212] Above, note 196.

[213] At Me-Turan, this may be a separate episode already; cf. above at note 196.

[214] Note that at Me-Turan, the former is the one episode missing from the repertoire of Sumerian Gilgamesh episodes.

[215] For the Enheduanna texts not further treated here, see below, ch. VIII 3.

[216] Partially edited by Limet 1971.

[217] Sjoberg 1975.

Amos. [218] And it is precisely this reverse order in which all three compositions are listed together at the beginning of a literary catalogue
which has only fairly recently come to light. [219]

If, then, the three great hymns by Enheduanna in honor of Inanna
are taken as forming an integrated cycle, then they constitute a the-
matic counterpart to her other principal work: the cycle of short
hymns to all the temples of Sumer and Akkad. [220] For while the
former may be said to celebrate the theme of "the king at war," the
latter reflects "the king at peace," solicitously caring for the temples
of all the country in a major attempt to satisfy the traditional requirements of Sumerian religion. [221] It achieves in exalted poetry what "the
Standard of Ur," found by Sir Leonard Woolley in the royal cemetery, had achieved in pictorial terms some three centuries earlier. This
precious object, variously interpreted as a wooden box, [222] a desk or
lectern [223] or, most recently, as the sound-box of a harp, has four
inlaid panels, of which the two largest show the king at war and at
peace respectively, presiding over battle on one side and libations on
the other. [224] Thus one could claim for the beginning of the Mesopotamian record, as Irene Winter has said of the end, that royal rhetoric
embraced art as well as literature.

In conclusion, it must seem somewhat audacious to defend the notion of "the birth of rhetoric in Mesopotamia." [225] And indeed, I admit that this notion, or at least this title, is Prof. Gitay's, not mine.
But I *am* prepared to defend it, along with the related notion that the
idea of *humanitas* goes back to Sumerian precedent. It has been said
that "the humanities were born in a rhetorical manger. The first re-

---

[218] Cf. already Hallo and van Dijk 1968:4, where, however, the assumed order
was Ebih-Stouthearted Lady-Exaltation.

[219] Mark E. Cohen, RA 70 (1976) 131f., lines 1-3.

[220] Åke W. Sjöberg and E. Bergmann S.J., *The Collection of the Sumerian Temple Hymns*
(= TCS 3, 1969).

[221] Hallo, Kutscher AV 17.

[222] Donald P. Hansen in Winfried Orthmann, *Der Alte Orient* (= Propyläen
Kunstgeschichte 14, 1975) 191 (VIII).

[223] André Parrot, *Sumer: the Dawn of Art* (New York, Golden Press, 1961) 144-150.

[224] *Ibid.*

[225] For the more conventional view, see e.g. Cole 1991. On the possible Mesopotamian background of specifically *political* rhetoric, see now (for older Babylonia)
Claus Wilcke, "Politik im Spiegel der Literatur, Literatur als Mittel der Politik im
alteren Babylonien" in Kurt Raaflaub, ed., *Anfänge politischen Denkens in der Antike* (=
Schriften des Historischen Kollegs, Kolloquien 24, 1993) 29-75, and (for later
Assyria) Peter Machinist, "Assyrians on Assyria in the First Millennium B.C.," *ibid.*
77-104.

corded use of the word *humanitas* is in the *Rhetorica ad Herrenium*, a text
roughly contemporaneous with Cicero." [226] But Latin *humanitas* may
fairly be described as a kind of calque or loan translation of Sumerian
nam-lú-ulu₆, an abstract noun formed from the Sumerian word for
"man, human being" (*lú*), perhaps via its Akkadian loan translation
amelūtu. Like the Latin abstract, the Mesopotamian terms have a double meaning, referring both to "humanity" in the sense of humankind
in the aggregate, and to "humanity, humanism," in the sense of that
special quality of breeding and deportment which distinguishes the
educated person from the masses. [227] A single quotation among many
may serve to illustrate. A dialogue in which a father berates his perverse son for nearly all of its 180-odd lines, includes this couplet: "Because you do not look to your humanity, my heart was carried off as
if by an evil wind / You are unable to make (your) words pay any
attention to your humanity." [228] The first recorded use of the
Sumerian term antedates Cicero by two millennia, but shares one of
his firm convictions: linguistic ability is at the heart of the scribal
curriculum of Hammurapi's Babylonia as much as it was the essence
of the Roman rhetorician's *facilitas*.

I cannot resist ending with a saying from the Jerusalem Talmud
cited by Richard Steiner in a recent study of colloquial Hebrew. [229]
In Megilla 71b we read that "Greek is good for singing, Latin for
warfare, Aramaic for lamentation, and Hebrew for (divine)
speech." [230] Had the sages, like Daniel's friends, mastered the "literature and script of the Chaldaeans" (Dan. 1:4), they might well have
added that Sumerian and Akkadian are good for rhetoric!

---

[226] E.D. Hirsch, Jr., *apud* James J. Murphy, ed., *The Rhetorical Tradition and Modern Writing* (New York, Modern Language Association, 1982) 20.

[227] Van Dijk, *La Sagesse Suméro-Akkadienne* (Leiden, E.J. Brill, 1953) 23-25; Limet, " 'Peuple' et 'humanité' chez les Sumériens," Kraus AV (1982) 258-267.

[228] Lines 70f. in Kramer 1957; *idem*, HBS 16; Sjöberg 1973:116.

[229] Steiner 1992.

[230] *Ibid.* 15. Hebrew *dibbur*, corrected by Steiner to *dibbēr*.

Bibliographical References

Abusch, Tzvi, 1986: "Ishtar's proposal and Gilgamesh's refusal: an interpretation of *The Gilgamesh Epic*, Tablet 6, lines 1-79," *History of Religions* 26:143-197; repr. in Krstovic 1989:365-374.

———, 1995: "The socio-religious framework of the Babylonian witchcraft ceremony *Maqlu* ...," Greenfield AV 467-494.

Alster, Bendt, 1990: "Sumerian literary dialogues and debates and their place in ancient Near Eastern literature," Lokkegaard AV 1-16.

Berlin, Adele, 1978: "Shared rhetorical features in Biblical and Sumerian literature," JANES 10:35-42.

———, 1986: "Narrative poetics in the Bible," *Prooftexts* 6:273-284.

———, 1994: *Poetics and Interpetation of Biblical Narrative* (Winona Lake, IN, Eisenbrauns) (reprint).

Cagni, Luigi, 1969: *L'Epopea di Erra* (= Studi Semitici 34).

Cavigneaux, Antoine and Farouk al-Rawi, 1993: "New Sumerian literary texts from Tell Haddad (ancient Meturan): a first survey," *Iraq* 55:91-105.

Cole, Thomas, 1991: *The Origins of Rhetoric in Ancient Greece* (Baltimore/London, Johns Hopkins U.P.).

Cooper, Jerrold S., 1977: "Gilgamesh dreams of Enkidu: the evolution and dilution of narrative," Finkelstein AV 39-44.

Dozeman, Thomas B. and Benjamin Fiore, 1992: "Rhetorical criticism," ABD 5:712-719.

Edzard, Dietz O., 1990: "Selbstgespräch und Monolog in der akkadischen Literatur," Moran AV 149-162.

Falkowitz, Robert S., 1982: *The Sumerian Rhetoric Collections* (Ann Arbor, University Microfilms).

Franke, S. and G. Wilhelm, 1985: "Eine mittelassyrische fiktive Urkunde zur Wahrung des Anspruchs auf ein Findelkind," *Jahrbuch des Museums für Kunst und Gewerbe, Hamburg* 4:19-26.

Freedman, David N., 1994: "The undiscovered symmetry of the Bible," BR 10/1 (February 1994) 34-41,63.

Gadd, C.J., 1933: "Epic of Gilgamesh, Tablet XII," RA 30:127-143.

Gitay, Yehoshua, 1981: *Prophecy and Persuasion: a Study of Isaiah 40-48* (= Forum Theologiae Linguisticae 14) (Bonn, Linguistica Biblica).

———, 1991: *Isaiah and his Audience: the Structure and Meaning of Isaiah 1-12* (= SSN 30).

Greenstein, Edward L., 1981: "Biblical narratology," *Prooftexts* 1:201-216.

———, 1982: "An equivocal reading of the sale of Joseph," in Kenneth R.R. Gros Louis, ed., *Literary Interpretations of Biblical Narratives* vol. II (Nashville, Abingdon) 114-125 and 306-310.

———, 1996: "A forensic understanding of the speech from the whirlwind," Haran AV 241-258.

Groneberg, B.R.M., 1971: *Untersuchungen zum hymnisch-epischen Dialekt der altbabylonischen literarischen Texten* (Ph.D. Thesis, Munich).

Hallo, William W., 1963: "On the antiquity of Sumerian literature," JAOS 83:167-176.

———, 1979: "Notes from the Babylonian Collection, I. Nungal in the egal: an introduction to colloquial Sumerian?" JCS 31:161-165.

———, 1983: "Lugalbanda excavated," JAOS 103:165-180; repr. in Kramer AV 2:165-180.

———, 1985: Back to the Big House: colloquial Sumerian, continued," Or. 54:56-64.

———, 1991: "Information from before the Flood: antediluvian notes from Babylonia and Israel," *Maarav* 7 (Gevirtz AV):173-181.

———, 1993: "Disturbing the dead," Sarna AV 183-192.

——— and J.J.A. van Dijk, 1968: *The Exaltation of Inanna* (= YNER 3) (repr. New York, AMS Press, 1982).

——— and W.L. Moran, 1979: "The first tablet of the SB recension of the Anzu-myth," JCS 31:65-115.

Heltzer, Michael, 1993: "Two ancient Oriental notes on Biblical issues," Dothan AV 57*-62*.

Hess, Richard, 1990: "Rhetorical forms in EA 162," UF 22:137-148.

Hunger, Hermann, 1968: *Babylonische und assyrische Kolophone* (= AOAT 2).

Jackson, Jared J. and Martin Kessler, eds., 1974: *Rhetorical Criticism: Essays in Honor of James Muilenburg* (Pittsburgh, Pickwick Press).

Kilmer, Anne D., 1982: "A note on an overlooked word-play in the Akkadian Gilgamesh," Kraus AV 128-132.

Kinnier Wilson, J.V., 1985: *The Legend of Etana: a New Edition* (Warminster, Aris & Phillips).

Kramer, Samuel N., 1944: "The Epic of Gilgamesh and its Sumerian sources: a study in literary evolution," JAOS 64:7-23.

———, 1957: "A father and his perverse son," *National Probation and Parole Association Journal* 3:169-173.

Krstovic, J. *et al.*, eds. 1989: *Classical and Medieval Literature Criticism* 2 (Detroit, Gale Research).

Limet, Henri, 1971: "Le poème épique 'Inanna et Ebiḫ': une version des lignes 123 à 182," Or. 40:11-28 and pl. I.

Michalowski, Piotr, 1991: "Negation as description: the metaphor of everyday life in early Mesopotamian literature," AuOr 9:131-136.

Moran, William L., 1993: "UET 6, 402: persuasion in the plain style," JANES 22:113-120.

Pearce, Laurie E., 1993: "Statements of purpose: why the scribes wrote," Hallo AV 185-193.

Porter, Barbara N., MS: "Language, audience and impact in imperial Assyria."

Rabinowitz, Isaac, 1993: *A Witness Forever: Ancient Israel's Perception of Literature and the Resultant Hebrew Bible* (Bethesda, CDL Press).

Reinink, G.J. and H.L.J. Vanstiphout, eds., 1991: *Dispute Poems and Dialogues in the Ancient and Mediaeval Near East* (= OLA 42).

Römer, W.H.Ph., 1967: "Studien zu altbabylonischen hymnisch-epischen Texten: ein *kummu*-Lied auf Adad (CT 15:3-4)," Falkenstein AV 185-199.

———, 1968: "Studien zu altbabylonischen hymnisch-epischen Texten (3): ein Lied mit Bezug auf einen Šubartum-Feldzug Hammurapis (CT 15:1-2)?" WO 4:12-28.

Savage, Mary, 1980: "Literary criticism and Biblical studies: a rhetorical analysis of the Joseph narrative," SIC 1:79-100.

Shaffer, Aaron, 1963: *Sumerian Sources of Tablet XII of the Epic of Gilgameš* (Ann Arbor, University Microfilms).

Sjöberg, Åke, 1971-72: " 'He is a good seed of a dog' and 'Engardu, the fool'," JCS 24:107-119.

———, 1973: "Der Vater und sein missratener Sohn," JCS 25:105-169.

———, 1975: "i n - n i n š à - g u r 4 - r a. A hymn to the goddess Inanna by the en-priestess Enheduanna," ZA 65:161-253.

Steiner, Richard C., 1992: "A colloquialism in Jer. 5:13 from the ancestor of Mishnaic Hebrew," JSS 37:11-26.

Sternberg, Meir, 1983: "The Bible's art of persuasion: ideology, rhetoric , and poetics in Saul's fall," HUCA 54:45-82.

———, 1985: *The Poetics of Biblical Narrative: Ideological Literature and the Drama of Reading* (Bloomington, Indiana U.P.)

Streck, Michael, 1993: "Kudurrus Schwur vor Muštešir-habli," ZA 83:61-65.

Tigay, Jeffrey H., 1977: "Was there an integrated Gilgamesh Epic in the Old Baby-lonian period?" Finkelstein AV 215-218.

Van Dijk, J.J.A., 1957: "La découverte de la culture littéraire sumérienne et sa sig-nification pour l'histoire de l'antiquité orientale," *L'Ancien Testament et l'Orient* (=OBL 1) 5-28.

Vanstiphout, Herman L.J., 1990, 1992: "The Mesopotamian debate poems," ASJ 12:271-318; 14:339-367.

————, 1991: "Lore, learning and levity in the Sumerian disputations: a matter of form, or substance?" in Reinink and Vanstiphout 1991:23-46.

Von Soden, Wolfram, 1932, 1933: "Der hymnisch-epische Dialekt des Akkadischen," ZA 40:163-227; 41:90-183, 236.

Vulpe, Nicola, 1994: "Irony and unity of the *Gilgamesh Epic*," JNES 53:275-283.

Watson, Duane J. and Alan J. Hauser, 1993: *Rhetorical Criticism of the Bible: a Compre-hensive Bibliography with Notes on History and Method* (= BIS 4).

Wilcke, Claus, 1977: Die Anfänge der akkadischen Epen," ZA 67:153-216.

Winter, Irene, 1981: "Royal rhetoric and the development of historical narrative in neo-Assyrian reliefs," *Studies in Visual Communication* 7:2-38.

Wiseman, Donald J., 1975: "A Gilgamesh Epic fragment from Nimrud," *Iraq* 37:157-163 and pls. xxxviif.

Wolff, Hope Nash, 1969: "Gilgamesh, Enkidu and the heroic life," JAOS 89:392-398.

CHAPTER SIX

KINGSHIP

The institution of kingship is spread widely across the face of the earth. Many states have been ruled by kings or queens over the centuries, and a number of kingdoms continue to exist to this day. Is this to say that the institution is a more or less universal response to the common challenge for political leadership? Or is it, once more, an example of diffusion from a common Near Eastern source, as we have averred in the case of writing, aspects of the calendar, and other fundamental innovations of civilization? If we confine the search to Western, i.e. essentially European kingship, we can argue that its models or sources of inspiration were basically two, Classical (more specifically Roman) and Biblical. As an example of the former influence, we may cite the very words for ruler in European languages. While the term "king" may have a native Germanic etymology, the term "Kaiser" or Russian "Tsar" goes back to Latin *Caesar*, and the English term "emperor" to Latin *imperator*. As an example of Biblical influence, one may point to the use of unction (anointing with oil) at the coronation of British monarchs, and indeed to much of the ritual of the British coronation ceremony. And while these features may be regarded as relatively external aspects of the institution, there are more substantial features which link modern and ancient kingship, such as the concept of the divine right of kings, their tenure for life, and the hereditary character of the office. Long ago, C.W. McEwan traced "the Oriental sources of Hellenistic kingship." [1] In what follows, I will attempt to outline some of the salient characteristics of these "Oriental" sources, by which of course he meant ancient Near Eastern precedent.

1. TITULATURY, INSCRIPTIONS, HYMNS

At the outset it must be emphasized that the "ancient Near East" does not present a unitary picture in this respect, any more than in most

---

[1] McEwan 1934.

others. In Egypt, for example, the Pharaoh enjoyed not only divine rights but divine status, especially under the Old Kingdom. This status followed him even into death; the great tombs erected during the Pyramid Age (especially Dynasties III-V) may be regarded as attempts to deny the mortality of the Pharaoh and to preserve the blessings of his divinity beyond his mortal reign.

In Israel, God was the only true king, and human kingship was a late and temporary aberration, a departure from the theocratic ideal. It was considered an accommodation to foreign norms and introduced by a reluctant Samuel only when the people insisted, in the face of foreign military pressure, that he "give us a king to judge us (i.e to govern us) like all the nations" (I Samuel 8:5; cf. 8:6). And indeed, the Israelite experience of kingship was every bit as disastrous as Samuel had "foretold" (ibid. 11-18). At the first opportunity, so to speak, a theocracy was restored. This happened when Jerusalem was destroyed and the monarchy and aristocracy exiled to Babylon, and more particularly when the Achaemenid Persians granted a measure of autonomy to Judaea. At the same time the hope for a restoration of the earthly monarchy was deferred to the end of time under the doctrine of Messianism, so called from the Hebrew word *mašiach*, literally "anointed," i.e. anointed king, understood as a descendant of the royal house of David.

In the Jewish view of matters, this "Messiah son of David," and the Messianic age which he is to usher in, lie in the distant future, although Jewish history is punctuated by doomed attempts to "hasten the Messiah" and by false Messiah's such as Shabbetai Zevi. In the Christian view, Jesus was the Messiah. His epithet *Christos* (Christ) is a calque or loan-translation of the Hebrew term *mašiach*. He was a descendant of David and condemned by the Romans as *rex Iudaeorum*, "king of the Jews." [2]

Passing on to the Hittites, their royal ideology again displayed traits of its own. They struggled repeatedly with questions of the succession, and may be said to have occupied an ideological middle ground between the veneration of kingship prevalent in Egypt and its ultimate rejection in Israel. The Hittite king allowed himself to be addressed as " (my) Sun," but he did not actually claim divine status

---

[2] Cf. the inscription on the cross, INRI, an acronym for *Iesus Nazarenus Rex Iudaeorum*, based on John 19:19.

in life. Only in death were Hittite kings and queens believed or said
to have "become god." [3]

Let us turn, then, to Mesopotamia, where the evolution of kingship
is perhaps most amply illustrated. I have traced this evolution in my
survey of Mesopotamian history. [4] Here it will suffice to highlight
some of its salient features.

We may begin, once more, with the very word for king in the
earliest native sources. It is *lugal* in Sumerian. On this point there is
no room for doubt, but there are several explanations of its etymology and hence of its origins and of the origins of the institution it
names. The word, like the word-sign or logogram with which it is
written, is clearly a combination of *lú* and *gal*, which can be translated
as "man" and "great" respectively, hence "great man." This would
imply that the king was simply a *primus inter pares*, a first or greatest
among equals and, indeed, early Sumerian texts refer to the election,
or rather divine selection, of the ruler out of the total body of the
citizenry—3600 of them in the case of Enmetena of the First Dynasty
of Lagash (ca. 2400-2375 B.C.), 36,000 in the case of Urukagina, last
ruler of the same dynasty (ca. 2350-2340 B.C.), [5] 216,000 in the case
of Gudea of the Second Dynasty of Lagash (ca. 2100 B.C.). [6]

A second interpretation may be mentioned only to be rejected.
The aforementioned logogram for *lugal* is actually written in the sequence GAL+LU, with the sign for "great" preceding the sign for
"man" on the left or, in the older, more nearly pictographic script,
lying on top of it. In appearance, then, it resembles very roughly a
man wearing a crown. But while Mesopotamian kings indeed wore
crowns, these did not resemble the sign GAL, nor does that sign have
the meaning "crown." It precedes (or surmounts) the sign for "man"
in keeping with a more general rule of the early orthography, according to which GAL also precedes other signs, such as UŠUM. We may
therefore abandon this effort at "Schriftarchäologie." [7]

We turn instead to lexicography, the study of the meanings of
words based on their occurrences in context and their equivalents in
lexical lists or bilingual texts, as well as their etymology. In this light,

---

[3] Otten 1958:119.
[4] Cf. below, ch. IX 1 and, in greater detail, ANEH.
[5] For proposals regarding the reading of his name see below, ch. VIII 1, n. 12.
[6] For all three passages see Falkenstein 1966:187, n. 1.
[7] Jaritz 1967:67; cf. the critique by Biggs 1969.

it is notable that Sumerian *lugal* is often—and early—used in the simple sense of "master" or "owner," e.g. of a slave, a meaning borne out
by its Akkadian equivalents, which are not only *šarru*, the usual Akkadian word for "king," but often also *bēlu*, the Akkadian word for
"lord" or "master." What this suggests is that the original sense of the
word was something like "householder," "head of a household," and
that the more exalted meaning became attached to the word only
gradually, when the relationship of a ruler to his polity came to be
perceived as an analogy to the status of the head of a household. [8]
The analogy survives, albeit in reverse, in the English saying that
"every man is king in his own castle." On this interpretation, the
terminology—and the institution—evolved on the analogy of many
cultic terms and practices, which are frequently seen to originate in
daily life before acquiring their specialized and in that case sacred
status. [9]

Finally, I may advance a rather controversial explanation of my
own. If we look once more at the two components of the Sumerian
word, *lú* and *gal*, there is no doubt that the first means, unambiguously, "man"; indeed, the cuneiform sign with which it is written can
be readily derived from an earlier pictogram clearly depicting a man.
But the pictogram for *gal* is not so easily explained. Obviously it does
not stand for "great," a concept hardly amenable to depiction. That
sense, rather, was secondarily assigned to the pictogram (and logogram) on the rebus-principle, i.e., the use of a sign depicting an
object easily pictured for a homophone of that object, that is to say
for another word having an identical or similar pronunciation—and
not easily pictured. In English orthography, where logograms survive
at best in the form of numerals, examples of the principle would be
" 4 sale" or " 2 let."

What, then, did the original pictogram and later logogram for *gal*
depict? Based on both the appearance of the pictogram and one of
the attested meanings of the logogram, the answer could well be: a
cup (Akkadian *kāsu*). If so, then the original sense of *lugal* may well
have been "man of the cup." We encounter the cup as a royal symbol, if not in the texts, then in the later iconography, notably in a
characteristic genre of neo-Sumerian cylinder seals inscribed with a

---

[8] Jacobsen 1957, reprinted in 1970.
[9] Levine 1974:15-20, 63f.

formulaic text which commemorates the presentation by the king of
the seal in question to a favored retainer. [10] Such seals depict the king,
often with strikingly individualized features, holding in his out-
stretched hand, not the seal (as was occasionally proposed in the
past), but a cup. Such a cup is also represented in an iconographic
theme known from both seals and reliefs and described as some kind
of lustration. [11] While not denying that cups also figure in the representations of lesser mortals, notably for example in the guise of votive
figurines, I therefore suggest that they may carry special symbolic significance for the king, and that he was, in fact as well as in etymology,
the proto-typical man of the cup, the goblet, or the chalice. [12]

The simple title of "king" or "king of the city X" developed by
stages into ever more elaborate forms reflecting the greater extent of
the royal power, both geographically and politically. The earlier
stages were fully traced in my book on "Early Mesopotamian Royal
Titles." [13] The later stages were subsequently presented, albeit according to less strictly historical principles, by M.-J. Seux. [14] These studies
need not be reviewed here, though it may be worth noting how many
of the more elaborate royal titles of Mesopotamia can be said to have
been introduced there from beyond its borders, whether by right of
conquest or by simple imitation. [15] What deserves a moment's notice
is rather the question of whether the borrowing ever went the other
way, i.e., whether Mesopotamia is the source of some royal titles in
the rest of the ancient world and so, ultimately, in our own.

When we look to the east, i.e., Iran, there is little doubt that this
is the case. The *cursus honorum* followed by the earliest Elamite rulers
known from Iran led them from the office of *lugal* to that of *sukkal* and
finally of *sukkal-mah*. All three of these titles are Sumerian, and the
last two clearly acquired their royal connotation only in Elam, precisely because under Sumerian rule the *sukkal* (literally "messenger,
envoy") and *sukkal-mah* (literally "chief messenger, vizier") had represented Sumerian authority in the Elamite provinces. A fourth title,
dumu-nin or "sister's son," was likewise expressed in Sumerian but
reflected the uniquely Elamite principle of succession. [16]

---

[10] Sollberger 1965; Franke 1977.
[11] Börker-Klähn 1974.
[12] Cf. also Winter 1986.
[13] Hallo 1957; see especially the summary on pp. 122-128.
[14] Seux 1967.
[15] Hallo 1980.
[16] See below, ch. VIII 2, nn. 67f.

When we look northward and westward, however, the view is less clear. The normal Akkadian equivalent of Sumerian *lugal* was, as previously noted, *šarru*. This term is cognate with West Semitic *śar*, a word which, however, means "prince" or "general" and never king. Rather, the West Semitic word for king is routinely formed from the root MLK, "to rule, to be or become king," as in Hebrew *melekh* or Aramaic *malka*. This distinction was duly noted by the Akkadian-speaking scholars of Mesopotamia, who taught the equation *malku* = *šarru* in a lengthy "synonym list" which began with that very entry and therefore took its name from it. [17]

But the differences between the Mesopotamian *lugal/šarru* on the one hand and the West Semitic *melekh* on the other extended far beyond mere terminology. We have already indicated some ideological divergences. We could add cultic ones that probably derive from these, for example the role of the king in the sacred marriage. Whether or not this ritual served to engender the crown-prince, [18] it was a rite already thoroughly transformed at Emar, a city situated on the boundary between Mesopotamia and the West Semitic world and active during the transition from Bronze Age to Iron Age. [19] The rite was thus hardly suited for export beyond those geographic and chronological borders, despite some fanciful interpretations to this effect of Biblical texts such as Psalm 45 and the Song of Songs. [20] On the level of courtly ceremonial, similarly, there is little in common between e.g. the coronation of Mesopotamian kings, [21] or their royal entertainments, and the comparable occasions at the Syro-Palestinian courts. In short, in the case of kingship, we cannot easily trace its Near Eastern origins further back than its Biblical antecedents.

More briefly, then, let us turn to aspects of Mesopotamian kingship other than the royal titulary, in particular the texts in which its ideology was expressed. These texts include both monumental inscriptions and canonical genres such as the royal hymns. An additional vehicle for royal propaganda was available in the form of the date formulas which served to name years in the millennium, approximately, between Sargon of Akkad (ca. 2300 B.C.) and the middle of the Kassite Dynasty. All these genres were linked to each other and to the royal

---

[17] Draffkorn 1963, 1965.
[18] See below, chapter VI 2.
[19] Dietrich 1990; Fleming 1992.
[20] Schmökel 1956.
[21] Below, chapter VI 2.

chanceries from which they presumably emanated according to a
" field theory" which postulates the emergence of an institutionalized
commemoration of royal achievements on a more or less annual basis
in three discrete but related formulations: at their briefest and most
prosaic in the date formulas; at greater length, though still in prose,
in the royal inscriptions, including both building and votive inscriptions; and at their most elaborate in the poems we describe as royal
hymns.

My " field theory," formulated in one brief paragraph in 1970, [22]
and endorsed by F.R. Kraus, [23] was put to the test in the Yale dissertation of Douglas Frayne, who successfully defended it in its essentials, while modifying it in details and greatly expanding the scope of
its application. [24] Many literary texts can now first be fully appreciated in the significance of their historical allusions thanks to his researches, while conversely isolated date formulas can in some cases be
arranged in their proper sequence thanks to their correlation with the
literary texts. [25] The royal inscriptions frequently serve as the bridge
between the two. [26]

More recently, I have even proposed to identify a fourth formula-
tion of the royal achievements, this time not textual but artistic, i.e.
in the form of statues, steles and other monuments depicting the king
in heroic guise carrying out the deeds described in words in date formulas, inscriptions and hymns. [27] Some of these monuments have
been rediscovered by modern excavations. Others, especially those of
the Sargonic kings, are described in copies made from them in Old
Babylonian times; what they may have looked like has been described
graphically by Giorgio Buccellati. [28]

The most notable example of the phenomenon may well be the
statue of "Shulgi the Runner," depicting that king as he performed
the incredible feat of covering the 150 kilometers between Nippur
and Ur (and back!) on foot in a single day in order personally to
celebrate on the appropriate day the lunar festival at both cities, respectively the religious and political capitals of his realm—and per-

---

[22] Hallo RAI 17:118f. Cf. Hallo 1983:19 with note 61; Renger, RLA 5 (1976)
130.
[23] Kraus *apud* Hallo 1983:19.
[24] Frayne 1981.
[25] Cf. also Frayne 1983.
[26] Frayne 1990, 1993, *passim.*
[27] Hallo 1988.
[28] Buccellati 1993.

haps incidentally to advertise the excellence of the road system he had commissioned. [29] Though the statue itself is lost, its description in a literary text of King Ishme-Dagan of Isin alerts us to the possibility that the actually surviving monuments of the Mesopotamian kings may also have their correlations in the texts.

Bibliographical References

Biggs, Robert D., 1969, review of Jaritz 1967 in BiOr 26:207-209.

Börker-Klähn, Jutta, 1974: "Šulgi badet," ZA 64:235-240.

Buccellati, Giorgio, 1993: "Through a tablet darkly: a reconstruction of Old Akkadian monuments described in Old Babylonian copies," Hallo AV 58-71.

Dietrich, Manfried, 1989: "Das Einsetzungsritual der Entu von Emar," UF 21:47-100.

Draffkorn Kilmer, Anne, 1963, 1965: "The first tablet of malku-šarru," JAOS 83:421-446; 85:208.

Falkenstein, Adam, 1966: Die Inschriften Gudeas von Lagaš I. Einleitung (= AnOr 30).

Fleming, Daniel, E., 1992: The Installation of Baal's High Priestess at Emar: a Window on Ancient Syrian Religion (=HSS 42).

Franke, Judith, 1977: "Presentation seals of the Ur III/Isin-Larsa period" in McGuire Gibson and Robert D. Biggs, eds., Seals and Sealing in the Ancient Near East (= BM 6) 61-66.

Frayne, Douglas R., 1981: The Historical Correlations of the Sumerian Royal Hymns (2400-1900 B.C.) (Ann Arbor, MI, University Microfilms).

———, 1983: "Šulgi, the runner," JAOS 103:739-748.

———, 1990: The Old Babylonian Period (= RIME 2).

———, 1993: The Sargonic and Gutian Periods (= RIME 2).

Hallo, William W., 1957: Early Mesopotamian Royal Titles (= AOS 43).

———, 1980: "Royal titles from the Mesopotamian periphery," AnSt 30:180-195.

———, 1983: "Sumerian historiography" in H. Tadmor and M. Weinfeld, eds., History, Historiography and Interpretation (Jerusalem, Magnes) 9-20.

———, 1988: "Texts, statues and the cult of the deified king," VTS 40:54-66.

Jacobsen, Thorkild, 1957, 1970: "Early political development in Mesopotamia," ZA 52:91-140; repr. in TIT 132-156, 366-396.

Jaritz, Kurt, 1967: Schriftarchäologie der altmesopotamischen Kultur (Graz, Akademische Druck- und Verlagsanstalt).

Levine, Baruch A., 1974: In the Presence of the Lord: a Study of Some Cultic Terms in Ancient Israel (=Studies in Judaism in Late Antiquity 5) (Leiden, Brill).

McEwan, C.W., 1934: The Oriental Sources of Hellenistic Kingship (= SAOC 13).

Otten, Heinrich, 1958: Hethitische Totenrituale (Berlin, Akademie-Verlag).

Schmökel, Hartmut, 1956: Heilige Hochzeit und Hohes Lied (= Abhandlungen für die Kunde des Morgenlandes 32/1).

Seux, M.-J., 1967: Epithètes Royaux Akkadiennes et Sumériennes (Paris, Letouzey et Ané).

Sollberger, Edmond, 1965: "Three Ur-Dynasty documents," JCS 19:26-30.

Winter, Irene, 1986: "The king and the cup: iconography of the royal presentation scene on Ur III seals," Porada AV 253-268 and pls. 62-64.

---

[29] Frayner 1983 and above, chapter III 1.

2. The Royal Lifetime: Birth, Coronation, Death

As we have seen, the ancient Near Eastern conception of kingship, and especially its Sumerian manifestation, involved leadership in a variety of functions—political, military, judicial and economic, among others. But it was fundamentally a religious conception, and can therefore also be studied from a cultic perspective, or in terms of what may be called the sacraments of the royal lifetime. One could include among these such crucial events as the young prince's induction into the scribal school, his marriage to an earthly princess as well as to a divine bride in the guise, perhaps, of a priestess, his construction of temples, installation of high-priests and priestesses, and dedication of sacred votive objects, even veneration of the king in statue form after his death. All these events are routinely commemorated in the three broad textual categories considered above: date formulas, building and votive inscriptions, and royal hymns. But I will confine myself to three other sacraments of the royal lifetime: birth, coronation and death. All three are universal elements of kingship; if there exists any link between the ancient Near Eastern institution and our own, it should be visible here.

"The birth of kings" was discussed by me in its relationship to the relatively novel ideology of divine kingship, which was introduced into Mesopotamia by the Akkadian rulers of the Sargonic Dynasty, and posed so many problems for the traditional Sumerian ethos. [30] How the religious establishment responded to the challenge has been considered in connection with the cult. [31] But even the monarchy faced a dilemma: how to reconcile the asserted divine status of the ruling king with his admittedly human status before his accession. One solution was to claim—retroactively— a divine parentage for the reigning king. [32] But this was not a completely satisfactory solution, since there was no attempt to combine this assertion of divine descent with any denial of human, albeit royal, parentage, a parentage which, moreover, tended to date back to a period *before* the royal father's own accession.

A more satisfying solution—indeed a genial one—was therefore found, in my opinion, in the age-old institution of the sacred mar-

---

[30] Hallo 1987.
[31] Hallo 1993a.
[32] Sjöberg 1972.

riage. Here the king, or future king, represented the god, ideally Dumuzi; his partner, whether a priestess or, more likely, the future queen, represented the goddess, typically Inanna. In my hypothesis, if a son was born of the union, he was declared the crown-prince and thus invested with a parentage that was at one and the same time human (though royal) and divine!

A chief basis for my argument, though by no means the only one, was a royal hymn conventionally designated as "Shulgi G," which describes that king's birth, if not actually his conception, in the Ekur, the great temple of Enlil in Nippur. The text had been frequently cited and given a wide variety of interpretations in discussions of the sacred marriage. [33] But it had never enjoyed a proper edition and full analysis. These needs have now been met by Jacob Klein in two separate articles. [34] In both of them he takes strong issue with my interpretation, questioning whether the hymn truly describes a sacred marriage [35] and, indeed, whether it records a historical event at all, or represents rather a theological apologia for Ur-Nammu's violent death and Shulgi's sudden accession. [36]

Much depends, I admit, on the identity of the female partner in the sacred marriage, for which this text remains potentially the best witness. She is described there with the term *en*, a Sumerian word that can be translated by Akkadian *ēnu*, " (high) priest" or *ēntu*, " (high) priestess," and we are told that "the *gipāru* served as the place of the fertility rite of the 'sacred marriage' and thus as the residence of the human partner in the rite, the *ēnu* or the *ēntu*." [37] Even Klein translates the crucial line 18 by: "the *en*-priestess gave birth to a 'faithful man' from (the semen) which has been placed in her womb." [38] Such high priestesses were often daughters of the king [39] and as such would, as Klein does not fail to point out, involve the king in an incestuous relationship for which there is otherwise absolutely no evi-

---

[33] See the summary in Hallo 1987:50.

[34] Klein 1987 and 1991.

[35] Klein 1987:105 top.

[36] Ibid. 105f.

[37] CAD G 84cd.

[38] Klein 1987: 99. Cf. his transliteration: *en-ne ša-tur-še gál-la-na lú-zi mi-ni-ù-tu*, based on Jacobsen (below, n. 41). For a different rendering, see S.N. Kramer, RAI 19 (1974) 166, n. 16.

[39] See ANEH 85 for examples from Shulgi's dynasty.

dence. [40] In particular it was the high priestess of the moon-god
Nanna who was daughter of the sovereign and appointed by him for
life or for a long term, and on one view it was such a priestess who
was involved here. [41] But on occasion the high priestesses were *not*
daughters of the king, but members of the aristocracy in general. [42]
All such priestesses were specifically prohibited from having children,
it is generally held—largely on the basis of the Laws of Hammurapi
(paragraphs 144-147, 178-184) and other Old Babylonian evidence. [43] But in my opinion they were denied this right only with
respect to ordinary mortals precisely *in order* to reserve their child-
bearing capacity for the king!

New and hitherto unpublished evidence now provides precious
new support for this interpretation. Among the incantations of the
Frau Professor Hilprecht Collection at Jena, J.J.A. van Dijk and J.
Oelsner have found one which specifically refers to Shulgi in terms
which I cite here with their permission as "the man of the *en*-priestess
(who) came forth from a 'virgin'." [44] Although it is technically possible that what is involved is rather the common personal name Lu-
enna, the interpretation offered here seems much more probable in
light of the parallels with the two preceding phrases: "the snake comes
out of the netherworld (*kur*), the scorpion out of the byre." Snake and
scorpion occur together in other topoi, once with birth-mother as
third element. [45] As to the Sumerian word translated by "virgin,"
(literally "pure place," Akkadian *ardatu*), it is moot whether it refers to
the precise physical condition of the priestess, for the legal status of
virginity in Mesopotamian law and custom remains a much-debated
question. [46] Suffice it to say that it presumably alludes, in poetic
terms, to her having reserved her sexual favors for the father of the
crown-prince, the founder of the Third Dynasty of Ur, Ur-Nammu.

Strange as it may seem, the coronation of this king is an equally
contentious issue. Thirty years ago I launched the debate with a

---

[40] For the possibility that Ibbi-Sin may have married his sister, see Jacobsen
1953:37, repr. TIT 174 and 408f., n. 6..

[41] T. Jacobsen, ZA 52 (1956) 126f., n. 80; repr. TIT 387f., n. 80; cited Hallo
1987:50 and n. 52.

[42] J. Renger, ZA 58 (1967) 126 Par. 20.

[43] A. Falkenstein apud Renger, ZA 58 (1967) 141, n. 233a.

[44] *lú-en-na ki-sikil-ta i-zi.*

[45] Hallo, 1990a:214.

[46] Cf. below, ch. VIII 1.

study based in part, once more, on a royal hymn. [47] Sollberger had previously shown that the coronation of the neo-Sumerian kings involved at least three cities of the realm, including the religious capital at Nippur, the political capital at Ur, and the prior home of the dynasty at Uruk. [48] This provided a close analogy to the sacred marriage, consummated in a number of different temples in various cities of the realm. In both rites, the blessings of relevant patron deities were invoked on the king and the country as a whole. The coronation ritual, in addition, involved the king's assumption of the insignia of office, or what may be called the regalia, including crown, scepter, staff and crook.

The last element may actually turn out to be, not another form of shepherd's staff, but rather the nose-rope (*eškiri*) by which oxherds led oxen and, by analogy, the king led his people. [49] Such a rope-like attachment is clearly pictured on the stele of Ur-Nammu, [50] and possibly on that of Hammurapi. [51] There was also a special garment reserved for royalty, but that is not mentioned in the hymn in question. [52] In addition, the king took his place on the royal throne to the accompaniment of the formula: "Oh youth of Suen, on your throne by Enlil (and) the lord Ashimbabbar!", [53] a formula that recurs in other contexts and has been subject to various interpretations. [54]

This scenario, inherently not unreasonable, was largely accepted by R.H. Wilkinson in his 1986 dissertation on the subject, [55] and has also found resonance among students of the comparable rites in Biblical Israel. [56] But it was rejected out of hand by Miguel Civil, who cited it as a veritable type-case of drawing inferences beyond the limits of the textual evidence. [57] While he did not adduce any specific reasons for his dissent, he seemed particularly to question the existence of a royal crown, or of a specific ceremony in which such a

---

[47] Hallo 1966.

[48] Sollberger 1956; differently Wilkinson 1986:210-212.

[49] Wilkinson 1986:36 n. 9.

[50] If it *is* Ur-Nammu's. Cf. Canby 1987.

[51] Porada and Hallo, Opificius AV 229, 234.

[52] Wilkinson 1986:227 s.v. *túg-ma6* (ME); cf, also *pala* (= *túg-nam-lugal*) and *túg-nam-nun-na*.

[53] Ashimbabbar is another name for or manifestation of the moon-god Suen (Sumerian Nanna).

[54] See above, ch. IV 2, at nn. 60-64.

[55] Wilkinson 1986.

[56] Ben-Barak 1980; Sauren 1971.

[57] Civil 1980:229.

crown was conferred on the king. I cannot accept his reservations. [58]
The king is routinely pictured on seals, steles and reliefs as wearing a
peculiar headdress, even if that headdress is not of a shape to justify
the interpretation of the pictogram for "king" as a man wearing such
a crown. [59] The literary texts, too, repeatedly speak of a royal crown,
and distinguish it lexically from the headdress of the high priest and
high priestess. [60] Archival texts detailing the expenditures incurred in
the coronation of Ibbi-Sin, and the cities involved, were assembled by
Sollberger to establish the ceremony in the first place (above), and
meantime one has been published dated to the last month of the
reign of his predecessor Shu-Sin and "on the day that Ibbi-Sin received the crown." [61] So Civil's objections leave me unconvinced.

A more serious objection comes from the subsequent discovery
that crucial lines from the presumed coronation-hymn of Ur-Nammu
recur verbatim in quite a different context, namely a collection of
antiphonal songs (*balbal-e*), perhaps love-songs, better suited to the sacred marriage than the coronation. [62] Does this make these lines little
more than clichés of the royal ideology, as Civil holds? There is at this
point simply no basis for deciding which context is the original,
though it is worth noting that the title (incipit) of the coronation
hymn has meantime been identified in a literary catalogue. [63] On the
other hand, there are by now several other candidates for inclusion in
the genre of coronation-hymns, or at least hymns that allude to a
prior coronation. Falkenstein had long ago, if tentatively, assigned the
hymn "Enlil suraše" to the genre, [64] Frayne suggested "Nanna-Suen's
Journey to Nippur" belonged there, [65] and Wilkinson has added several more. [66] Nor are neo-Sumerian kings the last to be honored by
the genre; the neo-Assyrian kings were likewise. [67] All over the ancient Near East, in fact, coronation ceremonies featured the compo-

---

[58] Cf. already Hallo 1990, esp. pp. 187, 199.

[59] Above, ch. VI 1.

[60] Falkenstein 1959:96f. For *muš* as the "corona" of land surrounding a city see
Hallo, JCS 23 (1970) 59 and nn. 17-24.

[61] Sollberger 1953: 48 and n.1. For the death and burial of Shu-Sin, see Sigrist
1989 and D. Charpin, N.A.B.U. 1992/4:80f. No. 106.

[62] Wilcke 1976:48ff.

[63] Hallo 1975:79. Same incipit in TMH n.F. 3:53 rev. 2'.

[64] Falkenstein 1959:10.

[65] Above, ch. IV 2, n. 64.

[66] Ur-Nammu C, Shulgi D+X (?), (G), P.

[67] For "Assurbanipal's Coronation Hymn" (LKA 31) cf. Livingstone 1989 No. 11.

sition and recitation, not just of brief hymns but of extended epics and other genres commemorating the heroic deeds of royal predecessors and ancestors. If this is the "Sitz in Leben" for the "Hebrew Epic" which some have proposed to see in much of Biblical narrative, [68] then we have here, at least, a bridge between Mesopotamian kingship and the modern variety.

Passing finally to the death of kings, it may be noted that *this* aspect has not been subject to debate. In fact, it has barely been taken up in research about Mesopotamia, or even Israel. Although the death of specific kings has been studied in individual articles, there had been no attention to the general topos as such (though it is frequent and distinct in both cultures) with one or two exceptions. [69] I was therefore entering virgin territory when I first broached the subject in 1987. [70] Since then at least two important studies have appeared on the subject, specifically on the burial rites of neo-Assyrian kings, [71] and some attention has also been paid to the funeral rites for the specifically neo-Assyrian institution of the substitute king (*šar pūhi*), [72] and to the neo-Assyrian mourning rites for Dumuzi. [73]

The original Dumuzi was, of course, himself a king, whether the antediluvian shepherd of Bad-tibira or the fisherman of the First Dynasty of Uruk. His death was mourned in numerous lamentations, while that of Gilgamesh, his successor at Uruk, was commemorated in myth and epic. [74] How Gilgamesh faced the Hobson's choice of achieving immortality by becoming ruler of the netherworld has been elucidated in an important study by Tzvi Abusch. [75] Moreover, according to a new reading of "The Death of Gilgamesh," "Gilgamesh makes a levy in his land and organizes the building of his tomb, reached by diverting the course of the Euphrates; then all his family and retinue is made to enter the tomb before the river returns to its course again." [76] This reading accords with the archaeological evi-

---

[68] Hallo, BP 78 and n. 8.
[69] Hallo 1991:150f., nn. 23 and 25, citing Cohn 1985 and Smit 1966.
[70] Hallo 1991:148, n. 1.
[71] McGinnis 1987; Deller 1987; cf. Scurlock 1991.
[72] Parpola 1970 No. 280 (= Parpola 1993 No. 352). For the funeral pyre (and cremation) implied here (and in No. 195 = 1993 No. 233) see K.R. Veenhof, *Phoenix* 38/1 (1992) 16f.
[73] Scurlock 1992.
[74] See below, ch. VII 2.
[75] See above, ch. V 3, n. 198.
[76] A. Cavigneaux and F. al-Rawi, *Iraq* 55 (1993) 93.

dence of the "Royal Graves" of Ur whose principal feature was the sacrifice, perhaps by mass suicide, of much of the royal court together with the royal couple—if indeed they are royalty. [77]

Did this grisly rite of the First Dynasty of Ur survive into the Third? There is some indirect evidence for the possibility that the widow of its founder, Ur-Nammu, expected to be interred with him, to judge by the moving lament for his death in battle which on that premise has been attributed to her. [78] But more startling still is the evidence for the rites surrounding the death of his son and successor Shulgi. It was previously known that on the second day of the eleventh month of his last (48th) year, this king was already receiving funerary offerings (ki-a-nag). [79] Now a routine archival document dating to the same month and newly published from the collection of Birmingham (England) [80] reveals that " 19 slave-girls working full-time and 2 slave-girls working 2/3 time worked for seven days, the equivalent of 142 1/3 woman-days, when the divine Shulgi was taken up into heaven to serve as doorkeeper." [81]

What this implies is nothing less than a revolution in our understanding of Sumerian funerary beliefs and customs, at least as they applied to royalty. For a period of seven days immediately following his death, the king was believed to have ascended to heaven, there to serve as one of two doorkeepers of heaven, roles normally assumed by the deities Dumuzi and (Nin)gizzida as we know from the myth of Adapa. [82] In particular, he seems to have served as a stand-in for Dumuzi, thus resuming in death the role he had already played in life during the rite of the sacred marriage. [83] Whether his consort followed him to the grave (as suggested above for the widow of Ur-Nammu) and thence to heaven to guard the other gatepost in (Nin)gizzida's place, or whether this role was filled by other members of his family or court (as suggested above for Gilgamesh) cannot as yet be shown.

In any case Shulgi's ascension presumably lasted no more than the

---

[77] Green 1975:46-53 questions whether the burials include royalty.
[78] See below, ch. VIII 3.
[79] Michalowski 1977:224f..
[80] Watson 1986 No. 132; cf. Horowitz and Watson 1991.
[81] Hallo 1991:158f.; *Maarav* 7 (1991) 180f.; cf. also below, ch. VII 2, n. 83.
[82] Foster, BP 1:429-434; FDD 97-101.
[83] See above at n. 33.

seven days specified in the account text from Drehem. Even if, as Horowitz and Watson suggest, the deceased king was cremated and according to later belief placed among the stars, [84] his earthly remains must have been buried at Ur, either in the hypogaeum recovered by the excavations or in the palace (possibly the *é-hur-sag*) attested by the texts, [85] along with material objects reflecting suitably on his royal status. As for the seven-day mourning period following burial, it is associated with Mesopotamian kings as far back as Gilgamesh [86] and Naram-Sin and for the queen-mother as late as Adad-guppi, while in Rabbinic exegesis it can be traced back to antediluvian times and the long-lived Methuselah. [87] The Jewish custom of an initial period of intense mourning lasting seven days and therefore known as *shiv'a* thus has hoary royal precedent.

The death of kings is a fact of life, but a problem for ideology. [88] If kingship in general is divinely sanctioned, and a particular king follows the divine behest, then he should die at a ripe old age and enjoy burial with his royal ancestors. But to the extent that kingship is an affront to the theocratic order, or if a particular king transgresses the divine norms, or even presumes to rival the gods, then he should meet an early or untoward end, and his departed spirit should know neither rest nor reverence. That such was not always the case in practice is obvious. As the problem of theodicy confronted theology, so the death of kings posed a challenge to historiography. In Egypt it was met by denial: the departed pharaoh was simply believed to live on after death. In the Mesopotamian tradition, where kingship was a divinely ordained norm from the beginning of history on, and where "the death of kings seems to have been a taboo subject for the ancient scribes," [89] any truly untimely or bizarre end required explanation, and this was often provided by alleged transgressions against the norms. In Israel, kingship represented a departure from a previously ordained theocratic order, and an assimilation to foreign norms. Only the special, and conditional, covenant bestowed on David allowed him and some of his descendants to merit ripe old age, a peaceful death and proper burial;   the prophetic sanction of

---

[84] Horowitz and Watson 1991. Cf. also above, note 72.

[85] Moorey 1984.

[86] T. Abusch, JANES 22 (1993) 8 and n. 5.

[87] Hallo, Gevirtz AV 178-180 for these and other Biblical and Apocryphal examples.

[88] What follows is essentially the conclusion of Hallo 1991.

[89] Michalowski 1977:224. But cf. Hallo 1991:164, n. 138.

Jeroboam's secession provided similarly for a minority of the kings of Israel. In each case, such a desirable end was deemed worthy of special notice by the Deuteronomic historian of the Book of Kings, and (where the Davidic house was concerned) by the Chronicler. Each of them struggled in his own way to justify the peaceful end of a wicked king such as Manasseh, or the violent death of a pious monarch such as Josiah. And all of Biblical historiography took a particular interest in the violent death of foreign kings. As a result, we have some intriguing convergences of Biblical and Mesopotamian traditions, as in the cases of Sargon and Sennacherib of Assyria, or of the last Chaldean king. In each case the objective records are to some extent reconcilable with each other, but the interpretation put on the event is different.

In fine, the theme of the death of kings looms large in the historiography of both Israel and Mesopotamia. In both traditions, the instances of unusual deaths predominate. We read of suicide, assassination, death in battle, if not in single combat, and by a variety of accidents, some so improbable as to defy belief. There can be little doubt that some of the tales are paradigmatic, i.e., intended to convey the lesson that royal excesses lead to king-sized grief. They thus serve the didactic purposes of the narrator: whether as a kind of mirror for princes, or to advance the claims of one royal house against another or, most significantly, to polemicize against the very institution of kingship from a non-monarchist or anti-monarchist perspective, be that priestly or, in Israel's case, prophetic.

Other tales may be more simply described as entertaining or edifying rather than didactic, i.e., intended to amuse an audience for whom royalty was a natural focus of interest. Such tales, too, need to be used with extreme caution when reconstructing the history of the ancient Near East.

But with all due allowance made for these two characterizations, there remains a residue of authentic memories, or tales with authentic cores, about the great kings of the Biblical and Mesopotamian traditions. And no matter which interpretation we favor, we can appreciate Shakespeare's summons as put into the mouth of King Richard II (*Richard II*, Act III Scene ii): [90]

---

[90] Cf. Julius Caesar II ii: "The heavens themselves blaze forth the death of princes."

For God's sake, let us sit upon the ground
And tell sad stories of the death of kings.
How some have been deposed, some slain in war,
Some haunted by the ghosts they have deposed;
Some poison'd by their wives, some sleeping kill'd;
All murdered: for within the hollow crown
That rounds the mortal temples of a king
Keeps Death his court ....

Bibliographical References

Ben-Barak, Zafrira, 1980: "The coronation ceremony in ancient Mesopotamia,"
    OLP 11:55-67.
Canby, Jeanny V., 1987: "A monumental puzzle: reconstructing the Ur-Nammu
    Stela," *Expedition* 29:54-64.
Civil, Miguel, 1980: "Les limites de l'information textuelle," in *L'archéologie de l'Iraq
    ...* (= Colloques Internationaux du CNRS 580) 225-232.
Cohn, Robert, 1985: "Conversion and creativity in the Book of Kings: the case of
    the dying monarch," CBQ 47:603-616.
Deller, K., 1987: "The sealed burial chamber," SAAB 1:69-71.
Falkenstein, Adam, 1959: *Sumerische Götterlieder I. Teil* (Heidelberg, Carl Winter).
Green, Alberto R.W., 1975: *The Role of Human Sacrifice in the Ancient Near East* (=ASOR
    Dissertation Series 1) (Missoula, MO, Scholars Press).
Hallo, William W., 1966: "The coronation of Ur-Nammu," JCS 20:133-141.
————, 1975, 1977: "Another Sumerian literary catalogue?" StOr 46:77-80, 48/3:3.
————, 1987: "The birth of kings," Pope AV 45-52.5
————, 1990: "The limits of skepticism," JAOS 110:187-199.
————, 1990a: "Proverbs quoted in epic," Moran AV 203-217.
————, 1991: "The death of kings," Tadmor AV 148-165.
————, 1993: "Disturbing the dead," Sarna AV 185-192.
————, 1993a: "Sumerian religion," Kutscher AV 15-35.
Horowitz, W. and P.J. Watson, 1991: "Further notes on the Birmingham Tablets Vol-
    ume I," ASJ 13:409-417.
Jacobsen, Thorkild, 1953, 1970: "The reign of Ibbi-Suen," JCS 7:36-47, repr. TIT
    173-186, 408-416.
Klein, Jacob, 1987: "The birth of a crownprince in the temple: a neo-Sumerian lit-
    erary topos," RAI 33:97-106.
————, 1991: "The coronation and consecration of Šulgi in the Ekur (Šulgi G),"
    Tadmor AV 292-313.
Livingstone, Alasdair, 1989: *Court Poetry and Literary Miscellanea* (= SAA 3).
McGinnis, J., 1987: "A neo-Assyrian text describing a royal funeral," SAAB 1:1-11.
Michalowski, Piotr, 1977: "The death of Šulgi," Or. 46:220-225.
Moorey, P.R.S., 1984: "Where did they bury the kings of the IIIrd Dynasty of Ur?"
    Iraq 46:1-18.
Parpola, Simo, 1970: *Letters from Assyrian Scholars* (= AOAT 5/1).
————, 1993: *Letters from Assyrian and Babylonian Scholars* (= SAA 10).
Sauren, Herbert, 1971: "L'intronisation du roi en Israël à la lumière d'une lettre de
    Mari," OLP 2:5-12.
Scurlock, JoAnn, 1991: " *Taklimtu*: a display of grave goods?" N.A.B.U. 1991/1:3 No.
    3.

————, 1992: "K 164 (*BA* 2, P. 635): new light on the mourning rites for Dumuzi?" RA 86:53-67.

Sigrist, Marcel, 1989: "Le devil pour šu-sin," Sjöberg AV 499-505.

Sjöberg, Åke W., 1972: "Die göttliche Abstammung der sumerischen Könige," Or. Suec. 21:87-112.

Smit, E.J., 1966: "Death- and burial formulas in Kings and Chronicles relating to the kings of Judah," in A.H. van Zyl, ed., *Biblical Essays* (Stellenbosch, Die Ou-Testamentiese Werkgemeenskap in Suid-Afrika).

Sollberger, Edmond, 1953: "Remarks on Ibbîsîn's reign," JCS 7:48-50

————, 1956: "Texts relating to Ibbî-Sîn's coronation," JCS 10:18-20.

Watson, P.J., 1986: *Neo-Sumerian texts from Drehem* (Warminster, Aris and Phillips).

Wilcke, Claus, 1976: *Kollationen zu den sumerischen Texten aus Nippur* ... (Berlin, Akademie-Verlag).

Wilkinson, R.H., 1986: *Mesopotamian Coronation and Accession Rites in the Neo-Sumerian and Early Old Babylonian Periods, c. 2100 - 1800 B.C.)* (Ann Arbor, University Microfilms).

3. THE ROYAL AFTERLIFE

In all ages of civilization, human beings have challenged the brutal reality of death with two unconquerable dreams: one the hope of longevity, and the other the illusion of immortality—the more so where royalty was concerned. In the ancient Near East, royal ancestors were venerated or even worshipped to an extent hardly imaginable today. [91] In what follows, the varieties of royal ancestor cults will be briefly reviewed, and then some ancient conceptions of death and the afterlife studied for their possible influence on our own.

In Egypt, where the king was considered a god, the death of kings was met by denial: the departed pharaoh was simply believed to live on after death. The enormous pyramids of the Old Kingdom gave monumental expression to this belief; by mummifying his physical remains, concealing them in a massive tomb, and providing for them ever after with daily offerings and prayers, the Egyptians hoped that the king would continue to assure the fertility and general well-being of his country long after his apparent demise.

Among the Hittites, departed royalty was believed, or at least said, to have "become a god," and enjoyed elaborate funerary rites, [92] followed by permanent offerings, not at the grave, but before the statue or image of the departed. [93]

Among the Western Semites, the spirits of long-deceased royalty, including both the king and his kin, assumed a semi-divine status as *repha' im*, who could become demonic threats to the living if not properly revered and provided for. [94] This was true in varying degrees at Ebla in the third millennium, at Ugarit in the second, and in Israel in the first. At Ebla, lengthy lists of departed kings were maintained, together with their offerings. [95] At Ugarit, where these spirits were probably called *rapi' uma*, their offerings were the subject of a whole group of special texts.[96] In the Bible, the *repha' im* were sometimes understood as an archaic ethnic group, or as the spirits of the dead in general, but also in the more specific sense of deceased kings and

---

[91] See in detail Hallo 1992, with previous literature, to which add especiallly Lewis 1989.
[92] Christmann-Franck 1971.
[93] Hallo 1992:383.
[94] Levine and de Tarragon 1984.
[95] Hallo 1992a:142f.
[96] Pitard 1987; 1992.

other chieftains (e.g. in Isa. 14:9) and subject to a royal cult of the
dead. [97] One curious feature that they share with what may be representations of these creatures in ancient Near Eastern art is their
"polydactilism," as illustrated by the six fingers and toes of the Philistine giant who was an offspring of the Rephaim in II Sam. 21:20 (=
I Chr. 20:6). Such polydactilism has been noted on Philistine coffins
as well as on the winged figures adorning cauldrons from Cyprus,
Greece and Urartu (Ararat). [98] It is also regarded as ominous in the
Babylonian mantic series *šumma izbu* which is devoted to freak births
and their interpretation (teratoscopy). [99]

In Mesopotamia, the cult of deceased royalty was intimately tied
to the evolution of the cult-statue, i.e., in effect, a life-size or near
life-size effigy. The development may be traced in a kind of dialectic
as follows: initially only the departed royal ancestors were worshipped
in the guise of cult-statues (a good illustration is provided by the silver
statue of Shagshag, wife of Urukagina of Lagash); [100] after the deification of kings Naram-Sin and Shar-kali-sharri of Akkad in the 23rd
century B.C., both living royalty and "real" gods were represented by
and worshipped as cult-statues; once the secular status of royalty was
restored by Hammurapi in the 18th century, cult-statues of the deceased royal ancestors continued to be worshipped alongside those of
the "living" gods. [101] At the same time the emphasis of the cult shifted
from the libations poured to the dead kings, *a-bal-bal* = *mê maqqiā-
tim* [102] and especially *ki-a-nag* (literally "the place of drinking—or caus-
ing to drink—water") to the meals ostensibly served to them but more
likely eaten by the living in their memory. [103] Such a meal is called
kispu (literally "morsel"?) in Akkadian, and *ki-sì-ga* ("grave") in
Sumerian, but a truer Sumerian equivalent may be *gizbun* ("banquet") written with (and thus replacing) an earlier Sumerian logogram *ki-kaš-gar* (literally "place where beer is put") and later
equated with Akkadian *takultu* ("divine repast"). [104]

---

[97] Hallo 1992:382-386.
[98] Barnett 1985, 1986, 1986-87.
[99] Leichty 1970:59f. (III 54-60).
[100] Cf. P. Steinkeller, *Iraq* 52 (1990) 22, n. 30, and especially Selz 1992. For a
cult-statue of Kubatum in the "gate of Enlil," see now R. de Maaijer, JEOL 33
(1995) 117-120.
[101] Hallo 1992:389; 1993:18-22. Note also the statue of Enkidu which Gilgamesh
made after the former's death according to an exemplar of Tablet VIII from Sultan
Tepe; cf. Gurney 1954:95; ANET 506; Lambert, RAI 7 (1960) 54.
[102] MSL 13:84:12-14.
[103] Tsukimoto 1985.
[104] Hallo 1993a:191f.

Although the term *kispu* does not actually occur in it, it is thought that the so-called Genealogy of the Hammurapi Dynasty is the record of such a cult-meal, perhaps on the occasion of the coronation of king Ammi-saduqa of Babylon in the 17th century; it included an invitation to all his royal predecessors and to their non-royal ancestors to eat and drink and bless the new king. [105] The emergence of the *kispu*-ritual in Old Babylonian times, and especially at Mari, may well have served in part to tie together the successive generations of each of the new Amorite dynasties, as well as to unite the separate dynasties under real or imaginary common ancestors, thus serving the purposes of their genealogical orientation. [106]

Another funerary repast thought to have figured at times in the cult of deceased kings (as well as commoners) is the rite asssociated with the institution known from the Bible as the *marze'ach* (Jer. 16:5; Amos 6:7). [107] It too may be attested as early as the texts from third millennium Ebla. [108] In the second millennium it is documented at Ugarit, [109] in the first in Israel and Judah, and in the "Israelian" colony at Elephantine in Egypt. At the turn of the millennium it is known from Phoenician and Punic settlements in the Piraeus near Athens and at Marseilles, and in Nabataean settlements at Petra in Jordan and Avdat in the Negev. Thereafter, it is frequently found in Palmyrene inscriptions, on the Madeba map, and in Rabbinic literature. [110] If Barnett is correct in describing the famous palace relief from Nineveh showing King Assurbanipal banqueting as illustrating a *marze'ach*, then it would be possible to argue that, in this case at least, it was meant to honor his royal ancestors. [111]

In all the ancient Near East, it may well be that the royal ancestor cult is best documented at Old Babylonian Mari, that great citadel on the middle Euphrates where east and west Semitic customs met and commingled. [112] We have already cited its evidence for the *kispu* ritual; this features prominently the "dead kings" (*maliku*) known also

---

[105] Finkelstein 1966.
[106] Hallo, Sachs AV (1988) 180-183.
[107] King 1989; Lewis 1989:80-94; Paul 1991:210-212, with full bibliography; Hallo 1992:383f. with nn. 27f., 400 n. 132.
[108] Pettinato, MEE 2:46 rev. i 2; cf. Paul 1980:211 n. 104 end.
[109] Loretz 1982.
[110] King 1989; Paul 1991:210-212.
[111] Barnett 1985.
[112] Malamat 1989, especially pp. 96-107: "The royal ancestor cult."

from Ugaritic ritual and comparable to the chthonic (underworld) demons of Mesopotamia known there as *malku*, [113] which may be the
restless spirits of departed kings. [114] Others compare these Mari
maliku rather to the "counselors, princes, or other high court function-
aries" of the Akkadian tradition, [115] or to the "ghosts of kings" (*ma-
al-ku-um lugal-lugal-e-ne*) at early Old Babylonian Isin. [116]

This overview, cursory as it is, will have to suffice to demonstrate
the importance attached to royal ancestors, and the cultic steps taken
to translate that concern into practical terms. This concern rested on
an underlying conception of the afterlife and the netherworld which,
for all its variations, is remarkably uniform and widespread in its essentials, and has passed into many of our own notions on these matters—all beyond empiric verification as they are. These essentials
include the following: (1) that the deceased descend below the earth,
though in the case of kings they might briefly ascend to heaven
first; [117] (2) that the deceased retain their status in death or even, in
the case of royalty, improve it in the sense that some of them could
acquire divine status even if they did not enjoy it in life; (3) that deceased kings could continue to secure the blessings of fertility for their
surviving subjects, provided the latter took care to provide adequately
for them. [118]

Echoes of these traditions survive in Christian belief, notably in
the concepts of heaven and hell, the canonization of worthy individuals—including royalty—in the guise of sainthood conferred upon them
posthumously by the Church, and their veneration in statue form. In
the Jewish tradition, the concept of Messianism involves belief in the
restoration of a Davidic king, the bodily resurrection of his subjects,
and the universal acknowledgement of a single divine kingship.

---

[113] CAD M/1:168f. s.v. *malku* B.

[114] Dietrich and Loretz 1981:69-74.

[115] Healey 1975, 1978, 1986; cf. D. Charpin and J.-M. Durand, RA 80 (1986)
168f.

[116] Hallo 1992:401, n. 138, based on BIN 9:440:31.

[117] See above, ch. VI 2.

[118] For a thorough review of the evidence, see now Schmidt 1996, which appeared too late to be incorporated here. Schmidt concludes (pp. 274-293) that there
was no organized ancestor worship or even simple veneration of (royal) ancestors in
the "Syro-Palestinian" world before Hellinistic times; for the "Syro-Mesopotamian"
situation he refers to my previous studies frequently if not always accurately (see esp.
pp. 18 n. 11, 42 n. 147, and 276 n.5).

Bibliographical References

Barnett, Richard D., 1985: "Assurbanipal's feast," EI 18:1*-6*.
————, 1986: "Sirens and rephaim," Mellink AV 112-120.
————, 1986-7: "Six fingers in art and archaeology," *Bulletin of the Anglo-Israel Archaeological Society* 6:5-12.
Christmann-Frank, L., 1971: "Le rituel des funéraires royales hittites," RHA 29:61-111.
Dietrich, M. and O. Loretz, 1981: "Neue Studien zu den Ritualtexten aus Ugarit (I): ein Forschungsbericht," UF 13:63-100.
Finkelstein, Jacob J., 1966: "The genealogy of the Hammurapi Dynasty," JCS 20:95-118.
Gurney, Oliver R., 1954: "Two fragments of the Epic of Gilgamesh from Sultantepe," JCS 8:87-95.
Hallo, William W., 1992: "Royal ancestor worship in the Biblical world," Talmon AV 381-401.
————, 1992a: "Ebrium at Ebla," *Eblaitica* 3:139-150.
————, 1993: "Sumerian religion," Kutscher AV 15-35.
————, 1993a: "Disturbing the dead," Sarna AV 183-192.
Healey, J.F., 1975: " *Malku:Mlkm:Anunnaki*," UF 7:235-238.
————, 1978: " *Mlkm/Rp'um* and the *kispum*," UF 10:89-91.
————, 1986: "The Ugaritic dead: some live issues," UF 18:27-32.
King, Phillip J., 1989: "The *marzeah*: textual and archaeological evidence," EI 20 (= Yadin AV) 98*-106*.
Leichty, Erle, 1970: *The Omen Series Šumma Izbu* (= TCS 4) (Locust Valley, NY, J.J. Augustin).
Levine, B.A. and J.-M. de Tarragon, 1984: "Dead kings and rephaim," JAOS 104:649-659.
Lewis, Theodore J., 1989: *Cults of the Dead in Ancient Israel and Ugarit* (= HSM 39).
Loretz, Oswald, 1982: "Ugaritisch-biblisches *marzh* 'Kultmahl, Kultverein' in Jer. 16,5 und Am. 6,7: Bemerkungen zur Geschichte des Totenkultes in Israel," Schreiner AV 87-93.
Malamat, Abraham, 1989: *Mari and the Early Israelite Experience* (= Schweich Lectures 1984) (Oxford, Oxford U.P.).
Paul, Shalom M., 1991: *Amos: a Commentary on the Book of Amos* (= Hermeneia) (Minneapolis, Fortress Press).
Pitard, Wayne T., 1987: "RS 34.126: Notes on the text," *Maarav* 4:111-155.
————, 1992: "A new edition of the 'Rāpi'ūma' texts,: KTU 1:20-22," BASOR 285:33-77.
Schmidt, Brian B., 1994: *Israel's Beneficent Dead: Ancestor Cult and Necromancy in Ancient Israelite Religion and Tradition* (Tübingen, J.C.B. Mohr). Repr. 1996 (Winona Lake, IN, Eisenbrauns).
Selz, Gebhard J., 1992: "Eine Kultstatue der Herrschergemahlin Šaša: ein Beitrag zum Problem der Vergöttlichung," ASJ 14:245-268.
Tsukimoto, A., 1985: *Untersuchungen zur Totenpflege (kispum) im alten Mesopotamien* (= AOAT 216).

CHAPTER SEVEN

RELIGION

For the modern world, religion is at best a part of life, but in the ancient world, religion was, in a sense, all of life. Characteristically, the languages of the ancient Near East had no special word for what in Latin is called *religio*. They made do with words of foreign origin, or of other meaning, or by coining circumlocutions like the later Hebrew "fear of heaven" (*yir'at shamayim*). Yet such is the modern debt to ancient Near Eastern religions that no survey of institutional origins would be complete without it. Three of the most distinctive aspects of those religions are sacrifice, prayer and lamentation. In what follows, these aspects will be surveyed, not for their influence on our own religious beliefs or practices, but in terms of the ancients' self-perceptions as compared with modern scholarly reconstructions.

1. The sacrificial cult [1]

In 1972, the classicist Walter Burkert published his "interpretations of ancient Greek sacrificial rites and myths" under the title *Homo Necans*, [2] "murderous humanity," no doubt with a nod to Jan Huizinga's earlier and equally famous treatment of *Homo Ludens*, [3] "playful humanity." Burkert surveyed the anthropological and more particularly the Greek literary evidence for the origins and motivations of animal sacrifice, and reconstructed them approximately as follows. Prior to the domestication of plants and animals, hunting-gathering groups divided the essential functions of victualling themselves between the sexes, with men assigned to the hunt and women to the gathering of edible plants. But the hunt required collective action and the aid of traps and weapons, and these mechanics held a potential threat in that they could conceivably be turned inward against members of the group. Hence the catching and dispatching of the animal prey was

---

[1] This is a modified and updated version of Hallo 1987.
[2] Burkert 1972, 1983.
[3] Huizinga 1955.

gradually hedged about with "ritualistic" restrictions designed to reduce the likelihood of internecine conflicts among the hunters.

With the domestication of plants and animals, the earlier sexual
specialization tended to disappear, but the replacement of wild prey
with domesticated victims created new problems. [4] Now the bull,
cow, goat or lamb led to the slaughter was not only defenseless but
more or less human-like in appearance and disposition. Thus dispatching it could not be justified in terms of self-defense or as an act
of manly valor but on the contrary evoked feelings of guilt to add to
those of terror previously present. To assuage these new feelings, the
earlier "ritual," which essentially consisted of *agenda*, or the performance of prescribed actions, was complemented by *dicenda*, or the recitation of prescribed formulas which, at their most elaborate, evolved
into mythologems. Myth and ritual, thus combined, invested what
otherwise might have constituted essentially "profane slaughter" [5]
with the aura of sanctity, literally "making it holy" —the etymological
sense of sacri-fice. [6] The sacrificial character of animal slaughter was
confirmed by dedicating the victim to the deity and treating the human consumption of the meat as a kind of fringe-benefit redounding
to the participants in the rite.

In the very same year that Burkert published his monograph,
René Girard published his *Violence and the Sacred*. [7] Girard covers much
of the same ground as Burkert and his premises are similar, but his
conclusions diverge. Thus he too postulates an inherent threat of internecine violence in the primitive group but sees it, not so much
activated by the hunting or slaughtering of the animal, but rather
defused by it. In other words the animal serves as a substitute for the
human victim of aggression, the hunt or the sacrifice as an outlet for
the innate disposition toward violence which, once aroused, must be
satisfied or assuaged. On this theory, the role of the deity recedes into
the background or rather becomes a secondary embellishment to an
essentially human or, at best, human-animal nexus of relationships.
(Often enough, the substitute victim is also human.) What counts, on
this view, is that the murder of the substitute-victim not be avenged,

---

[4] In a new survey of the subject, it is noted that animal sacrifice (henceforth)
always involved domesticated victims; Smith in Burkert, Girard and Smith 1982:197.

[5] See below.

[6] See the authorities cited in Hallo 1987:11, nn. 5f.

[7] Girard 1972; 1977.

as this might unleash an endless cycle of vengeance threatening to wipe out the entire group. It is to this end that the murder is invested with the mythic and ritual sanctions that turn it into a sacrificial act. And it is for this reason that sacrifice loses its significance in societies which have substituted a firm judicial system for more "primitive" notions of private or public vengeance.

Of these two comparable but discrete analyses, the former comes nearer to providing a clue to unraveling the mysteries of the sacrificial cult as these are enshrined in the Hebrew Bible, [8] while the latter bears comparison with the Mesopotamian situation. [9] Many gallons of ink have been spilled on this issue over the decades, but I may perhaps be permitted to simplify by way of orientation. According to Israelite belief, the shedding of animal blood was in some sense an offense against nature and courted the risk of punishment, although never on the level of human bloodshed. It was to obviate such punishment that successive provisions were made to invest the act of animal slaughtering with a measure of divine sanction. The common denominator of these provisions was to turn mere slaughter into sanctification. The sacri-fice was a sacred-making of the consumption that followed. [10]

Biblical attitudes toward the consumption of meat underwent three distinct transformations. In the primeval order of things, men and beasts alike were vegetarians by divine command. This is most explicit in the mythic version of creation prefaced to the priestly narrative: "See, I give you every seed-bearing plant that is upon all the earth, and every tree that has seed-bearing fruit; they shall be yours for food. And to all the animals ... [I give] all the green plants for food" (Gen. 1:29f.). It is only slightly less explicit in the epic version that begins the so-called J document: "Of every tree of the garden you are free to eat" (Gen. 2:16). It is also the state to which beasts, at least, are to revert in the messianic age when, according to the prophetic view, "the lion, like the ox, shall eat straw" (Isa. 11:7).

This original dispensation was superseded after the flood by a new promulgation which, while echoing it, reversed it completely: "Every creature that lives shall be yours to eat; as with the green grasses, I give you all these" (Gen. 9:3). The only restriction added immedi-

---

[8] For a new comparison of the Greek and Biblical evidence, see Katz 1990.
[9] Cf. especially Limet 1989.
[10] Hallo, BP 65f.

ately (Gen. 9:4) is: "You must not, however, eat flesh with life-blood in it." This act is virtually equated with homicide (Gen. 9:5). In the later rabbinic view, the new dispensation is one of the seven "Noahide laws" that are binding on all the descendants of Noah, that is, on all mankind. [11]

An entirely different principle was invoked in the legislation of the Holiness Code (Lev. 17-26), generally held to be one of the oldest strata surviving within the so-called Priestly Document (P). The levitical enactment postulates that "the life of the flesh is in the blood, and I have assigned it to you for making expiation for your lives upon the altar; it is the blood, as life, that effects expiation" (Lev. 17:11). In Jacob Milgrom's view, the expiation involved here is nothing less than ransom for a capital offense. Under the levitical dispensation, animal slaughter *except at the authorized altar* is murder. The animal too has life (older versions: "soul"), its vengeance is to be feared, its blood must be "covered" or expiated by bringing it to the altar. [12]

The final Biblical revision of the law of meat consumption was promulgated by Deuteronomy, presumably in the context of the Josianic reform of the seventh century. Again following Milgrom, [13] who in this instance, however, was preceded by A.R. Hulst, [14] we may see the repeated formulas introduced by "as I/He swore/com-manded/promised" as *citations* of earlier legislation, whether written or (in this case) oral. What King Josiah in effect instituted reconciled the older prohibition against "profane slaughter" with the newer cen-tralization of the cult: if the only authorized altar was to be in Jeru-salem, then slaughter without benefit of altar had to be permitted outside Jerusalem as a matter of practical necessity.

This reconstruction of the evolution of Israelite sacrifice, essentially based on Milgrom, differs significantly from earlier theories. [15] But it shows striking parallels with the Mesopotamian situation as this is emerging from a plethora of evidence. For here we have not only, as in Israel and elsewhere, the canonical (literary) formulations of how sacrificial rites are to be performed, or what can be designated "pre-scriptive rituals," but also the archival (economic) texts, the after-the-

---

[11] Novak 1983.
[12] Milgrom 1971.
[13] Milgrom 1976; 1978.
[14] Hulst 1963.
[15] For some of these see Hallo 1987:6.

fact accounts of the actual course of events taken by the ritual and duly recorded from the objective point of view of those charged with detailing the expenses incurred for each step of the ritual against the possibility of a future audit by a higher authority. These are the so-called "descriptive rituals" and they survive in far greater numbers than the "prescriptive" ones and from many successive periods. [16] The "economy of the cult" [17] that can be reconstructed with their help leaves no doubt that, in Mesopotamia, animal sacrifice, though ostensibly a mechanism for feeding the deity, was at best a thinly disguised method for sanctifying and justifying meat consumption by human beings. An Akkadian wisdom text best known from Ugarit seems to admit as much when it avers: "From of old our forefathers have held / Our fathers shared the sattukku-allotment [18] with the god!" [19] The privilege was routinely accorded to priesthood, aristocracy, and royalty, and sporadically, notably on holidays and holy days, to the masses of the population. [20] The practice is well attested at least as late as the ninth century B.C., [21] and the king's share of the divine "leavings" (rēhātu) even later. [22] The late Jewish author of the apocryphal "Daniel, Bel and the Dragon" saw through the Mesopotamian pretense involved in the "care and feeding of the gods" [23] and took a dim view of it, [24] as did the prophets of comparable practices in Israel, [25] the Hittites in their "Instructions to Temple Officials," [26] and an anonymous critic of late Egyptian usage. [27]

But the ritual texts, whether prescriptive or descriptive, tell us little about the true motivation for the sacrificial cult or the related question of its origins in the native conception. For this we must turn to literature in its higher forms, notably the mythology. Until recently, this served to underline the "official" interpretation which stressed the

---

[16] Cf. above, ch. III 2, with literature.

[17] For this concept, see Sigrist 1984 and apud Hallo, OLA 5 (1979) 104f.

[18] The sattukku is the regular daily offering, not necessarily of meat.

[19] From "The Instructions of Shube-awilim," cited Hallo, OLA 5 (1979) 105f. and Sigrist 1984:189; latest translations by M. Dietrich, UF 23 (1991) 49 and Foster, BM 332-335. Differently CAD S s.v. sattukku.

[20] S. Parpola, Reiner AV (1987) 261, lines 17-19 (rēhāti for "the forlorn scholar").

[21] McEwan 1983.

[22] Beaulieu 1990.

[23] Oppenheim, Ancient Mesopotamia 183-198.

[24] De Vaux, Ancient Israel 433f.; Reeves and Waggoner 1988:267f.

[25] Cf. especially Jer. 7:21.

[26] Kühne 1978:184 (iv 69-77).

[27] Steiner and Nims 1984.

divine need for sustenance. Indeed, if there is one common thread running through both Sumerian and Akkadian myths about the relationship between gods and humans, it is that the latter were created to relieve the former of the need to provide their own food—a notion even thought to find a faint echo in the primeval history of Genesis. [28] But a newly recovered Sumerian myth puts matters into a rather different light and permits considerably more precise analogies to be drawn with Biblical conceptions.

The myth, or mythologem, is embedded in an ostensibly epic tale dealing, like all other Sumerian epics, with the exploits of the earliest rulers of Uruk. They were preoccupied with heroic campaigns against distant Aratta, the source of lapis lazuli and other precious imports from across the Iranian highlands to the east, perhaps as far away as Afghanistan. [29] On one of these campaigns the crown-prince Lugalbanda fell ill and had to be left behind in a cave of the mountains by his comrades, with only enough food and fire to ease his dying days. Left for dead, he prayed to the sun at dusk, followed by the evening star, then the moon, and finally the sun again at dawn—and there the text effectively broke off in the first systematic presentation of the plot by Claus Wilcke. [30]

The thread of the epic is taken up at this point by a large tablet from the Yale Babylonian Collection published in 1983. [31] The prayers of Lugalbanda were answered: he arose from his sickbed and left the cave. He refreshed himself with revivifying "grass" and the invigorating waters of the nearest stream, but then he faced a problem: the food left for him by his comrades had given out; the fire they had left had died out. How was he to nourish himself henceforth? He was still in the mountains, or at least the foothills of the Zagros mountains, surrounded by wild plants and wild animals. The plants are pointedly contrasted with the domesticated varieties familiar to him from the cultivated plains of Uruk, and the animals consume them with relish. It is implied, however, that they are not fit for human consumption. In this extremity, Lugalbanda decides to make a virtue of necessity and turn carnivorous. But this is easier said than done when a solitary man confronts a thundering herd of aurochsen. He

---

[28] See Hallo 1987:7 and 12f., nn. 23-25, for details.
[29] See above, ch. II 3.
[30] Wilcke 1969.
[31] Hallo 1983, 1984.

must select one that is weak and languid from overeating and try to trap it as it mills about the meadow. To do this, he must bait the one trap he has presumably constructed. He does so, apparently, by baking some delectable cakes—admittedly a questionable procedure in these circumstances but one that would justify a subsidiary aetiology inserted in the text at this point, namely the invention of fire, or at least of fire-making! The embers of the last campfire left by his companions having died out, Lugalbanda must start a new fire by striking flintstones together until they generate a spark. And even then, 'not knowing how to bake a cake, not knowing an oven" (ll. 284, 289), he has to improvise. But one way or another, the aurochs is caught and then tethered by means of a rope made on the spot from the roots and tops of the wild juniper tree uprooted and cut with a knife. The process is then repeated with two goats, taking care to select healthy ones from those in sight.

But with the practical problems disposed of, Lugalbanda's real problems are just beginning. His companions have left him supplied with an ax of meteoric iron and a hip dagger of terrestrial iron (the latter presumably used already to cut the juniper trees), but how can he presume to wield them against his quarry? Only the appropriate ritual can solve this problem. Providentially, the answer is vouchsafed in a dream, by none other than Za(n)qara, the god of dreams himself. [32] He must slaughter the animals, presumably at night and in front of a pit, so that the blood drains into the pit while the fat runs out over the plain (where the snakes of the mountain can sniff it) and so that the animals expire at daybreak.

Upon awaking, Lugalbanda follows these prescriptions to the letter, needless to say. But he goes them one better—significantly better. At dawn he summons the four greatest deities of the Sumerian pantheon—An, Enlil, Enki and Ninhursag—to a banquet at the pit. This banquet is called a *gizbun*, a Sumerian word later equated with Akkadian *takultu*, the technical term for a cultic meal or divine repast. [33] Lugalbanda pours libations of beer and wine, carves the meat of the goats, roasts it together with the bread, and lets the sweet savor rise to the gods like incense. The intelligible portion of the text ends with

---

[32] Cf. CAD Š/3:405: ^{d}*zà-gar-(ra)*, ^{d}*za-gàr* = *ilu ša šutti/šunāti*; Klein 1981:110; Kutscher 1988.

[33] Cf. above, ch. VI 3.

these two lines (ll. 375f.): "So of the food prepared by Lugalbanda /
An, Enlil, Enki and Ninhursag consumed the best part."

What is offered here is a first glimpse at some tantalizing new evidence regarding early Sumerian religious sensibilities. As far as the
understanding of the text is correct, it permits the following tentative
conclusions.

1. The highest deities of the Sumerian pantheon—three gods and
one goddess who traditionally represent and govern the four cosmic
realms—physically partake of the best of the meat at a sacred meal
convoked in their honor. Presumably, then, they sanction the slaughter of the animals that has made this consumption of their meat possible.

2. The slaughter itself is carried out according to divinely inspired
prescriptions, by a divinely chosen individual, with weapons made of
rare metals. Presumably, then, we are to understand it as sacred, not
profane slaughter, indeed as the aetiology of the sacrificial cult.

3. The capture of the animals is related in the context of an elaborate narrative that is ostensibly of epic character but presumably has
the typical mythic function of explaining a continuing phenomenon
observed in the present by appeal to a real or, more often, an imaginary one-time event in the past. [34] In this case, then, we are presented
with an aetiology of meat-eating that explains its origins from the
straits in which Lugalbanda found himself, thus replacing a prior,
vegetarian order of things.

4. Other and perhaps lesser aetiologies are found in the epic cycle
of Uruk. Our own text thus seems to include the invention of fire
(making); another, the Epic of Enmerkar and the Lord of Aratta, includes the invention of writing [35] and perhaps of overland trade. [36]
That none of these inventions are placed chronologically quite where
modern research would date them does not detract from the deduc-
tion that Sumerian epic was a conscious vehicle for mythologems in
general and for aetiologies in particular.

5. Finally, the new text offers a fresh perspective on the comparable Biblical conceptions as current scholarship sees their evolution. In
both cases, an original dispensation provides for vegetarianism in the
divine as well as the human (and perhaps even the animal) realm,

---

[34] See above, ch. I 3, at nn. 183-187.
[35] *Ibid.*, at nn. 188-191.
[36] See above, ch. II 3.

with mankind assigned the task of domesticating and cultivating vegetation. Although in the Biblical case the domestication of animals
followed as early as the second generation (Abel), its purpose may be
construed as limited, in the time-honored Near Eastern manner, to
the exploitation of their renewable resources, such as wool, milk,
dung, and draft-power. [37] Although Abel sacrifices "the choicest of the
firstlings of his flock" (Gen. 4:4), [38] and his sacrifice is accepted, it is
not until Noah's sacrifice of the animals that he had brought safely
through the flood that humanity is specifically given permission to
consume them.

The cuneiform tradition may not have similarly linked the inaugu-
ration of meat-eating with the immediate aftermath of the flood—thus
again displaying a certain indifference to the exact dating of an aetiology. [39] But with this minor difference, Babylonian and Biblical
myths reflect remarkably similar conceptions of the origin of the sacrificial cult. Where the two cultures diverged widely was in its subsequent evolution. In Mesopotamia, the sacrificial cult was literally
taken as a means of feeding the gods and specifically, beginning with
the end of the third millennium, their cult statues. In Israel, where
anthropomorphic conceptions and representations of the deity were
proscribed, and where the worshipper already participated in the
consumption of the earliest (paschal) sacrifice, the later cultic legislation explicitly provided priesthood and laity with a share of the sacrificial offerings. Thus Israelite sacrifice, though in origin designed,
as in Mesopotamia, to sanctify the very act of consumption, ultimately served as well to sanctify other human activities and to atone
for other human transgressions. [40]

---

[37] See above, ch. II 2.
[38] So NJV. Literally: "from the firstlings of his flock and [specifically] from their
fat [parts or pieces]]," i.e., the parts later—in levitical legislation—especially reserved
for the deity or, in the Blessing of Moses, for strange gods (Deut. 32:38).
[39] Hallo 1987 10 and 13, nn. 35-38 for details.
[40] Hallo, BP 66.

Bibliographical References

Beaulieu, Paul-Alain, 1990: "Cuts of meat for King Nebuchadnezzar," N.A.B.U. 1990:71f. No. 93.

Burkert, Walter, 1972: *Homo Necans. Interpretationen altgriechischer Opferriten und Mythen* (= RVV 32).

———, 1983: *Homo Necans: the Anthropology of Ancient Greek Sacrificial Ritual and Myth* (Berkeley/Los Angeles, University of California Press).

———, René Girard and Jonathan Z. Smith, 1982: *Violent Origins* (Stanford, Stanford U.P.).

Girard, René, 1972: *La violence et le sacré* (Paris, Bernard Grasset).

———, 1977: *Violence and the Sacred* (Baltimore, Johns Hopkins U.P.)

Hallo, William W., 1983: "Lugalbanda excavated," JAOS 103:165-180; repr. as Kramer AV 2 (1984) 165-180.

———1987: "The origins of the sacrificial cult: new evidence from Mesopotamia and Israel," Cross AV 3-13.

Huizinga, J., 1955: *Homo Ludens: a Study of the Play-Element in Culture* (Boston, Beacon).

Hulst, A.R., 1963: "Opmerkingen over de ka'ašer-zinnen in Deuteronomium," NThT 18:337-361.

Katz, Marilyn A., 1990: "Problems of sacrifice in ancient cultures," SIC 3: 89-201.

Klein, Jacob, 1981: *Three Šulgi Hymns: Sumerian Royal Hymns Glorifying King Šulgi of Ur* (Ramat-Gan, Israel, Bar-Ilan U.P.).

Kühne, C., 1978: "Instructions," NERT 179-184.

Kutscher, Raphael, 1988: "The Mesopotamian god Zaqar and Jacob's maṣṣebāh," *Beer-Sheva* 3:125-130 (in Hebrew; English summary p. 12*.).

Limet, Henri, 1989: "La mort du mouton de sacrifice," in Méniel 1989:59-68.

McEwan, Gilbert J.P., 1983: "Distribution of meat in Eanna," *Iraq* 45:187-198.

Méniel, Patrice, ed., 1989: *Animal et Pratiques Religieuses: les Manifestations Matérielles* (= Anthropozoologica numéro spécial 3).

Milgrom, Jacob, 1971: "A prolegomenon to Leviticus 17:11," JBL 90:149-156.

———, 1976: "Profane slaughter and the composition of Deuteronomy," HUCA 47:1-17.

———, 1978: A formulaic key to the sources of Deuteronomy," EI 14:42-47 (in Hebrew; English summary pp. 123*f.).

Novak, David, 1983: *The Image of the Non-Jew in Judaism: an Historical and Constructive Study of the Noahide Laws* (New York, E. Mellen).

Reeves, John C. and Lu Waggoner, 1988: "An illustration from the Apocrypha ...," HUCA 59:253-268.

Sigrist, Marcel, 1984: *Les* sattukku *dans l' Ešumeša durant la période d' Isin et Larsa* (=BM 11).

Steiner, Richard C. and C.F. Nims, 1984: "You can't offer your sacrifice and eat it too: a polemical poem from the Aramaic text in Demotic script," JNES 43:89-114.

Wilcke, Claus, 1969: *Das Lugalbandaepos* (Wiesbaden, Harrassowitz).

2. Public Prayer [41]

Animal sacrifice has virtually vanished from the western world as expiation for the offense against nature and nature's God perceived in the consumption of animal meat, or for any other purpose. Its place has been taken by a variety of symbolic rites and especially by prayer, which in Biblical and pre-Biblical times co-existed with sacrifice. Typically both were employed together as a means of appealing to the divine, the one as a form of *dicenda*, or "things to be said," the other as a form of *agenda*, or "things to be done." Of the two, prayer has a much more obvious link to the Biblical and pre-Biblical past. Sometimes it has undergone manifold transformation, but sometimes, as in the case of the Psalms, it survives unchanged into our own times. The 150 separate poems of the Biblical Psalter serve to express a variety of human concerns, such as praise, petition, contemplation or even sheer artistry. The last is notably the case with Psalm 119, essentially one long disquisition on the law of God, which finds 176 different ways to describe that law in as many separate verses, grouped into 22 stanzas each of whose eight lines begin with a successive letter of the Hebrew alphabet.

One of the most persistent themes of the Psalter is the poetic response to collective or individual disasters that challenge human faith in the divine governance of the universe or of one's individual world. The Psalms that attempt to restore that faith are called lamentations, or laments, because they are characterized in the first place by expressions of dismay which serve as a catharsis for the grieving survivors. But they may also contain passages appealing to the deity for restoration of collective or individual fortunes and expressions of assurance in the ultimate experience of such restoration. The lamentations of the Psalter are preceded by a millennial tradition of comparable genres in the rest of the ancient Near East, especially Mesopotamia. Here, that tradition will be surveyed in respect to communal responses to disaster, while the following section will consider the individual responses.

Like those of the Bible, the lamentations of ancient Mesopotamia are poetic responses to disasters real or imaginary. [42] They can be

---

[41] This and the following section are a revised version of Hallo 1995.
[42] See in general Krecher 1980-83.

broadly divided into two groups which, in keeping with usage in Biblical criticism, can be described as congregational (communal) and individual laments respectively. Within each group, the material can be further classified according to the focus of the lament: a city or temple, a deity, or a deceased king on the one hand; a living king or a deceased individual on the other. In keeping with this classification, the native scribes recognized various specific genres, often labelling the compositions accordingly, and always adhering strictly to the traditional norms that featured a common, distinctive set of characteristics. In the millennial history of these genres, language is a useful index of date, with the earliest stages generally represented by main-dialect Sumerian, followed by dialectal Sumerian, Sumero-Akkadian bilinguals, and Akkadian unilinguals. In the survey that follows, the compositions will be organized by genre, and within each genre by language or dialect. They will be cited by the titles generally coined for them by current Assyriological usage, rather than by their ancient titles which normally consisted of their opening words or "incipit." In the conclusion, the genres will be compared and contrasted with their Biblical counterparts.

A. *Forerunners in main-dialect Sumerian*

The earliest example of a congregational lament dates from the Old Sumerian period and constitutes a kind of forerunner to the lamentations over the destruction of temples and cities of the neo-Sumerian canon. "The Fall of Lagash" is a unique composition preserved on a single clay tablet copy dating from, or at least referring to, the last ruler of the First Dynasty of Lagash, Uru-inimgina (Uru-kagina, around 2350 B.C.). [43] It catalogues the shrines of Lagash devastated by Lugalzagesi of Umma, and puts the blame squarely on that ruler or his patron-deity, absolving the ruler of Lagash. [44] Lugalzagesi went on to conquer all of Sumer but was in turn defeated by Sargon of Akkad (Agade) as related in a text better described as a legend than as a lamentation. [45] But the dynasty that Sargon founded came to grief in its own turn at the hands of the Gutians. [46] According to a

---

[43] For the latest view on the pronunciation of the name, see below, ch. VIII 1, note 12.

[44] Latest translation by Cooper 1986:78; discussion by Hirsch 1967.

[45] See above, ch. I 3, notes 192, 194f.

[46] Hallo 1971.

highly tendentious hymn, the destruction of Akkad occurred under Sargon's grandson Naram-Sin, although other evidence suggests a later date for the event; the "Curse of Agade" has many features in common with the city-laments. [47] A supposed parody of the genre, the assumed "Lament for Kirga," is rather a proverbial complaint about the loss of "standards" (*di-ir-ga*). [48] The linguistic evidence attests to the importance of musical accompaniment to formal lamentation. There are harps of lamentation (*balag a-nir-ra*) and of wailing (*balag ér-ra*) and reed-(pipes) of wailing (*gi ér-ra* = *qan bikīti*) which in turn gave rise to the technical term for ritual wailing (*gi-ra-num* = *girānu*). For percussion instruments see below, C.

B. *City Laments in main-dialect and dialectal Sumerian*

The Sargonic empire was restored to some extent by the Third Dynasty of Ur, whose own fall at the end of the third millennium was regarded as an especially devastating sign of divine displeasure. No less than six laments commemorated the event and did so in such vivid terms that they suggest the reaction of eye-witnesses. Because of their specific allusions to historic personages and events, they are sometimes described as "historical laments." Two of them, however, mention King Ishme-Dagan of Isin (ca. 1953-1935 B.C.), and were therefore written at least fifty years after the disaster, and this is probable for the others as well. In fact, they were designed as liturgical accompaniments to the royal rebuilding of the destroyed temples, which involved the inevitable razing of their remains—a potential sacrilege against their gods. Like their forerunners, therefore, the city-laments describe the earlier destruction in lurid detail, and they seek to absolve the royal rebuilder by heaping blame on the foreigners who caused the original devastation. But unlike their forerunners, they were intended for liturgical use, as indicated by their division into anywhere from four to twelve or more stanzas designated as "first, second (etc.) genuflection" (*ki-ru-gú*). Their specific allusions to particular destructions made them unsuitable for subsequent reuse in the liturgy, but they were adopted into the neo-Sumerian canon and widely recopied in the scribal schools of mid-Old Babylonian times (ca. 1800-1700). Three of them were written wholly or largely in the

---

[47] Latest edition by Cooper 1983.
[48] Jacobsen 1959.

main dialect of Sumerian. The "Lamentation over the Destruction of Sumer and Ur," which may be the first in the series, catalogued the devastation visited on all the major cities of the Ur III Dynasty in its second stanza, while concentrating on the capital city of Ur in the other four. [49] The laments for Eridu [50] and Uruk [51] bemoaned the fates of these two cities in at least eight and twelve stanzas respectively.

Three other city-laments bewailed the fate of the political capital at Ur, [52] the religious capital at Nippur [53] and, in fragmentary form, the more obscure town or temple of Ekimar. [54] They were written wholly or largely in the "Emesal" -dialect of Sumerian, literally "thin" or "attenuated speech" affected, in literary texts, by women or goddesses on the one hand and, on the other, by the liturgical singers who specialized in reciting lamentations (*gala* = *kalû*). The former were often described as bemoaning the fate of their cities, their husbands or their sons, and the theme of the weeping mother (sometimes compared to the "mater dolorosa" of the Christian tradition) has been recognized in several types of laments. [55] The *kalû*-singers may have included castrati singing in a kind of falsetto. Accordingly they became the butt of unflattering references, particularly in the proverbs. [56]

C. *Tambourine-laments and harp-songs in dialectal Sumerian*

Inevitably, the Dynasty of Isin too came to an end, meeting its doom at the hands of the rival dynasty of Larsa. The event was commemorated in a number of compositions in which Nin-Isina (the divine "Lady of Isin"), in one or another of her various manifestations, laments the fate of her city. [57] Most often, these compositions were labelled as "tambourine laments" (*ér-šèm-ma*, from *ér* = *tazzimtu*, lament or *bikītu*, wailing, and *šèm* = *halhallatu*, tambourine). There were once over a hundred compositions of this genre to judge by two catalogue

---

[49] Michalowski 1989.
[50] Green 1978.
[51] Green 1984.
[52] Kramer 1940; ANET 455-463.
[53] Kramer 1991.
[54] For the Kesh lament see Kramer 1971.
[55] Kramer 1982, 1982a, 1983.
[56] Gordon 1959:310f.
[57] See especially Krecher 1966.

texts listing their incipits (i.e., the first line or first words of each). [58]
They were addressed or attributed to a variety of deities, and probably composed under the First Dynasty of Babylon which, under its
greatest king Hammurapi, succeeded Isin and Larsa. At least twenty-
five of the tambourine-laments are preserved in whole or in part; they
are invariably composed in dialectal Sumerian. Except for those that
refer to Isin, they do not, like the city-laments, describe a specific,
historical destruction or reconstruction and can better be regarded as
wholly "ritual laments." They couched their complaints in such generalized language that they could be reused in the liturgy for many
centuries. [59] Indeed, some of the Old Babylonian examples of the
genre recur in copies of the first millennium, and new examples of the
genre were still being copied and perhaps even composed as late as
the first century B.C. [60]

But the late ershemma's served a new purpose: except when used
in certain ritual performances (*ki-du-du* = *kidudû*), the first millennium
ershemma's were now appended to another genre, the song of the
harp or lyre (*balag* = *balaggu*), alluded to already in the third millennium, known from three catalogues [61] and a dozen actual examples
in the second, and familiar from many more in the first. These harp-
songs included some of the longest of all Sumerian poems. They
were divided into liturgical stanzas like the city-laments but sometimes featured as many as sixty-five or more of them. Occasionally
they were accompanied by glosses (marginal annotations) possibly
representing musical notations or instructions. [62] In their late form,
each concluded with an ershemma, and the resulting combinations
were catalogued together as " 39 lamentations of gods" (literally "of
Enlil") and " 18 lamentations of goddesses." All were in dialectal
Sumerian, but the first millennium recensions often added a word-for-
word translation into Akkadian, inserted between the Sumerian lines
in interlinear fashion. [63]

A survey of the entire genre as well as the detailed history of par-

---

[58] Kramer 1975. Cf. also J.A. Black, AfO 36-37 (1989-90) 125 for nine fragments
of *eršemma*-catalogues, "probably ... all fragments of two tablets of the same catalogue."
[59] Cohen 1981.
[60] Cf. e.g. Maul 1991.
[61] Kramer 1981-82.
[62] Lambert 1971.
[63] Cohen 1974; 1988.

ticular examples shows clearly that the character of these long compositions became increasingly repetitive; they were filled with stock
phrases and sometimes with whole stock-stanzas, and the effect is best
described as litany-like. [64] That these compositions were employed in
the liturgy is clear from cultic calendars which specified their recitation on certain days of the cultic year, sometimes in identical form for
different deities on different days. [65] In this way, their divorce from
specific historical events became complete.

Another genre to be mentioned here is that of the "hand-lifting"
laments (šu-íl-la) of this or that deity. These are late compositions in
dialectal Sumerian with interlinear Akkadian translation. Like the
tambourine-laments and harp-songs, they typically seek to appease an
angry deity on behalf of the city, temple and community. [66] They are
to be clearly distinguished from the Akkadian incantations of the lifting of the hand which deal with individual distress. [67]

D. *Unilingual Akkadian City-Laments*

Although the liturgical lamentations in dialectal Sumerian often acquired (interlinear) translations into Akkadian in the first millennium
(above), their format and style were not much favored in new Akkadian compositions. Occasional lament-like passages were embedded in non-lament literature, as in the case of Marduk's "Lament
over the destruction of Babylon" found in the fourth tablet (chapter)
of the Myth of Erra, composed toward the end of the second millennium. [68] As late as the Seleucid period, an Akkadian text lamented
the destruction of the cities of Sumer and Akkad, apparently at the
hands of the Gutians. If this was an allusion to the historical Gutian
invasion in the third millennium it may represent a late copy of a
much earlier Akkadian original, or perhaps the Akkadian translation
of a lost Sumerian original. But more likely it constituted the use of
this ethnic label in a purely geographical sense to designate any warlike enemy on the northern or eastern frontier. [69] The text has also

---

[64] Cf. e.g. Kutscher 1975; Black 1985; Kramer 1985, 1990; Alster 1986; Volk
1989; Buschweiler 1990.
[65] Langdon 1925-26.
[66] Cooper 1970, 1988; Cohen 1989
[67] See below, ch. VII 3 (F).
[68] Pohl 1950-51. Latest translations by Foster, BM 796, FDD 155.
[69] Hallo 1971:717-719.

been regarded as "a neo-Babylonian lament for Tammuz," the Akkadian equivalent of the ancient Sumerian deity called Dumuzi (see
next section). [70]

E. *Dumuzi-Laments*

Ever since the domestication of plants and animals in the early neolithic period, Mesopotamian agriculture featured a mixed economy,
in which farmers and semi-nomadic pastoralists lived in an uneasy
but interdependent symbiosis. During the late spring and summer,
when vegetation dried up in the Tigris and Euphrates valleys, cattle
and sheep were driven to the highlands in the east, where verdure
continued to grow. Sumerian mythology equated these highlands or
mountains (*kur* in Sumerian) with the netherworld (likewise *kur*), and
the seasonal cycle with cosmic events. [71] The desiccation of the fertile
soil was thought to reflect the banishment to the netherworld of the
god of fertility. The rebirth of fertility in the winter (and early spring)
echoed his return to the world of the living. Most often this god was
called Dumuzi, whose name can mean "the healthy child," [72] but
other gods such as Damu son of Nin-Isina also filled the role. Dumuzi
was the son of Duttur (or Ninsun), the husband of Inanna, and the
brother of Geshtin-anna. These goddesses (and others) figured prominently as reciters of lamentations designed to assure the return of the
deceased deity to the world of the living. Even Inanna who, according to the mythology, had consigned Dumuzi to the netherworld in
the first place, participated in these appeals. [73] The "Death of Dumuzi" is recounted in a moving Sumerian lament [74] and incorporated
in a number of other compositions of a mythological character, such
as "The Descent of Inanna," [75] "Dumuzi's Dream," [76] and "Inanna
and Bilulu." [77]

Dumuzi was also regarded as a legendary or historical mortal—a
ruler of Pa-tibira (or Bad-tibira) before the Flood or of Uruk after the

---

[70] Lambert 1983, 1984.

[71] Cf. already Hallo *apud* Miller, SIC 1 (1980) 54, n. 19; Tadmor AV (1991) 154..

[72] Jacobsen 1985; earlier interpretations by Jacobsen 1953:165f., rep. TIT 57 and
338f., n. 23.

[73] See the Dumuzi-Inanna texts translated by Jacobsen, *Harps*, ch. 1.

[74] Jacobsen, *Harps*, 205-232.

[75] Kramer 1980.

[76] Alster 1972; Jacobsen, *Harps*, 28-46.

[77] Jacobsen 1953, rep. TIT ch. 5.

Flood and just before Gilgamesh. On the basis of late laments in which Dumuzi is associated (or even identified) with other kings from before the Flood, and of the epithet shepherd which he shares in many laments with the earlier Dumuzi, we may prefer to regard the antediluvian king as the mortal prototype of the deity. [78]

F. *Laments for Kings*

The deified Mesopotamian kings of the classical period (ca. 2250-1750 B.C.) were considered stand-ins for Dumuzi, especially in the rite of the "sacred marriage," and—albeit more rarely—in the ceremonies surrounding their death and burial. The death of kings was a major concern of Mesopotamian ideology, particularly if it was untimely or took a bizarre form. The topic was often addressed in the historiography, particularly in its characteristically Mesopotamian form of (historical) omens, which assumed connections between observed natural phenomena and historical events. [79] At other times, it was dealt with in the liturgy, assuming that some laments for Dumuzi really alluded to the newly deceased king.

There were also a number of compositions mentioning the king by name. Their prototype may be "The Death of Gilgamesh," a Sumerian epic which details the legendary fate of this celebrated ruler of Uruk. [80] Certainly this narrative has many points of resemblance with "The Death of Ur-Nammu," a poem about how the founder of the Third Dynasty of Ur met his death in battle, a fate Mesopotamian kings normally reserved for their enemies. [81] So moving was the lament composed for Ur-Nammu's burial, and so personal in its language, that it has sometimes been attributed to his widow. [82]

Lamenting the death of Mesopotamian royalty was also noted outside of strictly literary texts. Thus, for example, the founder of the First Dynasty of Isin (which succeeded the Third Dynasty of Ur) was mourned in a "great wailing" (*ér-gu-la*) according to a simple archival text which also records a banquet for his successor. [83] Nabonidus, the

---

[78] Alster 1985.

[79] See above, ch. VI 2.

[80] ANET 50-52. Additional references in Tournay and Shaffer, *Gilgamesh* 307. For this composition, see above, ch. VI 2, at n. 76.

[81] Kramer 1969; 1991a.

[82] Wilcke 1970:86. See also below, ch. VIII 3.

[83] Steinkeller 1992; previously Yoshikawa 1989.

last king of the last independent Mesopotamian dynasty, ordered a seven-day period of mourning for his mother when she died at the ripe old age of 104 in 547 B.C.E. This is recorded in a short third-person subscript added to her lengthy autobiography. [84] It turns that monument into a funerary inscription, another text-type occasionally attesting to laments for departed royalty. [85]

Bibliographical References

Alster, Bendt, 1972: *Dumuzi's Dream: Aspects of Oral Poetry in a Sumerian Myth* (= Mesopotamia 1).

————, 1985: "A Dumuzi lament in late copies," ASJ 7:1-9.

————, 1986: "edin-na ú-sag-gá: reconstruction, history and interpretation of a Sumerian cultic lament," RAI 32 19-31.

Black, Jeremy A., 1985: "A-še-er gi₆-ta, a balag of Inanna," ASJ 7:11-87.

————, 1987: "Sumerian *balag* compositions," BiOr 44:19-31.

Bottéro, Jean, 1982: "Les inscriptions cunéiformes funéraires," in G. Gnoli and J.-P. Vernant, eds., *La mort, les morts dans les Societés Anciennes* (Cambridge, Cambridge U.P.) 373-406.

Buschweiler, Francoise, 1990: " *La plainte du roseau*: eršemma de Dumuzi, MAH 16014," RA 84:119-124.

Cohen, Mark E., 1974: " *Balag*-compositions: Sumerian lamentation liturgies of the first and second millnnium B.C.," SANE 1:25-57.

————, 1981: *Sumerian Hymnology: the Eršemma* (= HUCAS 2).

————, 1988: *The Canonical Lamentations of Mesopotamia* (2 vv.) (Potomac, Md., Capital Decisions).

————, 1989: "A bilingual šuilla to Ningeštinanna," Sachs AV 79-85.

Cooper, Jerrold S., 1970: "A Sumerian šu-íl-la from Nimrud ...," *Iraq* 32:51-67.

————, 1983: *The Curse of Agade* (Baltimore/London, The Johns Hopkins U.P.).

————, 1986: *Presargonic Inscriptions* (New Haven, American Oriental Society).

————,1988: "Warrior, Devastating Deluge, Destroyer of Hostile Lands: a Sumerian šuila to Marduk," Sjöberg AV 83-93.

Gordon, Edmund I, 1959: *Sumerian Proverbs: Glimpses of Everyday Life in Ancient Mesopotamia* (Philadelphia, The University Museum).

Green, Margaret W., 1978: "The Eridu Lament," JCS 30:127-167.

————, 1984: "The Uruk Lament," JAOS 104:253-279.

Hallo, William W., 1971: "Gutium," RLA 3:708-720.

————, 1995: "Lamentations and prayers in Sumer and Akkad," CANE 3:1871-1881.

Hirsch, Hans E., 1967: "Die 'Sünde' Lugalzagesis," Eilers AV 99-10 106.

Jacobsen, Thorkild, 1953: "The myth of Inanna and Bilulu," JNES 12:160-187 and pls. lxvi-lxviii; rep. TIT 52-71 and 334-353.

————, 1959: "Lament for Kirga," *apud* Gordon 1959:473-475.

————, 1985: "The name Dumuzi," JQR 76:41-45.

Kramer, Samuel Noah, 1940: *Lamentation Over the Destruction of Ur* (= AS 12).

---

[84] ANET 560-562; latest translation by Longman, FAA 225-228; cf. ibid., 97-103.
[85] Bottéro 1982.

————, 1969: "The death of Ur-Nammu and his descent to the netherworld," JCS 21:104-122.

————, 1971: "Keš and its fate: laments, blessings, omens," Gratz College AV 165-175.

————, 1975, 1977: "Two British Museum iršemma-catalogues," Salonen AV 141-166; 48/3:4f.

————, 1980: The death of Dumuzi: a new Sumerian version," AnSt 30:5-13.

————, 1981-82: "Three Old Babylonian *balag*-catalogues from the British Museum," Diakonoff AV 206-213.

————, 1982: "Lisin, the weeping goddess," Kraus AV 133-144.

————, 1982a: "BM 98396: a Sumerian prototype of the *mater-dolorosa*," Orlinsky AV 141*-146*.

————, 1983: "The weeping goddess: Sumerian prototypes of the *mater dolorosa*," BA 46/X:69-80.

————, 1985: "BM 86535: a large extract of a diversified balag-composition," Birot AV 115-135.

————, 1990: "BM 96927: a prime example of ancient scribal redaction," Moran AV 251-269.

————, 1991: "Lamentation over the destruction of Nippur," ASJ 13:1-26.

————, 1991a: "The death of Ur-Nammu," Prince Mikasa AV 193-214.

Krecher, Joachim, 1966: *Sumerische Kultlyrik* (Wiesbaden, Harrassowitz).

————, 1980-83: "Klagelied," RLA 6:1-8.

Kutscher, Raphael, 1975: *Oh Angry Sea (a - a b - b a h u - l u h - h a): the History of a Sumerian Congregational Lament* (= YNER 6).

Lambert, W.G., 1971: "The Converse tablet: a litany with musical instructions," Albright AV 335-353.

————, 1983, 1984: "A neo-Babylonian Tammuz lament," JAOS 103:211-215; repr. in Kramer AV 2:211-215.

Langdon, Stephen, 1925-26: "Calendars of liturgies and prayers," AJSL 42:110-127.

Maul, Stefan M., 1991: " 'Wenn der Held (zum Kampfe) auszieht ...': ein Ninurta-eršemma," Or. 60:312-334.

Michalowski, Piotr, 1989: *The Lamentation over the Destruction of Sumer and Ur* (= Mesopotamian Civilizations 1).

Pohl, Alfred, 1950-51: "Die Klage Marduks über Babylon im Erra-Epos," HUCA 23/1:405-409.

Steinkeller, Piotr, 1992: "Išbi-Irras Himmelfahrt," N.A.B.U. 1992/1.

Volk, Konrad, 1989: *Die Balaĝ-Komposition úru àm-ma-ir-ra-bi* (= FSAO 18).

Wilcke, Claus, 1970: "Eine Schicksalsentscheidung für den toten Urnammu," RAI 17:81-92 + 2 pls.

Yoshikawa, Mamoru, 1989: "an-šè---a (=e' -e") 'to die', " ASJ 11:353.

3. INDIVIDUAL PRAYER

A. *Elegies*

The destruction of cities or temples, and the death of gods and kings—whether real or imaginary—were all alike cause for communal or congregational lament. The death of a private individual, however, or even the sickness or discomfiture of a king, were rather cause for individual lament. The former eventuality inspired a special text-type, the elegy, that is only sparingly attested so far. One such elegy bewails the fate of a virgin. [86] Two others are attributed to a certain Lu-dingirra ("man of God") and recited over his deceased father and wife respectively. [87] They end in a doxology, or perhaps a parody on a doxology, which identify their genre as an "elegy" (*i-lu* = *nubû* or *qubbû*). Since Lu-dingirra is known from another text, "The Message of Lu-dingirra to his Mother," as a citizen of Nippur living in a far country, it is possible that his elegies form part of a novelistic treatment of aristocratic life in that city, of which other episodes are also known. The fact that all six exemplars of the text appear to stem from Nippur may lend support to such a supposition. One of them, moreover, has interlinear glosses in Akkadian, and the genre may have survived in unilingual form in "An Assyrian Elegy" by and for a woman who died in childbirth, [88] in the "Lament of Gilgamesh for Enkidu" embedded in the eighth tablet of the Gilgamesh Epic, [89] and elsewhere.

B. *Private Letter-Prayers in Sumerian*

From a fairly early period on, the great gods of the Sumerian pantheon were imagined as having human form. They were so represented in the iconography, and human feelings were attributed to them in the religious literature. They were deemed subject to certain human weaknesses, such as anger or jealousy, and needed to be appeased by their mortal petitioners. Ideally, the penitent could be expected to become a priest or other officiant in the temple, there to stand in permanent personal attendance on the deity, the latter re-

---

[86] Kramer 1977.
[87] Kramer 1960; Sjöberg 1983, 1984.
[88] Reiner 1985:85-93; latest translations by Foster, BM 905, FDD 329.
[89] ANET 87f., 506. ; Lambert RAI 7 (1960) 53. Cf. Müller 1978.

presented by a divine symbol or, later, by an anthropomorphic statue. Where this was impossible, the same purpose could be served by replacing the worshipper with a statue of his own. Stone-carvers inscribed the statue with the name of the entreated deity and the name of the worshipper, as well as a formulaic prayer for the long life of the worshipper, his family and his king. More modest votive objects could also be commissioned: replicas in precious metal or in stone of tools, weapons and other objects used in the daily life of the worshipper. But even such votive offerings were beyond the means of most people, who therefore made do with commissioning a scribe to inscribe a clay tablet to be deposited at the feet of the divine statue. Private communication with the gods therefore typically assumed the form of a letter and the function of a prayer; the resulting text-type can best be described as a letter-prayer. [90]

Such letter-prayers can be traced back at least to the neo-Sumerian period at the end of the third millennium. They are directed to many of the great gods of the Sumerian pantheon, including Enki, [91] Nanna, [92] Nin-Isina, [93] Martu, [94] Nindinugga [95] and Nin-shubur. [96] In lieu of the deity, they may occasionally address a king or even a deceased(?) kinsman, [97] but here, too, at least sometimes in the form of their statues. [98]

The letter-prayers typically open with an elaborate salutation in which the deity is invoked by a succession of epithets selected to emphasize those divine qualities which will best respond to the petitioner's needs. Thus the sick penitent may praise the healing capacities of the healing god or goddess; the man deprived of his patrimony to the deity's sense of justice; the scribe undeservedly relieved of his duties to the wisdom of the scribal patron-deity. Beyond the simple salutation of the standard letters, the letter-prayers require a second and sometimes even a third salutation to accommodate all these invocations. The body of the letter follows; it prominently fea-

---

[90] See in detail Hallo 1968; 1981.
[91] Hallo 1968:82-88.
[92] Falkenstein 1959.
[93] TRS 60.
[94] Hallo forthcoming.
[95] Hallo 1968:89 *sub* B 17; for the connection to Nippur and the "house of Ur-Meme," cf. Hallo 1972:91f.
[96] Walker and Kramer 1982:78-83.
[97] Cf. Ali 1964; Hallo 1968:89 *sub* B 15, 16, 19, L, O, P.
[98] T. Jacobsen *apud* Hallo 1968:79, n. 74.

tures the complaints and protests of the petitioner, and reinforces the appeal for divine assistance by emphasizing the deity's past favors and the penitent's past deserts and innocence. The conclusion of the letter-prayer may include promises to sing the deity's praises if the prayer is answered, as well as a closing formulaic request for quick action typical of normal letters, or a new formula praying that the heart of the deity be appeased. [99]

C. *Royal Letter-Prayers in Sumerian*

Although in origin a private (and more economical) alternative to prayers inscribed on expensive statues and other votive objects, the letter-prayer came to be employed as well by royalty, especially under the dynasty of Larsa before that city succumbed to Hammurapi in 1763 B.C. The earliest example of "The Royal Correspondence of Larsa" is an intriguing document which recounts how Sin-iddinam commissioned a statue of his father and royal predecessor so that the latter might "forward" the son's prayers, in the form of two letters placed in the statue's mouth, to the sun-god Utu, patron deity of the dynasty. [100] The same Sin-iddinam is responsible for at least two other letter-prayers, one to Utu to lament the evil fate that has befallen Larsa, [101] and one to the healing goddess to plead for restoration of the king's health. [102] The correspondence climaxes in a letter-prayer addressed *to* Rim-Sin, last king of the dynasty. In it, the princess Nin-shatapada, daughter of the founder of the rival dynasty of Uruk, begs Rim-Sin to restore her to her priestly office, urging him to treat her with the same magnanimity he displayed towards Uruk after defeating its king. The terms in which she writes mirror those employed in the date-formulas, inscriptions and hymns of the dynasty; the incorporation of her letter-prayer in the correspondence of the dynasty suggests that her petition was granted. [103]

---

[99] For details see Hallo 1968:75-80. A new example of a third salutation can be restored in the letter-prayer to Zimri-Lim, for which see below, n. 106.

[100] Van Dijk 1965.

[101] Hallo 1982.

[102] Hallo 1976.

[103] Hallo 1983; 1991. Cf. also below, ch. VIII 3.

D. *Bilingual and Akkadian Letter-Prayers*

Letter-prayers were not as popular in Akkadian. The earliest examples may be two Old Babylonian letters addressed respectively to the goddess Ninsianna and to the writer's personal deity for transmittal to Marduk. [104] Others come from Mari under Yashmah-Addu and Zimri-Lim in the eighteenth century, and at least one of them is quite elaborately constructed. [105] Zimri-Lim is also the addressee of a letter-prayer, and this is in bilingual form, the Sumerian and Akkadian versions disposed in two parallel columns, though whether it was an authentic letter or the creation of a learned scribe is not certain. [106] The latter explanation seems to apply to some of the private letter-prayers known in Sumerian from the Old Babylonian schools at Nippur, Ur and elsewhere, many of them involving a certain Lugal-murub of Nippur, [107] and certainly to the bilingual letter *to* Lugal-murub known from schools of Late Babylonian date in Assyria (Assur), Anatolia (Hattusha) and Syria (Ugarit). [108]

There are other examples of letters to and even from the gods from Old Babylonian [109] to neo-Assyrian times, [110] but these cannot be said to function as prayers. The royal Assyrian letters to the gods, in particular, allow kings to report on their military triumphs in more imaginative style than the customary annals and other royal inscriptions. There is, however, one survival of the classical letter-prayer in late times. "The Appeal to Utu," originally created at Larsa by or for Sin-iddinam, is reproduced in a bilingual letter from Sippar of uncertain date and in another exemplar from the seventh century royal library at Nineveh. Babylon replaces Larsa of the original version and a king whose name is lost no doubt replaces Sin-iddinam. [111] So late a representative of the old genre encourages us to seek its reflexes also in the Hebrew Bible (below).

---

[104] Kraus 1971; YOS 2:141. Latest translations by Foster, BM 156f., FDD 294.
[105] Hallo 1968:78, n. 43; ARM 1:3, for which see ANET 627 and Charpin and Durand 1985: 339-342.
[106] Charpin 1992.
[107] Hallo 1968:88f. *sub* B 7, 8, 16.
[108] Nougayrol 1968:23-28 No. 15.
[109] Ellis 1987.
[110] Grayson 1983, 1984; von Soden, N.A.B.U. 1990:16f. No. 22; cf. in general Keller 1991.
[111] Borger 1991.

E. *Bilingual Laments for Appeasing the Heart*

The real successors of the Sumerian letter-prayers must be sought in
another genre altogether. This is the *ér-šà-hun-gá*, literally the "lament
(*ér*) for appeasing (*hun-gá*) the heart (*šà*) (i.e. of the angry deity)," so
called in the native terminology because such laments typically conclude with the wish "may your heart be appeased like that of a natural mother, like that of a natural father." This is a slightly expanded
form of the most common ending of the earlier letter-prayers: "may
the heart of my god (or king) be appeased." And other major characteristics of these laments also echo the earlier genre, abandoning only
its epistolary format. In place of one or more salutations, these laments begin with long invocations of the deity which stress, like the
earlier salutations, the divine qualities responsible for the penitent's
distress or his hoped-for salvation. The worshipper again catalogues
his sins, typically in multiples of seven, while claiming ignorance of
their specific nature. He promises to sing the deity's praises once he
is forgiven and rescued or cured.

The new genre begins to be attested already in Old Babylonian
times, probably at the end of that period, and possibly only at Sippar.[112] By the end of the Middle Babylonian period, King Tukulti-
Ninurta was carrying off examples of the genre to Assur, according to
his epic, and at least one Middle Assyrian example is known from
there. [113] But the genre really become popular in the first millennium.
At least 130 distinct compositions are known from surviving examples
and from catalogues. They are addressed to at least fifteen different
gods and six goddesses, as well as to "any god" or to a "personal
god." [114] Like the late congregational laments, [115] they are recited by
the lamentation-priest who is even described as "the one of the heart-
appeasing lament" in "The Fashioning of the *gala*" (i.e. the molding
of the lamentation-priest), an Old Babylonian harp-song. [116] Like
other compositions in his repertoire, they are invariably composed in
dialectal Sumerian and typically provided with an interlinear Akkadian translation. One lengthy ritual text prescribes the recitation of
numerous heart-appeasing laments together with congregational la-

---

[112] Michalowski 1987; *idem*, JNES 54 (1995) 50.
[113] Hallo 1992:779f. and nn. 19f.
[114] Maul 1988.
[115] Above, ch. VII 2 (C).
[116] Kramer ASJ 3 (1981) 3:21; Maul 1988:9, n. 22.

ments. But unlike those laments, the former are intensely personal in nature and concerned with the fate, not of city or country, but of the individual penitent, even when, on occasion, the king himself repeats the lament after the priest.

F. *Individual Prayer in Akkadian*

The typical Mesopotamian gesture of prayer, lifting the hand to the mouth, is attested both linguistically and in art; thus there arose a genre of "prayers (literally: incantations) of the lifting of the hand" (*inim-inim-ma šu-il-la-kam*). Because they combine the form of an incantation with the function of a prayer, they are often referred to in German as "Gebetsbeschwörungen" (incantation-prayers); in English they are more often known as "prayers in rituals of expiation." [117] Collectively they constitute a late and wholly Akkadian means of communication with the divine. They feature prominently a section devoted to complaint or lament, in which the individual penitent, speaking in the first person, or another party speaking on his behalf in the third, addresses the deity in the second. As in the earlier Sumerian and bilingual individual laments, these complaint sections are preceded by a salutation to the deity and introduction of the penitent, and followed by rehearsals of his virtues, his specific request and a conclusion that emphasizes his gratitude and vows to express it in material and other ways. [118] Unlike them, however, the late prayers include none, so far, on behalf of women.

G. *Just Sufferer Compositions*

All the genres so far reviewed are more or less liturgical in character. Demonstrably or by hypothesis, they served as librettos for such activities as razing ruined temples prior to rebuilding them; praying for the resurrection of Dumuzi and the fertility he symbolized; burying a sovereign or a relative; or offering sacrifice for one's health and welfare. As such, they belong to the broader category of prayers, individual or collective, and were presumably the product of the temples, and more particularly of such clerical poets as the lamentation-priests. But there was also an avenue for a more philosophical approach to the problem of human suffering and the related one of

---

[117] Mullo Weir 1934.
[118] Mayer 1976.

divine justice. This literature of "theodicy" debated the goodness and omnipotence of deity in the face of unpunished evil or unrequited good; it was unconnected with sacrifice, penitence, or any other liturgical rite or activity. Presumably the product of the schools, it belonged to the broad category of wisdom literature.

The theme of the "just sufferer" dealt with the apparent discrepancy between human deserts and divine rewards; if the sufferer was not wholly just, he was certainly more pious than many of those whose fortunes seemed better. While such themes are also struck in a number of letter-prayers and liturgical laments, they are central to a succession of wisdom texts, beginning with "Man and his God," sometimes regarded as a Sumerian parallel to the Biblical Job. [119] This composition is described in the colophon of one of its exemplars as a "supplication-lament to a man's (personal) god" (ér-šà-ne-ša₄ dingir-lù-lu₇-kam) but no other examples of such a genre are known, and it may be questioned whether it is liturgical in character. Like the later Akkadian treatments of the theme, it has a fairly simple tripartite structure, beginning with a description of the sufferer's condition, continuing with his complaints to the deity, and ending with divine relief or restoration.

The Akkadian treatments of the theme include one from the late Old Babylonian period, [120] one from the late Middle Babylonian period discovered at Ugarit (Syria), [121] and two from the first millennium, the "Poem of the Righteous Sufferer" also known by its native title as Ludlul bēl nēmeqi, "let me praise the lord of wisdom (i.e., Marduk)" —sometimes referred to as "The Babylonian Job" —and "The Babylonian Theodicy." [122] Of these first millennium examples, the former has the traditional structure, although spread over four tablets (chapters) with more than a hundred lines each. The latter has a much more elaborate structure. It comprises 27 stanzas of eleven lines each, and each of these eleven lines begins with the identical syllable. The 27 successive syllables in turn form an acrostic that spells out the sentence "I (am) Saggil-kinam-ubbib the incantation-priest, worshipper of god and king." The acrostic thus reveals (and at the same time

---

[119] Kramer 1955. ANET 589-917.

[120] Nougayrol 1952. Latest translations by Foster, BM 75-77, FDD 295-297.

[121] Nougayrol 1968:265-273. Latest translations by Foster, BM 326f., FDD 314f.

[122] Lambert 1960:21-90, 283-310, 343-345; Wiseman 1980. Latest translations by Foster, BM 308-325 and 807-814, FDD 298-313 and 316-323.

conceals) the name of the author (who may be the sufferer himself),
and asserts his religious and political loyalty lest the poem as a whole
be thought to suggest otherwise. [123] The poem features a dialogue
between the sufferer and his friend. The latter, well meaning but
stubborn in his defense of divine justice, insists, against all evidence
to the contrary, that suffering must always be deserved. Perhaps, then,
it would be better to refer to the sufferer as "pious" rather than
"just." [124]

H. *Possible Biblical Analogues*

It is never easy to document the relationship between Biblical and
Mesopotamian literature, even in the presence of striking parallels between phrases, passages or whole compositions on both sides of the
equation. Wherever borrowing is suspected, it is necessary to ask
where, when and even in what direction it might have occurred. If
many centuries separate a notion that is shared by Mesopotamian
and Biblical literature, it may be that they both relied independently
on a now missing third source. As an example, we can mention the
remarkably similar provisions concerning the goring ox in the "Laws
of Eshnunna" (20th or 19th century B.C.E.) and the Book of the
Covenant (Exodus 21:28-36). [125] But a likelier case for comparison
exists when the Mesopotamian analogue, or at least its genre, survives
in the late period. This is particularly the case with the various genres of lamentations.

The laments over the destruction of cities and temples, and their
successors, the tambourine laments and harp songs, display many features in common with the Biblical Book of Lamentations and with
the congregational laments of the Psalter such as Psalms 44,74, 79, 80
and 83, [126] as well as with the "jeremiads" of Jeremiah. [127] In both,
an angry deity has abandoned his city and caused or ordered its destruction, which he is invited to inspect. There are also features in
the former lacking in the latter, such as the special laments attributed
to goddesses, or the appeal to lesser deities for their intercession. Laments for Dumuzi are, of course, absent from the Bible as such, but

---

[123] On acrostics see above, chapter V 1 and notes 9-11.
[124] Mattingly 1990.
[125] See below, ch. VIII 1.
[126] Gwaltney 1983; Ferris 1992; differently McDaniel 1968.
[127] Dobbs-Allsopp 1993.

Ezekiel's condemnation of the women who sat at the gate of the Temple "wailing for the Tammuz" (8:14) shows not only that the practice was known in the exilic period, but that it was so widely accepted that Tammuz, the Akkadian name of Dumuzi, had become a generic noun in Israel. Of laments for kings, the outstanding Biblical example is David's lament for Saul and Jonathan, who perished in battle against the Philistines (II Samuel 1:17-27). It belongs to a genre (the *qînâ*) whose special meter has been linked to the peculiar dance accompanying a wake. Like some of its Mesopotamian analogues, it was entered in a larger written collection, the Book of Yashar or, perhaps, the Book of Song, and it was to be taught to the Judaeans. Similarly, Jeremiah's laments over King Josiah were entered in the anthology of *qînâ*-laments (II Chronicles 35:25). The genre was also used to mourn non-royalty, as in David's brief lament for Abner (II Samuel 3:33-34), an analogue of sorts to the Sumerian and Akkadian elegies for private individuals.

The royal letter-prayers in Sumerian find an echo in the Psalm of Hezekiah (Isaiah 38:9-20) who, like King Sin-iddinam of Larsa, pleads for divine release from illness by composing a prayer described as a *mikhtāv* ("written document"). It may be related to the genre of *mikhtām* in the Psalter (Psalms 16, 56-60) and to other forms of individual laments there. Like the late bilingual laments for appeasing the heart, the individual laments of the Psalter have lost the explicit epistolary structure and formulary of the earlier Sumerian letter-prayers, but retain many other echoes of possible prototypes in letter-form.

The obvious parallels between the Just Sufferer compositions in Sumerian and Akkadian and the Biblical Book of Job, including its ancient prose narrative frame, extend not only to their comparable treatments of a common theme but also, in the case of "The Babylonian Theodicy," to the dialogue structure familiar from the poetic core of the Biblical book. [128] Thus, while there are undoubtedly universal elements in the language of prayer and lamentation everywhere, its particular evolution in Mesopotamia permits the reconstruction of genre-histories and suggests the possibility that some features of this millennial tradition influenced Biblical psalmody and wisdom literature before and during the exilic period.

---

[128] Bottéro 1976; Mattingly 1990.

Bibliographical References

Ali, Fadhil A., 1964 : *Sumerian Letters: Two Collections from the Old Babylonian Schools* (Ann Arbor, University Microfilms).

Borger, Rykle, 1991: "Ein Brief Sin-iddinams von Larsa an den Sonnengott...," *Nachrichten der Akademie der Wissenschaften in Göttingen: I. Phil.-hist. Klasse* 1991:39-81.

Bottéro, Jean, 1976: *Le Problème du Mal et de la Justice Divine à Babylone et dans la Bible* (= Recherches et Documents du Centre Thomas More 14).

Charpin, Dominique, 1992: "Les malheurs d'un scribe ou: de l'inutilité du Sumérien loin de Nippur," RAI 35:7-27.

————, and Jean-Marie Durand, 1985: "La prise du pouvoir par Zimri-Lim," M.A.R.I 4:293-343.

Dobbs-Allsopp, F.W., 1993: *Weep, O Daughter of Zion: a Study of the City-Lament Genre in the Hebrew Bible* (= Biblica et Orientalia 44).

Ellis, Maria deJ., 1987: "The goddess Kititum speaks to King Ibalpiel: oracle texts from Ishchali," M.A.R.I. 5:235-266.

Falkenstein, Adam, 1938: "Ein sumerischer 'Gottesbrief'," ZA 44:1-25 + 2 pls.

————, 1959: "Ein sumerischer Brief an den Mondgott," *Analecta Biblica* 12:69-77.

Ferris, Paul W., 1992: *The Genre of the Communal Lament in the Bible and the Ancient Near East* (= SBL Dissertation Series 127).

Grayson, A. Kirk, 1983, 1984: "Literary letters from deities and diviners: more fragments," JAOS 103:143-148; repr. in Kramer AV 2:143-148.

Gwaltney, William C., 1983: "The Biblical Book of Lamentations in the context of Near Eastern literature," SIC 2:191-211.

Hallo, William W., 1968: "Individual prayer in Sumerian: the continuity of a tradition," JAOS 88:71-89; repr. in Speiser AV 71-89.

————, 1972: "The House of Ur-Meme," JNES 31:87-95.

————, 1976: "The royal correspondence of Larsa: I. A Sumerian prototype for the prayer of Hezekiah?" Kramer AV 209-224.

————, 1981: "Letters, prayers, and letter-prayers," PWCJS 7:101-111.

————, 1982: "The royal correspondence of Larsa: II. The appeal to Utu," Kraus AV 95-109.

————, 1983: "Sumerian historiography," in Tadmor and Weinfeld 1983: 9-20.

————, 1991: "The royal correspondence of Larsa: III. The princess and the plea," Garelli AV 377-388.

————, 1992: review of Maul 1988 in BiOr 49:777-780.

————, forthcoming: "Two letter-prayers to Amurru."

Keller, Sharon, 1991: "Written communications between the human and divine spheres in Mesopotamia and Israel," SIC 4:299-313.

Kramer, Samuel Noah, 1955: "'Man and his god': a Sumerian variation on the 'Job' motif," VTS 3:170-182.

————, 1960: *Two Elegies on a Pushkin Museum Tablet* (Moscow, Oriental Literature Publishing House).

————, 1977: The GIR$_5$ and the ki-sikil: a new Sumerian elegy," Finkelstein AV 139-142.

Kraus, Fritz R., 1971: "Ein altbabylonischer Privatbrief an eine Gottheit," RA 65:27-36.

Lambert, W.G., 1960: *Babylonian Wisdom Literature* (Oxford, Clarendon).

Mattingly, Gerald L., 1990: "The pious sufferer: Mesopotamia's traditional theodicy and Job's counselors," SIC 3:305-348.

Maul, Stefan M., 1988: *'Herzberuhigungsklagen': die sumerisch-akkadischen Eršahunga-Gebete* (Wiesbaden, Harrassowitz).

Mayer, Rudolf, 1976: *Untersuchungen zur Formsprache der babylonischen Gebetsbeschwörungen* (StPSM5).

McDaniel, Thomas F., 1968: "The alleged Sumerian influence upon Lamentations," VT 18:198-209.

Michalowski, Piotr, 1987: "On the early history of the ershahunga prayer," JCS 39:37-48.

Müller, Hans-Peter, 1978: "Gilgameschs Trauergesang um Enkidu und die Gattung der Totenklage," ZA 68:233-250.

Mullo Weir, Cecil J., 1934: *A Lexicon of Accadian Prayers in the Rituals of Expiation* (London, Oxford U.P.).

Nougayrol, Jean, 1952: "Une version ancienne du 'juste souffrant'," RB 59:239f.

———, 1968: "Textes suméro-accadiens des archives et bibliothèques privées d'Ugarit," *Ugaritica* 5:1-446.

Reiner, Erica, 1985: *Your Thwarts in Pieces / Your Mooring Ropes Cut: Poetry from Babylonia and Assyria* (=Michigan Studies in the Humanities 5).

Sasson, Jack M., 1987: "Yasmah-Addu's letter to God (*ARM* I:3)," N.A.B.U. 1987:63f., No. 109.

Sjöberg, Åke W., 1983, 1984: "The first Pushkin Museum Elegy and new texts," JAOS 103:315-320; repr. in Kramer AV 2:315-320.

Tadmor, H. and M. Weinfeld, eds., 1983: *History, Historiography and Interpretation* (Jerusalem, Magnes Press).

Van Dijk, J., 1965: "Une insurrection générale au pays de Larša avant l'avénement de Nūr-Adad," JCS 19:1-25.

Walker, C.B.F. and S.N. Kramer, "Cuneiform tablets in the collection of Lord Binning," *Iraq* 44:78-83.

Wiseman, Donald J., 1980: "A new text of the Babylonian poem of the righteous sufferer," AnSt 30:101-107.

CHAPTER EIGHT

WOMEN

Women's studies have made great strides in the past decade, and feminist interpretations have become fashionable in many fields of inquiry. The ancient Near East lends itself particularly well to such interpretations, and has begun to yield some valuable dividends, thanks in part to the fact that a considerable portion of the research is being carried on by women or by men sympathetic to a feminist approach. I am not referring here to relative "outsiders" like Ilse Seibert, who was the first to treat the subject of "Women in the Ancient Near East" in monographic form, [1] or Gerda Lerner, whose *The Creation of Patriarchy* made a big splash a few years ago but went far beyond the available evidence. [2] The same is true of Mary Wakeman's article on "Ancient Sumer and the women's movement." [3] Rather I am thinking of collective works like *Histoire Mondiale de la Femme*, [4] *La Femme dans le Proche Orient Antique*, [5] and *Women's Earliest Records from Ancient Egypt and Western Asia*, [6] in which Assyriologists, Egyptologists and other specialists have addressed and sifted the textual and other evidence to come up with reasoned conclusions. I would also call attention to recent anthologies of women's literature in which selections from the ancient Near East quite properly stand in first place. Among these I may single out those edited by Willis and Aliki Barnstone in 1980 and by Joanna Bankier and Deirdre Lashgari in 1983. [7] On the religious front, Merlin Stone's *When God was a Woman* is rather derivative, [8] but one should not overlook, in this connection, the pioneering book of Tikvah Frymer-Kensky, which illuminates the consequences of monotheism from a feminist perspective. [9]

---

[1] Seibert 1973: English translation: Seibert 1974; cf. the review by Cooper 1977. For translations into Hungarian and Polish see Or. 45 (1976) 65* Nos. 974f.

[2] Lerner 1986.

[3] Wakeman 1985.

[4] Bottéro 1965.

[5] Durand 1987.

[6] Lesko 1989.

[7] See below, ch. VIII 3, n. 110.

[8] Stone 1976.

[9] Frymer-Kensky 1992. Cf. now also the general surveys by Stol 1994, 1995.

For all the new attention devoted to women in the ancient Near East, however, we are still only at the threshold of a feminist reading or interpretation of the evidence. In what follows I will attempt to highlight three areas where new insights have been most produc-tive—law, public life, and literature.

1. In law

It stands to reason that the law is a fertile field for feminist investigation. The ancient Near East did not know the equivalent of an Equal Rights Amendment, and its legislation differentiated sharply between the sexes, as sharply as it did among the different social classes. Such legislation was at intervals collected in the form of wise precedents and judicious decisions, and promulgated under royal authority or, in Israel, under divine dispensation. Typically it was phrased in conditional form, or what we choose to translate as conditional forms. e.g., "If the ox of one man gore the ox of another man, so that he dies, then they shall sell the living ox, and divide its price equally, and the dead one too they shall divide equally." That happens to be a provision in the Biblical "Covenant Code" of the Book of Exodus (21:35), but it is anticipated almost verbatim by the laws of the Old Babylonian city-state of Eshnunna in the 19th century B.C. discovered in the outskirts of Baghdad in 1948; a partial duplicate was discovered during the recent Iraqi excavations of Me-Turan (Tell Haddad) [10]. Since this provision recurs in no other ancient law "code," not even in the section on goring oxen of the more famous and longer-lived Laws of Hammurapi (18th century BC), it raises the interesting question whether the lawgivers of Eshnunna and Israel arrived independently at the same ingenious solution or, if not, how knowledge of the precedent passed from one to the other, or perhaps from a common source to both. The last possibility cannot be excluded. To this day, oral law is widely shared by the Bedouin over the entire "Fertile Crescent," from the Sinai Peninsula to the Persian Gulf. [11] The same situation may have prevailed in the region at the beginning of the second millennium B.C., when Amorite tribes spread over all parts of the same area.

Suffice it to list here the major collections of precedent laws by language. In Sumerian, we have a forerunner of sorts in the "Reform Texts" of Urukagina, [12] last of the Old Sumerian rulers of Lagash. [13]

The first true precedent law is that attributed to the founder of the

---

[10] Al-Rawi 1982; Roth 1990.

[11] Bailey 1993:22.

[12] On the reading of this name, see Edzard 1991 and, most recently, Lambert 1992, Selz 1992.

[13] For the last treatment in English see Diakonoff 1958.

Third Dynasty of Ur, Ur-Nammu (ca 2100 B.C.), whose coronation
and death we have discussed earlier. [14] A new proposal to attribute
these laws to his son Shulgi [15] remains quite uncertain, given the fragmentary nature of the text, and may in fact be disproved by new
evidence. [16] The other Sumerian law code is that of Lipit-Ishtar of
Isin in the 20th century BC. It too has only been partially recovered
so far. The first law "code" in Akkadian may be one from Old
Assyrian Assur (20th century) which, though as yet not recovered,
seems to be alluded to (as *naru'ā'um*, "the stela") in letters, contracts
and court cases of the period, as Klaas Veenhof has shown. [17] The
first one actually recovered, at least in part, is that of the 19th century
kingdom of Eshnunna, already mentioned. The name of the king who
promulgated it is lost together with most of the prologue, but in any
case he was earlier than Hammurapi in the next (18th) century, who
collected many of the earlier precedents and augmented them to create the most extensive and carefully structured collection of all. It
lived on in the scribal schools as a model not only of legal expertise
but also of literary style and of calligraphy until well into the first
millennium. Later Akkadian collections include the Middle Assyrian
laws of the 12th century though perhaps going back as far as the
15th, and a fragment of neo-Babylonian laws. In Hittite, we have a
well-preserved collection thought to include an earlier as well as a
later recension. [18]

Finally, in Hebrew, the "Book of the Covenant" (Ex. 24:7) in Exodus 21-24, and the "Repetition of the Law" (Deut. 17:18) which supplements it in Deuteronomy 12-25, both include a preponderance of
laws phrased in the conditional or casuistic form. Additional laws in
these two books and in the other three books of the Pentateuch (including Genesis) are phrased in other than conditional form, such as
the anathematic, the participial and the apodictic. Anathemas (curses)
are typically invoked on crimes committed in secret. Apodictic legislation is unconditional, stating a rule for all time in peremptory sec-
ond-person imperatives or prohibitions as illustrated by the

---

[14] Above, ch. VI 2.
[15] Kramer 1983; cf. also J. van Dijk *apud* F. Yildiz, Or. 50 (1981) 93, n. 20a.
[16] Frayne and Hallo, forthcoming.
[17] Veenhof 1995.
[18] For all the preceding see ANET 159-198, 523-525, and now Roth 1995.

Decalogue. Rabbinic exegesis as summarized by Maimonides counts 613 Pentateuchal laws, 248 positive and 365 negative. [19]

All the collections of conditional laws are divided into three broad groups, described on the (somewhat doubtful) analogy of Roman law as the law of persons, of things, and of procedures—though not necessarily in the same order. [20] Of the three groups, the first two regularly comprise by far the biggest part, and among the laws of persons, in turn, those governing the behavior and treatment of women occupy a particularly prominent place. I would not try to summarize them even if I could, for this has been done in many expert syntheses, most recently by Raymond Westbrook. [21]

But I may single out here the case of "the slandered bride," which I identified over thirty years ago in an article of the same name. [22] It appears both in the Laws of Hammurapi and in those of Deuteronomy, and has the further and rarer advantage of being illustrated by an actual court case from the practice of law. (The court case is dated to the reign of Hammurapi's son and successor Samsu-iluna, ca. 1749-1712, specifically to his 23rd year, ca. 1727 B.C.) Or so I proposed in 1964. In the meantime a considerable amount of ink has been spilled on just that question, i.e., is the little dossier—made up of the lawsuit and two contracts related to it, all from Nippur—truly an illustration of the case provided for in the law codes?

The laws are clear. According to Hammurapi, if a bridegroom, between the time that he contracts a marriage and its consummation, attempts to renege, he must forfeit the bridal price according to Paragraph 159; in addition, if on examination the bride could demonstrate her virginity, she could renege according to Koschaker's interpretation of Paragraphs 142f. [23] In Deuteronomy (22:13-21), if he makes the attempt at the time of consummation by falsely impugning the virginity of the bride, he is not only required to pay a penalty but also prevented forever after from divorcing his wife. In my interpretation, the Nippur lawsuit constituted a striking illustration of the Biblical provision: the wife was cleared of false accusation against her husband, but the husband was convicted of slandering and abusing

---

[19] Posner 1972.
[20] Hallo 1995:87 and n. 41.
[21] Westbrook 1988 and 1988a.
[22] Hallo 1964.
[23] Hallo 1964:99f.; Finet 1973; differently Locher 1986:313 (below, n. 30).

his wife. Because of the exceptional participation in the court proceedings of what, borrowing a term from early English law, I called
"a jury of matrons," [24] it appeared to me that the proceedings must
have involved an "inspectio ventris," attested elsewhere in connection
with what we might call maternity suits, i.e. at the birth of a baby
whose maternity was potentially subject to dispute. [25]

The husband evidently pleaded guilty to the charge: he is quoted
as deposing "you may convict me (even) more than now." He ada-
mantly refused, however, to live out the rest of his life with his wife,
preferring fine, imprisonment or even (the word is ambiguous) hanging. "I will not have her," he insisted, using a form of the verb *aḫāzu*,
"to take possession of, to seize," which I interpreted here as meaning
"I will not consummate my marriage with her." Since the associated
contracts show that the marriage had been entered into as much as
ten years earlier, I posited a two-stage marriage in which betrothal
preceded consummation. In the interval, the bride could not be given
to another nor the groom renege without severe penalties.

The conception of the two-tier marriage, or the so-called "inchoate
marriage," had long been defended by Koschaker and others, and is
now generally accepted for Old Babylonian law. [26] But every other
part of my seemingly so coherent interpretation has been argued back
and forth in the last three decades. [27] I will not dwell on the details
of the debate, but simply refer to the most elaborate new treatment
of the case. In 1986, Clemens Locher devoted an entire book of almost five hundred pages to the relevant Biblical passage under a title
best translated as "The honor of a woman in Israel: exegetical and
comparative-legal studies to Deuteronomy 22:13-21." In a substantial
chapter of his book he dealt anew with the Babylonian case. He accepted the idea of betrothal (inchoate marriage) in both Babylonian
and Israelite law, and took over my translation almost verbatim, but
rejected the notion that virginity was a matter of substance in Baby-

---

[24] At the time I referred to A. Musil's phrase in describing the comparable situation among the Bedouin (1964:101 and n. 48), but I have since learned that he
borrowed the phrase from English law; cf. Forbes 1988.

[25] The parade example is PBS 5:100, for which see already Schorr 1915; cf. Hallo
1967:64 and *apud* Borger 1969:351; latest edition by Leichty 1989.

[26] Cf e.g. Owen and Westbrook 1992; Westbrook 1988:15f.

[27] Cardascia and Klima 1966:85f.; Landsberger 1968:90-92; Veenhof 1976:153ff.
Rofé 1977:25 and n. 22; Lipiński 1981; Carmichael 1985: 16, n. 2; Westbrook 1988
and 1988a:107; Lafont 1989; Malul 1991-92:76.

lonian law, and thus possible grounds for dissolution or non-consum-
mation of a marriage. He regarded the "jury of matrons" as simply
a matter of "female witnesses" and, since all the witnesses to the court
case were in fact men, reasoned that the women witnesses must have
been present when the original marriage contract was drawn
up—though he failed to explain why the more numerous male witnesses to that contract were *not* summoned back. Above all he argued
that the first of the two accusations against the husband, admittedly
involving a poorly preserved sign and a verb of uncertain meaning,
referred not to his "slandering" her but on the contrary to his " ne-
glecting" her, more specifically to his leaving her a virgin, literally
"not knowing her," albeit in the form of an otherwise unattested
Sumerian logogram in the middle of an Akkadian court case written,
as usual, in syllabic script for all but the most routine terms. [28]

Therewith, of course, the proposed parallel with the Biblical law
collapses, and indeed Locher avers that my reconstruction rests on
argumenta ex silentio and "Fehldeutungen," [29] and concludes his lengthy
discussion with the sad observation that, while he has not been able
to provide an alternative interpretation of the court case, he must
regard its relevance to the Biblical law as unproved. [30] The debate will
probably go on along these lines until new discoveries provide, as
they normally do in Assyriology, a sure means of choosing between
alternative interpretations and translations.

Meantime one further point needs to be emphasized about the
intriguing case. The woman in question originally contracted the
marriage on her own, without the intervention of a father although,

---

[28] Locher 1986:251, following Westbrook 1988:116: "she had been left a virgin."
Locher cites CADB (1965) 128a: *nu-un-zu-ša-ma*, "not having had intercourse with
her (lw. from Sum. n u - u n - z u)," but fails to cite the much more recent entry
from CADN/2 (1980) 357b: "either from Sum. n u ....z u 'having had no sexual
relations' or from an otherwise unattested *nezû*." One can certainly add to this entry
that the first explanation involves a vocable that is just as little "otherwise attested."
It is by no means clear whence CAD derived the meaning of the alleged Sumerian
etymology (literally "he/she does not know her/him"). If it was a supposed reading
of the Sumerian word for "widow" as *nu-mu-(un)-zu*, that is now disproved by a newly
found text from Me-Turan with the reading *nu-mu-un-kúš*, which shows that *nu-mu-un*-
su and *nu-ma*-su should also be read with final *kuš*, as in *nu-kúš-ù*, all equivalents of
Akkadian *almattu*; cf. Cavigneaux and al-Rawi 1993:94f. Cf. also Malul 1991-92: 68
for *giš dála nu-mu-un-zu-na*, "the pin of her virginity" in an Old Babylonian marriage
contract (TIM 4:48).

[29] Locher 1986:244.

[30] Locher 1986:313: "Aber unter inhaltlicher Rücksicht wird man die drei altbabylonischen Texte nur in einem entferntesten Sinne als 'Parallelen' zu Dtn [22,]
13-21 ... bezeichnen können."

to judge by the list of witnesses, a brother may have been involved, and she specifically claimed the right to initiate divorce proceedings in the future, on an equal basis with her husband, albeit on pain of forfeiting the sum(s) of money she had paid him for agreeing to marry her in the first place. That she acted on her own because she was a widow is excluded if my interpretation of the court case is correct, since her husband could not then have expected her to be a virgin. But whether it was because she was a priestess of a certain class, or whether, as an orphan, she was "given away" by her brother, is not clear. What *is* clear is that, as early as the time of Hammurapi's successor, there *were* women who enjoyed certain rights equally with men. That leads naturally to the next subject, the role of women in public life.

Bibliographical References

Al-Rawi, Farouk N.H., 1982: "Assault and battery," *Sumer* 38:117-120.

Bailey, Clinton, 1993: "The role of rhyme and maxim in Bedouin law," *New Arabian Studies* 1:21-35.

Borger, Rykele, 1969, review of Oppenheim AV in BiOr 26:351.

Bottéro, Jean, 1965: "La femme dans la Mésopotamie ancienne," in Pierre Grimal, ed., *Histoire Mondiale de la Femme* vol. 1 (Paris, Nouvelle Librairie de France) 158-223.

Cardascia, Guillaume and Joseph Klima, 1966: "Droits Cunéiformes," in Gilissen 1966:A/2.

Carmichael, Calum M., 1985: *Law and Narrative in the Bible* (Ithaca, NY, Cornell U.P.).

Cavigneaux, A. and F. al-Rawi, 1993: "New Sumerian literary texts from Tell Haddad (ancient Meturan): a first survey," *Iraq* 55:91-105.

Cooper, Jerrold S., 1977: review of Seibert 1974 in JNES 36:231-233.

Diakonoff, I.M., 1958: "Some remarks on the 'reforms' of Urukagina," RA 52:1-15.

——, 1986: "Women in Old Babylonia not under patriarchal authority," JESHO 29:225-238.

Durand, J.-M., ed., 1987: *La Femme dans le Proche Orient Antique* (= RAI 33).

Edzard, Dietz Otto, 1991: "Irikagina (Urukagina)," *Aula Orientalis* 9:77-79.

Finet, André, 1973: "Hammu-rapi et l'épouse vertueuse. À propos des §§ 133 et 142-143 du Code," Boehl AV 137-143.

Forbes, Thomas, 1988: "A jury of matrons," *Medical History* 32/1:23-33

Frayne, Douglas R. and W.W. Hallo, forthcoming: "New texts from the reign of Ur-Nammu."

Frymer-Kensky, Tikva, 1992: *In the Wake of the Goddesses: Women, Culture, and the Transformation of Pagan Myth* (New York, Free Press).

Gilissen, John, ed., 1966: *Introduction Bibliographique à l'Histoire du Droit et à l'Ethnologie Juridique* (Brussels, Université Libre de Bruxelles).

Hallo, William W., 1964: "The slandered bride," Oppenheim AV 95-105.

——, 1967: Review of RLA III/1 in JAOS 87:62-66.

——, 1995: "Slave release in the Biblical world in light of a new text," Greenfield AV 79-93.

Kramer, Samuel Noah, 1983: "The Ur-Nammu Law Code: Who Was Its Author?" Or. 52:453-456.

Lafont, Sophie, 1989: "*AEM* I/2, 488: une accusation contre la femme de Sîn-iddi-nam," N.A.B.U. 1989:29, No. 44.

Lambert, W.G., 1992: "The reading of Uru-KA-gi-na again," *Aula Orientalis* 10:256-58.

Landsberger, Benno, 1968: "Jungfräulichkeit: ein Beitrag zum Thema 'Beilager und Eheschliessung'," David AV 41-105.

Leichty, Erle, 1989: "Feet of clay," Sjöberg AV 349-356.

Lerner, Gerda, 1986: *The Creation of Patriarchy* (New York/Oxford, Oxford U.P.).

Lesko, Barbara S., ed., 1989: *Women's Earliest Records from Ancient Egypt and Western Asia* (Atlanta, Scholars Press).

Lipiński, Edward, 1981: "The wife's right to divorce in the light of an ancient Near Eastern tradition," *Jewish Law Annual* 4:9-27.

Locher, Clemens, 1986: *Die Ehre einer Frau in Israel: exegetische und rechtsvergleichende Studien zu Deuteronomium 22, 13-21* (= Orbis Biblicus et Orientalis 70).

Malul, Meir, 1991-92: " *şillâm paṭārum* 'to unfasten the pin.' *Copula carnalis* and the formation of marriage in ancient Mesopotamia," JEOL 32:66-86.

Owen, David I. and Raymond Westbrook, 1992: "Tie her up and throw her in the river! An Old Babylonian inchoate marriage on the rocks," ZA 82:202-207.

Posner, Raphael, 1972: "Commandments, the 613," *Encyclopaedia Judaica* (Jerusalem, Keter Publishing House) 763-782.

Rofé, Alexander, 1977: "Family and sex laws in Deuteronomy and the Book of the Covenant," *Beth Mikra* 22:19-36 (in Hebrew; English summary pp. 155f.).

Roth, Martha, 1990: "On LE §§ 46-47A," N.A.B.U. 1990:70f., No. 92.

―――, 1995: *Law Collections from Mesopotamia and Asia Minor* (= WAW 6).

Schorr, Moses, 1915: "Ein Anwendungsfall der *inspectio ventris* im altbabylonischen Rechte," WZKM 29: 74-96.

Seibert, Ilse, 1973: *Die Frau im Alten Orient* (Leipzig, Edition Verlag).

―――, 1974: *Women in the Ancient Near East* (New York, Abner Schram).

Selz, Gebhard J., 1992: "Zum Namen des Herrschers URU-INIM-GI-NA(-K): ein neuer Deutungsvorschlag," N.A.B.U. 1992:34-36, No. 44.

Stol, Marten, 1994: "Vrouwen in Mesopotamië," *Akkadia* 89-90: 14-26.

―――, 1995: "Women in Mesopotamia," JESHO 38: 125-143.

Stone, Merlin, 1976: *When God was a Woman* (New York/London, Harcourt Brace Jovanovich).

Veenhof, Klaas R., 1976: "The dissolution of an Old Babylonian marriage according to CT 45, 86," RA 70:153-164.

―――― 1995: " 'In accordance with the words of the stele': evidence for Old Assyrian legislation," *Chicago-Kent Law Review* 70/4:1717-1744.

Wakeman, Mary K., 1985: "Ancient Sumer and the women's movement: the process of reaching behind, encompassing, and going beyond," *Journal of Feminist Studies in Religion* 1/2:7-27.

Westbrook, Raymond, 1988: *Old Babylonian Marriage Law* (= AfO Beiheft 23).

―――― 1988a: *Studies in Biblical and Cuneiform Law* (= Cahiers de la Revue Biblique 26).

2. In Public Life

The prevailing form of government in the ancient Near East was monarchy, and women were rarely monarchs in their own right. Occasionally there were exceptions, like the semi-legendary Ku-Bau (or Ku-Baba) of Kish in the Third Early Dynastic Period of Sumer (ca. 2500-2300 B.C.). The Sumerian King List placed her at the boundary between its legendary rulers with impossibly long reigns, and historical rulers with reasonable regnal years, assigning her a reign of one hundred years, and making her the sole ruler of the Third Dynasty of Kish, albeit mother of the founder of its next dynasty. [31] But she was only the exception that proved the rule, for the same source gave her an unsavory reputation as a (former) tavern keeper or alewife (tapstress). [32]

Later historiographical tradition did not even seem sure of her gender, for in the omen literature she is linked with hermaphroditism: "if an anomalous birth has (both) penis and vulva, it is a case of the omen of Ku-Bau who ruled the land: the land of the king will become waste. If it has (both) penis and vulva but no testicle(s), a courtier will govern the land or (according to another interpretation) he will revolt against the king." [33] Since no revolts against Ku-Bau are known, the reference may be to the rise of the usurper Sargon, cupbearer to her grandson Ur-Zababa, and his establishment of the empire of Akkad. Indeed another tradition, in the form of a fictitious letter from the king of Isin to the king of Babylon(?), mentions all three rulers in succession. [34]

Whether historical or legendary, Ku-Bau was certainly the first queen of ancient Near Eastern tradition to rule in her own right. But there were others. In Anatolia, the Old Assyrian tablets from Kanish (Kültepe) refer not only to native princes with whom the Assyrian traders had to negotiate, but also princesses at such places as Ankuwa, Luhusatia and Wahshushana. [35] Whether sovereign or not, they may have laid the basis, in the later Hittite literary tradition, for a figure such as that of the Queen of Kanish in the "Legend of

---

[31] Jacobsen 1939:104f., 153.
[32] On this profession see Goetze 1965.
[33] Leichty 1970:8; cf. Hallo 1976:28.
[34] Previously known as the "Weidner Chronicle" or "Chronicle 19." New edition by al-Rawi 1990.
[35] Garelli 1963:214.

Zalpa." [36] There was also the Hittite queen who met her death in Shukzia, perhaps at the hands of its princes; but she was presumably no sovereign queen but only the wife of king Hantili. [37]

In Egypt, Nitokris (Nit-oqetry) ruled briefly at the end of the Sixth Dynasty (ca. 2180 B.C.) and a namesake of hers is already listed as queen and builder of the Third Pyramid at Gizeh (better attributed to Menkaure/Mycerinus) during the Fourth Dynasty (ca. 2600-2500 B.C.) by Manetho. [38] Less legendary and more famous is Queen Hat-shepsut of the Eighteenth Dynasty, daughter of Tuthmose I and wife of her brother Tuthmose II, upon whose death she first ruled for a year as regent for her young nephew, the future Tuthmose III, and then took the throne for twenty more years in her own name. Her inscriptions and statuary display both masculine and feminine attributes. [39] She sent a major trading expedition to Punt on the Somali coast of the Red Sea far to the south, and illustrated the event in vivid detail on her mortuary temple at Deir-el-Bahri. [40]

As the Egyptian example shows, a double claim to kingship (daughter of one king, wife of another) could help a princess to the supreme office. In Biblical Israel, the bloodthirsty Athaliah even had a triple claim: as daughter of Ahab and Jezebel of Israel, widow of Jehoram of Judah and mother of his short-lived son Ahaziah, she first sat behind, then beside, and finally on the king's throne. [41] Among the foreign queens mentioned in the Hebrew Bible, only the legendary Queen of Sheba is portrayed as ruling in her own right. She is the first of many pre-Islamic Arab queens known from other sources. [42]

More often, a queen came to prominence only after the death of her royal husband, when she achieved the status of queen-mother to the new king, assuming he was her son. This status became even more significant if her son succeeded to the throne while still in his minority. She could then function, de facto or even de jure, as his regent. This was perhaps most notably the case with Sammu-ramat

---

[36] See the latest discussion by Bayun 1994.
[37] Helck 1984.
[38] Smith 1971:179, 196.
[39] For some of her inscriptions see ANET 231; Lichtheim 1976 II 25-29.
[40] For Hat-shepsut II, wife of Amun-hotpe II(?), see ANET 246, n. 32.
[41] Cf. Spanier 1994 who, however, prefers to regard Omri of Israel as her father and Jehoshaphat of Judah as her probable husband.
[42] Abbott 1941.

of Assyria, the Semiramis of Greek legend. New studies of her record, and new additions to it, begin to make it possible to separate fact from fiction and outline her historical role. [43]

The name of the queen—and thus the lady herself—can be explained as West Semitic in origin, meaning approximately "high heavens" (cf. Luke 2:14). [44] She was the wife of Shamshi-Adad V (823-811 B.C.) and mother of Adad-nirari III (810-783 B.C.), who was a mere child when his father died. That Shamshi-Adad was mortally wounded in the midst of a battle at the gates of Babylon is repeatedly alleged by Pettinato, [45] but such a virtually unique royal demise would hardly go unremarked in the sources [46] and has in fact no basis in the evidence, as far as I can see. The only authority cited for the claim is Olmstead, who in turn had cited the "Assyrian Chronicle" or what we now call Eponym Canon Cb(I). But all that this reports for the king's last year is that "he went to—i.e. against—Babylon." [47]

In the moment of Assyrian weakness which followed, Sammu-ramat took the reins of state into her own hands and held them for at least four years. She was the first queen to inscribe a stele among the many erected at the capital in Assur, where she also built and dedicated a new temple to Nabu. Two statues at its entrance carried inscriptions on behalf of her and her young son respectively, each ending in the well-known lines: "In Nabu trust: trust in no other god!" [48] (A later and slightly milder echo of this henotheistic exclamation opens the divine love lyrics of Nabu and Tashmetu: "Let anyone trust in whomever he trusts—as for us, we trust in Nabu, we are devoted to Tashmetu.") [49] In 805, she led the Assyrian army across the Euphrates together with her son, as is revealed by the obverse of a boundary-stone newly discovered near Kahramanmaras (Maras) in Turkey and now in the museum of that city.[50] Shortly thereafter, probably later that same year, Adad-nirari took the reins of office into his own hands. [51]

---

[43] Cf. especially Eilers 1971, Nagel 1982, Pettinato 1985, and Capomacchia 1986.
[44] Weinfeld 1991.
[45] 1985:242, 263, 273, 277.
[46] Hallo 1991, esp. pp. 157, 161f.
[47] See simply Brinkman 1968:213 and n. 1325.
[48] ARAB 1 Par. 745.
[49] Cf. Foster, BM 902, FDD 344.
[50] Taşyürek 1975; Donbaz 1990.
[51] Page (Dalley) 1969.

Such was Sammu-ramat's prominence during the four years of her regency that later versions of her biography naturally grew by accretion with features more properly attributed to other, lesser queens in a process that can be described as "telescoping" and that is attested also elsewhere in Mesopotamian and Biblical historiography. [52] This is notably the case with the Greek legend of Semiramis reported by Ctesias, Diodorus Siculus and others. Diodorus, citing Ctesias, identified Semiramis as the wife of Ninos, the alleged founder of Nineveh, and credited her in addition with embellishing Babylon with the kind of palace reliefs more familiar from the Assyrian capitals. Similarly the notion that the great "hanging gardens," one of the seven wonders of the Classical world, were built in Babylon to please a queen may conceivably turn out to be a garbled reflection of the gardens built at Nineveh by Sennaherib (704-681 B.C.), the husband of Naqia. [53]

Naqia was in fact a rich source for the stories about Semiramis. Like her, she had a West Semitic name, though in her case she was also given an Akkadian equivalent, Zakutu. She was one of several wives of Sennaherib, and therefore in competition with the others for the succession of her son in preference to theirs. The assassination of Sennaherib by two of his sons, and their flight to Urartu-Ararat (Armenia) as reported in the Bible (II Kings 19:37) and confirmed to a large extent by cuneiform sources, removed some but not all other claimants. [54]

Naqia-Zakutu is widely credited—albeit with little solid evidence—for having secured the succession for her son Esarhaddon (680-669 B.C.) in the aftermath of the assassination and—with more likelihood—for inducing her son in 672 to regulate his own succession more carefully with the help of a number of treaties forcing each of Assyria's vassals to swear to abide by the projected division of the Assyrian empire between *his* two sons. But even though she exercised the traditional prerogatives of a queen-mother, and continued, for example, to present votive inscriptions on behalf of her son and herself, [55] there is little to indicate that she played a significantly larger role than her predecessors, let alone an independent one. [56]

---

[52] Evans 1983; cf. ANEH 63, 149.
[53] Dalley 1994.
[54] Parpola 1980.
[55] Van de Mieroop 1993.
[56] Melville 1994; cf. Arzt 1993.

Thus the role of monarch was normally closed to princely women in the ancient Near East, and a kind of "gold ceiling" limited their influence on public life. Nevertheless, in their roles as mothers, wives, and daughters of kings, they enjoyed considerable prestige and status. This was dramatically illustrated in 1989 by the sudden discovery, in the palace of Assurnasirpal II (883-859) in Kalah, of the intact tombs of three Assyrian queens, the wives, respectively, of Assurnasirpal himself, of Salmaneser III (858-824), and of Tiglat-pileser III (744-727). The tombs, found by the Iraqi Service of Antiquities, were filled with a veritable treasure-house of jewelry and other grave-deposits. Two of the accompanying inscriptions have already been published by Abdulillah Fadhil; they commemorate respectively Jaba, wife of an unnamed king, and Mullissu-mukannishat-Ninua, wife (literally "palace-woman") of the two ninth century kings in succession. [57] We are still waiting for the third but not, I dare say, because the queen in question bears, amazingly enough, the same name—Athaliah—as her Israelite-Judahite predecessor of a century earlier.

Of course the role of princely women changed over time in tandem with the evolution of kingship itself, as I tried to show some time ago in a study on women of Sumer. [58] The role was probably secondary in an early period of charismatic kingship when each new ruler had to win acclaim anew by his own prowess in battle or, conceivably, wisdom in judgment. But with the gradual emergence of dynastic succession, a proper wife and the ability to produce a suitable heir became crucial.

This concern was duly reflected in the literature. The Legend of Etana even projects it back, somewhat anachronistically, to the time of what it considers the first king of the first dynasty after the Flood, or what we would call the First Early Dynastic Period. The composition has still not been completely recovered, but all available fragments and recensions have been assembled by Kinnier Wilson [59] and newly translated by Foster. [60] Although the ending is lost, Etana's search for an heir, which is a theme of the legend, was presumably crowned with success, since his successor Balih was his son according to the Sumerian King List. A subsidiary theme is that, in his desper-

---

[57] Fadhil 1990 and 1990a; Harrak 1990.
[58] Hallo 1976.
[59] Kinnier Wilson 1985; cf. the reviews by Edzard 1986 and 1987.
[60] Foster, BM 437-460, FDD 102-114.

ate search for the plant of life, this first postdiluvian king went up to heaven on the wings of an eagle, a motif popular with the seal carvers of Mesopotamia long before it became a literary topos. [61]

The Ugaritic Legend of King Keret (or Kirta) shares this concern over an heir. Like Etana, Keret is the first king of all in this tradition. He rules, not at Ugarit itself but further east in Syria, perhaps near the Balih River. [62] He is married, but loses all his children according to one interpretation, [63] or all his wives according to another, [64] or all but two children in yet another. [65] Regardless of which solution is adopted, the point of the tale is the search for a new wife and heir.

But simple dynastic succession was not the only pattern to emerge from the experiments of the third millennium. In the "Second Dynasty of Lagash," succession often seems to have passed, not from father to son but from father-in-law to son-in-law, making the daughter rather than the wife of the ruler all-important. [66] And Elam, with its peculiar *cursus honorum*, [67] developed an equally peculiar system of succession via the *sister* of the ruler and on to her son(s). [68] Among the Hittites, the succession sometimes passed to the sister's husband, though by violence not by law. [69]

In some ways the most interesting role of princesses was in connection, not with the succession, but with the emergence of dynastic marriage, i.e., the use of marriage to cement diplomatic relations between separate dynasties. This institution is first attested under the Third Dynasty of Ur at the end of the third millennium, when numerous royal or high-born women left their mark, not only in the contemporary archives and monuments, but also in the later canons, as shown, i.a., by Edmond Sollberger, [70] Piotr Steinkeller, [71] and Piotr Michalowski. [72] The last, in particular, has combined these sources to show how a certain Kunshi-matum, daughter of King Shu-Sin of Ur,

---

[61] Baudot 1982.
[62] Astour 1973.
[63] Finkel 1955.
[64] Margalit 1976.
[65] Sasson 1988.
[66] Renger 1976.
[67] See above, chapter VI 1 at note 16.
[68] Van Soldt 1990.
[69] Wilhelm 1990.
[70] Sollberger 1967.
[71] Steinkeller 1981.
[72] Michalowski 1976, 1979, 1982.

was betrothed or married in succession to three Hurrian princes of
the distant city-state of Shimanum [73] in what appears to have been an
effort at establishing peaceful relations with the far end of the "Hurrian frontier." [74] Only when this effort failed did Shu-Sin resort to a
military campaign to try to conquer the city. [75]

In the Old Babylonian period that followed (ca. 2000-1600 B.C.),
dynastic marriage came into its own as a regular instrument of high
state policy. The many Amorite dynasties that eventually divided up
the empire of Ur considered themselves related to each other, and
constructed elaborate genealogies to stress that relationship. It was
only natural for them to marry their princesses off to each other in
order to cement these relationships. [76] So, for example, Nur-ahum of
Eshnunna married his daughter off to the son of Abda-El, the "gran-
dee" (*rabiānum*) of Amurru (or "sheikh of the Amorites") [77] and in turn
Abda-El's daughter became the wife of Nur-ahum's nephew and second successor Bilalama. [78]

But the princesses in question were not always equally willing and
pliant instruments of their royal fathers' will. Occasionally they complained bitterly about having to live in virtual exile from the attractions of the cosmopolitan city of their birth only to share the bed and
board of a doltish vassal-prince somewhere in the provinces. We are
especially well informed of such sentiments from the archives of the
great royal palace at Mari on the Euphrates, which dutifully shelved
and preserved all the letters received by the king, including a whole
volume of "feminine correspondence" as it was entitled by its modern
editor, Georges Dossin. [79] In his commentary, [80] in an edition of the
texts by Roemer, [81] and in review articles by Artzi and Malamat [82]
and others, we find, alongside the letters of Shibtu, the wife of the
king, also those of his daughters. I will cite just one, from the princess

---

[73] Michalowski 1975. For a new attempt to localize Shimanum see Astour
1987:42-47. For an interesting new reference to Kunshi-matum's intended, Arib-atal,
spelled A-ar-ba-tal(!), see Sigrist 1983 No.480.
[74] Hallo 1978, esp. p. 79.
[75] For other examples of Ur III dynastic marriages see Hallo 1976:31.
[76] See the examples and literature cited Hallo 1976:33.
[77] Stol 1976:87f.
[78] Franke 1977:63; see now Whiting 1987:26-29.
[79] Dossin 1967.
[80] Dossin and Finet 1978.
[81] Roemer 1971.
[82] Artzi and Malamat 1971.

Inib-sharri who had been married off to Ibal-Addu, ruler of Ashlakka. She wrote to her father Zimri-Lim, king of Mari, as follows: [83]

> Concerning my unhappiness I have written twice to my lord, and my lord wrote me (a reply) as follows: "Go and enter Ashlakka. Do not cry." This is what my lord wrote me. Now I have entered Ashlakka, but I am very unhappy. The wife of Ibal-Addu—she is the queen! And that woman herself constantly receives the gifts from (both) Ashlakka and the (other) cities, while she (he?) makes me sit in a corner and grasp my cheek in my hand like some female-simpleton.

If nothing else, this letter shows that Old Babylonian women, at least if they were princesses, could write cuneiform and express themselves in elegant idiom, without the aid, as far as can be seen, of any professional scribes. That naturally leads to our third topic, namely women as scribes and authors. [84]

Bibliographical References

Abbott, Nabia, 1941: "Pre-Islamic Arab Queens," AJSL 58:1-22.

Al-Rawi, F.N.H., 1990: "Tablets from the Sippar Library: the 'Weidner Chronicle': a suppositious royal letter concerning a vision," Iraq 52:1-13.

Artzi, P. and A. Malamat, 1971: "The correspondence of Shibtu, queen of Mari," Or. 40:75-89.

Arzt, Jennifer, 1993: "Neo-Assyrian Royal Women," Yale Graduate Journal of Anthropology 5:45-56.

Astour, Michael, 1973: "A North Mesopotamian locale of the Keret Epic?" UF 5:29-39.

———, 1987: "Semites and Hurrians in Northern Transtigris," SCCNH 2:3-68.

Batto, Bernard, 1974: Studies on Women at Mari (= JHNES (5)).

Baudot, Marie-Paule, 1982: "Representations in glyptic art of a preserved legend: Etana, the shepherd, who ascended to heaven," Naster AV II 1-10.

Bayun, Lilia, 1994: "The Legend about the Queen of Kanis: a historical source?" JAC 9:1-13.

Brinkman, John A., 1968: A Political History of Post-Kassite Babylonia 1158-722 B.C. (= AnOr 43).

Capomacchia, Anna Maria G., 1986: Semiramis, una femminilita ribaltata (= Storia delle religioni 4) (Rome, L'Erma di Bretschneider, 1986).

Dalley (Page), Stephanie, 1994: "Nineveh, Babylon and the Hanging Gardens: cuneiform and classical sources reconciled," Iraq 56:45-58.

Donbaz, Veysel, 1990: "Two neo-Assyrian stelae in the Antakya and Kahramanmaraş Museums," ARRIM 8:5-10.

Dossin, Georges, 1967: La Correspondance Féminine (= ARM 10 = TCL 31).

---

[83] Translation following Batto 1974:38.

[84] For dynastic marriages during the Late Bronze Age, see the comprehensive survey by Pintore 1978.

260 CHAPTER EIGHT

———— and André Finet, 1978: *Correspondance Féminine* (= ARMT 10).

Edzard, Dietz Otto, 1986, 1987: review of Kinnier Wilson 1985 in ZA 76:134-137, 77:303.

Eilers, Wilhelm, 1971: *Semiramis: Enstehung und Nachhall einer altorientalischen Sage* (Vienna, Böhlaus).

Evans, Carl D., 1983: "Naram-Sin and Jeroboam: the archetypal *Unheilsherrscher* in Mesopotamian and Biblical historiography," SIC 2:97-125.

Fadhil, Abdulillah, 1990: "Die in Nimrud/Kalhu aufgefundene Grabinschrift der Jabâ," BaMi 21:461-470.

————, 1990a: "Die Grabinschrift der Mullissu-mukanništat-Ninua aus Nimrud/Kalhu und andere in ihrem Grab gefundene Schriftträger," BaMi 21:471-482 + pls. 39-45.

Finkel, Joshua, 1955: "A mathematical conundrum in the Ugaritic Keret poem," HUCA 26:109-149.

Franke, Judith A., 1977: "Presentation seals of the Ur III/Isin-Larsa period," BM 6:61-66.

Garelli, Paul, 1963: *Les Assyriens en Cappadoce* (= BAHIFAI 19).

Goetze, Albrecht, 1965: "Tavern keepers and the like in ancient Babylonia," Landsberger AV 211-215.

Hallo, William W., 1976: "Women of Sumer," BM 4:23-40, 129-138.

————, 1978: "Simurrum and the Hurrian frontier," RHA 36(=RAI 24):71-83.

————, 1991: "The death of kings," Tadmor AV, 148-165.

Harrak, Amir, 1990: "The royal tombs of Nimrud and their jewellery," *Bulletin [of] the Canadian Society for Mesopotamian Studies* 20 (October, 1990) 5-13.

Helck, Wolfgang, 1984: "Die Šukzija-Episode im Dekret des Telipinu," WO 15:103-108.

Jacobsen, Thorkild, 1939: *The Sumerian King List* (= AS 11).

Kinnier Wilson, J.V., 1985: *The Legend of Etana: a new Edition* (Warminster, Aris and Phillips).

Leichty, Erle, 1970: *The Omen Series* šumma izbu (= TCS 4).

Lichtheim, Miriam, 1976: *Ancient Egyptian Literature*, vol. II: The New Kingdom (Berkeley, University of California Press).

Margalit, B., 1976: "The ill-fated wives of King Krt (CTA 14:14-21a)," UF 8:137-145.

Melville, Sarah Chamberlin, 1994: *The Role of Naqia/Zakutu in Sargonid Politics* (Ph.D. Dissertation, Yale University).

Michalowski, Piotr, 1975: "The bride of Simanum," JAOS 95:716-719.

————, 1976, 1979, 1982: "Royal women of the Ur III period," JCS 28:169-172; 31:171-176; ASJ 4:129-142.

Nagel, Wolfram, 1982: *Ninus und Semiramis in Sage und Geschichte* (Berlin, Volker Spiess).

Page (Dalley), Stephanie, 1969: "Adad-nirari and Semiramis: the stelae of Saba'a and Rimah," Or. 38:457-458.

Parpola, Simo, 1980: "The murderer of Sennacherib," RAI 26:171-182.

Pettinato, Giovanni, 1985: *Semiramide* (Milan, Rusconi, 1985).

Pintore, Franco, 1978: *Il matrimonio interdinastico nel Vicino Oriente durante i secoli XV-XIII* (Rome, Istituto per l'Oriente: Centro per le antichità e la storia dell'arte del Vicino Oriente).

Renger, Johannes, 1976: "The daughters of Urbaba: some thoughts on the succession to the throne during the 2. Dynasty of Lagash," Kramer AV 367-369.

Roemer, W.H.Ph., 1971: *Frauenbriefe über Religion, Politik und Privatleben in Mari* (= AOAT 12).

Sasson, Jack M., 1988: "The numeric progression in Keret 1:15-20. Yet another suggestion," SEL 5:181-188.

Sigrist, Marcel, 1983: *Textes Économiques Néo-Sumériens de l' Université de Syracuse* (Paris, Editions Recherche sur les Civilisations).

Smith, W. Stevenson, 1971: "The Old Kingdom in Egypt and the Beginning of the First Intermediate Period," CAH (3rd ed.) I/2 ch. xiv.

Sollberger, Edmond, 1967: "Ladies of the Ur III empire," RA 61:69f.

Spanier, Ktziah, 1994: "The Queen Mother in the Judaean Royal Court," PWCJS 11:75-82.

Steinkeller, Piotr, 1981: "More on the Ur III royal wives," ASJ 3:76-92.

Stol, Marten, 1976: *Studies in Old Babylonian History* (= PIHANS 40).

Taşyürek, O. Ayutuğ, 1975: "Some new Assyrian rock-reliefs in Turkey," AnSt 25:169-180.

Van De Mieroop, Marc, 1993: "An inscribed bead of Queen Zakutu," Hallo AV 259-261.

Van Soldt, W.H., 1990: "Matrilinearität. A. In Elam," RLA 7: 586-588.

Weinfeld, Moshe, 1991: "Semiramis: her name and her origin," Tadmor AV 99-103.

Whiting, Robert, 1987: *Old Babylonian Letters from Tell Asmar* (= AS 22).

Wilhelm, Gernot, 1990: "Matrilinearität. B. Bei den Hethitern," RLA 7:588-590.

3. As Authors

That Mesopotamian women could function as cuneiform scribes, albeit rarely, has long been known from scattered indications. To begin with, the traditional patron deity of all scribes was the goddess Nisaba. She is "chief scribe of Heaven (An), record-keeper of Enlil, all-knowing sage of the gods," and holds the lapis lazuli tablet on her knee. [85] The divine Geshtin-anna is "queen of the scribes;" [86] her Akkadian equivalent Belit-ṣeri served as scribe of the netherworld. [87] With these and other heavenly models, one is not surprised to find their earthly counterparts. Already Bruno Meissner mentioned female scribes of the late period in the chapter on schooling of his classic double volume *Babylonien und Assyrien*, citing in this connection two letters directed to the gods by king Assurbanipal which concluded as follows: "Disregard that a woman has written (this letter) and placed it before you." [88] In the latest edition of these letters, Ivan Starr notes that the two letters are in different hands. [89]

More recently, a survey of women scribes (and messengers) throughout the ancient Near East has been offered by Samuel Meier. [90] He notes the first (two) scribes identified as being female in an Ur III text. [91]

By Old Babylonian times, a single Mari text names nine female scribes. [92] In the "cloister" (*gagû*) of Sippar at least a dozen of them are known by name. [93] The most active and longest lived among them was called Inanna-amamu in Sumerian, or Ishtar-ummi in Akkadian. She was the daughter of Tiamat-tabum. She sometimes omitted the feminine determinative before (or after) the scribal title (*mi-dub-sar*; once *dub-sar-mi*). [94] This should alert us to the possible existence of other female scribes following the same practice. A certain "Belti-rimeni, female scribe," presumably from Sippar, copied an

---

[85] Hallo, RAI 17: 128f., lines 12f., 30; 130f. *ad locc.*

[86] Kramer, JANES 5 (1973) 247 line 24; cf. Alster JCS 27 (1975) 218 line 24.

[87] AHw s.v. ṭ/tupšarratu(m); cf. Meissner 1925:25 (with n. 16), 34, 145.

[88] *Ibid.* 329, with reference to ABL 1367f.

[89] Starr 1990:298f.

[90] Meier 1991.

[91] Meier 1991:541 n. 7, referring to Oppenheim 1948:21f.; cf. *ibid.* n. 44a. Copy republished by Sauren 1978 as No. 373.

[92] Meier 1991:542 and n. 15.

[93] Harris 1963:138f.; 1975:196f. Meier 1991:542 n. 14 adds one more.

[94] Meier 1991:541 and nn. 9f.

exemplar of the lexical series "Proto-Aa" (VAT 6574). [95] An exemplar
of the "Hymn to the Pickaxe" (VAT 6457+6492+6493) [96] is probably
by the same hand, [97] although this time the colophon says only "hand
of the/a female scribe" without mentioning her name; is the implication that female scribes were sufficiently rare to obviate the need for
further identification? For the later Old Babylonian period, it was
once thought that the scribe of the principal recension of the Atar-hasis Epic bore the female name Ellet-Aya, but that name more likely
has to be read as Nur-Aya. [98]

As late as neo-Assyrian times, female scribes are employed among
many other women in the queen's palace, both at Kalah [99] and at
Nineveh. [100] Both times the professional designation is written MÍ.A.BA
(at Kalah even LÚ.A.BA), now seen as standing for "ABC-man" or abe-
cedarian, i.e. specialist in Aramaic rather than Akkadian. [101] Thus,
the suggestion that the six Nineveh women scribes are further quali-
fied as "(scribes) of Aramaic" (ar-m[i-te] gains somewhat in probability. [102] Whether this has anything to do with the West Semitic
origin of some of the neo-Assyrian queens [103] must be left open here.

But even if there were women scribes, and if they wrote cuneiform
at least in earlier times, that does not, in and of itself, allow us to
speak of women authors. That awaited the rediscovery of Enheduanna and her oeuvre. Enheduanna was the daughter of Sargon
of Akkad who forged the first great empire on the soil of Western Asia
at the turn from the 24th to the 23rd centuries B.C. She compiled a
cycle of short hymns apostrophizing the temples of Sumer and Akkad, and probably intended to publicize her father's solicitude for the
cults of both halves of his newly established empire, the vanquished
Sumerian-speaking south, as well as the victorious Akkadian-speaking
north. She also composed a cycle of three lengthy hymns celebrating
her father's triumphs in war, though describing them as victories of

---

[95] MSL 9:148f.; MSL 14:135f.
[96] Published as SK 207.
[97] So Landsberger and Civil, MSL 9 (1967):148, followed by Sjöberg 1976:177,
n. 66 and Krispijn 1990:151 and n. 62.
[98] Walker 1982.
[99] Dalley and Postgate 1984:92-95; cf. Meier 1991:541 and n. 8.
[100] Fales and Postgate 1992:32-34.
[101] Parpola apud Tadmor 1982:459. Above, ch. I 3, nn. 251-253.
[102] Landsberger 1967:203 n.3; cf. Meier 1991:542 and n. 16.
[103] Above, ch. VIII 2.

his patron goddess Inanna. She had a retinue of officials who dedicated their seal inscriptions to her, and she herself dedicated an ala-
baster votive disk to the moongod at Ur. The reverse is inscribed
with her name, filiation, and priestly titles. The obverse is carved in
relief with a full-figure portrait of herself making an offering at an
altar in the company of three of her retainers. She was installed as
high priestess of the moongod at Ur by her father and thus became
the first of a long line of princesses to fill this newly created priestly
post. She was forcibly removed from her high office in the course of
a revolt against the authority of the Sargonic ruling house, and then
restored through what she regarded as the divine intervention of
Inanna. All this was set forth in detail in the description of her "life
and work" which opened the edition of one of her great poems to
Inanna by Van Dijk and myself in 1968. [104] What, then, has been
added to this record in the interim?

In the first place there has been renewed attention to Enheduanna's disk, found at Ur in the course of the joint British-Ameri-
can excavations conducted by Sir Leonard Woolley, and now on
display in the University Museum of the University of Pennsylvania.
The relief on its front has been scrutinized by Irene Winter, who even
suggests iconographic evidence for predecessors in her priestly office,
though there is as yet no textual basis for this hypothesis. [105] The disk
survived intact at least until Early Old Babylonian times at the beginning of the second millennium, since the inscription on its back, as
was noted by Edmond Sollberger, was at that time copied by a scribal
student at Ur by way of filling the space left on his clay tablet after
copying a longer and later inscription of King Ibbi-Sin of Ur. [106] It is
thus no longer possible to regard the present breaks in her disk as
dating all the way back to her own time and as further evidence of
the revolt against her royal house. The inscription and its late copy,
along with the seal inscriptions dedicated to Enheduanna, have been
reedited in new compendia of Sargonic monuments. [107]

In the second place, the publication of Enheduanna's "Exaltation
of Inanna," has been followed by many important reviews, new
translations, and additions to her corpus. Of the reviews, the most

---

[104] Hallo and van Dijk 1968, ch. 1.
[105] Winter 1987.
[106] Sollberger 1969.
[107] Gelb and Kienast 1990:64f., 190, 39; Frayne 1993:35f., 38f.

substantial ones are by Sauren, Heimpel, Römer (with what almost amounts to a new edition), and especially Wilcke. [108] Kramer provided a new translation of the composition under the title of "Hymnal prayer of Enheduanna: the adoration of Inanna in Ur," [109] and some or all of it has found its way into anthologies of women's poetry . [110] A new edition is in preparation by Annette Gunter, a doctoral candidate at the University of Pennsylvania. Roberta Binkley, a doctoral student at the University of Arizona, is writing a dissertation on Enheduanna's work from a feminist-rhetorical point of view. [111]

The additions to the corpus include Sjöberg's edition of her cycle of temple hymns and of the hymn "Stout-hearted lady" (in-nin šà-gur₄-ra), which describes Inanna's (i.e. Sargon's) triumphs over the rebellion that erupted in his old age. [112] A third major hymn, "Inanna and Ebih," recounts her (his) triumph over Mt. Ebih; though not yet published, it is widely available in a manuscript reconstruction by Barry Eichler. All three hymns to Inanna are listed together in a newly published literary catalogue, clarifying their relationship to each other and strengthening the case for attributing all three to Enheduanna. [113] Joan Westenholz has edited three shorter compositions which mention her by name or title and may be attributed to her, and added an appreciation of her priestly role. [114]

The new evidence tends to strengthen the impression that Enheduanna was a creature of flesh and blood, and not just the figment of later imagination to which it was deemed convenient, for whatever reason, to attribute so many highly stylized and elevated compositions, a notion which is at least theoretically conceivable and has even had its defenders. Joachim Krecher, notably, has entertained the possibility that the name may be explained as an epithet, 'high-priestess, ornament of Heaven (An),' and does not necessarily refer to the daughter of Sargon in her principal poems. [115] On present evidence,

---

[108] Sauren 1970; Heimpel 1971; Römer 1976; Wilcke 1976.
[109] ANET (3rd ed., 1969) 579-582.
[110] Barnstone and Barnstone 1980:1-8; Anne D. Kilmer in Bankier and Lashgari 1983:111-117.
[111] Cf. above, ch. V 3.
[112] Sjöberg and Bergmann, TCS 3; Sjöberg 1975.
[113] Cohen 1976:131f. lines 1-3; see above, ch. V 3, at nn. 215-219.
[114] Westenholz 1989.
[115] Krecher 1978:136.

Enheduanna is the first non-anonymous, non-fictitious author in world history—and a woman.

Nor was she the last of her sex to compose lofty Sumerian poetry. The death of King Ur-Nammu (ca. 2094 B.C.), whose broken body was left on the battlefield and had to be brought back to Ur for subsequent burial, was described in such moving terms that Wilcke, who after Kramer edited the relevant lamentation, is inclined to attribute its composition to the king's widow, possibly the lady called Watartum. [116] The plaintive tone of her(?) lamentation could be explained even better if it could be argued that the neo-Sumerian queens followed their husbands into the grave, as was notably the case with the much earlier and grisly "Royal Graves of Ur," as has recently been attested at least on a literary level for Gilgamesh from the new-found texts from Me-Turan, and as has been suggested for the next king of Ur, Shulgi. [117]

The wife of Shulgi, or one of his wives, is also candidate for author of a unique example of yet another Sumerian literary genre, the lullaby. In a composition called *ua-aua* after its opening words or, in this case, its opening sounds, she or perhaps her wet-nurse lulls her son to sleep. [118] If it is the queen, it may have been Abi-simti [119] now confirmed as the mother of Shu-Sin. [120] The name of the princely baby is not given in the preserved part of the poem, but it was very likely Shu-Sin, the intended crown-prince though destined to be preceded in the kingship of Ur by his brother Amar-Suen.

In any case it was Shu-Sin who, when grown to manhood, was the subject of a whole series of love-songs, some of them again arguably of female authorship. Shu-Sin claimed a degree of divinization exceeding even that of his father and brother, allowing or requiring himself to be worshipped in temples erected to him by his governors and inscribed with their dedications in precisely the style hitherto reserved for royal dedications of temples to the "real" gods. But he was also, no doubt, a stand-in for the divine Dumuzi in the rite of the sacred marriage, and some of the love-songs may reflect his partici-

---

[116] Wilcke, RAI 17(1970)86.

[117] Cf. above, ch. VI 2 at nn. 76-83.

[118] Kramer in ANET 651f. and 1971.

[119] Kramer in ANET 651, n. 1.

[120] Whiting 1976:178f. For the possibility that she may have been the wife of Amar-Suen rather than Shulgi see P. Steinkeller, ASJ 3 (1981) 79f. For Shu-Sin as son of Amar-Suen see now J. Boese and W. Sallaberger, AoF 23 (1996) 36-38.

pation in this rite, others his earthly union with mortal females. Both were equally and openly erotic in character.

Some or all of these love-songs have been attributed to the women who occasionally speak in them in the first person, from the priestess Kubatum, whose gift of a necklace of beads inscribed by Shu-Sin was excavated at Uruk, to the humble "tapstress" whom Thorkild Jacobsen has identified as the composer (and subject) of a bawdy drinking song probably directed at the king. (Perhaps she is the Il-ummiya whom Jacobsen has identified as a tapstress in the poem of Kubatum.) Jacobsen has translated these and several other compositions with flair, one may even say with relish, in the second chapter of his *The Harps That Once ...*, while in the first chapter he has included some of the equally erotic poetry centered on Dumuzi and Inanna, though without suggesting feminine (or masculine) authorship for them. [121]

A final example of Sumerian poetry by a woman, indeed a *chef d'oeuvre* of the genre, is the letter-prayer of Nin-shatapada. The letter is addressed to King Rim-Sin, last king of the Old Babylonian dynasty of Larsa, who conquered much of southern Babylonia during his long reign of sixty years (ca. 1822-1763), and thus paved the way for the still greater conquests of his younger contemporary Hammurapi of Babylon. Among Rim-Sin's victims was the rival dynasty of Uruk founded by Sin-kashid. It was Sin-kashid's daughter who appealed to the great conqueror to spare her as he had previously spared the king and people of Uruk, and to restore her to the high-priesthood of the city of Durum, a position to which she had been presumably appointed by her father in his lifetime. In addressing the king, the text utilizes some of the very same phrases employed in the official date formulas and inscriptions of the Larsa Dynasty, and with their help may be dated with some probability to the year 1800 B.C. Since it entered into the canon of the "Royal Correspondence of Larsa," we may suppose that it achieved its purpose. [122]

Here it may well be asked whether queens and princesses fluent in Sumerian were the only women in the ancient Near East to try their hand at authorship. The answer to this question is complicated by the noted reticence of the sources to identify authors altogether. More-

---

[121] Jacobsen, *Harps*, chs. 1-2; cf. Jacobsen 1987.
[122] Hallo 1983 and 1991; cf. Michalowski 1977 and above, ch. VII 3 at n. 103.

over when we do have an attribution, such as that of the Hittite ritual
against impotence to an "old woman" named Anniwiyanni, [123] we
may question whether she really composed it or whether it simply
circulated under her name. In all of Akkadian literature, I know of no
attributions to women authors, nor in Egyptian, and in Ugaritic literature no attributions to *any* authors, male or female.

That leaves Biblical literature. Here Richard Friedman has given
serious thought to the question, "who wrote the Bible?" and come up
with an answer: much of it was the work of two men, Jeremiah and
Ezra respectively. [124] The former had the help of his scribe Baruch
son of Neriyah, or Berach-Yahu son of Neri-Yahu as we can vocalize
the name found on a seal impression dating from the end of the First
Temple period. The discovery of this and other seals of the time inscribed with names familiar from the biographical details in the Book
of Jeremiah was unfortunately not made in a controlled archaeological context. Even so, it tends to inspire some confidence in the Biblical account of Baruch's role in recording Jeremiah's message, and
even in Friedman's hypothesis. Friedman also weighed the possibility
of a female author of one or more of the sources that went into the
redaction of the final Biblical text. He considered the so-called J
source of the Pentateuch as a conceivable candidate for such a hypothesis. [125]

This hypothesis was raised to the level of a virtual certainty, and
given wide publicity, when it was adopted by the prominent literary
critic Harold Bloom in *The Book of J*. The actual components of the
source referred to as "J" are far from agreed on even by those who
advocate the "documentary hypothesis" but, undaunted by these dis-
agreements, Bloom not only identified these components but also
provided a running translation—or rather perhaps paraphrase—of
them prepared by David Rosenberg, and then proceeded to assign
the entire source to a woman, possibly a princess, living in Jerusalem
at the time of Rehoboam in the aftermath of the break-up of the
United Monarchy— [126] much as Samuel Butler (1835-1902) assigned
the Odyssey to an "authoress." [127]

---

[123] Sturtevant 1935:100-126.
[124] Friedman 1987.
[125] Friedman 1987:86.
[126] Bloom and Rosenberg 1990. See Friedmann 1991 for his scathing view of
their effort.
[127] Butler 1922 (reference courtesy Baruch Halpern).

If I am not persuaded by Bloom's arguments, it does not mean that I rule out all possibility that other, and notably later parts of the Bible may reflect female authorship, or at least a feminist point of view. This has been suggested, at one time or another, for Ruth [128] and the Song of Songs. [129] My own favorite candidate is the Book of Esther, as I already noted in passing in 1983. [130] It not only displays its three female protagonists to considerable advantage, but in each case has them outshine their male counterparts. Queen Vashti is most certainly soberer and more majestic than her stumblebum buffoon of a husband, King Ahasueros. Zeresh is more straightforward and decisive than the devious Haman (Esther 6:13). And even Esther ultimately surpasses in wisdom and bravery her pious but stubborn uncle Mordechai. Whether this is a clue to the authorship of the scroll is for others to decide.

Bibliographical References

Bankier, Joanna and Deirdre Lashgari, eds., 1983: *Women Poets of the World* (New York, Macmillan).

Barnstone, Aliki and Willis Barnstone, eds., 1980: *A Book of Women Poetry from Antiquity to Now* (New York, Schocken).

Bloom, Harold and David Rosenberg, 1990: *The Book of J* (New York, Grove Weidenfeld).

Butler, Samuel, 1922: *The Authoress of the Odyssey* (London, Jonathan Cape, 1922).

Cohen, Mark E., 1976: "Literary texts from the Andrews University Archaeological Museum," RA 70:129-144.

Dalley, Stephanie and J.N. Postgate, 1984: *The Tablets from Fort Shalmaneser* (= CTN 3).

Fales, F.M. and J.N. Postgate, 1992: *Imperial Administrative Records, Part I: Palace and Temple Administration* (= SAA 7).

Frayne, Douglas R., 1993: *Sargonic and Gutian Periods (2334-2113 BC)* (= RIME 2).

Friedman, Richard E., 1987: *Who Wrote The Bible?* (New York, Simon and Schuster).

———, 1991: "Is everybody a Bible expert?" BR 7/2 (April 1991) 16-18, 50f.

Gelb, I.J. and B. Kienast, 1990: *Die altakkadischen Königsinschriften des dritten Jahrtausends v. Chr.* (= FAOS 7).

Hallo, William W., 1983: "Sumerian historiography," in Tadmor and Weinfeld, eds. *History, Historiography and Interpretation* (Jerusalem, Magnes) 9-20.

———, 1983a: "The First Purim," BA 46:19-29.

———, 1991: "The royal correspondence of Larsa: III. The princess and the plea," *Garelli AV* 377-388.

——— and J.J.A. van Dijk, 1968: *The Exaltation of Inanna* (= YNER 3).

---

[128] S. Sandmel, *Enjoyment of Scripture* (New York, 1972) 25, cited by Y. Gitay, *AJS Review* 18/2 (1993) 287.

[129] The psychiatrist Max N. Pusin in a letter of 1971 cited by M.H. Pope, *Song of Songs* (= AB 7C, 1977) 133f.; cf. *idem*, Childs AV (1988) 317.

[130] Hallo 1983a:24f.

Harris, Rivkah, 1963: "The organization and administration of the cloister in ancient Babylonia," *JESHO* 6:121-157.

———, 1975: *Ancient Sippar: a Demographic Study of an Old-Babylonian City* (= PIHANS 36).

Heimpel, Wolfgang, 1971: review of Hallo and van Dijk in JNES 30:232-236.

Jacobsen, Thorkild, 1987: "Two *bal-bal-e* dialogues," Pope AV 57-63.

Krecher, Joachim, 1978: "Sumerische Literatur," in Wolfgang Röllig, ed., *Altorientalische Literaturen* (= Neues Handbuch der Literaturwissenschaft 1) (Wiesbaden, Akademische Verlagsgesellschaft Athenaion).

Kramer, Samuel Noah, 1971: "u 5 - a a - ù - a: A Sumerian Lullaby," Volterra AV 6:191-205.

Krispijn, Th.J.H., 1990: "Tweetalige teksten in de oudere Mesopotamische literatuur" in W.J. Boot, ed., *Literatuur en Tweetaligheid* (Leiden, Rijksuniversiteit Leiden) 131-161.

Landsberger, Benno, 1967: "Akkadisch-Hebräische Wortgleichungen," Baumgartner AV 176-204.

Meier, Samuel A., 1991: "Women and communication in the ancient Near East," JAOS 111:540-547.

Meissner, Bruno, 1925: *Babylonien und Assyrien* II (Heidelberg, Carl Winters).

Michalowski, Piotr, 1977: "Durum and Uruk during the Ur III period," *Mesopotamia* 12: 83-96.

Oppenheim, A. Leo, 1948: *Catalogue of the Cuneiform Tablets* ... (= AOS 32).

Römer, W.H.Ph., 1976: review of Hallo and van Dijk 1968 in UF 4:173-206.

Sauren, Herbert, 1970: Review of Hallo and van Dijk 1968 in Bi.Or. 27:38-41.

———, 1978: *Les Tablettes Cunéiformes de l'Époque d'Ur des Collections de la New York Public Library* (= PIOL 19)

Sjöberg, Åke, W., 1975: "i n - n i n š à - g u r₄ - r a. A hymn to the goddess Inanna by the e n -priestess Enḫeduanna," ZA 65:161-253.

———, 1976: "The Old Babylonian Eduba," AS 20:159-179.

Sollberger, Edmond, 1969: "En-ḫedu-anna's inscribed disk from Ur" (= Notes Brèves 16), RA 63:180.

Starr, Ivan, 1990: *Queries to the Sungod* (= SAA 4).

Sturtevant, Edgar and George Bechtel, 1935: *A Hittite Chrestomathy* (Philadelphia, Linguistic Society of America).

Tadmor, Hayim, 1982: "The Aramaization of Assyria: aspects of Western impact," RAI 25:449-470.

Walker, C.B.F., 1982: "Nur-Ajja, the copyist of Atrahasis," RA 76:95f.

Westenholz, Joan Goodnick, 1989: "Enḫeduanna, en-priestess, hen of Nanna, spouse of Nanna," Sjöberg AV 539-556.

Whiting, Robert M., 1976: "Tiš-atal of Nineveh and Babati, uncle of Šu-Sin," JCS 28:173-182.

Wilcke, Claus, 1976: "nin-me-šár-ra - Probleme der Interpretation," WZKM 68:79-92.

Winter, Irene, 1987: "Women in public: the disk of Enheduanna, the beginning of the office of en-priestess, and the weight of visual evidence," RAI 33:189-201.

CHAPTER NINE

APPENDIX
THE FIRST HALF OF HISTORY [1]

History in the strict sense begins when writing begins. It begins in
any given area of the world where writing begins; and it depends in
the first instance on written documents. Only in a secondary sense
can it avail itself of the supplementary evidence of art and artifacts,
of legend and oral traditions, of alleged parallels from later periods or
the biased testimony of neighboring observers. Strictly speaking,
then, the conditions for writing true history are met first in the ancient Near East, beginning about five thousand years ago with the
invention of full writing—after a long prehistory of writing and counting techniques "before writing" —in Sumer near the end of the fourth
millennium B.C., and it is no exaggeration to say that "history begins
at Sumer." Writing spread from Sumer gradually to all of the Near
East, but beyond the Near East only in the course of the first millennium B.C. Hence, the ancient Near East is the setting for half of
recorded human history.

To write "half of history" in the compass of a single chapter may
seem an impossible task. Mountains of textual evidence have been
uncovered by nearly two centuries of Near Eastern excavations. Two
new humanistic disciplines—Assyriology and Egyptology—have
evolved to cope with the data in the cuneiform and hieroglyphic
scripts which were employed by the highly literate civilizations of

---

[1] The text of this section was originally written in or about 1970 for *History of the
World* edited by John W. Hall. When that project finally appeared in 1988, it was
replaced by an earlier version. It is here reproduced in essentially its original form
but without the illustrations envisaged for it. More recent formulations of the historical views expressed in it, and full bibliographical documentation, may be found in
Heritage: Civilization and the Jews (2 vols.) by William W. Hallo, David B. Ruderman
and Michael Stanislawski (New York, Prager, 1984); in *The Book of the People* by William W. Hallo (= Brown Judaic Studies 225) (Atlanta, Scholars Press, 1991); and in
The Ancient Near East: a History by William W. Hallo and William Kelly Simpson (2nd
ed.) (Fort Worth, Harcourt Brace, forthcoming). Full documentation may also be
found, for selected topics, in the pages of the present work. What follows will therefore dispense with further footnotes.

Mesopotamia and Egypt respectively. The adjacent lands that came under their influence have also left substantial bodies of evidence in a variety of scripts and languages. In Anatolia (Asiatic Turkey) these include the Hittite inscriptions, in Syria, Lebanon and the rest of the Levant those in various West (or "Northwest") Semitic dialects closely related to Hebrew, in Arabia the various North and South Arabic languages, in Iran successive stages of Persian. In addition, the study of the Hebrew Bible is an independent field of great antiquity and complexity. No one specialist can master all these sources, and no one specialty embraces all the skills they demand.

And yet the historian's task is aided by a certain underlying unity that informs the grand themes of ancient Near Eastern history. A common heartbeat seems to characterize its major trends. The ups and downs, the crests and troughs of the story appear to suggest a kind of pattern. Historians must be ever careful not to impose an unwarranted unity from without. At the same time, they need to rise above the local interests of the textual specialist to appreciate the larger picture. For despite the diversity of its languages and other cultural traditions, the Near East was an arena small enough to transmit the effects of major developments in short order from one end to the other. The introduction of new ideas, the invention of new techniques, the discovery of new resources, the rise or fall of empires, the movements of populations, the effects of major natural disasters—all were factors which radiated quickly from their origin to the rest of the area. In consequence, it is possible to delineate and characterize the major chronological subdivisions of ancient Near Eastern history before focusing on some of its separate geographical units.

The Early Bronze Age (ca. 3100-2100 B.C.) began with the emergence of civilization in both Mesopotamia and Egypt. Some of the components of civilization, such as urbanism, appeared in Canaan at the same time. The Old Kingdom and its imposing pyramids marked the high point of the Age in Egypt, and the Sargonic empire in Mesopotamia. With the beginning of the First Intermediate Period in Egypt, and the fall of Akkad in Mesopotamia, both empires, and the Early Bronze Age, came to a dramatic end.

The Middle Bronze Age (ca. 2100-1600 B.C.) began with a brilliant renaissance of urban civilization, spearheaded by the Third Dynasty of Ur in Mesopotamia and the Eleventh Dynasty, based at Thebes, in Egypt. But the greatest renown of the Age was achieved by the Dynasty of Hammurapi of Babylon and the Twelfth Dynasty of Egypt, consolidators of the Middle Kingdom. In the Syro-Palestinian area, the Age is sometimes equate with Patriarchal times. The fall of Babylon and Memphis marked its end.

The Late Bronze Age (ca. 1600-1200 B.C.) began inauspiciously for the traditional seats of empire, with Mesopotamia in the grip of a dark age, and Egypt in that of a Second Intermediate Period. Their leadership was contested by rival kingdoms in Syria and Anatolia, and a balance was struck in which New Kingdom Egypt and Kassite Babylonia had to contend with Hurrians, Hittites and Assyrians. Following the fall of Troy, "Sea Peoples" and Aramaeans swept into the established kingdoms of the Near East from all sides and created a new balance of power.

The Iron Age (ca. 1200-539 B.C.) dawned with Egypt and Assyria alone relatively unscathed. But Egypt soon plunged into an extended Third Intermediate Period, while in Syria and Palestine, Aramaeans and Hebrews established independent kingdoms to stem the Assyrian advance. At its height, the Assyrian empire included Syria, Palestine and briefly even Egypt, but it fell before the combined onslaught of Babylonia and the Medes, the latter ready to usher in a more lasting unification of the Near East under the Achaemenid dynasty of Persia.

1. THE LAND BETWEEN THE RIVERS

The Early Bronze Age

Sumer may well owe its early prominence to its strategic location athwart the intersection of the trade routes which brought the two essential ingredients of bronze-making together, for indications are that the heavier copper came by sea from the southern coasts of Iran, and the lighter tin overland from sources in the highlands of northern Iran or even further afield. Certainly it became a paramount object of Mesopotamian foreign policy to maintain control of the trade routes leading to these key sources throughout the Bronze Age. Hence most of the great campaigns recorded for the 3rd and 2nd millennia were fought on the Tigris or eastern frontier, while the Euphrates frontier was allowed to play a more passive role: though timber may have come downstream from the Levant, there were no riches to be found in the barren wastes of the Syrian and Arabian deserts which lay across the Euphrates from the fertile plain between the rivers. On the contrary, the poverty and hardships of nomadic life in the desert constantly tempted these Westerners to prefer the attractions of semi-nomadic or fully settled agriculture and to gravitate toward the urbanized plain. Hence the Euphrates became a defensive frontier (with varying success) against their incursion.

If the invention of writing marks the beginning of the historic period in Mesopotamia, and the introduction of bronze metallurgy ushers in the Bronze Age, then a third innovation, more or less contemporaneous with the first two, can be most truly said to signal the emergence of civilization, namely: the appearance of cities. Cities are distinguished from villages by two principal factors: they are surrounded by fortifications, and they include monumental buildings. At first the latter were generally temples; later, royal palaces were added. Now while there are isolated forerunners in other parts of the Near East to either fortifications (as at Jericho in Palestine) or monumental buildings (as at Çatal Höyük in Turkey), the combination seems to appear first in Southern Mesopotamia. Archaeological excavations and native literary traditions are in impressive agreement that the very first true city was Eridu, on the shore of the Bitter Lake which linked up with the Persian Gulf. Apparently, the Sumerians or their ancestors had entered Mesopotamia from the Gulf and built their first city where they first touched solid ground. But in short order urban settlement pushed upstream to fill all the lower half of the valley of the two rivers. Archaeological evidence to this effect, and to the spread and consolidation of many other aspects of civilization, comes from numerous sites about the turn of the 3rd millennium (ca. 3100-2900 B.C.). The literary tradition, ever disposed to prefer illustrative examples to exhaustive completeness, recalls just four cities succeeding Eridu in this first urban period, each ruled by one or two kings of legendary longevity. These are the antediluvians, or people before the Deluge (Flood), whose stories are closely parallelled in the Hebrew Bible (Genesis 4 and 5). They witnessed the invention of many other aspects of civilization: in the native traditions such characteristic Mesopotamian skills as divination (see below); in the Biblical version others such as music or the cultivation of the vine; according to archaeological evidence, fundamental socio-economic changes such as the accumulation of capital, specialization of crafts and trades, and the replacement of family and clan by new political systems.

The great flood, or deluge, that temporarily threatened all these new developments is a firm fixture both in the native and the Biblical traditions at this point. Again, legend has exaggerated and embellished what was, no doubt, a much more restricted event in historical terms—or simply a metaphor for ethnic migrations moving downstream along Tigris and Euphrates. If a major natural disaster did strike lower Mesopotamia about 2900 B.C., its consequences were very likely aggravated by (and metaphorically equated with) a simultaneous invasion of Westerners from the desert, sweeping down the still defenseless course of the Euphrates. These Westerners were of "Semitic" speech, related to Hebrew, Aramaic and Arabic, and very different from Sumerian. They settled upstream from the Sumerians, in a part of the Valley later known, after its principal city, as Akkad. But their first major city was called Kish, and it was here that, traditionally, kingship began (in the native conception "came down from heaven") after the Flood.

The first kings of Kish are as legendary as the antediluvians, as are the lengths of reign credited to them by the Sumerian King List. In fact, they (or the real figures who inspired these legends) probably reigned no more than some 200 years (ca. 2900-2700 B.C.). All we can say about them historically is that some of them bore Semitic (or "Akkadian") names and that they probably claimed undisputed rule over all of lower Mesopotamia (later known as "Sumer and Akkad") since there are no rival Sumerian claimants to kingship in their time. But some versions of the King List begin a second dynasty of Kish with a certain En-Mebaragesi and with him we leave the realm of legend and enter the realm of documented history, for this king has left us two inscriptions with his name including one with his title ("king of Kish") and henceforth the soil of Mesopotamia yields an uninterrupted stream of monuments to many of the kings that followed.

By this time, however, the Sumerian south had recovered sufficiently to contest Kish's sole claim to kingship. Two Sumerian cities in particular stand out both in the later literature about and in the excavations from this period (ca. 2700-2500 B.C.), Uruk and Ur. Uruk was sacred to the deified Heaven, An (called Anu in Akkadian), the chief god of all the Sumerians, and to the great goddess of love and fertility Inanna (equated with the warlike Ishtar in Akkadian). Her high priests assumed both religious and military leadership at Uruk, and their exploits are enshrined in a remarkable cycle of epics, originally composed in Sumerian, and later recast in Akkadian. The most enduring and best known is the Epic of Gilgamesh, which in its latest form told how this heroic leader built the walls of Uruk, struggled with demons and men, and set out in search of eternal life. Though the search was doomed to fail, it led him to Uta-napishtim, the Babylonian Noah, who told him the tale of the great Flood of which he was the lone survivor.

Ur too boasted an early line of rulers contemporaneous with En-Mebaragesi of Kish though they did not, like Gilgamesh, engage him (or his son) in battle. Some of them have left their names in the Sumerian King List, in inscriptions and in occasional literary allusions. Others have left a more startling—indeed frightening—memorial: the famous royal graves of Ur. Discovered by Sir Leonard Woolley in 1929, these graves revealed not only bodies of deceased kings and queens, but of whole retinues of servants, teams of oxen, and treasures of a royal household which apparently were destined to accompany the deceased rulers into the netherworld. Some of the finest examples of Sumerian jewelry, musical instruments, and golden vessels were painstakingly reconstructed from their crushed remains in these graves by Woolley. There is no evidence of struggle in the orderly disposition of the bodies, and since many of them were found with cups in or near their hands, it has been theorized that poison or sleeping potions may have been administered to the humans and animals before they walked to their involuntary interment. But this gruesome evidence of human sacrifice seems not to have recurred in Mesopotamia.

In the period that followed (ca. 2500-2300 B.C.) Uruk and Ur were ruled by a single dynasty, and in general the heroic pattern of rule by religious and charismatic leaders was succeeded by a more formal kingship in which royal families maintained themselves for many generations by alliance with a separate priesthood which conferred legitimacy upon them in return for lavish endowments to ever more elaborate temples. The resulting "dynastic age" can best be studied at Lagash, a city whose rulers regarded themselves as defenders of the faith and who forged a formidable fighting instrument out of a phalanx of armed foot-soldiers recruited from the free citizenry and led by a royalty and nobility in clumsy chariots drawn by onagers, an early forerunner of the domesticated horse.

The Lagash supremacy came to grief chiefly because of the resulting dislocations in the traditional socio-economic structure. Temples and nobility enriched themselves at the expense of the "little men"; when Urukagina (Urninimgina), the "first reformer in history," attempted to restore the old order, he was toppled from his throne by an invading army from the neighboring city of Umma.

But though Lagash fell, the dynastic principle survived, and it was soon to be wedded to another, the imperial. Centuries of internecine fighting had weakened the Sumerian city-states, and power shifted back to the north. At the court of Kish, a young retainer born, according to some of the later legends, of the illicit union of a priestess and a gardener, was destined to seize power under the name of Sargon, to found a new capital at nearby Akkad, and to erect history's first true empire. So extensive was this empire, and so impressive the achievements of Sargon and his descendants, that the entire ensuing period (ca. 2300-2100 B.C.) has become known as the Sargonic or Akkadian period. In native terms, however, it was the "Dynasty of Ishtar," for Sargon credited that goddess, whom he equated with the Sumerian Inanna, with all his conquests. In this he was ably aided by his gifted daughter Enheduanna, a princess who served also as priestess and prophetess, and who as poetess ranks as the first non-anonymous author in history. The poems directly attributed to her celebrate the exaltation of Inanna and the unification of Sumer and Akkad. Future princesses for another five hundred years emulated her priestly and poetic roles, though few approached her literary talents. Her life illustrates the high status to which women, at least at court, could aspire in Mesopotamia.

At various times certain professions were open to all women: as scribes, as priestesses, as ale-women. Their labor was valued not only in the home but in certain industries such as textiles. At the same time, their rations were typically only half those of men, and their legal status, though protected and defined by the laws (see below), was usually inferior to that of men.

At its height, the Sargonic empire embraced not only the lower half of the valley ("Sumer and Akkad") but its upper half as well, and its influence was felt far beyond the borders of the valley, from Anatolia (Turkey) in the northwest to the Persian Gulf in the southeast. Much of the enduring impact of Mesopotamian culture in the peripheral areas can be traced to this period, as cuneiform writing, the Akkadian language, and Sargonic styles in art all spread far and wide through the Asiatic Near East.

Successful campaigns reopened the trade-routes to the Iranian highlands in the east and as far as the Mediterranean in the west, and a flourishing economy at home supplied the internal markets.

Yet this first great empire was not destined to endure. Exposed on its long Tigris frontier to the assaults of rude and warlike mountain tribes, and ever open on the Euphrates frontier to new waves of Semitic-speaking nomads seeking settlement in the valley, the empire collapsed. The city of Akkad was destroyed so thoroughly that, alone among the great capitals of Mesopotamia, it has not been recovered by excavation; anarchy ensued as short-lived kings fought for the succession; and the old Sumerian city-states of the south reasserted their independence. Only a small rump state remained of the proud empire, with which the contrast was so impressive that later kings dated events of their own reigns as so many years "after the fall of Akkad," much as other cuneiform texts referred to "before the Flood" and "after the Flood" as an earlier fixed point. In modern terms, the collapse of Akkad may be correlated with the end of the Early Bronze Age, that first millennium during which civilization had spread its many innovations from Sumer through the Near East (3100-2100 B.C.).

The Middle Bronze Age

The restoration of the ancient independence of the Sumerian city-states of the south was to be short-lived, for the new imperial ideal was not forgotten in the collapse of the Sargonic empire. Briefly at Uruk and more lastingly at Ur, a new empire rose to take its place. The two cities were still linked dynastically: when Uruk assumed the mantle, its king appointed his son viceroy at Ur, and vice versa. Although not strong enough to recapture the lands beyond the rivers, they quickly turned all the city-states of the valley into provinces and ushered in a renaissance based on both Sumerian and Akkadian traditions. Each city administered its own province under a governor loyal to the king at Ur, worshipping its own deities in temples built by or on behalf of the king, and at the same time contributing to the upkeep of the great national shrines at the religious capital of Nippur, located midway between Sumer and Akkad, and to the maintenance of the royal court at Ur. The king's own attention was lavished in special measure on the great temples of Nippur and Ur, and monumental architecture, a hallmark of urban civilization, literally reached new heights. The great ziggurat, or stepped tower, built at Ur was emulated or imitated in many other cities of Babylonia and neighboring Elam (southwestern Iran), inspiring the Biblical tale of the Tower of Babel (Genesis 9).

Its first builder was the founder of the dynasty, Ur-Nammu, also generally held to be the promulgator of the first "code" of laws of the kind more familiar from Hammurapi (see below), and his four successors added to it and to the great sacred precinct surrounding it at Ur. They also built themselves a great new royal palace, constructed elaborate underground tombs for themselves, and figured as patrons of the arts, including learning, literature and music. It was in the schools endowed by them that the literary heritage of the Sumerians, hitherto perhaps largely transmitted orally, probably took its permanent written form.

This so-called Third Dynasty of Ur lasted for only a century (ca. 2100-2000 B.C.), but it has left an unequalled mass of economic and administrative texts in numerous great archives of clay tablets which attest to the smooth functioning of an active economy, largely state-administered by an impressive bureaucracy and the allied priesthood, though leaving room as well for a smaller private sector. When Ur fell to invading enemies from beyond the Valley, and the imperial mantle passed to the city of Isin, its kings ruled for another century as kings of Ur and respected and nourished the Sumerian traditions of their predecessors (ca. 2000-1900 B.C.). Even while allowing an ever greater penetration of the Valley by Amorite semi-nomads from the west, they encouraged the quick assimilation of the newcomers to the older patterns of the settled agricultural-urban society of the Valley. Trade and industry too continued to flourish.

There was, however, one inexorable natural development whose economic consequences could not be avoided: the increasing salinization of the land in the river valley required ever greater efforts at irrigation, and this in turn demanded a united effort. With Amorite chieftains establishing themselves in ever more of the old city-states, however, the desperately needed cooperation was often replaced by bickering and outright warfare over the diminishing fresh-water courses. For a century (ca. 1900-1800 B.C.), a dozen of the old Sumerian city-states under their new Amorite rulers contested with Isin and each other the rightful succession to Ur and access to fresh-water canals and sea-water ports, to the ultimate detriment of them all.

With the southern half of the Valley thus embroiled, the northern half enjoyed its first real chance to emerge from obscurity and play a significant role of its own. As we have already seen, Mesopotamian cultural influence had been carried upstream and beyond the rivers at least as early as the Sargonic period. Now the north was prepared to show that it too could combine Mesopotamian institutions with Amorite leadership into a potent force for advancing the frontiers of civilization. At Assur on the Middle Tigris an independent kingdom arose in the wake of the fall of Ur (ca. 2000 B.C.) prepared to take advantage of that city's strategic location at the convergence of the trade routes from Anatolia (Turkey) in the northwest and Northern Iran in the northeast. By ca. 1900 B.C., the city had become the focus of a lively trade between these two termini, importing tin (probably from Iran) to be shipped to Anatolia (specifically to that part known later as Cappadocia) where it was alloyed with native copper into bronze. In addition, Cappadocia was an eager market for bolts of cloth manufactured in Assur. On the return trip, the donkey caravans of the Assyrian traders were laden with finished bronze, and with silver and gold. Apart from sizeable tolls exacted by the native princes in Cappadocia and on the way back to Assur, the caravans confronted brigandage, price fluctuations, loss of credit, default by debtors, or cheating by partners. But along with the high risk went high profits (a 100 percent markup was standard), and the leading families of Assur enriched themselves throughout the century (1900-1800 B.C.), with the king himself eagerly involved as the biggest of the merchant-capitalists.

Meantime on the Middle Euphrates, an Amorite dynasty was establishing itself at Mari. This city, long an outpost of Mesopotamian culture strategically located to head off nomadic movements downstream toward the south, now developed into a massive citadel crowned by one of the greatest palaces ever excavated in Mesopotamia. Among its most startling features are wall paintings (otherwise rare in Mesopotamia) depicting the cult of the goddess Ishtar and the investiture of the king.

Mari was a true meeting place of "the desert and the sown," as revealed by tens of thousands of cuneiform tablets recovered from its archives. These indicate, for example, that the nomads and semi-nomads of the adjoining desert were still organized along tribal lines; that treaties were ratified by passing between the pieces of ceremonially slaughtered sacrificial animals; that genealogies were memorized, recited (and, sometimes, altered for political purposes) to a depth of many generations—and in many other respects parallel or supplement the memories of "patriarchal" times preserved in the Hebrew Bible (see below). One of the most striking illustrations of this is the use of prophecy and dream reports at Mari so different from the highly disciplined system of divination in use elsewhere in Mesopotamia.

It was left for yet another city in the north to unite both Mari and Assur into a great northern empire. Shubat-Enlil, a site on a tributary of the Habur River, itself a tributary of the Euphrates, became the seat of a great conqueror, Shamshi-Adad I (ca. 1813-1781 B.C.), who installed his two sons as viceroys at Mari and Ekallatum (near Assur) respectively and kept close watch over their stewardship, as a lively correspondence among all three reveals.

But by now Southern Mesopotamia had once more recovered its strength and, once reunited, found a worthy challenger to Shamshi-Adad. This was Hammurapi, Amorite king of Babylon, hitherto just one of the many competing city-states of the south. Hammurapi (ca. 1792-1750 B.C.) was destined to raise Babylon to preeminence in the south (which henceforth can accurately be named Babylonia) and, after Shamshi-Adad's death, to conquer all of the North as well. His empire thus ultimately—if only briefly—embraced the entire Valley of the two rivers. But his fame in later tradition, and to our own time, rests less on his military exploits than on his achievements in literature, administration, and above all in law. Under Hammurapi and his immediate successors, the scribal schools flourished as never before, preserving in numerous copies all the Sumerian literary and learned texts which had been composed since Ur III times. His administrative zeal is revealed by a far-flung correspondence with his lieutenants throughout the realm, over whom he exercised a tireless supervision extending to the smallest details of local affairs. Most significantly, Hammurapi collected the legal precedents dating back to Ur-Nammu of Ur (above) and arranged them into a corpus of laws which, though too selective to qualify as a true code, remains nonetheless the most systematic statement of civil and criminal law in the Ancient Near East outside the Bible, with which it shares many provisions both in general and in detail. The Laws, sandwiched between poetic prologue and epilogue, were incised in great steles set up in the marketplace of each city to be admired and read by or read to all (but increasing numbers were now literate). One of these has fortunately survived nearly intact, and its missing portions have been partly recovered from the many copies made ever after in the scribal schools.

Hammurapi's enduring fame among his later countrymen, like that of certain other great Mesopotamian rulers, may owe something to the stark contrast he provided to his relatively feeble successors. A mere decade after his death (ca. 1740 B.C.), rival dynasties had established themselves on all the borders of the empire, blocking its further expansion and ready to reduce its size at every opportunity. Three of them in particular helped seal the fate of the so-called "First Dynasty of Babylon" whose last five kings, though they succeeded each other in orderly fashion for another century and a half, ruled over a continually diminishing domain. These are the Hittites of Anatolia, the Sealand Dynasty in the extreme south, and the Kassites along the Middle Euphrates.

The Late Bronze Age

The fall of Babylon (ca. 1600 B.C.) was the result of an invasion from the far north—specifically Anatolia (central Turkey) where, not long after the period of the Assyrian traders (above), a new ethnic group had superseded the native princes and established a formidable empire in the mountain strongholds of the central plateau. Conventionally referred to today by the Biblical term of Hittites, this group spoke a language related to Greek, Latin and, ultimately, our own; indeed, having adopted the cuneiform script of Mesopotamia (perhaps via Mari), it has left the oldest documents of any "Indo-European" language, together with others in Sumerian, Akkadian and various Anatolian languages and dialects. From their capital at Hattusha (not far from the modern Turkish capital at Ankara), these Hittites were destined to play an important role in Near Eastern warfare and diplomacy for the next four centuries. On the whole, these centuries were characterized by the widening orbit of countries which, while indebted to Babylonia for many of their cultural advances, at the same time moved into a position to challenge its political preeminence in the Asiatic Near East.

The Hittites' ability to strike so far from their home was probably largely due to the horse-drawn chariot which they helped introduce to the Near East. But they themselves did not hold Babylon. Rather, that city was seized first by the Sealand and then by the Kassites, another people who had entered the Valley a century and a half earlier, and who presently established their rule over all of Babylonia and maintained themselves longer than any other Mesopotamian dynasty (ca. 1740-1160 B.C.; since ca. 1590 at Babylon; since 1415 throughout Babylonia). The new rulers soon adopted the cultural traditions—including languages, script, and literature—of the ancient civilization they had conquered, but they introduced a new socio-economic pattern which has certain analogies to the feudal system of medieval Europe. In order to maintain the chariotry that the new age demanded, the Kassite kings tended to endow loyal cavalry officers with ever more royal land or, what amounted to the same thing, to exempt them from taxation in return for past or future military help, including the maintenance of horses, chariots and auxiliary infantry at their own expense. Deeds to this effect were inscribed on large "boundary-stones" deposited in the temples and on the properties involved and serve as graphic symbols of the inevitable decline in the power and wealth of a central monarchy, and consequently of its influence in the international arena. Compared to the glorious age of Hammurapi that lay behind them, and the imperialist grandeur of neo-Assyrian and neo-Babylonian times to come, the Kassite era indeed represents a kind of Babylonian Middle Age.

At the same time, the Kassites provided a long period of relative peace and stability at home when Babylonian culture enjoyed prestige and expansion to ever new parts of the Near East. The characteristic elements of Babylonian culture were now exported and imitated abroad: in architecture, the stepped tower or ziggurat; in minor arts, the cylinder seal, carved (in reverse, so that when rolled in clay its impression was "printed" on a tablet or jar) with elaborate designs often inspired by the mythology and with inscriptions identifying the seal owner and sometimes including a prayer for his well-being; in writing, the cuneiform script; in literature, the millennial traditions of Sumerian myths and epics, hymns and prayers, proverbs and other "wisdom" compositions; in law, the precedents codified by Hammurapi; in technology, the manufacture of bronze, textiles, leather and other goods; in trade, the sophisticated management of long-distance mercantile ventures over land or sea, financed by great capitalist combines at home; in statecraft the elaboration of a royal bureaucracy at home and the cultivation of an enlightened and essentially pacific diplomacy abroad; in education, the evolution of a traditional pattern of scribal schools, adhering to a fixed curriculum and now organized along guild or ostensibly family lines.

All the lands on the periphery of Babylonia now began to imitate one or more of these elements of its culture. Elam in southwestern Iran boasts the best preserved ziggurat; the Hittites and (a little later) the Assyrians wrote their own law codes in the traditional "precedent" form; cylinder seals in the Kassite style have been found as far away as Thebes in Greece; a fragment of the Gilgamesh epic has turned up at Megiddo in Israel and dates to this period; and that this is no isolated coincidence is proved by the discovery of well-stocked libraries of cuneiform literature and flourishing schools for the study of Sumerian and Akkadian at the Hittite capital of Hattusha and the Egyptian capital at Amarna respectively, during the Late Bronze Age. A particularly dramatic illustration of all this is provided by the city-state of Ugarit on the Mediterranean coast in North Syria, traditionally a meeting-place of many cultures. Here a trading center of mixed population speaking a northwest Semitic dialect closely related to later Biblical Hebrew, but at pains to assimilate the ancient wisdom of Babylonia, studied traditional cuneiform script while developing a new and simpler one which provides the oldest evidence for the order of letters in our own alphabet.

But for all its cosmopolitanism, the Bronze Age was drawing to an end, an end precipitated by new technologies and new peoples. Iron was discovered to be a far superior medium for tools and weapons, and the fate of the old empires was sealed when the new discovery fell into the hands of new peoples, notably various seafaring peoples originating from the Aegean and beyond who invaded the Near East in the 13th century and are collectively known as Sea Peoples. The fall of Troy (ca. 1250 B.C.) may be said to have ushered in a whole succession of population shifts which sent these peoples on expeditions against all the coasts of the Mediterranean. Wherever they gained a foothold, they displaced the settled populations. At the same time, Aramaean tribes from the desert were pushing successfully against the interior land frontiers, so that by about 1200 B.C. the whole map of the Near East had altered dramatically.

The Iron Age

In Mesopotamia itself, one city-state managed to survive the catastrophes of the outgoing Bronze Age: Assur. It had already been an outpost of the Sargonic and neo-Sumerian empires at the end of the third millennium, and we met it as the base of independent and enterprising merchant-princes at the beginning of the second. Then followed five obscure centuries (ca. 1850-1350 B.C.) when the city was simply an appendage of greater neighbors who ruled upper Mesopotamia; but during all this time its population maintained a firm belief in its own identity and destiny. This belief was centered in the worship of the god Assur, for whom the city was named, and was cemented in the struggle, not only against rulers from the superior powers to west and south, but also against the warlike mountaineers who ever threatened to overwhelm the city from north and east. It required only the talents of an able leader to combine the Assyrians' determined sense of history with their fierce fighting abilities in order to propel them onto the world stage as a political power in their own right. This happened first under Assur-uballit I (ca. 1362-1327 B.C.) and continued under a succession of strong military figures who for the first time created a true kingdom of Assyria. By 1200 B.C., they had extended the boundaries of the new kingdom to embrace much of the Middle Tigris region and even, once more, to sack Babylon, one of whose last Kassite kings they carried into captivity.

Thus Assyria was prepared to face the dangers of the new Iron Age and, though it too suffered reverses, to emerge gradually as the foremost military machine the Near East had yet seen. The resonant names repeatedly assumed by its great conqueror-kings are often familiar from the Bible, for Israel was a frequent target of their ambitions, and conversely some of the first documented allusions to Biblical kings are found in the detailed historical records which the Assyrian monarchs commissioned in praise and memory of their triumphs.

For almost three centuries, Assyria dominated the Near East (ca. 890-610 B.C.), its long sway on the pinnacle of power based not only on its superb army but also on new departures in statecraft, diplomacy and economics. Each of these facets deserves to be illustrated by some examples.

The path from pure militarism to imperialism was a gradual one. During the outgoing Bronze Age the Assyrian army had originally achieved its vaunted proficiency in essentially defensive actions, designed to maintain the integrity and independence of the city of Assur and its immediate environs—that is, as much of the surrounding cultivated terrain as was, on the one hand, necessary to feed its urban population of absentee landlords, traders and warriors and, on the other hand, close enough to the city to send its population behind its fortifications for shelter in the event of outside attack. Even during the early Iron Age, as the needs and appetites of the urban population grew in tandem, and the military leadership adopted a more aggressive strategy, the favorite solution was basically an annual plundering expedition only thinly disguised in the royal annals as a military campaign. The various cities, chiefly to the west of Assur and by now frequently under the rule of independent Aramaic chieftains, were given the choice of submission or siege; if they chose the former, they were forced to pay a pre-determined tribute, if the latter, they were (except in the rare case of an Assyrian defeat) plundered without restraint. In either event, Assur was enriched as a result. But gradually the greater utility of annexation was recognized, and by the time of Salmaneser III (858-824 B.C.) the Assyrians had evolved a highly efficient system of provincial administration. Each new conquest was now entrusted to an Assyrian governor, appointed by the king, together with a large administrative and military staff. Under weak kings, such governors might prove rebellious, but their loyalty was usually insured by roving royal commissars directly responsible to the court at Assur or one of the other royal residences. There a massive central bureaucracy supervised the affairs of the imperial army and treasury while keeping an ever watchful eye on the provinces. Archives recovered from the various capitals as well as from some of the provincial centers attest to the effectiveness of a system which thus neatly balanced local and national interests.

A growing empire required, among other things, a uniform calendar, and the Assyrian administrative genius is nowhere better illustrated than in this regard. The traditional Babylonian system had allowed each independent city-state to name its years after an outstanding event of the previous year in its own realm or from its own point of view, and the Kassites had replaced this with a regnal year system. But the Assyrians reverted to an older one of their own, naming each year after a high official, or eponym, and now spliced this system with the new order by choosing the eponyms from the highest ministers and governors of the empire. At first the order of eponyms was determined by lot but presently it was found more convenient to have a predetermined order, usually headed by the king, then followed by the five or six highest imperial officers, and then by the governors of the provinces in set sequence. Long lists were then drawn up as aids to learning the sequence of years and some of these so-called eponym canons added for each year its outstanding political, military or natural event. The fortunate mention of a solar eclipse, dated by modern astronomical calculation precisely to 763 B.C., provides a fixed point for all Assyrian chronology (and thereby for all Near Eastern chronology) back to the beginning of the canon (911 B.C.) and thus obviates the necessity of adding "ca." (approximately) to our first millennium dates. Month names, too, were standardized, though this was done on the Babylonian model, i.e., on the luni-solar basis. In this calendar, the new month was based on actual observation of the moon, and the year consisted of twelve lunar months of twenty-nine or thirty days each. The calendar was brought back in line with the solar year, and hence with the seasons, by intercalating a thirteenth month seven times in nineteen years.

Assyrian arms were, moreover, not all-powerful. Though rarely defeated, they had to be content with something less than annexation when an enemy proved, for a time, too distant (particularly in the west) or too formidable (particularly in the difficult mountain terrain to the east). In such cases, diplomacy was invoked to impose a treaty on an as yet independent opponent. Parity-treaties, or treaties between equals, had been concluded in the Late Bronze Age, notably between the Hittites and Egyptians, but the Assyrians preferred vassal-treaties, in which they imposed a client-relationship, with explicit and dire penalties for infractions, on subject kingdoms as the price of their continued if somewhat nominal independence.

Court scribes and court artists celebrated the imperial monarchy that evolved under this system, and tended to give it a rather uniform cast over the centuries. But the kings around whom it was built were individuals, and they stamped each reign with their own character. This is dramatically illustrated by those who moved the capital city from Assur, either adding lavishly to an older city for this purpose or building a whole new one and naming it after themselves. In this way Nineveh, Kalah (Nimrud), and Dur-Sharrukin ("Sargonsburg") each served at times as the royal residence. Forced deportation of captive populations helped to swell the numbers of their residents beyond anything the surrounding countryside could maintain, and the twin needs of food and water for the new urban concentrations became a prime concern of royal policy. Taxation of the provinces and tribute from vassal-states furnished the former, while a veritable revolution in hydraulic technology supplied the latter. But it was a fragile base on which to found the economy, as events were to show.

The Assyrian Empire had successfully defended and extended its borders against the perennial pressures of newcomers from the deserts which faced it across the Euphrates and those from the mountains which loomed beyond the Tigris. But it could not seal these borders against an equally relentless but subtler process of infiltration which characterized the whole history of the Valley. Drawn as if by a magnet to the superior attractions of its urban-agricultural civilization, the Aramaeans in particular began to assume an increasing importance in the population. Armed with an active and widespread net of commercial relations and blessed with a vastly simpler script than the cumbersome cuneiform, they were soon making themselves an indispensable adjunct in Assyrian administration.

In Babylonia, the Aramaean role was even more pervasive. Here they and the kindred Chaldeans began to establish themselves as rulers early in the Iron Age, and when the Assyrian empire grew to include Babylonia, they served as natural rallying-points for resistance to Assyrian domination. They adopted the same traditional elements of Babylonian culture as the Assyrians themselves, and contributed a special emphasis on mathematics and astronomy. Some of the latter was in the interests of astrology, and the very word Chaldean became synonymous with astrologer or diviner, but much of it was objective and directed toward ends that, to us at least, seem more practical, such as the calendar. It was probably as early as the accession of Nabonassar in 747 B.C. that they perfected a system for calculating the 19-year intercalary cycle (see above) which freed the calendar from the necessity of actual observation of the moon. They also showed a lively and objective interest in history and, at this same time, the learned Babylonian priests inaugurated an annual recording of key events in political and military affairs, the so-called Babylonian Chronicle, a dispassionate record which serves as a welcome corrective to the self-serving and bombastic annals of the Assyrian kings.

By 626 B.C., with the Assyrian Empire in decline, the Chaldeans were ready to proclaim the tenth (and last) native Dynasty of Babylon. This neo-Babylonian, or Chaldean, Dynasty, contributed to the final demise of the Assyrians, though that was primarily the work of the Medes (see below). The final fall of Assyria (615-612 B.C.) was a precipitate one. Without the tribute of provinces and vassals to fill their coffers or the captive labor of deported subject populations to man their massive waterworks, the great Assyrian cities were deprived of their means of subsistence almost at a single blow, and most of them disappeared so totally that only the spade of the excavators was able even to locate them again. The greatest neo-Babylonian king, Nebukadnezar II (604-562 B.C.), inherited much of the Assyrian empire and briefly united the Asiatic Near East when he captured Jerusalem and added Judah to his conquests (586 B.C.). But the turmoil of the sixth century (see below) proved too much for the neo-Babylonian empire in its turn, and by 539 B.C. the capital itself welcomed a new conqueror as Cyrus the Mede entered Babylon to usher in the Achaemenid Empire. Not till Abbasid times (A.D. 750) was the Valley of the Two Rivers again to rule the world.

2. The Gift of the Nile

The Early Bronze Age

Like western Asia, Egypt in the outgoing Stone Age had a substrate population which already boasted a flourishing culture ready to make the transition to civilization. In Egypt's case, both physical and cultural links point to African connections for this substrate population. The general progress of culture seems to have been downstream along the Nile, from south to north; in some cases it may have been from west to east along the coastal trade routes or across the desert. The earliest pottery cultures of neolithic Egypt have been identified in the south of the country, and by the end of the Stone Age the use of pottery is attested in central Egypt. But northern or Lower Egypt is devoid of any clear evidence of prehistoric settlement.

As in Mesopotamia, so in Egypt an immigrant element seems to have acted upon the substrate population and interacted with it to stimulate the transition to civilization. Indeed, the same immigrant element may have been involved. For there are many striking similarities between the specific products of the emerging Bronze Age in Egypt and Sumer. They include the invention of writing; the evolution of the cylinder seal; the recessed niche pattern in monumental architecture; the symmetrical disposition of paired figurines around a central axis and other artistic motifs. Possibly, then, the Sumerians (or their ancestors) reached Egypt (as they had Mesopotamia) by sea (specifically via the Red Sea), and may have had some direct influence on the first Egyptian civilization.

But this foreign stimulus, even if conceded, was no more than a catalyst. Almost immediately, the innovations mentioned, and many others, were radically transformed and developed along lines that clearly and permanently distinguished Egyptian civilization from Mesopotamian. Egyptian history can be said to begin as early as Sumerian, i.e., about 3100 B.C., with a First Dynasty of eight kings which, like the antediluvians of the Mesopotamian (and Biblical) traditions, must have spanned a period of some two centuries (ca. 3100-2900 B.C.). The greatest achievement of this First Dynasty was the unification of the two great halves into which Egypt has always been divided by geography: Upper (or southern) and Lower (or northern) Egypt. Upper Egypt is the long, narrow (at times extremely narrow) strip of cultivatable lowland which the Nile River has carved out over the millennia between the mountains and deserts lying to either side. It reaches from the Nubian border at the First Cataract near Aswan in the south to what is now Cairo in the north. Lower Egypt is essentially the region of the Delta. All the evidence suggests that Upper Egypt was already ruled by kings of some stature in pre-dynastic times, and that unification involved their conquest of Lower Egypt and their consequent assumption of the double crown of Upper and Lower Egypt. The Egyptians continued to call their country "The Two Lands" in conscious recognition of the many disparities between its two parts, and this is also the etymology of the standard Biblical name for Egypt, Miṣrayim.

Like the contemporary "antediluvian" period in Mesopotamia, the time of the First Dynasty in Egypt was one of astonishing creativity. The most impressive monuments of the dynasty are the tombs of the kings and their favored retainers, especially at Abydos in the south and Sakkara in the north. They introduce us to an abiding characteristic of ancient Egyptian civilization: its real or apparent emphasis on burial and proper provision for the afterlife. The emphasis is real enough in absolute terms, as attested by an undeniably vast investment of art, architecture, and literature devoted to the dead. It is more apparent than real in relative terms, for while the barren rocks on the western side of the Nile Valley which served for burials have preserved a disproportionate share of evidence from the realm of the dead, the valley itself has been continually occupied, and most traces of the life of the living Egyptians has vanished in the wake of the uninterrupted occupation and cultivation there. A similar disproportion applies to the evidence from Lower Egypt, for the moist conditions in the Delta are far more destructive of organic antiquities, notably including papyrus texts, than the dry soil of Upper Egypt. These limitations need to be remembered when evaluating the surviving testimony for the reconstruction of Ancient Egyptian history. Thus while it is highly likely that an urban revolution took place in Egypt too at this time, the archaeological evidence for it is less conclusive than in Mesopotamia. One of the oldest well-preserved Egyptian myths tells of a sinful mankind and its deliverance from destruction. But no event of the magnitude of the Babylonian flood separated the first two Egyptian dynasties. Both ruled, or at least derived, from the southern city of This. They are thus jointly referred to as the Thinite dynasties and their four centuries of rule as the Protodynastic Period. They have left a number of contemporaneous inscriptions though not enough to permit a connected history of the period.

For the Second Dynasty (ca. 2900-2700 B.C.), the single most important event that can be reconstructed from later evidence is the introduction of the calendar. The regular recurrence of the seasons has, of course, led to an approximation of the solar year among many peoples, but in Egypt such approximations were very early refined by the observation of the annual rise of the Nile. The Nile, swollen by the melting snows of the equatorial mountains of East Africa, each year flooded its banks, depositing a rich topsoil on which Egyptian agriculture subsisted for the ensuing year. It was further observed that this event regularly coincided with the "heliacal" rising of the Dog Star (Sirius, in Egyptian: Sothis), i.e., with the day when this star, the brightest in the Egyptian sky, first emerges from the sun's rays and becomes visible before sunrise. The interval between these occurrences was established as 365 days, and gave rise to a calendar year just short of the true solar year. It takes 1460 solar years to restore the resulting discrepancy, and since such convergences of the Egyptian year and the solar year were recorded for A.D. 140 and 1320 B.C., it is assumed that the calendar originated at a previous convergence. By this calculation, the year 4241 B.C. was once regarded as "the earliest date in human history" (Breasted), but this date has since had to be lowered by one Sothic cycle to about 2776 B.C. The introduction of the Egyptian calendar, ancestral to the Julian calendar and thus ultimately to our own, may then be dated hypothetically to the time of the Second Dynasty.

The successful unification of Egypt under the Thinite dynasties elevated the position of the king above any of the individual cities and their rulers. The royal figure served as the warrant for maintaining the newly achieved unity. Soon the king came to be regarded and worshipped as a god. This peculiarly Egyptian conception of kingship reached its fullest expression under the Old Kingdom, which began with the Third Dynasty (ca. 2700-2600 B.C.). The Old Kingdom introduced a host of major cultural and political innovations destined to mark out Egypt's course for the subsequent millennia. The many and diverse achievements of the period include sculpture, painting and the beginning of literature. But the one that ever since has aroused the greatest admiration is the pyramids.

In the Thinite period, the kings had been buried in modest graves surmounted by squat piles of brickwork in the form of trapezoidal solids (so-called mastaba's). But the Third Dynasty kings enlarged the base of these tombs and piled successively smaller replicas of the same shape on top of it. They thus expressed their superiority—even in death—over their favored courtiers, who were allowed to build their own tombs in mastaba-style surrounding that of the king. The result was at first a simple "step-pyramid" such as those of King Djoser at Sakkara. But the aggrandizement of political and economic power by the king combined with the genius of semi-legendary architects such as Im-hotep soon led to the construction of the true pyramid, a massive structure designed to support (like the more modest tombs and obelisks) a small pyramidion or apex at the very top, while guarding the royal burial chamber in its innermost recesses. By the Fourth Dynasty (ca. 2600-2500 B.C.), each king provided for an entire pyramid complex for himself, his queen and his court, and some like Snefru even built more than one, perhaps to foil would-be despoilers. To the later Greeks, the great pyramids thus erected at Gizeh, and the famous Sphinx which was built together with Chephren's pyramid, constituted one of the seven wonders of the world, and to this day they symbolize the might of the Old Kingdom and the total deification of its monarchs. The pyramids were all located west of the Nile, to which they were connected by a long ramp, each end of which had its own chapel. An elaborate cult not only marked the entombment of the pharaoh, but also secured his continuing beneficence toward Egypt thereafter.

But the pyramids of the Old Kingdom were only the most visible outward symptom of Egypt's break with the cultural stimuli that it owed to or shared with the earliest Mesopotamian civilization (above). A more fundamental distinction was the consolidation of the provincial structure in the form of the traditional " nomes" in Egypt. The " nomes," originally clans united by ties of kinship, shared a common totem and divided the productive agricultural land of Upper and Lower Egypt among them; but they did so without the kind of urbanization that resulted in the emergence of the city-state distinctive for Mesopotamian political structure. Thus, they readily formed the basic units of a monarchic structure, constituting provinces under strong kings and only asserting their independence under weak central administrations. At the same time, urbanization took a different form in Egypt. Although new towns were founded with as many as 10,000 inhabitants, they lacked the fortifications and monumental architecture necessary for independence. These features instead were concentrated in a few capital cities or even a single one in any given period. For the Old Kingdom, Memphis emerged in this role; located at the border of Upper and Lower Egypt, its cultic function paralleled in some measure that of Nippur, at the border of Sumer and Akkad. But in the absence of rival centers, its emergence did not immediately involve the displacement of an earlier theology, as in Sumer. Instead, the chief deity of Memphis, Ptah (in cosmic terms the god of the earth, like the Sumerian Enki), figured as the universal creator and protagonist of the "Theology of Memphis," and this in turn as the theoretical justification for the new political reality. Though attested only in much later copies, this text probably originated at this time, which marks the beginning of Egyptian literature generally. Other arts too began to flourish under royal patronage, notably sculpture. Some of the finest portraiture dates from this period, as for example the bust of Ankhaef, architect of the pyramid of Chephren at Gizeh. In the economic realm, too, the new state proved its initiative: it is probable that the mines of Sinai were exploited for turquoise and metals as early as the Third Dynasty.

During most of the succeeding two centuries (ca. 2500-2300 B.C.), while Mesopotamia was consolidating its city-state pattern during its "dynastic age," Egypt was ruled by the Fifth Dynasty. The pyramids of this dynasty were less imposing than those of its immediate predecessor whose heroic standards were compromised, like those of their Sumerian contemporaries, in a close alliance with the priesthood. But where the Sumerians venerated different gods in each of their many city-states, the political centralization of the Old Kingdom was reflected in the corresponding supremacy of a single god. Specifically it was Re, the sun-god, who was the major object of worship at this time. Great temple complexes were dedicated to Re by the first six of the nine kings of the Fifth Dynasty on the testimony of the inscriptions, and two of them have been identified and excavated. And whereas in Sumer, the temple complex occupied the most prominent place within each city, in Egypt, where there were no comparable cities, these sun-temples were built in the necropoles ("cities of the dead") in the western desert. They seem in fact to have played a part in the cult of the deceased king, and thus to have helped to compensate for the more modest size of the Fifth Dynasty pyramids.

Apart from Re, another deity prominently worshipped at this time was Hat-hor, the "Mistress of Dendera." Dendera was one of the more strategically located nomes (provinces) of Upper Egypt during the Old Kingdom, and the worship of its principal goddess spread to the court at Memphis and to a number of other nomes. At the Fifth Dynasty sun-temples, a number of priests served both Re and Hat-hor. Like many lesser deities, Hat-hor was conceived of in animal form, in her case in the form of a cow. This conceptualization took a number of forms, not all consistent with each other from a modern, rational point of view: from a merely metaphoric attribution of certain bovine characteristics to the goddess, via a hybrid representation with selected bodily features grafted onto a human torso (either in the art or in the orthography), to an outright identification of goddess and animal. In the last case, the result was frequently the actual worship of living animals as manifestations of the deity. Such animal worship, which may have had its roots in Africa, represented a striking contrast to the worship of Re and other hypostases of cosmic and natural forces such as are familiar from Mesopotamian polytheism. But it is of a piece with the Egyptian's characteristic respect and reverence for the stable and predictable in a world of erratic turmoil and human caprice. The great gods of the Mesopotamian pantheon were most often conceived and represented in human guise; hence much of the cult was calculated to "appease" them, to wean them from their anthropomorphic caprice back to their divine immutability. But the Egyptian gods emulated animals, not men, and men on the contrary strove to emulate them. (Yet another pattern is true of Biblical theology, where man was conceived as created in the image of God.)

In the particular case of Hat-hor, one of the immutable characteristics was that of exemplifying the progenitress, the maternal principle par excellence. As the cow is destined for patient breeding and suckling (and little else) throughout her placid life, so Hat-hor evolved in the emerging ideology as a mother-goddess, first in general, then more particularly of the sun-god and his earthly manifestation, the king. In this development, we may see a significant parallel with contemporary Sumer, where the divine progeniture of kingship emerged at this time as a concomitant of the dynastic principle.

One further parallel may be noted, for in Egypt too, the second half of the third millennium marked the first significant archives of economic texts. Though written on papyrus and thus less durable than cuneiform records on clay, they survive in sufficient numbers—either in the safety of tombs high above the annual inundation, or in copies on stelas—to illuminate the many facets of an expanding economy. Together with the rich representational art, notably in the

wall-paintings and wooden carvings which decorated graves, they
provide priceless insights into daily life of both nobleman and commoner.

The Sixth Dynasty of Egypt (ca. 2350-2200 B.C.) marked far less
of a break with its predecessor than the approximately contemporaneous Sargonic Dynasty in Mesopotamia, nor were its achievements
nearly so memorable. Rather, it meant the continuation and conclusion of the Old Kingdom, whose principal innovations were perpetu-
ated and institutionalized. The outstanding rulers of the dynasty, if
only by sheer length of reign, were Pepi I (40 or 49 years) and his son
Pepi II (94 years), but they were not otherwise the equals of Sargon
and Naram-Sin. Pepi II, having ascended the throne at the age of
six, died in his one hundredth year. His was thus the longest reign in
the history of Egypt, and perhaps of Near Eastern history generally.
(The neo-Babylonian queen-mother Adad-guppi boasted an even
longer biography when she died at 104.) During Pepi II's minority
and again in his old age, co-regencies were instituted to help assure
the succession, and effective power was in the hands of the vizier, and
throughout the Sixth Dynasty the vizierate grew in importance.
Other royal prerogatives were dissipated in the direction of the provincial nomarchs (rulers of nomes) and temples, thus further under-
mining the powers of the central government and setting the stage for
the disintegration that ensued. Characteristically, the nomarchs began to carve their tombs out of the cliffs overlooking their respective
provinces from the Western Desert, in preference to being buried in
the mastaba's that surrounded the earlier Old Kingdom pyramids.

The practice of building pyramids continued at this time; indeed,
each of the Sixth Dynasty kings contrived to have an entire pyramid
complex built in his honor, with the smaller ones intended for the
several queens and other members of the court. But whereas the
earlier Old Kingdom pyramids were scattered along the Western Desert some distance from Memphis, the Sixth Dynasty pyramids were
all concentrated at Sakkara in the immediate vicinity of the capital;
indeed, the name of the city (Mempi in Akkadian, Moph or Noph in
Hebrew) is thought to derive from Men-nefer, the name given to the
pyramid of Pepi I. Other funerary practices also thrived, with mummification, first attested in the Second Dynasty, becoming a fine art.
Funerary inscriptions assumed a canonical form, and the great collection known as the Pyramid Texts date from this period, though the
first known example goes back to the last king of the Fifth Dynasty.

These texts were essentially collections of spells designed to assure the deceased king of safe passage, nourishment and other necessities of the after-life, but they also incorporated and preserved many of the mythological and theological conceptions of earlier periods. They were inscribed on the walls of the funerary chamber and adjoining portions of the pyramid, and were subsequently copied for the benefit of lesser mortals as well.

The long reign of Pepi II came to an end about 2180 B.C., i.e., in one estimate, about the same time as that of Naram-Sin of Akkad. The great empires that they ruled survived the two kings by only a few years. By about 2150 B.C., a collapse ensued in both areas that was as dramatic as it remains enigmatic. The last, obscure members of the Sixth Dynasty (including the Queen Nit-oqrety or Nitocris) were contemporary with the numerous ephemeral pretenders of the Seventh and Eighth Dynasties. There were at least eighteen of these in thirty years or, if Manetho is to be believed, seventy in as many days for the Seventh Dynasty alone. A novel hypothesis would account for these traditions by positing the institution of the murder or suicide of the king for his failure to harness the natural cosmic order for the benefit of his people. Extreme conditions of famine over an extended period of time could indeed have shaken the Egyptians' traditional faith in the powers of their king, whom they worshipped precisely as the embodiment of the annual Inundation by the Nile which, within proper limits, was the prerequisite of a successful agricultural year in Egypt. The Sed-festival, whose origins go back to proto-dynastic times at least, was intended to insure the king's continuing powers for fertility; it was celebrated as a kind of jubilee in the thirtieth year of long-lived rulers, and at two or three year intervals thereafter, and must have become a commonplace in the long reign of Pepi II. That his successors were unable to stem the economic and agricultural disaster that overtook Egypt is graphically depicted in "The Admonitions of Ipuwer," an Egyptian sage whose eyewitness accounts almost certainly reflect conditions of the First Intermediate Period. As he describes it, law and order broke down, the peasant abandoned his plot in despair, the birth rate declined and the death rate increased, corpses were abandoned to the Nile yet its waters, thus polluted, were drunk for want of better; the sand dunes advanced over the arable land; foreign commerce came to a halt; royal tombs were plundered; the Delta and all Egypt were laid open to invasion; even cannibalism was not unheard of. In these circumstances, the position of the king became indeed untenable. People could at best look to local governors who, with greater foresight or luck than their fellow nomarchs, had prepared for the worst in better years. Such individuals have left telling memorials to their role in their tomb inscriptions, and it is from them that the reconstruction of Egyptian society and monarchy was to ensue.

The Middle Bronze Age

The half millennium from 2100 to 1600 B.C. is generally regarded by archaeologists as the Middle Bronze Age of Palestine, Syria and Anatolia, and the term can usefully be extended to cover most of the civilized world of the time, for it marked a definable mid-point—indeed a high point—of Bronze Age civilization. Mesopotamia entered its classical phase during the neo-Sumerian and Old Babylonian periods, and Egypt rose to new heights under the Middle Kingdom. In the Aegean world, the age is roughly coterminous with the Middle Minoan of Crete, the Middle Cycladic of the lesser islands, and the Middle Helladic of the mainland, as these areas began to reflect the stimulus of contacts with the older centers of culture. Throughout the Near East, there was a perceptible regeneration of urban life as the high civilizations recouped from the disasters that marked the end of the Early Bronze Age.

The reunification of Egypt, and its emergence from the chaos of the First Intermediate Period, lagged by a few decades behind that of Mesopotamia. Its impetus came from the south, specifically from the fifth nome of Upper Egypt, whose nomarchs began to distinguish themselves even before the end of the Tenth Dynasty. They founded a new dynasty at Thebes about 2130 B.C. and raised that city to a commanding position which it was to retain through most of the second millennium. Three pharaohs of the Eleventh Dynasty (ca. 2100-2000 B.C.) bore the dynastic (or personal) name In-yotef and three or four that of Montu-hotpe. Of these, it was Montu-hotep II (ca. 2060-2010 B.C.) who most deserves attention. A worthy counterpart and near contemporary of Shulgi, he succeeded in asserting himself over his fellow nomarchs. Although these retained a greater measure of autonomy than was true in contemporary Sumer, they did not dispute Montu-hotpe's assumption of the double crown of Upper and Lower Egypt about 2050 or 2040 B.C. In later tradition, he was regarded as the equal of Menes and Ahmose, the founders of the Old

Kingdom and New Kingdom respectively. In short, he may be credited with establishing the Middle Kingdom.

The new king's building program was worthy of these pretensions. Though concentrating on mortuary architecture, he broke entirely with the specific forms this had taken in the pyramid age. The single small pyramid that he erected contained no burial chamber, and the royal tomb instead formed part of an elaborate complex of buildings overlooking Thebes from the Western Bank of the Nile at Deir-el-Bahri. Only slightly less monumental structures provided for his deceased queens and the officials and ladies of his court. A colonnaded mortuary temple dominated the whole complex which is therefore sometimes known in its entirety by the king's throne name as the Temple of Neb-hepet-Re. It attests the continuing vitality of the Egyptian concept of divine kingship; even though the ravages of the First Intermediate Period had shaken the faith in the absolute and automatic divinity of the pharaoh, it was still possible for outstanding kings (and even for lesser mortals) to command divine honors during and sometimes long after their lifetime in proportion to the measure of greatness that they had evinced on earth and to their effectiveness particularly with respect to the orderly maintenance of fertility and the other bases of a stable society.

That the Egyptian economy enjoyed good health in the later Eleventh Dynasty is shown by a small group of letters and accounts from Thebes dating ca. 2000 B.C. They belong to a typical farmer-priest of moderate means who amassed a modest fortune in rentals of land and commodities without, however, appearing interested in expanding his land holdings as such. Perhaps he was saving his money and other liquid assets toward a decent burial, for the funerary practices of private persons in the Middle Kingdom were proportionately as costly as those of the wealthier nobility. In any case, these examples of economic texts from the outgoing third millennium, rare as they are by comparison to the overflowing archives of contemporary Sumer, suggest that agricultural wealth had filtered downward in the Eleventh Dynasty, a process that probably originated in the First Intermediate Period as a concomitant to the political decentralization of the same time.

In tracing the history of the Near East thus far we have used noncommittal geographical terms to describe the inhabitants of Mesopotamia, Egypt, and the intervening areas, and avoided virtually all racial or ethnic labels. Our reticence on this point, though not shared by all historians, is imposed by the third millennium sources, whose evidence is too slight or too ambiguous for drawing firm inferences. As far as physical differences go, these were subject to progressive erosion as the isolation of human groups gave way to increasing movement and intermingling even before the beginning of the Bronze Age. Ethnic distinctions, for their part, are acquired rather than inherited, and therefore difficult to associate conclusively with any given demographic component over any length of time. This applies in the first instance to cultural traits such as kinship patterns and social organization, or industrial techniques and artistic styles. It applies less stringently to the other principal ethnic trait that the individual shares with his group, namely language. As textual data increase, the linguistic criterion therefore becomes a more reliable clue to ethnic affiliations and movements and, in judicious combination with other cultural indicators, may be employed to elucidate some major historical trends.

It is within these limits that we can characterize the beginning of the second millennium as the era of the Amorites. Amurru (or Amaru) was, in its earliest cuneiform attestations, simply a geographical name for the deserts bordering the right bank of the Euphrates. This area, which stretched without apparent limit into the Syrian and Arabian deserts, was traditionally the home of nomadic tribes of Semitic speech who were drawn to the civilized river valley as if by a magnet and invaded and infiltrated it whenever opportunity beckoned. In the process they became progressively acculturated—first as semi-nomads who spent part of the year as settled agriculturalists in an uneasy symbiosis with the urban society of the irrigation civilizations, and ultimately as fully integrated members of that society, retaining at most the linguistic traces of their origins.

The "staging-area" for the Amorite expansion was probably the Jebel Bishri (Mount Basar) which divides or, if one prefers, links the Euphrates River and the Syrian Desert. From here it was a comparatively short and easy march down the river to Babylonia or across the river to Assyria. The way to Egypt was not only longer, but led through more hilly and intractable land. This may be one reason that the Amorite wave was somewhat longer in reaching the Egyptian border. When it did, it confronted just such a wall as Shu-Sin (ca. 2036-2028 B.C.) had built "to keep Didanum at bay": in one of those curious parallels that punctuate ancient Near Eastern history, they met the "Wall-of-the-Ruler, made to oppose the Asiatics and crush the Sand-Crossers," as it is described in the story of Sinuhe (below). This wall is attributed by the "Prophecy of Nefer-tohu (Neferti)" to Amon-em-het I (ca. 1991-1961 B.C.), whose accession marked the beginning of the Twelfth Dynasty (ca. 2000-1800 B.C.). But the extraordinary revitalization of the Egyptian monarchy by this dynasty was the real reason that the Amorite wave broke harmlessly at the Egyptian border and the characteristic petty-statism that it brought in its train was deferred for two centuries.

The successive Amon-em-het's and Sen-Usert's (Sesostris) who made up the Twelfth Dynasty enjoyed long reigns and smooth patrilinear successions. But this was not by accident. They consciously adopted policies calculated to reestablish the political authority of the king, if not his divine status, as it had existed in the Old Kingdom, and Snefru of the Fourth Dynasty figured prominently both in the literature and the cults of the time. The Eleventh Dynasty had tolerated a large measure of local autonomy on the part of the separate nomarchs—possibly, indeed, these princes had tolerated the Eleventh Dynasty kings and their reestablishment of a united monarchy because, from their relatively remote capital at Thebes in Upper Egypt, they posed no threat to the particularist ambitions of the more powerful nomes. But the new dynasty changed this balance: while continuing to endow Thebes lavishly with public buildings, and confirming the nomarchs in their hereditary offices, the new kings moved the political capital back to the Memphis region, specifically to the new town of It-towy. (In its full form, the name means "Amon-em-het takes possession of the two lands," thus stressing the geographical and political role of the site.) Situated somewhere on the way to the Fayyum, this area was now opened for development. They erected their tomb complexes, including more modest sized pyramids, nearby at Lisht and other sites south of Memphis favored in the Pyramid Age. They redrew the provincial boundaries and curbed the powers of the nomarchs by appointing court officials to supervise them and to insure that tax quotas were properly met. The office of the vizier was reduced in importance, and the practice of co-regency was institutionalized, with the designated crown prince joining his father in the kingship at an early enough date to ensure a smooth succession, and to avoid a repetition of the assassination which ended the reign of Amon-em-het I. This event is described in detail in his posthumous instructions to his son and successor, a pseudepigraphic work which nonetheless gives valuable insights into the operations of the Middle Kingdom.

An even more important literary source from the same time is the story of Sinuhe, an autobiographical narrative describing a courtier's self-imposed exile to Asia at the time of the assassination, and his ultimate reprieve and return to Egypt. In the course of the story, it becomes clear that the Egypt of the Twelfth Dynasty was successful in restoring not only royal prestige but concomitantly also a healthy economy and successful military and foreign policy whereby the borders of the state were successfully defended on the east against the Asiatics and on the west against the Libyans, while they were aggressively expanded southward into Nubia. The gold of Nubia and the turquoise of Sinai flowed into royal and private hands as a result and are only two examples of the prosperity that ensued. The material remains of the Twelfth Dynasty, chiefly recovered from tomb deposits, are eloquent testimony to the high standard of living in these two centuries.

With the beginning of the 18th century B.C., the political geography of the Asiatic Near East can for the first time be rendered with reasonable accuracy, and many previously blank spots filled in. This was a period of intense commercial and diplomatic activity, punctuated by military campaigns and sieges conducted at considerable distances from home. The fortuitous recovery of archives from many diverse sites reveals a host of geographical names, and many of these can be approximately located, or even identified with archaeological sites, with the help of occasional itineraries. Such itineraries were guides to travellers or, more often, records of their journeys, and come closest to maps in the absence of any real cartography.

No small-scale map can, of course, show all the minor vassal and petty states in all their complexity. And even the larger kingdoms and city-states add up to a bewildering number. But certain patterns can be detected. The Syrian Desert was populated by loosely organized tribal groupings still maintaining a largely nomadic way of life; the mountainous border regions beyond the Tigris and the Upper Euphrates were being organized under various non-Semitic peoples who came under varying degrees of Mesopotamian cultural influence; the "Fertile Crescent" itself (that is, the valley of the two rivers together with the eastern Mediterranean littoral) was firmly in the hands of urbanized Amorite rulers. Within this great arc, the largest and most central position was occupied by the kingdom of Shamshi-

Adad I (ca. 1813-1781 B.C.) destined to be incorporated into the even greater empire of Hammurapi of Babylon (ca. 1792-1750 B.C.).

Contemporary Egypt produced no comparable kings. Though the Thirteenth Dynasty (ca. 1786-1633 B.C.) attempted to govern along the lines laid down by the strong kings of the Twelfth, the royal power was diluted in many ways. The most obvious was the sheer number of kings attested—from fifty to sixty—which implies a fratrilinear succession and must have precluded the development of long-term policies by royal initiative. The patrilinear principle was, instead, reserved for the vizierate, a post that grew proportionately in influence. Moreover, a rival dynasty, the Fourteenth, ruled in the Western Delta from the first, and others followed to begin the dismemberment of the pharaonic kingdom. The Amorite threat, which had been kept at bay under the Twelfth Dynasty, became more insistent. The Execration Texts, directed against the princelings of Syria and Palestine among others, suggest the growing inability of Egypt to keep them at arm's length, while Amorite names in lists of domestic slaves (chiefly women) from this period indicate one of the ways in which Egypt itself was increasingly infiltrated and the stage set for the "Rulers of Foreign Lands" (i.e., the Hyksos) to take over much of the country.

As the fall of Akkad ushered in the end of the Early Bronze Age, so the end of the Middle Bronze Age was marked by the capture of Babylon and Memphis. The two great capitals fell to different captors, but a common source may have set in motion the train of events that culminated in their defeat. For to the north of both the high civilizations, an entirely new ethnic element had made its entry onto the stage of history early in the Middle Bronze Age: the Hittites (see above).

For the Amorite kingdoms of the Mediterranean littoral also reacted to the stirrings set in motion by the Hittites. Cut off from their kinsmen in the east, they evolved distinct variations of the common cultural traditions and looked in the opposite direction, toward Egypt, for new lands to conquer. Their peaceful penetration of Lower Egypt had begun together with the Thirteenth Dynasty, and before the end of that Dynasty, they had succeeded in setting themselves up as rulers of the Eastern Delta (ca. 1720 B.C.). By about 1675 B.C., they had acquired sufficient prestige, and assimilated Egyptian patterns of government to the point that they were recognized as an Egyptian dynasty in their own right, probably the Fifteenth. At least six of their rulers are known by name. At first, these shared power with the legitimate pharaohs at Memphis, as well as with the other contemporary dynasties which had assumed power in the Western delta (the Fourteenth Dynasty) and in Upper Egypt (the Seventeenth Dynasty). They were known in the native sources as Hyksos, or "Rulers of Foreign Lands," and their ethnic identification has been much debated. Probably they included a mixture of stocks, but many of them, including most of their kings, were evidently Amorites. By 1600 B.C. at the latest, they had captured Memphis, supplanted the Thirteenth Dynasty, and reunited all of Lower Egypt while reducing Upper Egypt to vassal status. But their rule was felt as an alien one, and has left few monuments. Though the Second Intermediate Period ended sooner here, a dark age settled over Egypt as it had over Asia.

The Late Bronze Age

When the Dark Age lifted at the end of the 16th century B.C., Western Asia emerged to a radically new political and ethnic configuration. In place of the numerous small and medium-sized Amorite states of the outgoing Middle Bronze Age, a few non-Semitic royal houses now ruled the Fertile Crescent with the help of a more or less feudal nobility. The indigenous Semitic population was, at least for the time being, reduced either to the status of a semi-free peasantry or to that of roving mercenaries.

In Egypt, too, military and political hegemony was meantime passing out of the hands of Semitic-speaking peoples. A new dynasty of Theban rulers, the Eighteenth, had succeeded by the middle of the sixteenth century B.C. in driving the Hyksos from Egypt and reuniting the country. Its first king, Ahmose, previously a vassal ruler of Thebes, is thus regarded as the founder of the New Kingdom, which his successors transformed into a true empire when they crossed the frontier into Asia and brought all of Palestine and most of Syria under Egyptian control for the first time. First, however, the southern frontier had to be secured. The first four pharaohs of the new dynasty (1558-1490 B.C.), while they conducted punitive raids into Asia, concentrated their greatest efforts against Nubia and the Sudan, where they created a virtual African empire. Queen Hatshepsut, who as a widow of Tuthmose II ruled Egypt for twenty years, first as a regent and then in her own right (1490-1469 B.C.), even sent a commercial expedition down the Red Sea as far as Punt (the Somali coast) to bring back its exotic products, and the record of this celebrated, if not entirely unique, voyage decorated the magnificent mortuary temple which she erected for herself at Deir-el-Bahri, opposite Thebes, near the Valley of the Kings, which this dynasty turned into the preeminent royal burial site.

But it was left for her successor to forge a real Egyptian empire in Asia. Tuthmose III (1490-1436 B.C.) had been pharaoh in name only during Hatshepsut's lifetime, but she had no sooner died than he launched a succession of campaigns into Retenu, as the Egyptians called Palestine and southern Syria. Seventeen campaigns in twenty years (ca. 1468-1448 B.C.) carried Egyptian arms as far as the Euphrates and reduced the intervening city-states to vassalage. His greatest victory was won on the very first campaign, when he defeated the armies of the Asiatics combined, if not exactly united, under the prince of Kadesh, at the great battle of Megiddo; Megiddo itself fell after a siege of seven months. This first "Armageddon" (the Graecized form of Har-Megiddo, "hill of Megiddo") was duly commemorated in loving detail on the walls of the great temple at Karnak, a part of Thebes that was now wholly given over to the worship of Amon-Re, that is the patron deity of the New Kingdom conceived as a manifestation of the ancient sun-god. With Retenu firmly in his grasp, Tuthmose III even challenged the armies of Mitanni and eventually extracted a treaty that recognized a common frontier running between Hama and Qatna (ca. 1448 B.C.). His successors Amonhotep II and Tuthmose IV continued to maintain the Asiatic empire by repeated incursions into Palestine and Syria to receive the submission of loyal vassal-princes and secure that of the recalcitrant ones. Sporadic finds of cuneiform tablets from Palestine (Ta'anakh, Gezer, Aphek) seem to include royal exhortations to this effect.

Thus the subjugation of the indigenous Amorites was completed before the end of the fifteenth century B.C. throughout the Near East. There was, however, one exception to this rule. Since the emergence of the Amorites, cuneiform texts from very diverse regions had begun to make mention of a group of people called Habiru with ever increasing frequency until, by the fifteenth century, they appear in texts from all over the Near East. On philological grounds, these Habiru can be conclusively equated with the Apiru of the Egyptian texts and with the Hebrews of the Bible, where the term is used most often in a slightly derogatory connotation. Their name was explained, tellingly if not scientifically, as meaning "robbers," "dusty ones," or "migrants" respectively. These Habiru were thus not an ethnic, but a social entity: though largely of Amorite stock, they constituted that portion of the population unwilling to submit to Amorite rule or, subsequently and more particularly, to that of their non-Semitic conquerors. Instead they chose to serve as roving mercenaries under successive masters or, alternatively, to band together in order to impose their own rule in areas beyond the reach of the various imperial armies. The latter was particularly true of the wooded hill country of Syria and Palestine. There they maintained a tenacious and much maligned independence even while the great powers were dividing up the cleared lowlands.

Thus far, the history of Egypt in the Bronze Age has been correlated with that of western Asia only sporadically; whenever key personalities or recognizable trends in both areas could be described as parallel they have been expressed as contemporaneous developments or reactions to common underlying causes. But the Near East of the fourteenth century B.C. witnessed the convergence of so many of the factors that we have already isolated—ethnic, economic, ecologic, military, technical, and others—that its history can hardly be written other than in international terms. Not only does the region enter upon a period of thorough-going cosmopolitanism, but the nature of the sources is such as to impose a regional view. These two factors are not unrelated. It was because imperialism had enlarged the vistas of each area that the documents concern themselves preponderantly with international relations. The texts, in short, only reflect the experience of the men and women of the time, which featured an unprecedented amount of foreign travel and exposure to foreign influences. Because the records found at El-Amarna in Egypt, and similar texts from Asia, are characteristic of the period, and because the revolutionary events at Amarna itself were among the most dramatic of the time, it is appropriate to designate the entire period as the Amarna Age.

The immediate source of the new cosmopolitanism, and the locus where it flourished most readily, was the royal court. In each of the major states, the capital city featured a courtly society where arts and learning blossomed under royal patronage, where foreign princes were educated while serving as hostages for their fathers' loyalty, and where foreign princesses graced the royal harem. The last factor was perhaps most characteristic of the age, for although individual queens of considerable personal stature were known earlier, the practice of dynastic marriage was now elevated to a high principle of statecraft, and much of the history of the period could be written in terms of such marriages and of the protracted negotiations that surrounded them. The new internationalism thus implied at the same time a new high in the status of women, and even a commoner of character and energy could rise to the rank of princess and first wife of a pharaoh such as Amon-hotep III.

The leading proponent of the dynastic marriage (as of the education of foreign hostage princes) appears to have been the Eighteenth Dynasty of Egypt (ca. 1550-1300 B.C.). This dynasty derived its original legitimacy from an ancestress related by descent to the Seventeenth (Theban) Dynasty and perhaps to the Nubians, and by marriage possibly to the Hyksos (Fifteenth and Sixteenth Dynasties). It displayed a strong matriarchal tendency in its early phase, climaxed by Queen Hatshepsut (above). When her stepson Tuthmose III finally assumed sole reign after her death (1468 B.C.), he may have already been married to the three queens whose graves have been recovered, thoroughly pillaged, near Deir-el-Bahri. These are thought to have been Syrian princesses, thus inaugurating the practice of dynastic marriages. The practice became official policy under Tuthmose IV (1412-1402 B.C.), who recognized the importance of an alliance with Mitanni to counter the growing strength of the Hittites. After four rounds of negotiations, a daughter of Artatama of Mitanni finally entered his harem to seal the agreement. His son Amon-hotep III (1402-1363 B.C.) pursued the policy most consistently. Although he made the Egyptian Tiy his principal wife, his marriage to Gilu-Hepa, daughter of Shuttarna of Mitanni, was celebrated on an elaborate scarab, and he sought the hand of a second Mitanni princess. In addition, he succeeded in acquiring two Kassite princesses and one from Arzawa in southwestern Anatolia for his harem. His son, Amon-hotep IV (1363-1347 B.C.), succeeded to some of these queens by right of inheritance, but is most famous for his marriage to the beautiful Nefertiti, and for the lavish attention he bestowed on her and her daughters after abandoning the traditional cult of Amon at Thebes for that of the sun-disc (Aten) at the new capital which he constructed at Akhet-Aten (Amarna) and where he ruled under the new name of Akhen-Aten. The many novel, artistic, literary, and theological concepts spawned in these surroundings have suggested to modern historians a veritable "Amarna revolution."

After Akhen-Aten's death, the succession eventually passed, through one of his daughters, to her husband Tuth-ankh-Aten, but now the Amon priesthood reasserted itself, the new capital was abandoned again, and the king changed his name, significantly, to Tuth-ankh-Amon. His tomb near Thebes, miraculously escaping ancient pillage, has preserved for modern excavators the most elaborate burial deposits of any pharaoh. But he was himself a minor ruler of a declining power, for the Amarna interlude had exacted a high price in terms of Egypt's military posture and international prestige. It had been firm Egyptian policy, while accepting foreign princesses for the royal harem, to refuse to send Egyptian princesses abroad. But now the widow of the pharaoh appealed to the Hittite king Shuppiluliuma (ca. 1375-1335 B.C.), who had by this time displaced the Mitanni king as the greatest monarch of this time, to give her a son of his own as her consort. This remarkable request was fraught with consequences. When the Hittite king finally granted the request, the prince despatched for the purpose was slain on the way to Egypt. The Eighteenth Dynasty came to an end in the hands of Ay (1337-1333 B.C.) and Horemheb (1333-1303 B.C.), two generals of non-royal lineage. Shuppiluliuma, for his part, avenged the death of his son by declaring war on Egypt and taking captives from the populations under Egyptian protection. Although the Egyptians were powerless to oppose him, both of these actions constituted breaches of the treaties which by now bound Egypt and the Hittites. According to the "Confessions" of Shuppiluliuma's surviving son and successor, Murshili II (ca. 1334-1306 B.C.), these treaty violations triggered their own penalty, for the captives brought a plague with them which devastated the Hittite country and counted Shuppiluliuma himself among its victims.

The delicate balance of power constructed on the novel ideas of international negotiation and accommodation in the fourteenth century B.C. survived even the ambitions of particularly strong rulers such as the Hittite Shuppiluliuma. But it was not equal to the threat from below; in the end it succumbed to the tidal waves of diverse new ethnic groups which broke on all the shores of the Near East and destroyed the last vestiges of the age of diplomacy. At the outset of the thirteenth century B.C., however, these momentous developments could hardly have been foreseen by contemporaries. Instead, war and peace revolved as before around the major powers. In the east, Assyria fought the Kassites of Babylonia about the turn of the century and, at least in the Assyrian historical and epic versions of the event, won the day. In the west, the Nineteenth Dynasty ruled Egypt throughout the century; it is also known as the First Ramesside Dynasty after its most illustrious member, the long-lived Ramses II (ca. 1290-1224 B.C.), who is sometimes regarded as the unnamed pharaoh of the oppression in the Biblical book of Exodus. There is actually little to recommend this identification beyond the tenuous equation of the "storage city" called Ramses in Exodus 1:11 with Per-Ramses, "the House of Ramses," which was the name given by Ramses II to Tanis (elsewhere in the Bible called Zo'an), a city in the Eastern Delta which his dynasty, true to its Lower Egyptian origins, used as its capital. What is beyond dispute, however, is that his reign, whose length was exceeded only by that of Pepi II at the end of the Old Kingdom, left its monuments all over Egypt and inspired a cult of the ruler that survived his reign by many centuries. Most of the inscriptions and reliefs commemorate the pharaoh's great battle with the Hittites at the Battle of Kadesh on the Orontes River. Here, in his fifth year (ca. 1285 B.C.), Ramses encountered Muwatalli (ca. 1306-1282 B.C.), son of Murshili II, and a worthy successor to his father and his grandfather Shuppululiuma. The battle of Kadesh, one of the best-documented in antiquity, and one of the great battles of history, ended in something of a stalemate, and left the Hittites in firm possession of northern Syria. Some fifteen years later, however, it led Ramses and Hattushili III, a brother and successor of Muwatalli, to conclude an elaborate treaty of peace which is one of the more remarkable examples of its genre. Alone among the rather numerous treaties of its time, it is preserved in two versions, one in Egyptian and one in Hittite. Though not the first treaty between the two powers, it was observed more sedulously, for both countries now faced a common danger, the so-called Sea Peoples. The spearheads of this massive migration had already made their presence felt at Kadesh, with Dardanians and Philistines allied to the Hittites and Sherden ("Sardinians") fighting on both sides. But by the middle of the century, these and other newcomers were ready to assume an independent role and one that proved fateful for the balance of power in the entire Near East. They sought new lands to conquer and settle wherever the established powers were too weak to withstand them, and left their names scattered across the Mediterranean littorals and islands to this day, from Cilicia and Philistia (Palestine) in the east to Sicily, Etruria (Tuscany) and Sardinia in the west. The populations displaced by their arrival fled elsewhere to spread the process in a chain-like reaction, until confronted by corresponding migrations from an opposite direction. Thus the Hurrians of Cilicia fled northeast into Hittite Anatolia, putting an end to the Hittite empire there; the Hittite refugees in turn moved southeast into the former Mitanni area of northern Syria. Here they encountered and joined forces with the Aramaeans, a new wave of Semitic-speaking semi-nomads moving north out of the Syrian desert. The Hurrians of Mitanni, in turn, fled northeast toward the area of Lake Van, where they coalesced with the ancestors of the Urartians. Further south, the Amorite and other peoples of Canaan were squeezed between and subjected to the Philistines occupying the coast and the Israelites moving into the land from the south and east.

In an inscription of Pharaoh Merneptah (ca. 1224-1214 B.C.), the collective name of Israel first appears in an extra-Biblical source. Merneptah himself managed to hold off the Sea Peoples, and about 1190 B.C. they were decisively defeated in the Delta in a great land and sea battle which sent many of them westward across the Mediterranean. But this victory belongs to Ramses III and the Twentieth (or Second Ramesside) Dynasty. The Nineteenth Dynasty itself had come to an undistinguished end by 1200 B.C., Egypt fell briefly under the domination of a foreign usurper called Irsu (who may be identical with the Cushan-Rishataim of Judges 3:8, 10), and the many Ramses' who restored Egyptian authority at home in the twelfth century B.C. were unable to save her Asiatic empire or to stave off for long the end of the New Kingdom.

The Iron Age

The fall of the Twentieth Dynasty about 1085 B.C. marked the end of the New Kingdom or Empire period of Egyptian history. Politically it was followed by half a millennium of decline, an interval so long as to almost belie the term Third Intermediate Period sometimes attached to it. For most of this period, Egypt was ruled by foreign dynasties: Libyans from the west, Nubians from the south, and Assyrians from the northeast. Although a native dynasty reasserted itself at Sais as the Saite or Twenty-sixth Dynasty (664-525 B.C.), the era of innovation had ceased. Egyptian culture continued in the molds cast by earlier precedent, and this is a convenient point at which to characterize that culture and its bequests to later ages.

In both respects, pride of place may well be given to the technique of writing. The Egyptians of the Third Millennium had adapted this non-Egyptian invention to their own peculiar genius. Blessed with an unmatched gift for draftsmanship and proportions, they developed the elegant hieroglyphic system. Like Sumerian writing, this was a mixture of word-signs and syllabic signs, hence a so-called logo-syllabic system of writing. A large number of signs was needed for the system, and artistic skill was required to represent them. Repeatedly, therefore, it spawned simpler systems. One of these was the "hieratic" script, a cursive hand far easier to write (though harder to read) than the hieroglyphic. A more significant offshoot affected the inner structure of the system when confronted by the challenge of writing growing numbers of foreign names: in the Empire period with its increasing foreign contacts, a purely syllabic orthography was devised. It not only dispensed with word-signs entirely but also distinguished the vowels of each syllable, where the traditional hieroglyphic system represented only the consonants. It is now generally held that, by the middle of the Second Millennium, this system inspired the first West Semitic syllabic orthographies; for at that time Semitic-speaking laborers came into contact with their Egyptian task-masters in the turquoise mines of the Sinai. In simple dedications to their own deities, they devised a syllabic script that paved the way for a whole series of Semitic systems of at most some thirty signs. Ultimately adopted and simplified by the Phoenicians, this script was passed by them to the Greeks. They in turn added the vowel signs that converted this syllabary into a true alphabet. The Aramaic script subsequently spread the same invention eastwards and between them the offshoots of Greek and Aramaic alphabets conquered most of the world.

The early mastery of writing by the Egyptians meant that they also developed, along with the Sumerians, the world's oldest corpus of written literature. The richness and variety of this corpus remains a source of fascination even to the modern reader. Only a few representative examples have been cited for each period: the Pyramid texts of the Old Kingdom, the Admonitions of Ipuwer for the First Intermediate Period, the story of Sinuhe for the Middle Kingdom, or the Hymns to the Aten (sun-disc) from the Amarna Age. And the same scribes who composed and transmitted these purely literary texts were also available to record the daily transactions of a bustling economy, or the great royal inscriptions, treaties and other memorials

of the state. For the late period, perhaps the single most characteristic literary monument is the story of Wen-Amon. Set at the very
end of the New Kingdom, it tells of the misadventures of an Egyptian
emissary and his fruitless attempts to reassert Egypt's traditional
trade relations with the great commercial centers of the Phoenician
coast. But another literary genre may be said to have had the most
enduring impact, and that is the so-called Wisdom Literature. In the
form of "instructions" and proverbs, it passed into the Hebrew Bible.
The clearest instance of this is found in the "thirty sayings of admonitions and knowledge" (Proverbs 22:17-24:22; cf. 22:20), with their
numerous affinities to the Instructions of Amon-em-Ope. By this and
other means, a modest fraction of Egyptian heritage has indirectly
passed into world literature.

A much more direct and visible legacy of ancient Egypt is its
monumental architecture and sculpture. Like Mesopotamia, Egypt is
poor in timber. The Sumerians resorted to perishable clay and reed
to make up for this lack, and their monuments have been destroyed
by fire and covered by sand in the interim. But the valley of the Nile
was squeezed between mountains of granite and limestone on either
side, and while these restricted the expansion of agriculture, they furnished an inexhaustible supply of stone, both hard and soft, for ma-
son and sculptor. After a brief period of clay construction (probably
in imitation of Sumerian practices), the Egyptians soon took full advantage of the more durable medium. The pyramids, tombs, temples
and statuary of all periods surpass in quantity and quality the stone
monuments of any other Near Eastern culture. Many of them were
never fully destroyed or buried; others have been restored or excavated and form a magnificent setting for the equally sophisticated arts
of the painter and calligrapher.

From the modern point of view, an inordinate proportion of surviving monumental Egyptian art was devoted to the burial and cult
of the dead; in the Old Kingdom, the deceased king was the particular object of these attentions, including the Pyramid Texts. But by
Middle Kingdom times, the Coffin Texts that succeeded them were
used for the graves of nobles as well, and in New Kingdom times a
new synthesis called the Book of the Dead was inscribed on papyrus
or leather and available even with the humbler burials. Increasingly
in the later periods there was a growing popular concern with death,
and the characteristic Egyptian practice of preserving the body by
means of embalming (mummification) spread to ever wider circles.

But this should not lead to a distorted view of Egyptian conceptions. In most periods they viewed death as a continuation of life "in the West," and they duly prepared for a well-provided life after death. They also had a very healthy love of *this* life. Literature and art both attest to their ability to enjoy the blessings of this world. When the Nile Inundation appeared in its regular course the economy flourished, and under the friendly skies of the Egyptian sun there was ample leisure time for enjoying an abundant surplus of the necessities and luxuries of life. Wall paintings and secular songs record in loving detail the revels of the Egyptian at play or relaxing at banquets. When the Hebrew psalmist referred to "anointing his head with oil" (23:5) or more specifically to "the precious oil upon the head, running down upon the beard . . . running down on the collar of his robes" (133:2) he was probably preserving a fragment of standard Egyptian extravagance.

In these and other ways too numerous to catalogue here, the millennial legacy of Egypt passed on to later history. Because of the protracted period of decline which preceded the Persian conquest, the transmission was often more effective than in the case of Mesopotamia. There both Assyria and Babylonia fell abruptly at the height of their power, the former to the Medes, the latter to the Persians. But Egypt's slow descent from the imperial heights of the New Kingdom meant that its institutions were often adopted by its conquerors in a subtler and less conscious manner. To this day, the Arab fellahin of the Nile Valley feel an innate kinship for the scenes of daily life recovered by the excavations from Ancient Egypt, while the educated Egyptian considers himself an heir to the scribes, nobles and pharaohs of old.

3. The Land of Milk and Honey

Lying between the two great rivers valleys, the eastern shore of the Mediterranean forms the land bridge between Egypt and Mesopotamia. Throughout the Bronze Age, it shared in the historical and cultural developments of these two centers of high civilization. The urban revolution of the Early Bronze Age embraced both its southern end (Canaan) and its northern end (Syria) and the discovery of the royal archives and libraries at Ebla reveal a major city-state with a sophisticated culture and far-flung commercial and diplomatic contacts. In the Middle Bronze Age, hieroglyphic and cuneiform sources throw additional light on Canaan and Syria respectively. But it is only in the Late Bronze Age that the area became the persistent object of direct intervention by the great powers that surrounded it. Egyptians, Hurrians and Hittites all strove to incorporate parts of the area in their empires. Native city-states like Ugarit in the north and Hazor further south attempted to maintain and extend their own borders in the face of foreign conquerors. And in all the less urbanized areas the ubiquitous Habiru wrested a meager living from the countryside. The contemporary texts, especially the Amarna correspondence, describe the aggressive tactics of these "outlaws" who may have been ancestral to the Hebrews. But none of them know of Israel.

The oldest epigraphic evidence for the name of Israel dates from the very end of the Bronze Age (above) and some historians are disinclined to begin the history of Israel before the Iron Age. Others, however, regard this as an unwarranted overestimation of epigraphic evidence. Since the Bible is far and away the best—and often the only—source for our knowledge of Israelite history, its testimony must, according to this view, be taken seriously even in the absence of direct epigraphic corroboration, that is, the testimony of inscriptions contemporary with the evidence described. This is not to say that patently literary recastings of oral traditions such as the Patriarchal narratives (above) are all to be accepted uncritically; there can be no theological justification for exempting Biblical literature from the standards applied to other ancient Near Eastern texts. But neither should it be subjected to standards demanded nowhere else. On this basis, Israelite traditions about its own Bronze Age past, though these traditions were written down in the Iron Age, have to be given as much credence as, for example, Middle and neo-Assyrian notions about the Old Assyrian past. Just as the Assyrian historians gave formal expression, by various means, to a very real sense of continuity which centered on the worship of Assur, the deity from whom their city took its name, so the Biblical authors wrote their history in terms of the worship and worshippers of the God of Israel. In both instances, it was the reality of an unbroken religious tradition which permitted an ethnic group to lay claim to the memories or monuments surviving from the Bronze Age and to link them to later political institutions.

In this sense the prelude to Israelite history can be legitimately said to include the events enshrined in Genesis, from the primeval history of mankind set in Mesopotamia, through the patriarchal wanderings in Syria-Palestine, to the sojourn in Egypt. It continues with the traditions of the Exodus from Egypt, the revelation at Sinai, and the wanderings in the desert as preserved in the rest of the Pentateuch. The Exodus in particular had such a perennial impact on later Israelite belief and thought that to reject its historicity is to rob subsequent (and even prior) Biblical historiography of its basic paradigm. And though unattested in extra-Biblical sources, the Exodus led to an exaltation of the God of Israel that has a striking and near-contemporary parallel in the exaltation of Marduk to the apex of the Babylonian pantheon and thereby a further warrant for its inherent probability. Details, needless to say, remain open to debate: whether there was one Exodus or two, whether the "twelve tribes" were as closely related as later genealogical schemes made them out to be, whether the conquest of Canaan took place all at once as the Book of Joshua would have it or gradually as implied by the Book of Judges. But in outline the situation at the start of the Conquest is clear: a group of tribes related by common worship and traditions both to each other and to a segment of Hapiru-Hebrews of Late Bronze Palestine began to claim that land for themselves in a concerted effort.

This conquest took fully two centuries to consummate (ca. 1200-1000 B.C.) and involved both sides of the Jordan. In this period, the various tribes retained their separate identities under the rule of temporary judges, who occasionally united a number of tribes under their leadership, but conspicuously rejected a hereditary kingship even when this was offered to them. Instead, the basic governmental principle seems to have been a so-called amphictyony, a loose confederation, partly military, partly sacral, which centered on one or another

religious shrine and was modelled on the tribal organization encountered by the Israelites among some of their neighbors, especially
across the Jordan.   It registered some successes under charismatic
leaders such as Deborah, Gideon and Samson, alternating with as
many setbacks in the struggles against the indigenous population and
against other newcomers seeking a foothold in the country at the
same time, notably the Philistines.   But in the end the attractions of
a more successful model proved irresistible, and Samuel, the last of
the judges, was forced to accede to the popular demand: " now ap-
point for us a king to govern us like all the nations" (I Samuel 8:5).
His choice fell on Saul (ca. 1020-1000 B.C.) of Benjamin, a tribe
whose modest pretensions may have inspired the hope that the cen-
tralization of authority and aggrandizement of power inevitably inherent in the monarchical system could somehow be minimized.   But
the lesson of the signal military successes initially won under Saul's
effective leadership were not lost on the united tribes.   Only seven
years after his disastrous defeat at the hands of the Philistines at Mt.
Gilboa, they restored the United Monarchy under David of Judah
(ca. 1000-960 B.C.) and he and his successor Solomon (ca. 960-920
B.C.) successfully constructed a true empire reaching from the Orontes River in the north to the Gulf of Aqaba in the south.   They maintained a commanding position on the international scene by a
combination of military conquests, diplomatic alliances (including
marriages to foreign princesses), overseas trade, and internal reorgani-
zation which attempted to submerge the old tribal organization and
allegiances under a new system of administrative districts directly responsible to the king.   David's conquest of Jerusalem and Solomon's
construction of the First Temple there laid the basis, at the same time,
for the centralization of both political power and religious worship as
the priesthood, too, became subservient to the crown.   A process of
urbanization ensued as the Israelites absorbed the wealth accruing
from trade and war abroad, and conquered the Canaanite towns that
had held out in the time of the Judges.

The Israelite ascendance was in large measure made feasible by
the concurrent impotence of Babylonia and Assyria, and of Egypt.
With a line of High Priests of Amon ruling upper Egypt from Thebes,
the Twenty-first Dynasty was content to give its tacit support to the
Davidic kings, whom they considered on the one hand a useful check
to the more immediate threat from the Philistines of the seacoast and
the Shosu of Transjordan, and on the other a valued partner of their

traditional Phoenician allies. The precipitate decline of Egypt's stature in Asia is tellingly illustrated by the story of Wen-Amun. But the United Monarchy was itself not without its built-in weaknesses, political, diplomatic, and ideological, as the sequel was to show.

On the political side, the House of David was unable to eradicate the vestiges of tribal particularism, especially the separatist tendencies of the northern tribes. These tribes refused to forget the southern (Judahite) origins of the dynasty, or to forgive its ruthless elimination of the survivors of Saul's Israelite family. They threatened secession at every crisis with the cry "To your tents, oh Israel!" (I Kings 12:16; cf. II Samuel 20:1), a threat made good under Solomon's son Rehoboam (ca. 920 B.C.). It coincided with a brief Egyptian resurgence under two concurrent Libyan dynasties (the Twenty-second and Twenty-third) whose first ruler, Sheshonk I (ca. 935-914 B.C.), attempted to reassert Egypt's Asiatic pretensions. Though unsuccessful in this effort in the long run, his massive attacks throughout Palestine (cf. I Kings 14:25) frustrated whatever hopes Rehoboam may have entertained of reuniting the monarchy. The ten northern tribes constituted themselves a separate kingdom under Jeroboam I, lately returned from political asylum at Sheshonk's court, and for two hundred years the United Monarchy became the Divided Monarchy (922-722 B.C.). The political and military history of the two rump states in this interval was largely determined by the vagaries of the international situation, with Syria and especially Assyria looming ever more importantly on the northern horizon.

The rupture of the kingdom did not, however, estrange the two groups of tribes permanently. They still shared a common heritage and observed to some extent the same cult. The royal houses of both states were often linked by marriage or other alliances even though the Judahite throne remained firmly in the House of David whereas the succession of Israel passed from one short-lived dynasty to another in the search for ever new charismatic leadership. Most importantly, both states were subject to similar socio-economic forces, and in the long run the most significant resistance to the emerging urban-monarchic structure in both states was neither political nor diplomatic in origin, but ideological. This resistance was based on a deep-seated attachment to certain traditional virtues and beliefs associated (rightly or wrongly) with the simpler past in the period of the desert wanderings and the conquest: a strict monotheism free of the taint of polytheistic cults as practiced by the indigenous population and the higher civilizations of Syria, Mesopotamia and Egypt; opposition to the social injustices and economic exploitation associated with an expanding economy; and a firm belief in the importance of cultic and ethical propriety, not only on the part of the king (as was notably true in Mesopotamia) but of the people as a whole. The most articulate champions of these essentially conservative positions were the prophets, who originated as popular wonder-workers and teachers, but who eventually became a counterforce to kings and priests alike. Beginning with Amos and Hosea in the eighth century B.C., their speeches were preserved in the form of literary prophesy, a unique genre in ancient Near Eastern literature. The high moral commitment of these prophetic writings, their political realism, and their emergent universalism combined to give them an influence that drastically shaped Biblical religion and all its subsequent derivatives.

The humiliating defeat of the Northern Kingdom by Tiglath-pileser III and its incorporation into the Assyrian Empire by Sargon II in 722 B.C. provided the first dramatic vindications of the prophetic calls to national rectitude. Isaiah, whose ministry began "in the year that King Uzziah (Azariah) died" (Isaiah 6:1), i.e., in 740 B.C., and who still confronted King Ahaz (731-716 B.C.) as something of an adversary, thus found himself an honored counselor at the court of King Hezekiah (715-687 B.C.). The new king accepted the prophetic message and inaugurated a policy of religious reform and a determined anti-Assyrian stance that represented a clear break with his predecessor. Although the long reign of Manasseh (686-642 B.C.) reversed these policies for a time, they were revived with renewed vigor by Josiah (639-609 B.C.) and became the veritable constitution of Judah in 622 with the promulgation of the Deuteronomic code (cf. II Kings 22). This work, essentially the Book of Deuteronomy, at one stroke restored the authority of the ancient Mosaic legislation, canonized the prophetic doctrine of national responsibility, and declared Judah's political independence. The last purpose was achieved, more subtly than the first two, by employing the very terms of vassalage that had hitherto bound the country to Assyria, and transferring them instead to God. Assyria was in fact losing her grip on the west, and Josiah was presently able to extend his rule, and his reforms, also to the former territory of the Northern Kingdom. In the eyes of the "Deuteronomic historian," that is the unknown author or editor who is responsible for the "Deuteronomic" framework of the historical books (the so-called "Former Prophets"), Judah thus entered into a new covenant with God (II Kings 23:3) and Josiah ranked as its most pious king (*ib.* 25).

The religious reforms thus inaugurated proved, however, to be more durable than the political gains that they accompanied. For the decline of Assyria was advantageous not only to Judah, but also to more substantial powers, notably Egypt and Babylonia and, looming just over the horizon, the Medes and the Persians. Egypt was the first to make its weight felt in Palestine. The Libyan dynasties (above) had been succeeded by a Nubian (Twenty-fifth) Dynasty which fell under Assyrian vassalage after Esarhaddon's conquest of Egypt (671 B.C.). The Saite (Twenty-sixth) Dynasty which followed similarly began as vassals of Assurbanipal. But as Assyrian power waned in the later seventh century B.C., they reasserted Egyptian independence and unity, and Pharaoh Necho (609-594 B.C.) had visions of reviving Egypt's Asiatic role when he marched north in his first year to meet Josiah at the ancient battlefield of Megiddo. The king of Judah was mortally wounded and Necho proceeded north. Unable to save the last remnants of Assyrian power at Harran, the Egyptians soon found themselves confronting the revitalized Babylonian army at Carchemish (605 B.C.). Nebukadnezar, unmindful of the fact that Judah had so recently made common cause with Babylon against Assyria, followed up his triumph at Carchemish with the capture of Jerusalem in 597 B.C. and the first exile of its aristocracy. Eleven years later, dissatisfied with the tenuous loyalty of the vassal kingdom, he returned to destroy Jerusalem, including the Solomonic temple, and to complete the exile of its leading citizens.

Once again political events had vindicated the dire warnings of the great Prophets. But this time they had exacted so heavy a toll that prophecy turned from reproach to consolation. The Second Isaiah began his message with "Comfort ye, comfort ye, my people . . . (Jerusalem) has received from the hand of the Lord double for all her transgressions" (Isaiah 40:1-2). Jeremiah advised the exiles in Babylonia to make the best of their new lives, and himself reluctantly fled to Egypt. Ezekiel, living among the Babylonian exiles, encouraged them with visions of a restored Jerusalem. And indeed the exile proved less of a hardship than life in Jerusalem for the impoverished remnants left behind there. When Cyrus entered Babylon in 539 B.C., he permitted and even encouraged the exiles to return to Jerusalem and there to rebuild the temple. Many took advantage of this offer, but many more preferred to remain in the hospitable Babylonian environment where they had meantime struck roots. In 525 B.C., Cambyses conquered Egypt, put an end to the Saite (Twenty-sixth) Dynasty, and found Israelite mercenaries settled at Elephantine far up the Nile. Thus the Persian Achaemenids brought both Judaea and the diaspora under their rule, and indeed united the entire Near East under a single far-flung empire for the first time. The convergence of Israelite and Persian history thus coincides with a major turning-point in the development of the entire Near East, and forms an appropriate conclusion to its ancient history here as it does in the Hebrew Bible (cf. II Chronicles 36:22-23=Ezra 1:1-2).

The Near East United

Mesopotamia, Egypt and Israel—the three principal foci of attention in our historical survey up to this point—were united under one administration for the first time by the Assyrian Empire. That empire occupied the approximate center of what then constituted the civilized portion of the inhabited world, or what the Greeks like to call the oikoumene. The death of Assurbanipal (627 B.C.?) deprived the Assyrian Empire of its last really effective ruler, and plunged the Near East into nearly a century of tumultuous readjustment. The Chaldeans of Babylonia, the Saites of Egypt, the Judaean kings of Palestine, and other former subject peoples all contended for the political spoils of the falling and fallen empire. The shock waves set off by this military turmoil at the center were accompanied by even wider repercussions on the cultural plane. It was a time of intellectual and religious ferment from one end of the oikoumene to the other. The founders of the seminal philosophic and theological movements that have shaped subsequent thought and belief were all born during this turbulent century, or active in it: the pre-Socratic philosophers of the Greek world, the great exilic prophets of Israel, Zoroaster in Iran, Buddha in India, Lao-tse and Confucius in China. One cannot demonstrate any connection between these five discrete cultural movements, widely separated as they are in space, but their virtually contemporaneous appearance suggests yet another convergence of underlying causes such as supplied the common troughs and crests of the history of the oikoumene in its earlier and more constricted phases.

As far as the Near East was concerned, the intellectual ferment of the period seemed to parallel some kind of growing disenchantment with the political convulsions of the age. Assyrian rule had been harsh, but to some extent predictable. The feuding heirs of the Assyrian imperium were equally harsh on each other, and less predictable. Witness, for example, the decisive break which Nebukadnezar's destructions of Jerusalem and the ensuing Babylonian exile implied in Jewish history. In Chaldean Babylon, meanwhile, the short-lived successors of Nebukadnezar fell to warring among themselves until Nabonidus stepped in and, to all appearances, abandoned the ancient city and the cult of Marduk in favor of the centers of moon worship at Ur, at Harran and at Teima deep in the Arabian Desert. Thus it was that, when Cyrus the Persian arrived at the gates of Babylonia in 539 B.C., he was welcomed by Babylonians and exiles alike. Deferring to the sensibilities of the Babylonian priesthood, he allowed that ancient land to delude itself that it was once again to be the center of the oikoumene. His imperial rescripts employed the "script and language of the Chaldeans" (cf. Daniel 1:4); his royal titulary proclaimed him the legitimate successor to the Chaldean kings; his court and provincial administrators copied many of the time-tested practices of the Assyrians. The loyalty of the provinces was won over by giving them a measure of local autonomy, encouraging native cults, and permitting the return of exiled populations. This policy is best attested for the Judaeans, who even briefly restored the Davidic monarchy under Persian overlordship, but other groups formerly subject to the neo-Babylonian empire also enjoyed the same privileges.

But behind this outward benevolence there can be detected the elements of a grand design. Cyrus envisioned an empire greater than any the world had yet seen, and to this end he needed unity at the center and loyalty on the frontiers. He did not live to see all his aims fulfilled, but when he died in 530 B.C. after a reign of 30 years (including eight over Babylonia), his conquests passed smoothly and intact to his son and successor Cambyses. Cambyses completed the unification of the Near East by defeating the Saites and annexing Egypt, but like his father he strove for legitimacy in Egyptian eyes and the Persians came to be regarded as simply another (the twenty-seventh as it happens) in the long line of "native" dynasties by the Egyptians. He may not have been equally solicitous of Babylonian sensibilities for rebellions broke out there during his absence in Egypt, led by pretenders flaunting such names as Nebukadnezar. But the royal Achaemenid line, albeit in the form of a collateral branch,

reasserted itself with a vengeance when Darius I swept all the pretenders aside and gained the throne for no less than 36 years (522-
486 B.C.). He raised the empire to its heights, and carved an
indelible monument for himself on the rock at Behistun, a monument
which not only dramatically immortalized his triumphs, but also
served (like the Rosetta Stone in the case of Egyptian hieroglyphics)
as key to the decipherment of cuneiform in the nineteenth century
A.D.

Darius' descendants all enjoyed lengthy reigns, so that throughout
the fifth and most of the fourth centuries B.C. the Achaemenid dynasty held undisputed sway "from India to Ethiopia, one hundred
and twenty-seven provinces" as it is phrased in the Bible (Esther 1:1).
But like other great monarchies before and since, the Persian Empire
contained within itself the seeds of its own destruction. It failed to
extend its sway to the western shore of the Aegean in the confronta-
tion with Greece made famous by Herodotus and later Greek historians; the Ionian Greeks of the eastern Aegean, though subject to
Achaemenid rule, proved hard to govern; and all the while Greek
ideas, artistic techniques and military tactics infiltrated the Persian
court administration and army. Their superiority once recognized, it
was only a matter of time before the Persians, with their vast financial
resources, began to purchase the services of Greek thinkers, craftsmen
and soldiers. And what began with the royal court, was soon enough
imitated at the provincial level: the satraps who ruled the far-flung
provinces began to employ the foreigners at their own courts, to build
and decorate their own palaces in the western style, and to enlist
Greek mercenaries or generals to supplement their provincial armies.
Soon their power rivalled that of the king himself, and set the stage
for intrigues against the crown. The rebellion of Cyrus the Younger
(died 401 B.C.) is a case in point: aided by 10,000 Greek mercenaries,
he marched almost unopposed through half the empire before meeting his death in battle against Artaxerxes II. The retreat of the
10,000, made famous by Xenophon's record of it in the *Anabasis*, only
confirmed the Greeks in their suspicion that the great Achaemenid
empire was ripe for dismemberment or worse. And while the city-
states of Greece were too divided among themselves to take advantage of the opportunity, it became the sacred mission of Philip of
Macedon. He lived long enough to rally the cities to his cause, at
first intending or perhaps pretending to seek no more than the libera-
tion of the Greek cities of Ionia. But upon his death, his son Alexan-

der dropped all restraints and drove to the heart of the Persian empire. The battle of Issus (333 B.C.) virtually sealed its doom. The Near East was united to the Greek world and, though the successors of Alexander were unable to maintain the union, nonetheless Near Eastern and Greek traditions fused on the cultural level in the Hellenistic world. In a sense, that cultural unity survived and outweighed the political diversity which characterized the Near East until the advent of Islam.

CHAPTER TEN

CONCLUSION
THE LEGACY OF THE ANCIENT NEAR EAST

Our debt to the ancient Near East has been documented in a variety
of fields in the preceding pages. It goes almost without saying that any
one book can do this only by way of illustration. In what follows, a
rapid review of the illustrations offered above will be joined to a few
of the many more areas that had to be left out of account. The combined effect should serve to underline the continuities that characterize the civilizations of the ancient Near East and those of the
modern West. This effect is the more remarkable as most of its constituent elements are the results of rediscovery rather than of straightforward survival. In a sense, the recovery of many of our cultural
origins in the Ancient Near East constitutes an analogy, if not to the
scientific revolution of the seventeenth century, then at least to the
renaissance of the Quattrocento and the Cinquecento.

In some measure, it was the fall of Constantinople in 1453 A.D.,
and the prior and subsequent arrival of Greek émigré scholars in Italy, that sparked the rediscovery of the Classical, and especially the
Hellenic, antecedents of Western culture. Often enough, these scholars brought with them the classics of the Greek tradition. To cite just
one instance, all the extant manuscripts of Callimachus' Hymns "descend from a Byzantine sylloge which contained the *Hymns* of Homer,
Callimachus, Orpheus, and Proclus. A MS containing this collection
was brought from Constantinople to Venice in 1423 by Joannes Aur-
ispa." [1] Through such manuscripts, recopied or printed at Venice and
other centers of learning, all of Europe gradually awoke to a new
appreciation of its common past.

Of course, Greek civilization had never been entirely lost. Aristotle, Galen, and many other authors lived on in more or less faithful
translations or imitations in Arabic, Hebrew, and Latin, whence they
began to enter the various European vernaculars even before their
originals were rediscovered in the Renaissance. Still, to cite an editor

---

[1] Pp. 13f. of the Loeb Classical Library edition (vol. 129) of Callimachus' Hymns.

of Galen's *On the Natural Faculties*, "The year 1453, when Constantinople fell into the hands of the Turks, is often taken as marking the commencement of the Renaissance. Among the many factors which tended to stimulate and awaken men's minds during these spacious times was the rediscovery of the Greek classics, which were brought to Europe by, among others, the scholars who fled from Byzantium. The Arabo-Scholastic [i.e. Latin] versions of Aristotle and Galen were now confronted by their Greek originals. A passion for Greek learning was aroused." [2]

Can comparable claims be made for the legacy of ancient Near Eastern antiquity and its rediscovery? Selected examples will have to do by way of approaching this question.

We may begin with the linguistic evidence, specifically with the survival of ancient Near Eastern words in European languages. Often enough this is the case with products at home in the ancient Near East which travelled thence together with the words identifying them. Some indeed may have originated outside the Near East and be merely documented there for the first time in their global wanderings. They are aptly described as "Wanderwörter" or "Kulturwörter" by our German colleagues.

Writing on "the debt of Europe to Babylon" in 1925, R. Campbell Thompson, the noted British expert on cuneiform botany and chemistry (as well as lexicography), listed some fifty Greek and Latin words, most of them with cognates in modern European languages, which could with some likelihood be traced back to Akkadian and thence, one may add, often enough to Sumerian. [3] The spice cummin, for example, is called *kamūnu* in Akkadian and *gamun* in Sumerian (and *kappani* in Hittite); it is sometimes written with a word-sign (Ú.DIN.TIR.SAR) that means the "Babylon-plant." [4] The carob-tree appears as *harūbu* in Akkadian and *harub* in Sumerian; the terebinth (and its derivative turpentine) reflect Akkadian *šurmēnu* and Sumerian *šur-mìn*. The mineral jaspar derives from Akkadian *jašpû*, of unknown origin. The chemical sal ammoniac is presumably a calque (loan translation) from Akkadian *ṭābat amānim* and Sumerian *mun a-ma-nim*. English "cane" (and "canon") may be ultimately related to Semitic words for "reed," and French marre ("hoe") almost certainly derives

---

[2] P. xxi of the Loeb Classical Library edition (vol. 71).
[3] CAH 3:248-250. Cf. more generally Partridge 1958.
[4] Cf. already A. Deimel, Or. o.s. 13 (1924) 330.

(via Arabic) from Akkadian *marru* and Sumerian *mar*, with the same meaning.

To these familiar standbys catalogued by Thompson one may add others. The word "gum" derives, perhaps via Greek *kommi*, from Egyptian *kmj.t* according to some opinions, or from Sumerian *(šim)-gam-gam-ma* according to others. Modern saffron has been compared with Akkadian *azupīru* and its derivative *azuprirānu*, which figures as the native city of Sargon of Akkad in the (late) legend of his birth. [5] The chameleon, with its improbable Greek etymology as the "on-the-ground lion," is more likely related to Akkadian *hulamēšu* and to the "lion of the ground" (*nēšu ša qaqqari*) in Gilgamesh XI 296 with which *hulamēšu* is equated in a commentary text. [6] Å. Sjöberg has even suggested a relationship to the Hebrew *nāḥāš* (= Akkadian *nēšu*, Eblaite *na'išu* ?) in the story of Eden. [7] This daring suggestion receives a curious sort of support from an unexpected quarter: the autobiography of an English physician's wife who spent many years in Kenya records the local belief that the snake of Eden was in fact a chameleon. [8]

If most of us are understandably ignorant of these scattered survivals of ancient Near Eastern terminology in our contemporary animal, vegetable and mineral vocabulary, there are other lexical survivals in the realm of proper names, geographical and otherwise, including some that go back before Akkadian and Sumerian to the substrate languages which often survive longest in toponyms. These names have become familiar parts of our own vocabulary via Biblical or classical intermediaries, and include among many others the garden of Eden, from *edin*; the rivers Euphrates from *buranun* (via Akkadian *purattu*) and Tigris from *(i)diglat* (interpreted as Sumerian *i-dagala*, "the wide river"); the cities Ur (*urim*), Akkad (*agade* or *aggide*), Babylon (*babil*) and Nineveh (*ninua*). Similarly, Memphis goes back (via Greek) to Egyptian *mr-nfr* (and appears in Biblical Hebrew as *moph* or *noph*); but Thebes is known to us by the name of the Greek city of the same name instead of its Egyptian name *nt*, " (the) city" (which however

---

[5] ANET 119; Foster, BM 819f., FDD 165f.

[6] B. Landsberger, MSL 8/2 (1962) 58:205d; M. Civil, OA 21 (1982) 11f., n. 14. Cf. also CAD s.vv. *ajar ili* and *hurbabillu*; Syriac *arya di 'afra* or *arya diar'a* (chameleon-plant).

[7] Sjöberg 1984.

[8] Gallman 1994:9=1995:37. My thanks to Marcelle Schyns, Advertising Manager of Media Partners International (Amstelveen) for furnishing me with a copy of the *Holland Herald*.

survives in Biblical *no* or *no amon* and in Assyrian *ni' u*). Among many other personal names we may cite those of Mordechai and Esther, derived from the Akkadian divine names Marduk and Ishtar, and the legendary Biblical name Nimrod which may be ultimately a reflex of the Old Akkadian (and Old Babylonian) royal name Naram-Sin.

Less obvious than these purely verbal survivals—but more significant—are the *ideas* which the ancient Near East contributed to later civilization, beginning with the very idea of civilization itself. All of its basic components were present in Sumer at the dawn of history, and bequeathed by the Sumerians to later ages. To take only one example, the high yields made possible by irrigation agriculture in Sumer early made it the breadbasket of the Near East—and, on one theory, the agricultural techniques evolved in Sumer were spread far and wide by the oral transmission of wisdom literature and its subsequent fixation in texts such as "The Instructions of Ninurta" and others. [9]

The agricultural surpluses produced in Sumer and exported beyond its borders permitted the import of products not available there, including tin and copper. Before the end of the fourth millennium, these metals were combined together to create the alloy called bronze and to usher in the Bronze Age. Indications are that such bronze metallurgy may have begun in Sumer. Certainly it is well attested there throughout the third millennium and all over the ancient world by the second. [10]

Another essential ingredient of civilization is writing, invented in Sumer but studied in scribal schools far beyond its confines. The early writing systems of Elam and Egypt probably arose in response to the Sumerian stimulus. The Egyptian system of hieroglyphics inspired the earliest system of West Semitic writing, the Proto-Sinaitic found in the Sinai Peninsula and, together with the Mesopotamian system of cuneiform, the Ugaritic writing system of the Syrian coast, which operated with a mere 30 (consonantal) signs compared to the more than six hundred syllable-signs and word-signs of the earlier script. Ugaritic, in turn, preserves the oldest evidence of the order of the letters in the form of abecedaries dating to the fourteenth and thirteenth centuries B.C. and already displaying, in essence, the same sequence as our own alphabet. [11]

---

[9] See above, ch. II 2; Hallo, JNES 37 (1978) 270. Cf. also Proverbs 27:23-27.
[10] Above, ch. II 1.
[11] Above, ch. I 3.

Writing is associated with reading and arithmetic in the "Three
R's"—and in history. Number signs (or tokens) are, if anything, even
earlier than signs standing for words or syllables, and the Sumerians
early developed a high aptitude for mathematical calculation. One
key to their success in this area was the utility of the base 60, with its
multiple factors and the simplicity and elegance of the numeral notation based on it. The sexagesimal base survives in such conventions
as the 60 seconds in the minute, the 60 minutes in the hour, and the
360 degrees in a circle. [12]

There was also a system of notation built on the base 10 which
found its way, via India (about 500 B.C.) and the Arabs (ninth or
tenth century A.D.) back to Italy by about 1200, though not widely
used till about 1300. [13]

The Egyptians, meantime, while handicapped (as were the later
Greeks and Romans) by a much more cumbersome numeral notation
and therefore behind the Mesopotamians in the sophistication of
their algebraic mathematics, bested them in applied geometry, im-
pelled by the annual inundation of the Nile, and the consequent necessity to rechart the boundaries of real estate. [14]

Armed with the necessary mathematical skills, the Sumerians and
their Babylonian heirs were able to make formidable strides in astronomy. They were responsible for the identification and naming of
many of the constellations in the northern sky. To this day, many of
these continue to carry, in Latin or English translation, the names
first assigned to them in Sumerian by imaginative observers, who
thought they saw in them such likenesses as the lion, the bull, the
scorpion, or the waterman—still to this day present in the Zodiac as
Leo, Taurus, Scorpio and Aquarius, and in our perception of the
starry sky as featuring the corresponding constellations. [15]

One "practical" application of astronomy was to astrology, defined
by David Pingree as "the forecasting of earthly ('mundane') and human ('sublunar') events by means of observing and interpreting the
fixed stars, the Sun, the Moon, and the planets." [16] Although
Mesopotamian astrology in its most sophisticated form evolved under

---

[12] Above, ch. IV 1.
[13] EB 15th ed. (1978) 11:673.
[14] Above, ch. IX 2.
[15] Wallenfels 1993; Porada 1987. Cf. also Borger 1964 and Heimpel 1989 for
these and other Mesopotamian survivals.
[16] EB 15th ed. (1978) 2:219.

Akkadian auspices, there is little reason to doubt that its foundations were laid in Sumerian-speaking times. A whole volume of A. Deimel's Sumerian Lexicon is devoted to star-names and the field retained a largely Sumerian terminology. [17] Traces of the sophisticated late Babylonian complex of astrological techniques survive in the naive and simplistic casting of horoscopes that passes for astrology in the Western world today. India may retain a little more of the Babylonian legacy here. [18]

A more enduring application of Mesopotamian astronomy took place with respect to the calendar. Already the Sumerians divided the day into 24 hours (or twelve double-hours), albeit unlike ours these were not yet of equal length—except on two days of the year, the vernal and autumnal equinox. Otherwise the daylight hours were longer in summer and the nighttime hours in winter. [19]

The week, however, corresponds to no astronomical or other natural phenomenon. On present indications it was an original creation of the Israelite genius, though combined subsequently with Hellenistic (and Egyptian) calculations based on the "planetary week" before it became the perpetual sequence familiar the world over today. [20]

The solar year in use in the Western world today represents the result of a number of adjustments to the Egyptian year of 365 days, inspired by the annual recurrence of the inundation of the Nile and the average length of the intervals between its recurrences as calculated over long periods of time. The Egyptian year was based on twelve months arbitrarily given thirty days each, plus a period of five days at the end of the year to make up the difference. On the other hand the luni-solar year still in use among Jews goes back to Babylonian precedent, with its twelve lunar months based on the actual observation—or, later, calculation—of the new moon, and hence varying between 29 and 30 days each for a total of 354 days. The discrepancy with the solar year that resulted is made good by a leap-month regulated, probably since the time of Nabonassar, who became king of Babylon in 747 B.C., as occurring seven times in every 19 years (so-called Metonic cycle). [21]

---

[17] Gössmann 1950.

[18] Pingree 1987.

[19] Above, ch. IV 1.

[20] Above, ch. IV 2.

[21] See above, ch. IV 1 with nn. 2f.; Hallo 1988; Bowen and Goldstein 1988; Toomer 1988:353.

And one more calendaric innovation. When we count the present year as 1996, we are availing ourselves of an "era" system of dating—in this case the Christian era introduced in the sixth century A.D., for *anno domini*, "according to the year of the Lord," i.e. the approximate birth of Christ. But the idea of an era, a tremendous convenience, goes back at least to the fourth century B.C. (i.e., "before Christ") when the Seleucid Era was introduced in the Seleucid Empire which encompassed most of Mesopotamia and Syria. And perhaps it goes back further still, to the time of Nabonassar (above). [22]

If the calendar governs our lives in one sense, the law does so in another. And here it is possible to trace a link back to the earliest systematic collection of laws, generally attributed to Ur-Nammu of Ur in the 21st century B.C., which inaugurated a tradition of assembling legal precedents that continued with Babylonians, Assyrians, Hittites, and Israelites. [23] These collections of precedents are not really codes in the Roman sense, and to speak of the "Code of Hammurapi," for example, is to perpetuate something of a misnomer for, long as it is, this collection is far from covering all possible contingencies—nor does it aspire to. And the other collections are considerably briefer and even more selective in their coverage. What they rather constitute can better be described as a codification of extremes, an attempt, that is, to collect for posterity those precedents where criteria of guilt or innocence are so massive that there was no difficulty applying them—while a wise judge would be able to deal with the borderline cases that fell between these extremes. [24] In short, they are "judicious" precedents rather than statutory law, and as such more nearly forerunners of our own Anglo-Saxon precedent law than of Roman and Continental codified law.

If the law collections represent legal ideals, then legal practice, the practical side of law, is represented by contracts—and in a literate, writing-happy society like that of Mesopotamia, there are contracts by the thousands. Such contracts typically conclude with the names of witnesses and the date. But there is a group of contracts that substitutes instead "Its witnesses, its date," and this conclusion characterizes the "model contracts" by which future scribes training in the

---

[22] Above, ch. IV 3.

[23] Above, ch. VIII 1.

[24] Hallo, Oppenheim AV (1964) 99 and n. 35; B. Eichler, Reiner AV (1987) 72, n. 9.

law learned their craft. Such model contracts have their place in the Anglo-American tradition of legal education too, and while they owe nothing directly to the ancient precedent, the pedagogic technique in question is the same, and its durability is impressive. [25]

Real contracts differ from model contracts in another respect: they are sealed, usually by the witnesses and routinely by the contracting parties, or at least by the obligating party. To this day, we tend to use the expression "signed and sealed" to describe a binding agreement, even though signatures have largely replaced seals except for the most formal compacts. But it was not so long ago that seals were in almost universal use, and certainly that was so in the ancient Near East. Here too we may give the priority to the Sumerians, at least for replacing the archaic stamp seals with the characteristic cylinder seals that were ideally suited for rolling around the neck of a jar or across the surface of a tablet in order to impress the wet clay with a design to which soon enough there was added an inscription. Cylinder seals were in short order imitated in proto-dynastic Egypt and everywhere else in the Near East where Mesopotamian influence radiated. They represent an uninterrupted and unrivalled record of art in miniature, mirroring changes and continuities in taste and surviving by the thousands to enrich the museums of the modern world. [26]

So far I have described a rather materialistic society: fertile fields producing an agricultural surplus, crowded cities manufacturing textiles and bronze, spices and other luxuries imported from abroad, and all this economic activity regulated by sophisticated calendars and judicious legislation. Is it any wonder if such a society produced the world's first rudimentary banking system. In fact, although the historians of banking remain to be convinced, it can be argued that we have the indirect ancestors of our own bank drafts, or checks, in Sumer. They are routine clay tablets, formally indistinguishable from the great majority of other archival texts, but saying in effect: Pay to the order of the bearer so-and-so-much, and signed by the payee. Such documents may be called letter-orders because they employ the form of the contemporary letters while functioning as orders. [27]

What they ordered to pay was usually grain, or wool, or other staples on deposit in the great granaries and other storage-centers of

---

[25] Cohen 1985.
[26] For a recent survey see Collon 1987.
[27] Above, ch. I 2.

the public sector. But that was not for want of money. The Sumerians already used silver in all the classical functions of money: as a medium of exchange, a measure of value, and a unit of account. They did not coin it (that was left for the Lydians of the seventh century) but they did carry it with them in the form of spiral rings worn on the arm which could be broken off and weighed when needed, or in the form of lumps carried in money-bags. Merchants, in particular, used silver as money, and they have left us the first examples of double-entry bookkeeping which, like banking, is usually traced no further back than the Italian Quattrocento. But how else shall we describe a system in which each merchant made a semi-annual inventory of his assets and liabilities, carefully recording the unit-prices of each of his staples on hand, and all of his purchases of imports, before balancing his account to see whether he carried forward a positive or negative balance. [28]

With so much commercial activity, society was in danger of economic dislocation, of widening the gap between the successful entrepreneurs and the simple farmers and toilers possibly struck by misfortune or simply unable to meet the payments due on their loans. The intervention of a higher power was needed to redress the resulting imbalance—and typically that power, once institutionalized, took the form of kingship. The first social reforms in documented history are those of Uruinimgina (Urukagina), ruler of the Sumerian city-state of Lagash at the end of the Early Dynastic period. His intervention on behalf of widows, orphans and impoverished citizenry generally became a tradition repeatedly emulated in Old Babylonian times in the form of royal edicts proclaiming liberty (from debt-slavery) throughout the land. The tradition found its way into the Biblical legislation of the sabbatical year and the jubilee year, and thence even onto Philadelphia's Liberty Bell, whose inscription is a straight translation of Leviticus 25:10 and a fitting final illustration of the longevity of some ancient Near Eastern innovations, as well as their transformations over the millennia. [29]

---

[28] Above, ch. I 2 and II 3.
[29] See most recently Hallo 1995.

Bibliographical References

Borger, R., 1964: "Ausstrahlungen des Zweistromlandes," JEOL 18: 317-330.

Bowen, Alan C. and Bernard R. Goldstein, 1988: "Meton of Athens and astronomy in the late fifth century B.C.," Sachs AV 39-81.

Cohen, Morris L., 1985: "Legal forms," *Yale Law Report* 31/2 (Spring 1985) 25-28.

Collon, Dominique 1987: *First Impressions: Cylinder Seals in the Ancient Near East* (London, British Museum Publications).

Gössmann, Felix, 1950: *Planetarium Babylonicum, oder: Die sumerisch-babylonischen Stern-Namen* (= ŠL 4/2).

Gallman, Kuki, 1994: *African Nights* (New York, Viking).

————, 1995: "African Nights: an excerpt," *Holland Herald* (June 1995) 35-41.

Hallo, William W., 1988: "The Nabonassar Era and other epochs in Mesopotamian chronology and chronography," Sachs AV 175-190.

————, 1995: "Slave release in the Biblical world in light of a new text," Greenfield AV 79-93.

Heimpel, Wolfgang, 1989: "The Babylonian background of the term 'Milky Way', " Sjöberg AV 249-252.

Partridge, Eric, 1958: *Origins: a Short Etymological Dictionary of Modern English* (New York, Macmillan).

Pingree, David, 1987: "Venus omens in India and Babylon," Reiner AV 293-315.

Porada, Edith, 1987: "On the origins of 'Aquarius'," Reiner AV 279-291.

Sjöberg, Åke W., 1984: "Eve and the chameleon," Ahlström AV 217-225.

Toomer, G.J., 1988: "Hipparchus and Babylonian astronomy," Sachs AV 353-362.

Wallenfels, Ronald, 1993: "Zodiacal signs among the seal impressions from Hellenistic Uruk," Hallo AV 281-289.

ABBREVIATIONS

AASF = Annales Academiae Scientiarum Fennicae Ser. B

AASOR = Annual of the American Schools of Oriental Research

AB = Anchor Bible

AbB = Altbabylonische Briefe in Umschrift und Übersetzung

ABD = *Anchor Bible Dictionary* (1992)

ABL = R.F. Harper, *Assyrian and Babylonian Letters* (14 vols., Chicago, University of Chicago Press, 1892-1914)

ADD = C.H.W. Johns, *Assyrian Deeds and Documents* (Cambridge, 1898)

AfO = Archiv für Orientforschung

AGSK = Abhandlungen der Geistes- und Sozialwissenschaftlichen Klasse

Ahlström AV = *In the Shelter of Elyon: Essays on Ancient Palestinian Life in Honor of G.W. Ahlstrom*, ed. W. B. Barrick and J.R. Spencer (= JSOTS 31, 1984)

AJA = American Journal of Archaeology

AJSL = American Journal of Semitic Languages and Literatures

AJS Review = Association for Jewish Studies Review

ALASP = Abhandlungen zur Literatur Alt-Syrien-Palästinas (Münster)

Albright AV (1971) = *Near Eastern Studies in Honor of William Foxwell Albright*, ed. Hans Goedicke (Baltimore/London, The Johns Hopkins U.P., 1971)

AMT = R.C. Thompson, *Assyrian Medical Texts* (London, 1923)

ANEH = W.W. Hallo and W.K. Simpson, Jr., *The Ancient Near East: a History* (New York, Harcourt Brace Jovanovich, 1971)

ANET = James B. Pritchard, ed., *Ancient Near Eastern Texts Relating to the Old Testament* (3rd ed., Princeton, Princeton U.P., 1969)

ANET 1950 = the same (1st ed., 1950)

ANET 1955 = the same (2nd ed., 1955)

ANETS = Ancient Near Eastern Texts and Studies (Lewiston, Edwin Mellen Press)

AnOr = Analecta Orientalia

AnSt = Anatolian Studies

AOAT = Alter Orient und Altes Testament

AoF = Altorientalische Forschungen

AOS = American Oriental Series

AOS 32 = A.L. Oppenheim, *Catalogue of the ... Eames Babylonian Collection* (1948)

AOS 55 = H.A. Hoffner, Jr., *Alimenta Hethaeorum* (1974)

ARAB = Daniel D. Luckenbill, *Ancient Records of Assyria and Babylonia* (2 vols., Chicago, 1926-27)

ARET = Archivi Reali di Ebla - Testi

ARRIM = Annual Review of the RIM Project

ARM = Archives Royales de Mari

ARMT = Archives Royales de Mari (texts in transliteration and translation)

Arnaud, *Emar* = Daniel Arnaud, *Recherches au Pays d'Astata : Emar VI/1-4* (Paris, Editions Recherches sur les Civilisations, 1985-87)

Artzi AV = *Bar-Ilan Studies in Assyriology Dedicated to Pinhas Artzi*, ed. Jacob Klein and Aaron Skaist (Ramat Gan, Bar-Ilan U.P., 1990)

AS = Assyriological Studies (Chicago)

AS 20 = Jacobsen AV

ASJ = Acta Sumerologica (Japan)

ASOR = American Schools of Oriental Research

ASSS = Acta Sumerologica Supplementary Series

AUCT = Andrews University Cuneiform Texts

AuOr = Aula Orientalis

AUW = *Ausgrabungen der Deutschen Forschungsgemeinschaft in Uruk- Warka* (Leipzig, Harrassowitz).

AV = Anniversary Volume

AVO = Altertumskunde des Vorderen Orients (Münster, Ugarit- Verlag)

AWLM = Akademie der Wissenschaften und der Literatur, Mainz

BA = Beiträge zur Assyriologie

BA = Biblical Archaeologist

BAH = Bibliothèque Archéologique et Historique

BAHIFAI = Bibliothèque Archéologique et Historique de l'Institut Français d'Archéologie d'Istanbul

BaMi = Baghdader Mitteilungen

BAR = Biblical Archaeology Review

BASOR = Bulletin of the American Schools of Oriental Research

Baumgartner AV = *Hebräische Wortforschung: Festschrift zum 80. Geburtstag von Walter Baumgartner* (Leiden, Brill, 1967).

BBVO = Berliner Beiträge zum Vorderen Orient (Berlin, Dietrich Reimer Verlag)

BE = Babylonian Expedition of the University of Pennsylvania

Beek AV = *Travels in the World of the Old Testament: Studies Presented to Professor M.A. Beek*, ed. M.S.H.G. Heerma van Voss et al., (Assen, Van Gorcum, 1974)

Bezold = C. Bezold, *Babylonisch-Assyrisches Glossar* (Heidelberg, Carl Winter, 1926)

BIN = Babylonian Inscriptions in the Collection of J.B. Nies (New Haven)

BIN 9 = V.E. Crawford, *Sumerian Economic Texts from the First Dynasty of Isin*

BiOr = Bibliotheca Orientalis

Birot AV = *Miscellanea Babylonica: Mélanges offerts a Maurice Birot*, ed. J.-M. Durand and J.-R. Kupper (Paris, Editions Recherche sur les Civilisations, 1985)

BIS = Biblical Interpretation Series (Leiden, E.J. Brill)

BM = Bibliotheca Mesopotamica (Malibu)

BM 3 = Robert D. Biggs, Inscriptions from Al-Hiba—Lagarh (1976)

BM 4 = Denise Schmandt-Besserat, ed., *The Legacy of Sumer* (1976)

BM 6 = McGuire Gibson and Robert D. Biggs, eds., *Seals and Sealing in the Ancient Near East* (1977)

BM 11 = M. Sigrist, *Les sattukku dans l' Ešumeša* (1984)

BM 25 = Mark W. Chavalas and John L. Hayes, eds., *New Horizons in the Study of Ancient Syria* (1992)

Bobrinskoy AV = *Languages and Areas: Studies Presented to George V. Bobrinskoy* (Chicago, University of Chicago Press, 1967).

Böhl AV = M.A. Beek et al, eds., *Symbolae Biblicae et Mesopotamicae Francisco Mario Theodore de Liagre Böhl Dedicatae* (Leiden, Brill, 1973).

Boorstin, *Discoverers* = Daniel J. Boorstin, *The Discoverers* (New York, Random House, 1983)

Borger, HKL = Rykle Borger, *Handbuch der Keilschriftliteratur* (3 vols., Berlin, de Gruyter, 1967-1975)

Bottéro, Gilgamesh = J. Bottéro, *L' Épopée de Gilgameš. Le grand homme qui ne voulait pas mourir* (Paris, NRF, 1992).

BR = Bible Review

BRM = Babylonian Records in the Library of J. Pierpont Morgan

BSA = Bulletin on Sumerian Agriculture

Buchanan, ENES = Briggs Buchanan, *Early Near Eastern Seals in the Yale Babylonian Collection* (New Haven/London, Yale U.P., 1981)

CAD = The Assyrian Dictionary of the Oriental Institute of the University of Chicago

CAH = Cambridge Ancient History (1st ed., 1925; 3rd ed., 1970ff.)

CANE = J.M. Sasson, ed., *Civilizations of the Ancient Near East* (4 vols., New York, Scribners, 1995)

CBQ = Catholic Biblical Quarterly

Childs AV = *Canon, Theology, and Old Testament Interpretation: Essays in Honor of Brevard S. Childs*, ed. G.M. Tucker *et al.* (Philadelphia, Fortress, 1988)

CILL = Cahiers de l'Institut de Linguistique de Louvain

Clarke AV = Ian Hodder *et al.*, eds., *Pattern of the Past: Studies in Honour of David Clarke* (Cambridge, Cambridge U.P., 1981).

CNRS = Centre National de la Recherche Scientifique (Paris)

CoS = W.W. Hallo and K.L. Younger, Jr., eds., *The Context of Scripture* (Leiden, Brill, forthcoming)

CRAIBL = Comptes Rendus de l'Académie des Inscriptions et Belles Lettres

Cross AV = *Ancient Israelite Religion: Essays in Honor of Frank Moore Cross*, ed. P.D. Miller, Jr. *et al.* (Philadelphia, Fortress, 1987)

CT = *Cuneiform Texts from Babylonian Tablets in the British Museum* (58 vols., London, The British Museum, 1896-1990)

CTA = A. Herdner, *Corpus des Tablettes en Cunéiformes Alphabétiques découvertes à Ras Shamra-Ugarit* (Paris, 1963)

CTN = Cuneiform Texts from Nimrud (London, British School of Archaeology in Iraq)

Dalley, Tell Rimah = S. Dalley *et al.*, *The Old Babylonian Tablets from Tell al Rimah* (London, British School of Archaeology in Iraq, 1976)

David AV = *Symbolae Iuridicae et Historicae Martino David Dedicatae*, ed. J.A. Ankum *et al.* (2 vols. Leiden, Brill, 1968)

Deimel, ŠG = Anton Deimel, *Šumerische Grammatik* (2nd ed., Rome, Pontifical Biblical Institute, 1939).

Deimel ŠL = Anton Deimel, *Šumerisches Lexikon* (4 vols., Rome, Pontifical Biblical Institute, 1927ff.)

De Vaux, *Ancient Israel* = Roland de Vaux, *Ancient Israel: its Life and Institutions*, tr. John McHugh (New York, McGraw-Hill, 1961).

Diakonoff AV = *Societies and Languages in the Ancient Near East: Studies in Honor of I.M. Diakonoff*, ed. M.A. Dandamayev *et al.* (Warminster, Aris and Phillips, 1982)

Dothan AV = *Studies in the Archaeology and History of Ancient Israel in Honor of Moshe Dothan*, ed. Michael Heltzer (Haifa, Haifa U.P., 1993)

DP = M. Allotte de la Fuÿe, *Documentes Présargoniques* (Paris, 1908-1920)

EA = El Amarna

EB = Encyclopaedia Britannica

Edzard, SR = D.O. Edzard, *Sumerische Rechtsurkunden des III. Jahrtausends* (= VKEK A4, 1968)

Edzard, ZZB = D.O. Edzard, *Die "zweite Zwischenzeit" Babyloniens* (Wiesbaden, Harrassowitz, 1957)

EI = Eretz-Israel

Eilers AV = *Festschrift für Wilhelm Eilers*, ed. Gernot Wiessner (Wiesbaden, Harrassowitz, 1967)

EJ = Encyclopaedia Judaica (Jerusalem, Keter, 1971).

E.Y. Kutscher AV = *Studies in Hebrew and Semitic Languages dedicated to the memory of Prof. Eduard Yechezkel Kutscher*, ed. G.B. Sarfatti *et al.* (Ramat-Gan, Bar-Ilan U.P., 1980).

Falkenstein AV = *Heidelberger Studien zum Alten Orient: Adam Falkenstein zum 17. September 1966*, ed. D.O. Edzard (= HSAO 1, 1967)

Falkenstein NG = Adam Falkenstein, *Die neusumerischen Gerichtsurkunden* (3 vols. = VKEK A2, 1956-57)

FAOS = Freiburger Altorientalische Studien (Stuttgart, Franz Steiner)

Finkelstein AV = *Essays on the Ancient Near East in Memory of Jacob Joel Finkelstein*, ed. Maria deJ. Ellis (= MCAAS 19, 1977)

Fohrer AV = *Prophecy: Essays presented to Georg Fohrer ...*, ed. J.A. Emerton (Berlin/New York, de Gruyter, 1980)

Foster, BM = Benjamin R. Foster, *Before the Muses: an Anthology of Akkadian Literature* (2 vols., Bethesda, MD, CDL Press, 1993)

Foster, FDD = Benjamin R. Foster, *From Distant Days: Myths, Tales, and Poetry of Ancient Mesopotamia* (Bethesda, MD, CDL Press, 1995)

Freedman AV = *The Word of the Lord Shall Go Forth: Essays in Honor of David Noel Freedman ...*, ed. C.L. Meyers and M. O'Connor (Winona Lake, IN, Eisenbrauns, 1983)

Friedrich AV = *Festschrift Johannes Friedrich ...*, ed. R. von Kienle *et al.* (Heidelberg, 1959)

Garelli AV = *Marchands, Diplomates et Empereurs: Etudes sur la civilisation mesopotamienne offertes à Paul Garelli*, ed. D. Charpin and F. Joannès (Paris, Éditions Recherche sur les Civilisations, 1991)

GCCI = R.P. Dougherty, *Goucher College Cuneiform Inscriptions* (2 vols., New Haven, Yale U.P. 1923-33)

Gelb, MAD = I.J. Gelb, *Materials for the Assyrian Dictionary* (5 vols., Chicago, University of Chicago Press, 1952-70)

Gevirtz AV = *Let Your Colleagues Praise You: Studies in Memory of Stanley Gevirtz* (2 vols. = Maarav 7-8, 1991-92)

Gordon, SP = S.P. 1, 2.

Gratz College AV = *Gratz Collge Anniversary Volume*, ed. I.D. Passow and S.T. Lachs (Philadelphia, Gratz College, 1971)

Greenfield AV = *Solving Riddles and Untying Knots: Biblical, Epigraphic, and Semitic Studies in Honor of Jonas C. Greenfield*, ed. Z. Zevit *et al.* (Winona Lake, IN, Eisenbrauns, 1995)

Greengus, OBTIV = Samuel Greengus, *Old Babylonian Tablets from Ishchali and Vicinity* (= PIHANS 44, 1979)

Güterbock AV = *Anatolian Studies Presented to Hans Gustav Güterbock...*, ed. K. Bittel *et al.* (= PIHANS 35, 1974)

Hallo AV = M.E. Cohen *et al.*, eds., *The Tablet and the Scroll: Near Eastern Studies in Honor of William W. Hallo* (Bethesda, MD, CDL Press, 1993)

Hallo, BP = W.W. Hallo, *The Book of the People* (= Brown Judaic Studies 225) (Atlanta, GA, Scholars Press, 1991)

Haran AV = *Texts, Temples, and Traditions: a Tribute to Menahem Haran*, ed. M.V. Fox *et al.* (Winona Lake, IN, Eisenbrauns, 1996)

Heerma van Vos AV = *Funerary Symbols and Religion: Essays Dedicated to Professor M.S.H.G Heerma van Vos*, ed. J.H. Kamstra *et al.* (Kampen, Kok, 1988).

Hestrin, *Catalogue* = Ruth Hestrin and Michal Dayagi-Mendels, *Inscribed Seals: First Temple Period ...* (Jerusalem, Israel Museum, 1979)

Hospers AV = *Scripta Signa Voces: Studies about Scripts, Scriptures, Scribes and Languages in the Near East, Presented to J.H. Hospers ...*, ed. H.L.J. Vanstiphout *et al.* (Groningen, Forsten, 1986).

Hrouda AV = *Beiträge zur Altorientalischen Archäologie und Altertumskunde: Festschrift für Barthel Hrouda ...*, ed. P. Calmeyer *et al.* (Wiesbaden, Harrassowitz, 1994)

HSAO = Heidelberger Studien zum Alten Orient

HSM = Harvard Semitic Monographs (Atlanta, GA, Scholars Press)

HSS = Harvard Semitic Series

HSS = Harvard Semitic Studies (Atlanta, GA, Scholars Press)

HTS = Harvard Theological Studies

HUCA = Hebrew Union College Annual

HUCAS = HUCA Supplements

ICO = International Congress of Orientalists

IEJ = Israel Exploration Journal

IRSA = E. Sollberger and J.-R. Kupper, *Inscriptions Royales Sumériennes et Akkadiennes* (= LAPO 3) (Paris, Cerf, 1971)
IUONsm = Istituto Universitario Orientale (Napoli) Seminario di Studi Asiatici, series minor
JAC = Journal of Ancient Civilizations
Jacobsen AV = *Sumerological Studies in Honor of Thorkild Jacobsen* ..., ed. S.J. Lieberman (= AS 20, 1975)
Jacobsen, *Harps* = Thorkild Jacobsen, *The Harps that Once...: Sumerian Poetry in Translation* (New Haven/Lonmdon, Yale U.P., 1987).
Jacobsen, TIT = Thorkild Jacobsen, *Toward the Image of Tammuz*, William L. Moran, ed., (= HSS 21, 1970).
JANES = Journal of the Ancient Near Eastern Society of Columbia University
JAOS = Journal of the American Oriental Society
JBL = Journal of Biblical Literature
JCS = Journal of Cuneiform Studies
JEA = Journal of Egyptian Archaeology
JEOL = Jaarbericht ... van het Vooraziatisch-Egyptisch Genootschap "Ex Oriente Lux"
JESHO = Journal of the Economic and Social History of the Orient
JHNES = Johns Hopkins Near Eastern Studies
JJP = Journal of Juristic Papyrology
Jones AV = *Studies in Honor of Tom B. Jones*, ed. M.A. Powell, Jr. and R.H. Sack (= AOAT 203, 1979).
JKF = Jahrbuch für Keilschriftforschung
JNES = Journal of Near Eastern Studies
JPS = Jewish Publication Society
JQR = Jewish Quarterly Review
JSOTS = Journal for the Study of the Old Testament Supplement Series (Sheffield, JSOT Press).
JSS = Journal of Semitic Studies
KAR = Erich Ebeling, *Keilschrifttexte aus Assur Religiösen Inhalts* (2 vols.) (= WVDOG 28, 34, 1915-23)
Kramer AV = *Kramer Anniversary Volume: Cuneiform Studies in Honor of Samuel Noah Kramer*, ed. B.L. Eichler *et al.* (= AOAT 25, 1976)
Kramer AV 2 = Jack M. Sasson, ed., *Studies in Literature from the Ancient Near East ... dedicated to Samuel Noah Kramer* (= AOS 65, 1984; also appeared as JAOS 103/1, 1983)
Kramer, HBS = Samuel Noah Kramer, *History Begins at Sumer* (Chicago, University of Chicago Press, 1981).
Kraus AV = zikir šumim: *Assyriological Studies Presented to F.R. Kraus* ..., ed. G. van Driel *et al.* (= Studia Francisci Scholten Memoriae Dicata 5) (Leiden, Brill, 1982)
KTU = M. Dietrich, O. Loretz and J. Sanmartin, *Die keilalphabetischen Texte aus Ras Shamra-Ugarit* (= AOAT 24/1, 1976).
Kupper AV = *De la Babylonie a la Syrie ...: Mélanges ... Kupper*, ed. O. Tunca (Liège, 1990)
Kutscher AV = kinattūtu ša dārâti: *Raphael Kutscher Memorial Volume*, ed. A.F. Rainey (Tel Aviv, Tel Aviv University Institute of Archaeology, 1993)
LAK = A. Deimel, *Liste der archaischen Keilschriftzeichen* (= WVDOG 40, 1922)
Landsberger AV = *Studies in Honor of Benno Landsberger* ..., ed. H.G. Güterbock and T. Jacobsen (= AS 16, 1965)
LAPO = Littératures Anciennes du Proche-Orient (Paris, Les Éditions du Cerf)
LeSor AV = *Biblical and Near Eastern Studies: Essays in Honor of William Sanford LaSor*, ed. G.A. Tuttle (Grand Rapids, MI, Eerdmans, 1978)
Limet AV = forthcoming

Lipiński AV = *Immigration and Emigration within the Ancient Near East: Festschrift E. Lipiński*, ed. K. van Lerberghe and A. Schors (= OLA 65, 1995).

Lipiński, STE = Edward Lipiński, ed., *State and Temple Economy in the Ancient Near East* (2 vols. = OLA 5-6, 1979)

Liverani, *Akkad* = Mario Liverani, ed., *Akkad the First World Empire: Structure, Ideology, Traditions* (Padua, Sargon srl, 1993).

LKA = Erich Ebeling, *Literarische Keilschrifttexte aus Assur* (Berlin, Akademie-Verlag, 1953)

LKU = Adam Falkenstein, *Literarische Keilschrifttexte aus Uruk* (Berlin 1931)

Lokkegaard AV = *Living Waters: Scandinavian Oriental Studies Presented to Professor Dr. Frede Lokkegaard*, ed. Egon Keck *et al.* (Copenhagen, Museum Tusculum, 1990).

Longman, FAA = Tremper Longman III, *Fictional Akkadian Autobiography: a Generic and Comparative Study* (Winona Lake, IN, Eisenbrauns, 1991)

Malamat AV = *Avraham Malamat Volume*, ed. S. Ahituv and B.A. Levine (= Eretz-Israel 24, 1993)

MANE = Monographs on the Ancient Near East (Malibu, CA)

M.A.R.I. = Mari: Annales de Recherches Interdisciplinaires

Matouš AV = *Festschrift Lubor Matouš*, ed. B. Hruška and G. Komoróczy (2 vols. = Assyriologia 5) (Budapest, 1978)

MCAAS = Memoirs of the Connecticut Academy of Arts and Sciences (Hamden, CT, Archon Books)

MCS = Manchester Cuneiform Studies

MDOG = Mitteilungen der Deutschen Orientgesellschaft

MDP = Mémoires de la Délégation en Perse

MEE = Materiali Epigrafici di Ebla

Meissner, BuA = Bruno Meissner, *Babylonien und Assyrien* (2 vols., Heidelberg, Carl Winter, 1920-25)

Mellink AV = J.V. Canby *et al.*, eds., *Ancient Anatolia: Aspects of Change and Cultural Development: Essays in Honor of Machteld J. Mellink* (Madison, The University of Wisconsin Press, 1986)

Mesopotamia (Copenhagen)

Mesopotamian Civilizations (Winona Lake, IN, Eisenbrauns)

MKNAWL n.r. = Mededelingen der Koninklijke Nederlandse Akademie van Wetenschappen Afd. Letterkunde, nieuwe reeks

Moran AV = T. Abusch *et al.*, eds., *Lingering Over Words: Studies in Ancient Near Eastern Literature in Honor of William L. Moran* (= HSS 37, 1990)

MS = Manuscript (unpubl.)

MSL = Materialien zum šumerischen Lexikon; Materials for the Sumerian Lexicon

Muilenburg AV = *Israel's Prophetic Heritage: Essays in Honor of James Muilenburg*, ed. B.W. Anderson and W. Harrelson (New York, Harper & Brothers, 1960)

Muilenburg AV 2 = *Rhetorical Criticism: Essays in Honor of James Muilenburg*, ed. Jared J. Jackson and Martin Kessler, (Pittsburgh, Pickwick, 1974)

MVAG = Mitteilungen der Vorderasiatisch-Aegyptischen Gesellschaft

MVN = Materiali per il vocabolario neo-sumerico

N.A.B.U. = Nouvelles Assyriologiques Brèves et Utilitaires

Naster AV = *Archéologie et Religions de l'Anatolie Ancienne: Mélanges en l'honneur du professeur Paul Naster*, ed. R. Doncel and R. Lebrun (= Homo Religiosus 10, 1984)

NEB = New English Bible

NERT = W. Beyerlin, ed., *Near Eastern Religious Texts Relating to the Old Testament* (Philadelphia, Westminster, 1978).

n.F. = neue Folge

NRVN = M. Çiğ and H. Kizilyay, *Neusumerische Rechts- und Verwaltungsurkunden aus Nippur*, vol 1 (Ankara, Türk Tarih Kurumu Basimevi, 1965)

NJV = New Jewish Version

NThT = Nederlands Theologisch Tijdschrift
OA = Oriens Antiquus
OBL = Orientalia et Biblica Lovaniensia
OIC = Oriental Institute Communications (Chicago)
OIP = Oriental Institute Publications (Chicago)
OIP 99 = Robert D. Biggs, *Inscriptions from Abu Salabikh* (1974)
OLA = Orientalia Lovaniensia Analecta
OLA 5 = Lipiński, STE
OLP = Orientalia Lovaniensia Periodica
Opificius AV = *Beschreiben und Deuten in der Archäologie des Alten Orients: Festschrift für
    Ruth Mayer-Opificius*, ed. M. Dietrich and O. Loretz (= Altertumskunde des Vor-
    deren Orients 4) (Münster, Ugarit-Verlag, 1994)
Oppenheim, Ancient Mesopotamia = A.L. Oppenheim, *Ancient Mesopotamia: Portrait
    of a Dead Civilization* (Chicago, University of Chicago Press, 1964)
Oppenheim, AOS 32 = A.L. Oppenheim, *Catalogue of the Cuneiform Tablets of the Wil-
    berforce Eames Collection in the New York Public Library* (1948)
Oppenheim AV = *Studies Presented to A. Leo Oppenheim*, ed. R.D. Biggs and J.A. Brink-
    man (Chicago, Oriental Institute, 1964)
OPSNKF = Occasional Publications of the Samuel Noah Kramer Fund (Philadel-
    phia)
Or. = Orientalia (nova series)
Orlinsky AV = *Harry M. Orlinsky Volume*, ed. B.A. Levine and A. Malamat (= Eretz-
    Israel 16/,1982)
Or. Suec. = Orientalia Suecana
Owen, NSAT = D.I. Owen, *Neo-Sumerian Archival Texts* (Winona Lake, IN, Eisen-
    brauns, 1982)
Özgüç AV = *Anatolia and the Ancient Near East: Studies in Honor of Tahsin Özgüç*, ed. K.
    Emre *et al.* (Ankara, Türk Tarih Kurumu Basimeri, 1989)
PAAJR = Proceedings of the American Academy for Jewish Research (Jerusalem
    and New York)
PBS = Publications of the Babylonian Section, University Museum, University of
    Pennsylvania
Pedersen AV = *Studia Orientalia Ioanni Pedersen ...dedicata* (Copenhagen, 1953).
PIHANS = Publications de l'Institute Historique et Archéologique Néerlandais de
    Stamboul
PIOL = Publications de l'Institut Orientaliste de Louvain
Plaut, *Torah* = W.G. Plaut, B.J. Bamberger and W.W. Hallo, *The Torah: a Modern
    Commentary* (New York, Union of American Hebrew Congregations, 1981)
Pope AV = *Love and Death in the Ancient Near East: Essays in Honor of Marvin H. Pope*,
    ed. J.H. Marks and R.M. Good (Guilford, CT, Four Quarters, 1987)
Porada AV = *Insight through Images: Studies in Honor of Edith Porada*, ed. Marilyn Kelly-
    Buccellati (Malibu, Undena, 1986)
Porada AV 2 = *Monsters and Demons in the Ancient and Medieval Worlds*, ed. A.E. Farkas
    et al. (Mainz, von Zabern, 1987)
Prince Mikasa AV = *Near Eastern Studies dedicated to H.I.H. Prince Takahito Mikasa*, ed.
    M. Mori *et al.* (Wiesbaden, Harrassowitz, 1991)
PSD = The Sumerian Dictionary of the University Museum of the University of
    Pennsylvania
PThMS = Pittsburgh Theological Monograph Series
PWCJS = Proceedings of the ... World Congress of Jewish Studies. Section A: The
    Bible and the Ancient Near East
R = Rawlinson (cited as I R, II R, etc.)
RA = Revue d'Assyriologie et d'Archéologie Orientale
RAI = Rencontre Assyriologue Internationale

RAI 7 = P. Garelli, ed., *Gilgameš et sa Légende* (Paris, 1960)

RAI 17 = Andre Finet, ed., *Actes de la XVIIe RAI* (Ham-sur-Heure, Comité Belge de Recherches en Mésopotamie, 1970)

RAI 19 = Paul Garelli, ed., *Le Palais et la Royauté* (Paris, Geuthner, 1971)

RAI 20 = *Le Temple et le Culte* (= PIHANS 37, 1975)

RAI 23 = *Iraq* 39 (1977) 1-231; rep. as J.D. Hawkins, ed., *Trade in the Ancient Near East* (London, Britsh School of Archaeology in Iraq, 1977).

RAI 24 = M. Astour *et al.*, *Les Hourrites* (= RHA 36 (1978)

RAI 25 = H.J. Nissen and J. Renger, eds., *Mesopotamien und seine Nachbarn* (2 vols. = BBVO 1, 1982).

RAI 26 = B. Alster, ed., *Death in Mesopotamia* (= Mesopotamia 8)

RAI 32 = Karl Hecker and Walter Sommerfeld, eds., *Keilschriftliche Literaturen* (= BBVO 6, 1986)

RAI 33 = Jean-Marie Durand, ed., *La Femme dans la Proche-Orient Antique* (Paris, Éditions Recherche sur les Civilisations, 1987)

RAI 35 = Maria deJ. Ellis, ed., *Nippur at the Centennial* (= OPSNKF 14, 1992)

RAI 38 = D. Charpin and F. Joannès, eds., *La Circulation des biens, des personnes et des idées dans le Proche-Orient ancien* (Paris, Editions Recherche sur les Civilisations, 1992).

RB = Revue Biblique

Reiner AV = *Language, Literature, and History: Philological and Historical Studies presented to Erica Reiner*, ed. F. Rochberg-Halton (= AOS 67, 1987)

RG = W. Röllig, ed., *Répertoire Géographique des Textes Cunéiformes* (Wiesbaden, Reichert)

RHA = Revue Hittite et Asianique

RHDFE = Revue Historique de Droit Français et Étranger

Richerche = Istituto Orientale di Napoli, Pubblicazioni del Seminario di Semitistica

RIMA = The Royal Inscriptions of Mesopotamia: Assyrian Periods (Toronto)

Rimah = Stephanie Dalley, C.B.F. Walker and J.D. Hawkins, *The Old Babylonian Tablets from Tell al Rimah* (London, British School of Archaeology in Iraq, 1976)

RIME = The Royal Inscriptions of Mesopotamia: the Early Periods (Toronto)

RLA = Reallexikon der Assyriologie

RS = Ras Shamra

RSF = Rivista di Studi Fenici

RSO = Rivista degli Studi Orientali

RTC = F. Thureau-Dangin, *Récueil des Tablettes Chaldéennes* (Paris, 1903)

RVV = Religionsgeschichtliche Versuche und Vorarbeiten

SAA = State Archives of Assyria (Helsinki, Helsinki U.P.)

SAAB = State Archives of Assyria Bulletin

Sachs AV = *A Scientific Humanist: Studies in Memory of Abraham Sachs*, ed. Erle Leichty *et al.* (= OPSNKF 9, 1988)

Salonen AV = *Studia Orientalia* 46 (1975), corrections *ib.* 48/3 (1977) 4f.

SANE = Sources from the Ancient Near East (Malibu, CA)

SAOC = Studies in Ancient Oriental Civilization (Chicago)

Sarna AV = *Minḥah le-Naḥum: Biblical and Other Studies Presented to Nahum M. Sarna ...*, ed. M. Brettler and M. Fishbane (= JSOTS 154, 1993)

SB = Standard Babylonian

SBA = Saarbrücker Beiträge zur Altertumskunde

SBL = Society of Biblical Literature

SBT = *Studien zu den Boğazköy-Texten*

SCCNH = *Studies on the Civilization and Culture of Nuzi and the Hurrians*

Schreiner AV = *Künder des Wortes: Beiträge zur Theologie der Propheten: Josef Schreiner zum 60. Geburtstage*, ed. L. Ruppert *et al.* (Würzburg, 1982).

SD = Studia et Documenta ad Iura Orientis Antiqui Pertinentia (Leiden, Brill)

SEb = Studi Eblaiti (Rome)
SEL = Studie Epigrafici e Linguistici
SF = Anton Deimel, *Schultexte aus Fara* (= WVDOG 43, 1923)
SHAW = Sitzungsberichte der Heidelberger Akademie der Wissenschaften, phil.-hist. Klasse
SIC 1 = C.D. Evans, W.W. Hallo and J.B. White, eds., *Scripture in Context: Essays on the Comparative Method* (PThMS 34, 1980)
SIC 2 = W.W. Hallo, J.C. Moyer and L.G. Perdue, eds., *Scripture in Context II: More Essays on the Comparative Method* (Winona Lake, IN, Eisenbrauns, 1983)
SIC 3 = W.W. Hallo, B.W. Jones and G.L. Mattingly, eds., *The Bible in the Light of Cuneiform Literature* (= ANETS 8, 1990)
SIC 4 = K.L. Younger, Jr., W.W. Hallo and B.F. Batto, eds., *The Biblical Canon in Comparative Perspective* (= ANETS 11, 19910
Sjöberg AV = *Dumu-e₂-dub-ba-a: Studies in Honor of Åke W. Sjöberg*, ed. Hermann Behrens *et al.* (= OPSNKF 11, 1989)
SK = H. Zimmern, *Sumerische Kultlieder* (= VS 2 and 10, 1912f.)
ŠL = A. Deimel, *Šumerisches Lexikon* (Rome, Pontifical Biblical Institute)
SLB = Studia ad Tabulas Cuneiformes Collectas a F.M.Th. de Liagre Böhl Pertinentia (Leiden)
Sollberger, CIRPL = Edmond Sollberger, *Corpus des Inscriptions " Royales" Présargoniques de Lagaš* (Geneva, Droz, 1956)
S.P. 1, 2 = Edmund I. Gordon, *Sumerian Proverbs* (= Museum Monographs) (Philadelphia, The University Museum, 1959)
S.P. 3 = Robert S. Falkowitz, *The Sumerian Rhetoric Collections* (Ph.D. Thesis, University of Pennsylvania; Ann Arbor, MI, University Microfilms, 1980)
Speiser AV = *Essays in Memory of E.A. Speiser*, ed. W.W. Hallo (= AOS 53, 1968; also appeared as JAOS 88/1, 1968)
SRT = E. Chiera, *Sumerian Religious Texts* (Upland, PA, Crozer Theological Seminary, 1924)
SSA = J.J.A. van Dijk, *La Sagesse Suméro-Accadienne* (Leiden, Brill, 1953)
SSN = Studia Semitica Neerlandica (Assen/Maastricht, Van Gorcum)
Stith Thompson, *Index* = Stith Thompson, *Motif-index of Folk-literature* (rev. ed., 6 vols., Bloomington, IN, Indiana U.P. 1955-58)
StOr = Studia Orientalia (Helsinki)
StPSM = Studia Pohl Series Maior (Rome)
STT = O.R. Gurney *et al.*, *The Sultan Tepe Tablets* (2 vols., British Institute of Archaeology at Ankara, 1957-64)
Šurpu = Erica Reiner, *Šurpu, a Collection of Sumerian and Akkadian Incantations* (= AfO Beiheft 11, 1958)
s.v. = *sub verbo*
s.vv. = *sub verbis*
Tadmor AV = Ah, Assyria ...:*Studies ... Presented to Hayim Tadmor*, ed. M. Cogan and I. Eph'al (= Scripta Hiersolymitana 33, 1991)
Talmon AV = "Sha'arei Talmon": *Studies ... Presented to Shemaryahu Talmon*, ed. M. Fishbane and E. Tov (Winona Lake, IN, Eisenbrauns, 1992)
TAPhS = Transactions of the American Philosophical Society
TCAAS = Transactions (of) the Connecticut Academy of Arts and Sciences
TCL = Textes Cunéiformes du Louvre
TCS = Texts from Cuneiform Sources (Locust Valley, NY, J.J. Augustin).
TCS 1 = Edmond Sollberger, *The Business and Administrative Correspondence under the Kings of Ur* (1966)
TCS 3 = Å.W. Sjöberg and E. Bergmann S.J., *The Collection of the Sumerian Temple Hymns* (1969)
TCS 4 = Erle Leichty, *The Omen Series Šumma Izbu* (1970)

Tigay, *Evolution* = Jeffrey H. Tigay, *The Evolution of the Gilgamesh Epic* (Philadelphia, University of Pennsylvania Press, 1982)
TIM = Texts in the Iraq Museum

TIM 9 = J. van Dijk, *Texts of Varying Content* (Leiden, Brill, 1976)
TLB = Tabulae Cuneiformes a F.M.Th. de Liagre Böhl Collectae
TMH = Texte unde Materialien der Frau Professor Hilprecht Collection (Jena)
Tournay and Shaffer, *Gilgamesh* = Raymond J. Tournay and Aaron Shaffer, *L' Épopée de Gilgamesh* (LAPO 15, 1994)
TRS = Henri de Genouillac, *Textes Religieux Sumeriens du Louvre* (2 vols. = TCL 15-16)
UET = Ur Excavations, Texts
UET 5 = H.H. Figulla, *Letters and Documents of the Old-Babylonian Period* (1953)
UET 6 = C.J. Gadd and S.N. Kramer, *Literary and Religious Texts* (2 vols., 1963-66)
UET 7 = Oliver R. Gurney, *Middle Babylonian Legal Documents and Other Texts* (1974)
UF = Ugarit-Forschungen
Unger AV = *In Memoriam Eckhard Unger*, ed. M. Lurker (Baden-Baden, Valentin Koerner, 1971)
U.P. = University Press
UVB = Vorläufiger Bericht über die ... Ausgrabungen in Uruk-Warka
VAT = Vorderasiatische Abteilung Tontafel (Berlin)
VE = Vocabulario di Ebla = MEE 4:115-343
VKEK = Veröffentlichungen der Kommission zur Erschliessung von Keilschrifttexten (Munich, Bayerische Akademie der Wissenschaften, Philosophisch-historische Klasse, Abhandlungen, neue Folge)
Volterra AV = *Studi in Onore di Eduardo Volterra* 6 (Rome, Giuffré, 1969)
VS = Vorderasiatische Schriftdenkmäler (Berlin)
VT = Vetus Testamentum
VTS = Supplements to Vetus Testamentum
WAW = Writings from the Ancient World, SBL (Atlanta, Scholars Press)
Wilcke, *Kollationen* = C. Wilcke, *Kollationen zu den ... Texten aus ... Jena* (Berlin, Akademie-Verlag, 1976)
Wilcke, *Lugalbanda* = C. Wilcke, *Das Lugalbandaepos* (Wiesbaden, Harrassowitz, 1969)
WO = Welt des Orients
WVDOG = Wissenschaftliche Veröffentlichungen der Deutschen Orientgesellschaft (Leipzig)
WZKM = Wiener Zeitschrift für die Kunde des Morgenlandes
WZUH = *Wissenschaftliche Zeitschrift der Universität Halle* G.H.
YBC = Yale Babylonian Collection
YNER = Yale Near Eastern Researches
YOS = Yale Oriental Series: Babylonian Texts (New Haven/London)
ZA = Zeitschrift für Assyriologie
ZATW = Zeitschrift für die Alttestamentliche Wissenschaft

Abbreviations of Biblical books

Gen. = Genesis
Ex. = Exodus
Lev. = Leviticus
Num. = Numbers
Deut. = Deuteronomy
Sam. = Samuel
Isa. = Isaiah
Jer. = Jeremiah

Ez. = Ezekiel
Hos. = Hosea
Nah. = Nahum
Ps. = Psalm(s)
Prov. = Proverbs
Chron. = Chronicles
Sir. = Sirach

GENERAL INDEX

Akk. = Akkadian
AN = Author's name
ANf = Author's name (female)
Aram. = Aramaic
CN = Composition name
DN = Divine name
DNf = Divine name (female)
Ebl. = Eblaite
EN = Era name, dynasty name
GN = Geographical name
GNm = Geographical name (modern)
Gk. = Greek

Heb. = Hebrew
Hitt. = Hittite
Lat. = Latin
LN = Language name, ethnic name, writing system
PN = Personal name
PNf = Persoanl name (female)
RN = Royal name
RNf = Royal name (female)
Sum. = Sumerian
TN = Temple name, palace name
Ug. = Ugaritic

INDEX OF BIBLICAL PASSAGES CITED

STUDIES IN THE HISTORY AND CULTURE
OF THE ANCIENT NEAR EAST

EDITED BY

B. HALPERN AND M.H.E. WEIPPERT

ISSN 0169-9024

1. G.W. AHLSTRÖM. *Royal Administration and National Religion in Ancient Palestine*. 1982. ISBN 90 04 6562 8

2. B. BECKING. *The Fall of Samaria*. An Historical and Archaeological Study. 1992. ISBN 90 04 09633 7

3. W.J. VOGELSANG. *The Rise and Organisation of the Achaemenid Empire*. The Eastern Iranian Evidence. 1992. ISBN 90 04 09682 5

4. T.L. THOMPSON. *Early History of the Israelite People*. From the Written and Archaeological Sources. 1992. ISBN 90 04 09483 0

5. M. EL-FAÏZ. *L'agronomie de la Mésopotamie antique*. Analyse du «Livre de l'agriculture nabatéenne» de Qûtâmä. 1995. ISBN 90 04 10199 3

6. W.W. HALLO. *Origins*. The Ancient Near Eastern Background of Some Modern Western Institutions. 1996. ISBN 90 04 10328 7

7. K. VAN DER TOORN. *Family Religion in Babylonia, Syria and Israel*. Continuity and Change in the Forms of Religious Life. 1996. ISBN 90 0410410 0

8. A. JEFFERS. *Magic and Divination in Ancient Palestine and Syria*. 1996. ISBN 90 04 10513 1

9. G. GALIL. *The Chronology of the Kings of Israel and Judah*. 1996. ISBN 90 0410611 1